Capital Gains Tax Planning 2007–08

Capital Gains Tax Planning 2007–08

First Edition

LexisNexis®
Butterworths

Members of the LexisNexis Group worldwide

United Kingdom	LexisNexis Butterworths, a Division of Reed Elsevier (UK) Ltd, Halsbury House, 35 Chancery Lane, London, WC2A 1EL, and London House, 20–22 East London Street, Edinburgh EH7 4BQ
Argentina	LexisNexis Argentina, Buenos Aires
Australia	LexisNexis Butterworths, Chatswood, New South Wales
Austria	LexisNexis Verlag ARD Orac GmbH & Co KG, Vienna
Benelux	LexisNexis Benelux, Amsterdam
Canada	LexisNexis Canada, Markham, Ontario
Chile	LexisNexis Chile Ltda, Santiago
China	LexisNexis China, Beijing and Shanghai
France	LexisNexis SA, Paris
Germany	LexisNexis Deutschland GmbH, Munster
Hong Kong	LexisNexis Hong Kong, Hong Kong
India	LexisNexis India, New Delhi
Italy	Giuffrè Editore, Milan
Japan	LexisNexis Japan, Tokyo
Malaysia	Malayan Law Journal Sdn Bhd, Kuala Lumpur
Mexico	LexisNexis Mexico, Mexico
New Zealand	LexisNexis NZ Ltd, Wellington
Poland	Wydawnictwo Prawnicze LexisNexis Sp, Warsaw
Singapore	LexisNexis Singapore, Singapore
South Africa	LexisNexis Butterworths, Durban
USA	LexisNexis, Dayton, Ohio

First published in 2007
© Reed Elsevier (UK) Ltd 2007
Published by LexisNexis Butterworths

A CIP Catalogue record for this book is available from the British Library.

ISBN for this volume
ISBN 978 0 7545 31401

Typeset by Columns Design Ltd, Reading, England
Printed in the United Kingdom by Polestar Wheatons Ltd
Visit LexisNexis Butterworths at www.lexisnexis.co.uk

About the authors

Winter Rule is the largest accountancy practice in Cornwall, having originally been set up in the 1920s. The firm has seven partners and nearly 80 staff and its clients are predominately owner managed businesses and private clients. The Winter Rule Tax Team were short listed in the category of Best Tax Team in a Small Firm at the LexisNexis Tax Awards in both 2004 and 2006.

John Endacott BSC (Econ) FCA CTA (Fellow)

John has considerable experience of advising on capital gains tax (CGT). He has been the tax partner at Winter Rule for the last ten years and prior to that worked for KPMG and Coopers & Lybrand.

John has written widely in the professional journals on CGT and is a co-author of the CGT planning chapter in Tolleys Tax Planning. John's CIOT Fellowship Thesis was on CGT taper relief.

John has been a member of the Technical Committee of the ICEAW Tax Faculty and is also a tax examiner for both the ICAEW and the CIOT.

Alice Gunn BA (Hons) ACA

Alice started her career with Pridie Brewster in London before joining Winter Rule where she advised both business owners and private individuals on CGT planning. She is currently on secondment at H M Revenue and Customs with their Individual Customer Unit dealing with the Complex Personal Tax Returns Unit.

Anthony Meehan BA (Hons) MA CTA ATT

Anthony started his career with KPMG before joining Winter Rule. He won the Spoforth Medal for the best paper on taxation and trust in his CTA exams and specialises in advising high networth individuals on CGT planning.

Steve York, BSC ATT

Steve trained with Winter Rule and has specialised in advising high networth individuals on CGT planning. He is a co-author of the chapter on CGT planning in Tolley's Tax Planning.

Richard Wadman BA ACA

Richard started his career with KPMG before joining Winter Rule in 1999. Richard advises on corporate finance and corporate restructuring and as well as dealing with corporate tax issues, advises business vendors on CGT planning

Other individuals at Winter Rule have also been involved in the production in this book and by far the biggest contribution has been by Fiona Windsor, in helping to project manage the process and typing over 135,000 words.

While every care has been taken to ensure the accuracy of this work, no responsibility for loss or damage occasioned to any person acting or refraining from action as a result of any statement in it can be accepted by the authors, editors or publishers.

Contents

Contents

Contents

Stop Press – Pre-Budget Announcement 9 October 2007

On 9 October 2007, Alistair Darling, the Chancellor of the Exchequer, announced wide-ranging changes to capital gains tax (CGT) (just as this book was going to press). It is not possible to amend the text of this book to comment on those proposed changes, and indeed there is insufficient detail available at this time to make meaningful statements about many of the implications for CGT planning that may follow. However, it does seem appropriate to include some very early comments and we have also included a copy of the Pre-Budget Report Note PBRN17 entitled 'Capital Gains Tax Reform' as part of this book. At the time of writing, that is all any adviser has to go on in terms of the implications of the changes.

The CGT changes take effect from 6 April 2008 and as such, the CGT planning outlined in this book will continue to be in place until that time. Indeed, it is likely to be a very busy time for CGT planning in order to take advantage of the existing regime. However, there were also three other announcements of tax changes in the Pre-Budget Report that are relevant to the planning contained in this book:

- the proposed changes on 'income shifting' which are to take effect from 6 April 2008 will have implications for the long-term ownership of assets between married couples and civil partnerships and this needs to be borne in mind when reading Chapter 10;

- the proposed changes on residency and the remittance basis for non-domicilliaries need to be borne in mind when reading Chapter 14; and

- the proposed transferability of the nil rate band which takes effect from 9 October 2007 for inheritance tax (IHT) purposes needs to be considered when reading Chapter 15.

The changes to CGT proposed are set out in PBRN17 but in short amount to:

- the abolition of taper relief;

- the withdrawal of any entitlement to indexation allowance;

- deemed global rebasing elections as at 31 March 1982;

- the abolition of the rebasing transitional halving relief for hold-over and roll-over relief purposes;

- a return to a single share pool; and

- the introduction of a single rate of CGT of 18%.

These changes finish the unwinding of Nigel Lawson's reforms of 1988 and take us back to something close to the original 1965 rules except that there is no tax on short term gains, as there was at that time, and there is no form of retirement relief. There is also no form of protection against inflation (at a time when inflation is coming back onto the agenda) and therefore, the long-term ownership of assets is positively discouraged as individuals will be paying tax on inflationary gains. This inconsistency is compounded by the fact that companies continue to be entitled to indexation allowance and none of the changes affect the taxation of companies.

The obvious CGT planning ideas are as follows:

- the acceleration of gains into 2007/08 where the vendor is entitled to full business asset taper relief (BATR);

- where short-term assts have been held with minimal entitlement to taper relief, such as on quoted shares or buy to let properties, then it is probably better to defer disposals until after 5 April 2008;

- consideration will need to be given to crystalising gains prior to 5 April 2008 where the owner has full entitlement to BATR such as by transfer to a settler-interested interest in possession trust; and

- investment planning for individuals and trustees after 5 April 2008 is going to focus much more heavily on CGT planning because of the entitlement to both the annual exemption and a maximum tax rate of 18%.

It remains to be seen whether there are any significant changes to these proposals between now and the Finance Bill next year. Whilst there has been significant comment on the implications for entrepreneurs of an increase from a tax rate of 10% to one of 18%, that must surely have been fully considered by the government before making such announcements. Not the least of which because the current Prime Minister was so closely associated with the taper relief policy. However, it would seem that there will be lobbying for some form of retirement relief at least and even more so, it seems hard to believe that even gains held over the shortest time periods will qualify for the 18% tax rate. Whether this leads to some rules on the taxation of very short term gains as income or just on the imposition of the existing anti–avoidance provisions remains to be seen. However, advisers will need to carefully consider whether activities need to be construed as trading as considered in Chapter 1, employment income as considered in Chapter 4 and the full remit of anti-avoidance provisions as set out in Chapter 13.

Some other points to consider are:

- roll-over relief is likely to become more important again and this is considered in Chapter 7;

- EIS relief will be slightly more attractive on business assets and this is considered in Chapter 6;

- whether or not to apply s 138A on earnouts in 2007/08 as considered in Chapter 5;

- the position for EMI option holders on a sale has not got any easier and this is considered in Chapter 4; and

- the planning issues in respect of capital losses in Chapter 12 now require even more careful thought.

The point on capital losses only seeks to emphasise the disconnection between taxation of capital gains and income. The claiming of trading losses against capital gains for a higher-rate taxpayer now looks very unwise as the losses will only be relieved at 18%, whilst losses on shares subscribed for in unlisted trading companies are now subject to an 18% rate on gains but relievable against income on losses. All of this only serves to emphasise that there is some more water to flow under the bridge before these rules finally bed down. I would also anticipate further changes in the next few years.

John Endacott

12 October 2007

Chapter 1

Introduction to Capital Gains Tax Planning

Purpose of this book

1.1   This book has been designed to sit alongside Tolley's Capital Gains Tax, which provides an explanation of the various rules relating to the tax. The purpose of this book is to provide a planning guide and is primarily aimed at those advising individuals and trustees although it is of course very difficult to neatly segregate the advice that could be relevant to such persons away from that which is relevant to companies. Inevitably, some matters are covered in more depth than others and whole books have already been written and published dedicated to many of the chapter subjects in themselves. Whilst acknowledging these limitations the aim of this book is to provide planning ideas, to act as a source of convenient reference on various matters and where possible to highlight some potential pitfalls. In writing the book it has been assumed that the readership already have a few years of practical experience working in tax and are perhaps recently qualified Chartered Tax Advisers, experienced general practitioners or even tax experts looking for guidance!

In writing this book, the authors have tried to take a fresh look at the planning ideas. Although capital gains tax (CGT) is a relatively new tax, it is noteworthy that none of the authors were even born in 1965. What is even more pertinent is that whilst all of the authors were born prior to 1982, several of them have no real memories of that year, and in particular of the circumstances existing at 31 March 1982.

At that date (which was just prior to the invasion of the Falkland Islands by Argentina), Seven Tears by the Goombay Dance Band was number 1, Liverpool were on the way to winning the football league, and Fulham were on their way to winning promotion out of the old third division. More relevantly, the bank base rate was 13%, inflation was around 8% and the yield on government stock was 15% to 16%. The average house price in 1982 was £23,644 and under the tenancy laws then in place (prior to assured shorthold tenancies), many tenants had significant occupation rights, such that the values of properties were significantly reduced by sitting tenancies.

Turning to businesses, the European formats for statutory accounts, including the vertical balance sheet and with the disclosure categories that are now so well known, were only just coming in, with the result that the historic accounts will often look pretty alien to modern eyes. In 1982, the highest rate of income tax on investment income was 75% and on earned income the rate of tax was 60%, whilst the main rate of corporation tax was 52% with the small companies' rate at 40%. The CGT rate was 30%.

All of this will be entirely familiar to many readers, but if the book is to achieve its objective, it is important that tax advisers understand both the background to, and the nature of, CGT. It is clear that one needs to look back over the history of CGT as many of these historic issues will be relevant to previous decisions that have been made and to base costs.

All statutory references in this chapter are to TCGA 1992 unless otherwise stated.

A brief history of capital gains tax prior to 1982

1.2 Whilst taxation of income was originally introduced over 200 years ago, this did not extend to the taxation of capital gains. As a result, capital gains were encouraged and this was seen as providing a tax break for asset strippers and profiteers in much the same way as comments are made today about the private equity industry. After the Second World War pressure grew for capital gains to be taxed and a Royal Commission on the Taxation of Profits and Income was appointed in the early 1950s.

The Commission noted that whilst the USA had taxed capital gains as income since the introduction of the Federal Code in 1913, this had been mitigated by the introduction of a lower tax rate for long-term gains in 1922. The Commission objected to taxing capital gains at marginal tax rates as the profit may have accrued over a period of time. The Commission also objected to the offset of capital losses against income, felt that the tax would be a disincentive to saving and would generate a low tax yield as well as reducing tax receipts from stamp duty and estate duty.

The Report concluded that 'we have said enough to show that a tax on capital gains if put into operation cannot be expected to prove a tax of simple structure or one that would be free from a number of rather arbitrary solutions of its various problems'. The Commission did not recommend taxation of either short or long-term capital gains.

The key political driver for change was the high taxation of income at a time that favoured the retention of profits. The absence of a tax on gains enabled tax-free profits to be taken on the disposal of shares where their value had increased through the retention of profits. R H Tawney of the LSE was influential in policy development and referred to this 'immunity from taxation which ...such speculative plunder continues to enjoy has as much justification as a close season for sharks'.

Even for the Conservatives, the taxation of capital gains was about politics rather than tax generation. Anthony Eden referred to such a tax as a 'gesture [that] would out-weigh the dangers and even the inefficiency of the tax'. Reginald Maudling stated that a short-term tax on capital gains would be 'a fundamental act of justice in a society where the rewards for ownership are disproportionate to the rewards for effort' and that 'it would be politically very welcome to many of our supporters'. The Conservative's political agenda was to remove the worst excesses of the mergers and takeover boom of the late 1950s and early 1960s and the infamous asset-stripping that went with it. This also explains the decision to introduce the transactions in securities legislation in 1960. Selwyn Lloyd had discussed the possibility of a CGT in his Budget Statement on 17 April 1961 but at the time he did not think it was worthwhile. In his statement of 9 April 1962 he said:

> 'my objections to a capital gains tax ... is that such a tax would militate against saving, genuine investment and economic growth. I have not, therefore, come here today to propose a capital gains tax, but to suggest that what may loosely be called speculative gains be subject to tax.'

This change to introduce what became the Schedule D Case VII charge, was on the grounds of equity and not yield.

The Labour agenda promoted by James Callaghan was a corporation tax so that a lower rate of taxation applied to companies which sought to retain their profits in order to reinvest. However, unless this was introduced in tandem with CGT, it would only open the door to further 'profiteering' via tax-free gains on shares.

When CGT was originally introduced, there was a charge on death. The CGT payable on death was deductible from the estate duty due so the position was consistent with a net of tax calculation of the estate. The removal of the charge on death considerably weakened the tax and created the modern choice of CGT or inheritance tax (IHT) for estate tax planning.

Gilts were brought within CGT as to exclude them 'would leave a wide open door for avoidance' and an exemption for them was not introduced until 1970. Given the use of such exempt assets in more recent financial arrangements for individuals, there is probably considerable truth in this original view.

There was then the issue as to how to introduce such a tax and the valuation issues that arise. James Callaghan did not want to rebase, other than for shares for which were created Budget Day Values (ie partial rebasing). For other assets, except development land, gains were to be calculated by time apportionment up to a maximum of 20 years (ie 6 April 1945).

The major exception that James Callaghan made to CGT in his Budget Statement was the 'owner-occupied house'. What is now ss 222 to 224 were poorly drafted, in particular, s 223(1) which deals with the position where the property is only a principal private residence (PPR) for part of the period of ownership. At issue here is the final 36 months of ownership which are deemed to count 'in any event'. The wording is loose and leaves considerable planning opportunities especially where property prices rise over a very short period of time (as is the pattern in this country). The planning is especially possible for those with more than one property and is allowed by the curious drafting of the election in s 222(5). The initial two-year qualification period is potentially restrictive, but subsequent changes have total flexibility subject to qualification of the property as a residence. Some overlap in entitlement is clearly essential, especially as in the 1960s bridging was more common. However, the original final period was 12 months but this was extended to 24 months in the housing market slump of the early 1980s and then to 36 months in that of the early 1990s. As with the other reliefs in the original legislation, the drafting was inadequate, but whilst those other reliefs have been substantially amended, for political reasons the relief on owner occupied property has been regarded as largely untouchable. PPR is considered in detail in CHAPTER 9.

Retirement relief existed at the outset of CGT and was always an important consideration for those contemplating the disposal of business assets. The relief was misnamed as retirement was never required, merely the existence of a gain on the disposal of qualifying business assets after the transferor had reached a certain age. Whilst this approach tended to be misleading to taxpayers (who were often surprised that the relief was available to them) it did have the benefit of relative simplicity as it did not require a definition of retirement. It was clearly designed as a relief for those who had been in business for many years and to help give them something in the nature of a tax-free lump sum.

The original retirement relief provided for a maximum relief of £10,000 at age 65 for a disposal by an individual of the whole or part of the business or on the disposal of securities in a family trading company. The maximum relief was doubled to £20,000 in 1974, although there was little change to the statutory requirements which had to be supplemented by various statements of practice and extra-statutory concessions (ESCs). For disposals after 11 April 1978 (the same time that hold-over relief was introduced) the relief was increased to £50,000 and the original provisions redrafted. The ESCs and statements of practice were codified, amended and reissued. Geoffrey Howe increased the maximum relief to £100,000 in 1983 and then, following a review, the legislation was redrafted and statutory effect given to the various statutory concessions and statements of practice in 1985. The maximum relief was further increased in 1987 and then again in 1988 with a two-tier relief being introduced. Further increases followed in 1991 and 1993 as well as reductions in the age of entitlement in 1991 and in 1995. By 1995 the relief was available to those aged over 50 with a 100% exemption on gains up to £250,000 and 50% on a band of gains between £250,000 and £1,000,000. This amounted to a maximum relief of £625,000.

Other original elements of the CGT legislation from 1965 are roll-over relief and the no gain/no loss rule on transfers between spouses (and now civil partners). There were significant deficiencies in the drafting of the legislation on both these provisions which had to be supplemented in the form of interpretations, ESCs and statements of practices. These played a major part in the tax adviser's role when advising on CGT and knowledge of them is still important. However, the tax law rewrite project has led to much codification of these non-statutory documents and this together with a less conciliatory tone by HMRC has reduced their importance to tax advisers. Despite this, much reference is still made in this book to tax planning opportunities presented by such documents.

The mid to late 1970s were dominated by concerns over inflation, which were relevant to the consideration of CGT as the tax was levied on gains caused only by monetary de-valuation. This, together with concerns over high tax rates, led to the formulation of aggressive tax planning schemes (such as the Rossminster Schemes) which were based around a literal interpretation of the tax law and a pre-determined set of transactions. In turn, these schemes led through to the case law decisions in the 1980s, such as *WT Ramsay v CIR* [1981] STC 174, *Furniss v Dawson* [1984] AC 474, [1984] 1 All ER 530, HL and *Craven v White* [1989] AC 398, [1988] 3 All ER 495, HL. These form the bedrock of a judicial principle of setting aside tax planning schemes where certain circumstances apply. These principles are considered in CHAPTER 13.

As far as inflation was concerned, pressure grew for some relief in the calculation of capital gains. This extended to the Conservative party including a pledge in its 1979 manifesto for the general election to take action to prevent the taxation of inflationary gains. However, after the election, it was still cautious in its approach to the issue. In his 1980 Budget speech, Geoffrey Howe said:

> 'I am fully conscious of the impact inflation has had [on gains]. It can rightly be argued that the tax often falls on what are no more than paper gains. Proposals for indexation or tapering as a means of meeting this problem have been put forward on many occasion …but the conclusion to which I have come is that both would result in an unwelcome increase in the cost of administration …while reducing the yield of tax to negligible proportions.'

Capital gains tax since 1982

1.3   In broad terms, CGT does not apply prior to 1982 although as will be clear from the various chapters of this book, and from the above, it is still necessary to consider events that took place prior to that date. It is also important to understand the course of events which took place throughout the 1980s. This is because despite the fact that 31 March 1982 is such a key date for CGT, nothing that was announced actually changed at that point in time. Indeed, partial rebasing was not introduced until 1985.

What was introduced in 1985 was an indexation allowance that applied to a market value as at 31 March 1982. However, it was only the indexation allowance that was calculated by reference to the March 1982 value and the unindexed gain was still calculated by reference to cost. However, the indexation allowance could not create or augment a loss and so it was necessary to calculate the gains both on a basis by reference to cost and then a basis including the indexation allowance.

Three years later, this bizarre system was replaced by full rebasing. Nigel Lawson introduced a CGT system that only taxed real gains, but this was by aggregating gains with income. However, even in this supposedly all inclusive system, capital losses brought forward from earlier years were not indexed. So from 6 April 1988, gains were then calculated both by reference to cost and by reference to a re-based March 1982 value. At that time, it was (and still is) necessary to calculate gains both by reference to cost and by reference to their March 1982 value unless a global rebasing election was made under FA 1988, s 96(5) or as it has since become, s 35(5). A further change was that from that point, indexation allowance could create or augment a loss.

It is worth explaining that the 31 March 1982 date was chosen in particular because it was the proposed re-rating date for all properties in England before the Conservative government pulled the rates revaluation. This was because inflation had led to a significant rise in the value of properties since the previous rates valuation in 1973 and the Conservative government looked for a different form of local government taxation until they eventually decided upon the Community Charge, or Poll Tax as it was otherwise known. The important, ongoing point is that the District Valuer had already been required to revalue all properties in England and this database is available to the District Valuer in terms of negotiating property values as at 31 March 1982.

A further change introduced in 1988 is that whilst the highest rate for income tax was dramatically cut from 60% to 40%, at the same time, CGT was increased from 30% to 40%. Therefore, what had prior to that date been an effective 50% rate of taper relief on all gains was withdrawn overnight and the whole focus of CGT planning shifted. There became an increasing acceptance that the rate of CGT was unduly harsh and this prompted the introduction of the Enterprise Investment Scheme (EIS), reinvestment relief and Venture Capital Trusts (VCTs). As explained in CHAPTER 6, these reliefs were very important throughout the 1990s because otherwise the capital available for investment was depleted by the high rate of CGT. The Labour opposition appreciated this and this in turn led to the introduction of taper relief which is considered further below. If inflation is low, then there is unlikely to be any major campaign for an allowance for inflation. However, the position could change again in the future.

Taper relief

1.4 Gordon Brown announced the introduction of taper relief, as follows:

'The ...regime we inherited rewards the short-term speculator as much as the committed long-term investor. So it is time also for a fundamental reform ...I have decided to phase out complex allowances and instead will introduce a new structure of CGT which will explicitly reward long-term investment and is based on a downward taper and lower tax rates.'

Geoffrey Robinson MP was Paymaster General in Tony Blair's first administration and was heavily involved with the introduction of taper relief. He comments on the reforms to CGT in his book *The Unconventional Minister*. In this book, he explains that he believes that Nigel Lawson, whilst simplifying the tax, fixed the rate of CGT at too high a rate. Prior to 1988, the rate of taxation applied to long-term capital gains had always been lower than the top income tax rate. Nigel Lawson had said in his Budget Speech of that year:

> 'In principle, there is little economic difference between income and capital gains, and many people effectively have the option of choosing to a significant extent which to receive. And insofar as there is a difference, it is by no means clear why one should be taxed more heavily than the other. Taxing them at different rates distorts investment decisions and inevitably creates a major tax avoidance industry.'

Geoffrey Robinson believed that the rate of CGT should differentiate between short and long-term gains. He accepted that this meant additional complexity by having more than one rate but wanted 'to encourage and reward long-term investment by the portfolio investor and more importantly by the entrepreneur'. Interestingly the original proposals were put together by Andersen just prior to the general election of 1997.

Whilst Geoffrey Robinson was keen to get rid of the annual exemption, the political situation was such that a compromise was required and the end result was half-hearted reform. However, the implication in his book, and also of other statements by Ministers at the time, was that the further changes would take place once the taper had started to bite. As far as abolishing existing reliefs was concerned, Geoffrey Robinson 'took the view from the beginning that retirement relief should be phased out over as long a period as possible. The aim would be to protect those who would soon retire and enable those who were five or more years away from retirement to benefit from the taper'.

The idea of a longer process in the book ties in with the statements by him in the House of Commons and also by Dawn Primarolo, who, for instance, commented that 'the introduction of the taper relief will make it possible progressively to withdraw the complicating features ...from the CGT system. Chief among those is the indexation allowance'. The expectation was that future changes could be achieved because taper relief would reduce the benefit of other tax reliefs and so enable them to be later removed.

As a result of taper relief the following tax rates would apply for higher rate personal taxpayers from April 1998:

Number of whole years of ownership	Business assets	Non-business assets
1	37%	—
2	34%	—
3	31%	38%
4	28%	36%
5	25%	34%
6	22%	32%
7	19%	30%
8	16%	28%
9	13%	26%
10 plus	10%	24%

It is notable that whilst the long-term reduction in tax rates was substantial, the short-term impact was not that great because of the delay in the taper applying for non-business assets. Even for business assets, it would be five years before the rate of CGT fell to the equivalent of the higher rate tax charge on dividends.

Whilst the non-business rate of taper has remained unchanged, taper relief for business assets has been substantially amended twice since taper relief was introduced, in 2000 and 2002 as follows:

Number of whole years of ownership	Business assets 1998	Business assets 2000	Business assets 2002
1	37%	35%	20%
2	34%	30%	10%
3	31%	20%	—
4	28%	10%	—
5	25%	—	—
6	22%	—	—
7	19%	—	—
8	16%	—	—
9	13%	—	—
10 plus	10%	—	—

The rate of accrual of relief is now considerably faster than was originally proposed in the Andersen policy document. The two-year period can also be contrasted with the five-year period of ownership in the purchase of own shares legislation which is considered in CHAPTER 4.

Operation of taper relief

1.5   By far and away the most important relief throughout the CGT legislation is now taper relief. In providing planning advice on CGT, it is particularly important not to make ill-judged assumptions about the entitlement to this relief. The core of the taper relief rules are contained in s 2A and Sch A1, para 2. These introduce the order of events, the table of accrual rates, and the definitions of 'qualifying holding period' and 'relevant period of ownership'. Section 2A applies taper relief to gains of a person eligible for taper relief and by reference to the year of assessment. It is applied on a gain by gain basis with the result being aggregated.

Taper relief is calculated by reference to the qualifying holding period throughout which an asset has been held. Only complete years count, and the period will commence on 6 April 1998 or at the time of acquisition, if later, and end on the date of disposal. For non-business assets acquired before 17 March 1998 an extra 'bonus' of one year increases the qualifying holding period. For these assets the maximum non-business asset taper rate of 40% has applied since 6 April 2007.

Although taper relief has been described as a replacement for the indexation allowance, its computational treatment is different. Whilst indexation allowance is deducted in establishing the amount of a gain, taper relief is given after the chargeable gain has been established. The computational approach is therefore as follows:

(a)   calculate the unindexed gain;

(b)   deduct indexation allowance;

(c)   deduct reliefs (ss 152, 222 etc);

(d)   deduct losses; and

(e)   apply and deduct taper relief.

Where a gain is relieved under a provision that reduces the cost of a replacement asset (eg s 152), the amount of the rolled-over gain is the gain before any taper relief is given. On any subsequent disposal of the new asset, no account is taken of the period during which the original asset was held. For the purposes of taper relief, the qualifying holding period on the subsequent disposal begins on the date that the replacement asset is acquired. Roll-over relief is considered in CHAPTER 7.

Schedule A1, para 2 introduces the concept of 'relevant period of ownership'. This is a period of up to ten years (although not before 5 April 1998) during which the ownership of the asset is considered for the purposes of taper relief. The relevant period of ownership ceases when the asset is disposed of and so is measured backwards from the date of disposal.

Where an asset was not acquired but was created by the person making the disposal, for example goodwill, the date of acquisition is the date the asset was created. The date the asset was created is determined as a question of fact on the basis of the evidence available. The revised Statement of Practice D12 suggests that this is the date when a business commences trading.

When taper relief was introduced, it was announced that the capital gains treatment of companies would be reviewed and amended. Companies are not entitled to taper relief, and instead have continued to receive the benefit of indexation allowance. However FA 2002 introduced the new Substantial Shareholdings Exemption (SSE) of Sch 7AC and the changes to the taxation of intangible fixed assets contained in FA 2002, Sch 29. The UK tax legislation now contains a participation exemption enabling companies to dispose of subsidiaries and other strategic shareholdings without a liability to tax. These corporate rules are relevant when considering individual versus a corporate ownership structure.

Impact of development of capital gains tax for planning

1.6 It is easy to dismiss most of the above as being of only academic interest now and of no relevance to those practising in tax. However, there are a number of important points that can be drawn out and that are relevant on an ongoing basis, both in terms of understanding the nature of CGT and also in many ways as an indication to likely future changes. Future changes are important, bearing in mind that the tax adviser is providing advice on how to structure a client's affairs to minimise CGT in the long term and it must be assumed that there will be changes in the tax legislation over that period.

The specific points that can be learnt from the development of CGT are as follows:

(a) CGT is fundamentally an anti-avoidance provision to prevent the diversion of income profits into capital gains.

(b) Short-term gains are viewed as much the same as income and taxed as such whilst longer-term gains should be subject to a lower tax rate than income. This was historically achieved by setting a lower CGT rate than the income tax rate, by having retirement relief and then more recently, by the introduction of taper relief.

(c) There is no inflation protection for base costs, such that over time inflationary gains are taxed. Whilst the retail price and consumer price indices have suggested a low level of inflation over the past few years, this is not borne out by asset price inflation or by a wider measure of inflation. A good example of the impact of this on tax planning has been for instance where a client wishes to sell a let property but then wants to invest the proceeds in another let property. Under the current structure of CGT, this is not tax efficient.

(d) The aggregation of gains onto income means that tax planning by minimising income is advisable particularly where it is possible to bring the income down out of higher rate such that CGT is saved at this rate.

(e) It is still necessary to consider all of the rules regarding CGT rebasing to 31 March 1982 especially where a loss arises as in the absence of a global rebasing election, this will probably not be available.

These planning considerations are best considered by way of the following examples.

Example – Pension contribution

Lucy was born on 2 March 1950. She owned a café for a number of years and intends to continue to run the café until she is 60. On 30 November 2006, she sells a number of shares she inherited from her late Auntie. Lucy's friend had recently lost a lot of money when a company she had shares in collapsed, which made Lucy nervous and so she decided to sell her shares even if she would have to pay some tax.

The gain on the shares is £22,340. There is no taper relief available as the shares were owned for less than three years.

Lucy made profits from the café in the year to 31 October 2006 (her accounting year) of £25,000. Her accountant estimated her dividend income for the year to 5 April 2007 to be £4,500. She had no other sources of income. He then advised her that her tax position for 2006/07 would be as follows:

Income	£	£	£
Profits		25,000	
Dividends		5,000	
		———	
			30,000
Less: personal allowance			(5,035)
			———
			£24,965
Tax @ 10% on	2,150	= 215	
Tax @ 22% on	17,815	= 3,919	
Tax @ 10% on	5,000	= 500	
	———		
	£24,965		4,634
Less: dividend tax credits			(500)
			———
			4,134
Class 4 National Insurance contributions			1,597
			———
Income tax liability			5,731
Capital gain	22,340		
Less: annual exemption	(8,800)		
	———		

Taxable gain	13,540		
Tax @ 20% on	8,335	= 1,667	
Tax @ 40% on	5,205	= 2,082	
CGT liability			3,749
Tax payable			£9,480

Lucy's accountant advised her to make a personal pension contribution of £5,205 (gross) to wipe out the higher rate element of the gain. Lucy was at first opposed to investing anything into a pension fund, but relented when her accountant explained that she would only need to fund £3,019 after tax relief. This is calculated as follows:

	£	£	£
Income tax liability (as before)			5,731
Taxable gain (as before)	13,540		
Tax @ 20% on	13,540	= 2,708	
Tax @ 40% on	Nil	—	
CGT liability			2,708
Tax payable			£8,439

The tax liability has therefore reduced by £1,041. The tax relief on the pension contribution was therefore:

	£
Gross contribution	5,205
Tax relief at source (22%)	(1,145)
Additional relief (20%)	(1,041)
Net contribution	£3,019

Example – Re-basing

Fiona purchased some land with no business use on 1 October 1980 for £50,000 (including costs of acquisition) and sold it on 15 August 2007 for £160,000 (net of selling expenses). Its value at 31 March 1982 was £70,000.

	£	£
Net sale proceeds	160,000	160,000
Less: cost	(50,000)	
Market value 31.3.82		(70,000)
Unindexed gain	110,000	90,000
Indexation allowance (factor 1.047)	(73,290)	(73,290)
Gain after indexation	£36,710	£16,710
Chargeable gain (subject to taper relief)		16,710
Taper relief at 40%		(6,684)
Chargeable gain		£10,026

If the proceeds were only £60,000 then the position would be:

	£	£
Net sale proceeds	60,000	60,000
Less: cost	(50,000)	
Market value 31.3.82		(70,000)
Unindexed gain	10,000	10,000
Indexation allowance (factor 1.047) but restricted to	(10,000)	—
Gain/loss	£Nil	£10,000
Chargeable gain	£Nil	

There is also the possibility that the cost could be higher than the value at 31 March 1982. This is uncommon but can occur where antiques or artwork are involved or where quoted shares were acquired not long before 31 March 1982.

March 1982 values

1.7 It is important not to overlook the benefits of maximising the base cost where it is based upon the market value at 31 March 1982. It is still certainly worth spending time looking at the basis of the value and whether there are any arguments that can be put forward to suggest a higher value particularly where business valuations are concerned. In this context, it is important that there is good communication and dialogue between the tax adviser and the valuer (whether that it is a chartered surveyor or a colleague undertaking a share valuation).

The effect of indexation allowance from March 1982 up to April 1998 is to increase the base cost by just over 100% and so where tax is payable at 40%, then every increase of £1 in the March 1982 will reduce the tax payable by 80p. Often, opportunities to increase the March 1982 value may not be particularly obvious and can only be established through discussions with the client. For instance, it may be that there was a planning permission on land at that date which has since lapsed, or an offer was received for the shares in the company at that time, but not pursued, or that valuations were prepared for other purposes such as for bank finance or for capital transfer tax purposes. In the same way, it is also worth spending time going back over the enhancements made to the asset, a number of which may be many, many years ago. Whilst such planning may seem obvious, it can significantly cut the tax bill.

Connected persons

1.8   Throughout CGT it is necessary to consider the position where the parties to a transaction are connected. A list of those persons who are treated as connected for CGT purposes appears in s 286. The main problems commonly associated with transactions between connected persons can be summarised as follows:

(a)   If the parties to a disposal and corresponding acquisition of an asset are connected, the transaction is deemed to be undertaken otherwise than by way of bargain made at arm's length. In such situations, however, the parties may have negotiated an acceptable price with no thought of bounty, only for the price to be questioned, perhaps on reference to the District Valuer or Shares Valuation Division.

(b)   Where a loss arises on the disposal of an asset to a connected person, that loss may only be offset against chargeable gains attributable to the disposal of other assets to the same connected person and not against gains generally. This suggests that only in exceptional circumstances should an asset be transferred to a connected person where a loss is expected to arise on disposal.

(c)   There are provisions which may affect the determination of market value where assets transferred to a connected person are subject to enforceable rights or restrictions (eg see ss 18(6) and 29).

(d)   An individual may contemplate the disposal of an asset by a series of transactions. This action will usually be undertaken to reduce the aggregate disposal proceeds with the assistance of fragmentation. For example, an individual may retain virtually the entire issued share capital of an unlisted company. A single transfer of the aggregate holding to a connected person may well result in a substantial market value reflecting the notional disposal proceeds. In an attempt to reduce this value there may be successive transfers, each involving perhaps 10% of the holding. Section 19 seeks to nullify this attempt at tax avoidance where linked transactions are carried out between connected persons within a six-year period. The section requires that the market value will not be limited to the independent value of each transaction but will instead be based on the aggregate value of all transactions.

Approach to capital gains tax planning

1.9   The objective of CGT planning is to achieve the elimination or reduction of a liability to tax. This can be achieved by one of the following means:

(a)   taking advantage of an exemption such as principal private residence relief or non-residence;

(b)   reducing the rate of tax by maximising the available taper relief or minimising taxable income; or

(c)   deferring the chargeable gain by utilising one of the available reliefs such as hold-over or roll-over.

CGT planning should be approached in the order of priorities set out above. The first question is, can absolute exemption from tax be achieved? If not, then how much tax is payable? Then an assessment needs to be made as to whether this can or should be deferred. By claiming a deferral, hold-over or roll-over relief, an opportunity to subsequently claim a tax exemption may be lost.

That said, it could be that a combination of these tactics is required to achieve the tax saving. It may be that intermediate steps are required or that the timing or parties to the transaction need to be changed. Possibilities include phasing an asset sale or transferring an asset from one spouse/civil partner to another prior to eventual sale. It is also very important that other taxes are considered. The importance of flexibility must never be overlooked when planning as tax reliefs can and do change, and it is important that too much faith is not placed on current legislation when anticipating events designed to take place in the future.

Whether an item is revenue or capital account

1.10   Section 37(1) gives primacy to income tax over CGT. It is therefore necessary to consider whether a disposal is subject to CGT. As has already been explained above, prior to CGT, it was possible to escape taxation if an item was a capital gain. As a result, a significant body of case law built up in respect of whether or not an activity represented trading on the revenue account or proceeds from a capital disposal. Over time, HMRC have codified these into badges of trade and indeed the badges of trade were arrived at from the report by the Royal Commission referred to earlier in this introduction which reported in 1955.

A summary of badges of trade is contained in *Marson v Morton and others* [1986] STC 463. Badges of trade are identified as follows:

(1)   Whether or not a profit-seeking motive is present – evidence of the sole object of acquiring an asset being to re-sell it at a profit without any intention of holding it as an investment is an indicator that a trade is being carried on.

(2)   The frequency of transactions – whilst an isolated transaction can be a trading transaction, it is far more likely that in the trade, there will be repeated and systematic transactions. Therefore, an individual who enters into a number of property transactions is going to give an indication of trading.

(3)   The nature of the assets – can the asset be used to generate an investment return? Is the fixed asset used within a business or to provide personal enjoyment? In the absence of one of these factors, the assets concerned are more likely to represent stock in trade.

(4)   The existence of similar transactions or activities – the view will be coloured by the trade or occupation of the individual concerned. Many of the older cases that pre-date CGT concerned builders who had constructed properties and subsequently argued that they held them for investment on capital account so enabling them to sell them at a later date free of tax. The position was summed up in the case referred to above, *Marson v Morton and others* [1986] STC 463, in the comment that 'a one-off purchase of silver cutlery by a general dealer is much more likely to be a trade transaction than a purchase by a retired colonel'.

(5)   Has the asset been changed in any way to make it more saleable? – If there is expenditure on the asset after purchase and prior to sale, then this could suggest that trading is being carried on if the purpose is to make the item more saleable. Also, where an asset is purchased and then broken down into smaller lots for re-sale then it is indicative of trading. In *Cape Brandy Syndicate v CIR* [1921] 12 TC 358, the purchase of cape brandy which was imported into the UK blended with French brandy, recast and sold in numerous lots was always indicative of a trading activity.

(6)   The method of sale – is the nature of the transaction consistent with that of a trading activity or has it been forced by a change in circumstance or other event such as to raise proceeds in an emergency?

(7)   The financing of the transaction – has money been borrowed to finance the acquisition of the asset and if so, is this by way of bank overdraft or by term loan? If the financing is dependent upon the sale of the asset in the very short term then the nature of the financing is indicative of a trading activity.

(8)   The interval between purchase and sale – if there are a number of transactions with a short time scale between purchase and sale then this is likely to be indicative of trading.

(9)   Method of acquisition – where an asset is acquired by way of inheritance or is received as a gift, then it is less likely to be considered an item that is the subject of a trade. On the other hand, if it is purchased from a wholesaler, then this is likely to be indicative of trading.

In the context of CGT planning, the issue as to whether or not a trade has been carried on is normally considered in respect of the sale of either properties or shares (both quoted and unquoted).

Whilst an individual regularly buying and selling quoted shares with many transactions, and no intention to retain them in the long term is suggestive of trading, this is not borne out by the practice of HMRC or by the case law. Even though the purchase may be of shares which are not dividend yielding and by reference to many of the other badges of trade would seem to indicate trading, HMRC will not accept that a trade is being carried on. This is in part because an argument in favour of trading is normally made by the taxpayer where losses are involved and HMRC is of course anxious to try and resist a claim for loss relief. In such a case, the Inspector will normally quote that the individual concerned is unable to act as a trader because he is not qualified nor has the regulatory permissions to do so. In *Salt v Chamberlain (Inspector of Taxes)* [1979] STC 750, 53 TC 143 which concerned losses made by an individual through the buying and selling of quoted securities with the intention of making a profit, Oliver J said that 'where the question is whether an individual engaged in speculative dealings is carrying on a trade, the prima facie presumption would be that he is not'.

Therefore, as far as considering whether a trade is carrying on, we are left only with unquoted shares and property transactions to consider as a general rule. On the subject of unquoted shares, then the guidelines issued by the British Venture Capital Association (BVCA), as agreed with HMRC, suggests that investing in unquoted shares in not a trading activity, as long as matters are structured within the guidelines. This point is considered in CHAPTER 4. As far as properties are concerned, there remains the possibility that an activity could amount to a trade and this is most commonly argued by HMRC where there are a number of transactions and on which claims for PPR are made. This issue is considered further in CHAPTER 9.

The distinction between revenue and capital account is still important as far as CGT planning is concerned, not the least of which because of the opportunities presented by s 161. This concerns the appropriation of fixed assets to trading stock. Section 161(1) states that 'where an asset acquired by a person otherwise than as trading stock of a trade carried on by him is appropriated by him for the purposes of the trade as trading stock (whether on the commencement of the trade or otherwise) and, if he had then sold the asset for its market value, a chargeable gain or allowable loss would have accrued to him, he shall be treated as thereby disposing of the asset by selling it for its then market value'.

As a result, a disposal for CGT purpose arises where an asset is appropriated from fixed assets to trading stock. This may happen for instance where a property used as a fixed asset is going to be redeveloped, eg where a factory site is redeveloped as part of a property development trade. In such cases, it is possible to elect under s 161(3) for the capital gain not to arise at that point in time, but instead the gain to be effectively rolled over into the cost of the asset for trading stock purposes. The result of this is that the profit on appropriation will subsequently be taxed as trading income.

Example – Appropriation of fixed assets to trading stock

Len has owned a workshop business for many years, however, because of claims for roll-over relief it has a CGT base cost of only £1,000. He prepares accounts to 31 December each year.

In April 2007, a major customer goes into receivership giving rise to a large bad debt. He decides to close down the business and redevelop the site as it has a high residential value. He incurs a significant loss on the sale of the plant and machinery and because of redundancy costs. He instructs surveyors and architects to advise him, drafts a business plan and obtains bank finance to undertake the development. Planning permission is applied for.

On the appropriation of the fixed asset to trading stock, a capital gain will arise. The trading loss can be offset against this as otherwise it would be wasted on the cessation of the business.

Whether or not s 161 applies will be a matter of fact based upon proper accounting policies and the nature of the capital and revenue divide. However, where it does apply, it can present significant tax planning opportunities in terms of structuring the timing to fall into different tax years. For instance, it may be that an asset is appropriated from fixed assets to trading stock at its market value and is sold in a subsequent year, so generating a further profit. By splitting the transactions across two different tax years, it may be possible to cut the tax that would otherwise apply. There may also be circumstances that make a trading profit more desirable such as where there are trading losses or a desire to make significant pension contributions. Equally there may be other circumstances where a gain subject to CGT is more attractive, even though there will be no cash available to pay the tax that will arise. This may be for instance because a claim for roll-over relief is to be made on the gain arising from s 161(1).

Conclusions

1.11   It is important that tax advisers understand both the background to, and the nature of, CGT. It is a long-term tax and therefore matters that may seem a long way in the past may still be relevant. Moving on from that, it is important that advisers get the basics right and consider whether or not a transaction is a trading transaction or a capital transaction and then consider the basic rules of calculation and reliefs before turning to thinking about any more bespoke planning. Having considered these matters, it is then appropriate for the tax adviser to consider what other reliefs are available or how best to structure any disposal in order to minimise CGT. The remainder of this book is concerned with such further planning, as well as also considering some international tax planning implications and interaction with other taxes, notably IHT.

Checklist

Context and Background to Capital Gains Tax Planning	Cross Reference
Advisers need to understand the historical development of CGT in order to appreciate the implications of previous planning.	1.2
The context and operation of taper relief is important to all CGT planning.	1.4
The importance of March 1982 values and establishing them must be appreciated for all assets held prior to that date either by the existing holder or by a related party.	1.7
Whether a transaction is a capital gain or could instead be a trading transaction must be considered as part of any planning.	1.10

Chapter 2

Business Asset Taper Relief

Business or non-business status

2.1   Taper relief was introduced in 1998 as part of a wide ranging reform of capital gains tax (CGT). In order to encourage entrepreneurship it provides for a lower effective tax rate on business assets compared to non-business assets. Subject to some anti-avoidance provisions, all chargeable gains benefit from taper relief – the issue is therefore what taper rate will apply and what will be the effective rate of tax.

The distinction between business and non-business status is of the utmost significance because:

(a)   the maximum rate of taper on business assets is 75%, whereas it is 40% for non-business assets; and

(b)   the maximum taper on business assets is achieved after only two years whilst the maximum rate on non-business assets requires ten years of ownership.

An asset that does not achieve business asset status will represent a non-business asset. However, significant extensions were made to the relief from 6 April 2000, 17 April 2002 and 6 April 2004. Therefore it is not as simple as deciding what the status of an asset is at the time of disposal – it is also necessary to consider the position throughout the period of ownership. The goal of the planner is to establish business asset status and so achieve an effective tax rate of 10% or less.

Example – Importance of business asset status

Roy and Caren are both higher-rate taxpayers. They both sold some shares on 20 May 2007 that they have each owned for just over two years. The gain before taper relief for each of them is £36,800. Roy's shares qualify for business asset status throughout his period of ownership.

	Roy £	Caren £
Gain before taper relief	36,800	36,800
Taper relief @ 75%/0%	(27,600)	—
	9,200	36,800
Annual exemption	(9,200)	(9,200)
	£Nil	£27,600
CGT @ 40%	£Nil	£11,040

The basic mechanics of the operation of taper relief are set out in CHAPTER 1. Taper relief implications for planning feature throughout this book but particular areas include spouse holding periods which is considered in CHAPTER 10 and the interaction with other CGT reliefs which are considered in CHAPTER 8, CHAPTER 9, CHAPTER 7 and CHAPTER 6. The position of trustees and beneficiaries of settlements is considered in CHAPTER 11. This chapter is primarily concerned with CGT advice given in connection with a sale. All statutory references are to TCGA 1992 unless otherwise stated.

Business asset conditions

2.2   There are two classes of business assets:

(a)   shares or securities in a qualifying company by reference to an individual (Sch A1, para 4), and

(b)   assets other than shares (Sch A1, para 5).

The rules are different in certain circumstances and so consideration of the tax position should be approached separately for each category even where it may seem the position will be more or less identical eg where an owner/director of a company sells both his shares and business premises owned personally.

Whilst assets are categorised between business and non-business assets, the reference to business is misleading. It should more accurately be defined as 'Trading Asset Taper Relief'. In this context, trade is extended to include furnished holiday letting and farming.

The business asset status is determined by the nature of the asset and by its usage and ownership over a period of time. The period of time is the shortest of:

  (i) the actual ownership period;

 (ii) the period since 6 April 1998; and

(iii) ten years.

Although the business asset qualification criteria was significantly extended on 6 April 2000 and 2004, the period prior to those dates will continue to be relevant for many taxpayers until 6 April 2010 or 2014. When advising on taper relief it is necessary to review the position throughout the relevant period. If the asset has both business and non-business status during the period of ownership it is referred to as having 'tainted taper'.

Common taper relief issues

2.3   The most common situations are as follows:

(a) an owner-managed company carrying on some non-trading activities and whether these are substantial or not;

(b) whether or not share-owning employees qualify for business asset taper relief (BATR);

(c) to what extent BATR is available to landlords; and

(d) where assets are used for both business and non-business purposes at the same time (mixed use assets).

In each case the issue is to what extent the taper relief is tainted and the impact this has on the effective rate of tax to be paid on the disposal. Following on from these issues is how to restart the taper period to remove tainting and whether any planning falls foul of the specific taper relief anti-avoidance rules.

The taper status can be tainted either by reference to activity (trading status) or ownership. Both need to be considered. Whilst a minimum period of a year is required to qualify for taper relief, and whilst taper rates are only accrued on a whole year basis, the apportionment between business and non-business status is on a simple time basis (daily/monthly/annually).

Example – Tainted taper on private company shares

Annabel has held 2% of the shares in High Growth Limited since a management buy out in 1995. Annabel's taper period is tainted as High Growth Limited was not a qualifying company by reference to her throughout the entire period of ownership. The shares are sold on 6 April 2007. In calculating this gain, the two taper rates are apportioned on a time basis. For example, for shares that fall within this scenario and were held on 17 March 1998 (and so the bonus year applies for non-business assets), the taper rate is calculated as follows:

	%
6 April 1998 to 5 April 2000 2/9 × 40%	8.9
6 April 2000 to 5 April 2007 7/9 × 75%	58.3
	67.2%

The same time apportionment calculation is used in other situations where tainting occurs and this has to be performed for each separate holding.

Sometimes it will be advantageous to crystallise a capital gain if full BATR is available prior to any tainting of the taper.

For instance, this may be the case where it is intended to put a company into liquidation. In such a case, the cessation of trading will start a non-business asset period. If there is likely to be a significant delay in the making of the distribution on a winding up, and if the company has not had a long trading life, then the tainting of the taper could have a significant impact. In such a case, one approach would be to settle shares on oneself as this is a disposal for CGT purposes.

Shares and securities

2.4   Shares, in relation to a company, includes (a) any securities of that company, and (b) any debentures of that company that are deemed, by virtue of s 251(6), to be a security for the purposes of that section (Sch A1, para 22). There is no general definition of securities for CGT and s 251(6) only deals with debentures issued on a reorganisation. Where loan stock is acquired other than on a reorganisation, it is necessary to consider whether or not it satisfies the definition of 'debt on a security'.

The HMRC view, based on judicial interpretation, is that in order to qualify as a 'debt on a security' the loan note must be capable of being held as an investment and realised at a profit. In the drafting of any such loan note it is necessary to consider the rate of interest applying, the transferability of the loan note, and its term as well as any other factors that may make it unattractive as an investment. The same issue does not arise in relation to shares regardless of any restrictions placed upon them. The position of loan notes is considered further in CHAPTER 5.

For the first two years of BATR a company could only be identified as a qualifying company if it was a trading company, or the holding company of a trading group, in which at least 25% of the voting rights were exercisable by the individual holding the shares. The requisite voting rights could be reduced to 5% if the individual was a full-time working officer or employee of that company or some other concern with which the company was connected.

These requirements were substantially relaxed for periods falling after 5 April 2000. From that date, an individual's shareholding in a trading company, or the holding company of a trading group, may now be treated as a business asset and the company as a qualifying company if:

(a)   none of the company's shares is listed on a recognised stock exchange and the company is not a 51% subsidiary of a second company whose shares are so listed;

(b)   the individual is an officer or employee of the company, or of some other connected company; or

(c)   at least 5% of the voting rights in the company are exercisable by the individual.

In addition, and also for periods falling after 5 April 2000, an individual's shareholding in a non-trading company, or the holding company of a non-trading group, may be treated as a business asset, and the company as a qualifying company, if:

(i)   the individual was an officer or employee of the company, or some other connected company, and

(ii)   the individual did not have a material interest either in the company or in any company which at that time had control of the company.

An individual has a material interest if he or she has directly or indirectly more than 10% of the issued shares or securities, voting rights, rights to distributions or rights to surplus assets in a winding up. For the purposes of establishing whether a material interest exists, it is necessary to merge the interests of persons connected with the individual. The meaning of 'connected persons' is as set out in s 286 and broadly covers family relations, related trusts, business partners, related companies and certain shareholdings in those related companies. A material interest is defined as the possession of or the ability to control directly or by any other indirect means:

- more than 10% of the issued shares and securities in the company of any particular class;

- more than 10% of the voting rights in the company;

- such rights as would, if the whole of the income of the company were distributed among the participators (without regard to any rights of any person as a loan creditor), give an entitlement to receive more than 10% of the amount distributed; or

- such rights as would, in the event of the winding up of the company or in any other circumstances, give entitlement to receive more than 10% of the assets of the company, which would then be available for distribution among the participators.

A right to acquire shares or rights (however arising) is taken as a right to control them. These are rights that a person is entitled to acquire at a future date or which he will be entitled to acquire at a future date, eg deferred shares.

Definition of a 'qualifying company'

2.5   A 'qualifying company' is a company carrying on trading activities whose activities do not include to a substantial extent activities other than trading activities (Sch A1, para 22A). This is the same definition as for the Substantial Shareholding Definition (Sch 7AC, para 20) and so means that the objectives for individuals, trustees and corporate shareholders are consistent in terms of achieving trading status for a company.

'Trading activities' means activities carried on by the company:

1   in the course of carrying on its trade;

2   for the purposes of preparing to trade;

3   with a view to acquiring or starting to acquire a trade; or

4   with a view to acquiring a significant interest in the share capital of another company which is a 'trading company' or the holding company of a 'trading group' and which is not a member of the same group of companies as the company acquiring the shares.

Activities is not defined by statute and so takes its ordinary meaning. It includes trading operations, making and holding investments, preparing, planning, and monitoring any operations and company secretarial work. Trading activities may be undertaken both in preparation for and during trading. A company must commence to trade 'as soon as is reasonably practical in the circumstances' (Sch A1, para 22A(3)).

Substantial non-trading activities

2.6   The activities of a company or a group must not include to a substantial extent activities other than trading activities. When considering the activities of a group, intra-group activities are to be disregarded so that the activities of the members of the group are looked at as one business. Whilst the disregard for intra-group activities is a good thing, different trading structures can alter the calculation. For instance, property let to a subsidiary is ignored but if the tenant was not a subsidiary but was owned by the shareholders in parallel then the letting would probably be a non-trading activity and included. Intra-group loans and interest receipts give rise to the same issues.

HMRC have stated that they consider 'substantial' to mean 'more than 20%' and stated in Tax Bulletin 53 that:

'It is therefore necessary to consider what should form the basis for measuring whether a company's non-trading purposes are capable of having a substantial effect. We consider that this will vary according to the facts in each case but some or all of the following might be taken into account in reviewing a particular company's status:

• turnover receivable from non-trading activities,

• the asset base of the company,

• expenses incurred by or time spent by, officers and employees of the company in undertaking its activities.'

Further consideration of the issue is included in the HMRC Capital Gains Manual CG1795o. Four scenarios are stated as not necessarily indicating non-trading activities:

(1)   letting part of any trading premises;

(2) letting surplus property whilst trying to sell it;

(3) subletting leased property where it is impractical to assign or surrender the lease; and

(4) the acquisition of property where it is the intention to use it within the trade in the future.

It is interesting to explore the boundaries of these scenarios. For instance, the third scenario may enable leased property to be retained on the disposal of part of a trade without losing business asset status, even if the remaining trade is small.

Also, what if a pub and hotel group was considering the purchase of a portfolio of properties (both freehold and tenanted)? Could business asset status be maintained, even if the tenanted part of the combined portfolio was not insubstantial, as long as there was an intention to reduce, over time, the tenanted element so that it became insubstantial? *Farmer v IRC* [1999] STC SCD 321 also sets out that activities must in any event be looked at over a period of time and 'in the round'.

The IHT business property relief Commissioners' case of *Farmer v IRC* is relevant in considering these issues. This has been expanded upon by the Court of Appeal decision in *IRC v George* [2004] STC 147. This suggested that the following factors should be considered in determining trading status:

- the overall context of the business;

- capital employed;

- employer time;

- turnover; and

- profits.

The issue of non-trading activities has been an issue for several years as far as EIS relief is concerned. It is sometimes difficult to identify non-trading activities as they are subsumed within the overall trading activities. Eg, a pressure washer sales business that also installs and operates car washes, or a heavy plant sales business that hires out plant as well. The 20% limit does allow some room for manoeuvre but the downside is that it can restrict otherwise desired commercial decisions. This can lead to grey areas and the issue is often the extent to which other services are provided.

In practice, difficulties often arise where a longstanding trading company has reduced its level of trading activity for economic reasons and may have let former trading premises. The result may be a substantial source of rental income. The position can be particularly uncertain where the trade may recover and premises be brought back into trading use or perhaps where there is surplus land with residential development potential.

Another example of potential problems could be where a pub and nightclub operator decides, for good commercial reasons, to lease one of its premises to another operator.

If a business buys a building to use for its trade, but refurbishes it before occupation, HMRC's view is that while it is unoccupied during refurbishment, it is a non-business asset. Ideally, the business should use the building in some small way for trading purposes from the first day of ownership, perhaps as a storage area, which will result in full business asset taper relief applying. This is the same point as for roll-over relief (see CHAPTER 7).

Considerations as to trading status are an everyday planning aspect of advising owner-managed businesses. Shares may also cease to qualify because a company ceases trading. There are also other important planning considerations that arise in such situations including structuring to secure the Substantial Shareholding Exemption and inheritance tax and income tax issues.

Joint ventures

2.7 A 'joint venture company' is a trading company or the holding company of a trading group of which 75% or more of its ordinary shares are held by five or fewer persons (Sch A1, para 23). Prior to FA 2002 it was five or fewer companies. A 'qualifying shareholding' is greater or equal to 10%. A 'joint enterprise company' does not have a trading requirement unlike the position for a joint venture company (Sch A1, para 24). Joint venture companies are therefore a subset of joint enterprise companies.

Subparagraphs 4 and 6 apply a proportionate consolidation approach in order to bring in the activities of the joint venture company for the purposes of establishing the trading status of the investing company.

Case Study – Trendy Fashion Shops Limited

Trendy Fashion Shops Limited has been incorporated for 29 years. It originally had a single shop (Homestore) but then expanded to have a chain of five shops. Following a strategic review in 2004, a decision was made to cease trading from two of the shops (Old Town and New Town) which were then let to tenants. The trading shops are now Homestore, High Street and Retail Village. The company owns all of the shops with the exception of Retail Village which is leasehold.

The directors and shareholders are:

	No of shares (£1 ordinary)
Alan and Barbara Hazel (husband and wife)	4,500
Thomas Hazel (son)	5,500
	10,000

The directors have obtained planning permission to redevelop the top two floors of the Old Town shop and also to extend the property. This will create five apartments in addition to the letting shop. Alan Hazel intends to occupy one of the apartments.

The intention is to convert the New Town shop into two luxury apartments. No decision has yet been made as to whether these apartments are to be let or sold.

On a turnover basis, and by reference to the management time, the company is clearly a trading business. What is the position on the asset basis?

Trendy Fashion Shops Limited Balance Sheet as at *30 June 2007*	*£000s*
Fixed assets:	
Homestore	1,250
High Street	750
Old Town	500
New Town	400
Goodwill	500
Fixtures and fittings	100
	3,500
Working capital	(250)
Long-term bank loans	(600)
	£2,650
Represented by:	
Share capital	10
Profit and loss account	2,390
Revaluation reserve	250
	£2,650

After redevelopment, the Old Town property will be worth £1 million and £700,000 for New Town. The conversion costs are £250,000 for Old

Town and £150,000 for New Town. The conversion costs are to be funded by additional bank debt. The apartment to be occupied by Alan Hazel will be worth £200,000.

Profitability of the trade is declining such that the goodwill value may fall.

Forecast Position after Redevelopment

	Total	Alan Hazel's apartment	Remainder of Old Town	New Town	Trading Assets
	£000s	£000s	£000s	£000s	£000s
Homestore	1,250				1,250
High Street	750				750
Old Town	1,000	200	800		—
New Town	700			700	—
Goodwill	500				500
Fixtures and fittings	100				100
					2,600
Working capital	(250)				(250)
	4,050	£200	£800	£700	£2,350
Long-term bank loans	(1,000)				
	£3,050				

The pure trading assets represent £2,350,000 out of gross assets of £4,050,000 – 58%. Depending on the allocation of the bank loans, the proportion of trading to investment assets could vary. However, the intention is to use the rental income to repay the bank borrowing and so the bank debt should reduce over time in any event.

If the usage of the apartment by Alan Hazel is part of his remuneration arrangements, then it could be considered to be part of the trading assets of the business.

If the letting of the Old Town shop is only temporary and it could be brought back within the trade at a later date, then it could be a trading asset. A sale of the New Town apartments with reinvestment of the proceeds in the trade would increase the proportion of trading assets.

If the company is no longer trading then the taper position will be tainted. The company was certainly trading until 2004 and is probably a trading company afterwards. However, there is some uncertainty. The impact on the BATR will depend on the long term intentions. If the aim is to sell the shares in the company in the longer term then the BATR position by that time could be significantly worsened. Alternatively, if the objective is to form part of a gift of shares from Alan or Barbara to Thomas then entitlement to business asset hold-over relief will be important and this case study is further considered in CHAPTER 8.

Specific anti-avoidance rules for taper relief

2.8 When trying to identify and advise on planning opportunities, it is necessary to consider whether specific legislation exists to counter the approach being considered. There are three principal anti-avoidance rules for taper relief:

(a) limited exposure to fluctuations in value (Sch A1, para 10) which is referred to in the CGT Manual as 'freezing' – retaining ownership of an asset to increase the qualifying holding period while removing any economic exposure from that ownership;

(b) 'enveloping' (Sch A1, para 11A) – transferring an asset held for a short time period to a company whose shares have been held for a longer time period in order to take advantage of the longer qualifying holding period of the shares; and

(c) value shifting (Sch A1, para 12) – shifting value from shares held for a shorter time period to shares held for a longer time period in order to take advantage of that longer qualifying holding period.

The anti-avoidance legislation in each paragraph operates where a particular set of factual circumstances exists. There is no purpose test and therefore it does not matter whether the taxpayer had any intention to exploit the taper rules. Reference should also be made to CHAPTER 13 to consider whether any proposed planning is caught by wider anti-avoidance rules – such as whether the gain is subject to CGT in the first place.

The three rules apply to create periods that are:

(i) excluded from the qualifying holding period;

(ii) excluded when computing the last ten years ending with the time of the disposal that is taken into account in determining the relevant period of ownership; and

(iii) excluded from the relevant period of ownership.

The impact of these rules is different for value shifting which relates to a single event and so the effect of excluding the period prior to the event is to restart the relevant period of ownership. For freezing and enveloping the contravening activity can cease so that only the period of the contravening activity is excluded. This means that the relevant period of ownership start date can be more than ten years before disposal.

A transaction includes any agreement, arrangement or understanding, whether or not legally enforceable, and a series of transactions (Sch A1, para 22).

Freezing

2.9 Freezing applies where the person making the disposal, or a relevant predecessor, entered into a transaction that had the effect that he:

'(a) was not exposed, or not exposed to any substantial extent, to the risk of loss from fluctuations in the value of the relevant asset; and

(b) was not able to enjoy, or to enjoy to any substantial extent, any opportunities to benefit from such fluctuations.'

Once again the legislation relies upon the interpretation of 'substantial' and exposure to fluctuations in value is therefore limited if the potential movement is 20% or less either way. Reasonable insurance of the asset or foreign currency hedging are acceptable.

The Capital Gains Manual CG17916 states:

'Where the loan notes are issued as part of the normal commercial arrangements in an exchange the Inland Revenue do not consider that Paragraph 10 applies. This will usually be so even where the loan notes are underwritten by a third party guarantee (for example a bank guarantee) as part of those arrangements. In more complex or non-commercial circumstances, where the loan notes are issued to exploit the operation of taper Paragraph 10 may however apply.'

This guidance is helpful and is potentially concessionary, but it is subject to the caveat that it applies to 'normal commercial arrangements' and para 10 may apply where complex or non-commercial circumstances are used to exploit the operation of taper relief. Given that the major driving force behind structuring loan notes as non-Qualifying Corporate Bonds (QCBs) is to continue to obtain business assets status, care is certainly required.

Put and call options

2.10 Freezing would prevent future taper entitlement if put and call options are agreed. Therefore, it has been the practice to look at single options, or to include some exposure to a change in value on cross options by having differences in the price under each option and/or different time periods and exercise dates. Freezing could possibly be applied by certain non-standard provisions in the Articles of Association of a company.

Enveloping

2.11 The enveloping anti-avoidance provision operates by reference to activities. A company will be regarded as active if it is preparing, or actually carrying on a business of any description or if the business activity is being wound up. Note that the business need not be being carried on with a view to a profit nor conducted on a commercial basis. Further, the business can include the holding and managing of assets and so can include a business of investment. It should also be remembered that these definitions are only relevant to the question of whether or not the company is active and not the business asset qualification tests.

This test must be applied before considering business asset status. A company is not regarded as active solely because it holds cash on deposit, insignificant assets, shares in other non-active companies, is lending money to its participators or companies under their control or simply complying with the requirements of the Companies Act. An otherwise non-active company will be regarded as active if it has at least one active subsidiary, or a qualifying shareholding in a joint venture company or a subsidiary with such a shareholding. This is particularly relevant when one considers property consortia where very often there are companies involved that are link companies and are not otherwise engaged in much activity.

A company must be a close company throughout for para 11A to apply. A period when a company is inactive, but not close, will still count for taper relief purposes and the normal close company determination rules apply. A company in liquidation post winding up is inactive.

Tax Bulletin 61 comments on the meaning of business and cites authorities to support the views stated. The case of *Jowett v O'Neill and Brennan Construction Ltd* [1998] STC 482 succinctly rehearses the arguments as to whether activities amount to a business. In that case the activities were held not to amount to a business, and in fact only amounted to the placing of funds on deposit.

Paragraph 11A(4)(a) does make it clear that holding money on deposit can amount to a business otherwise it would not be necessary to include this exclusion. However, holding money on deposit could still be held to be a non-trading activity and so lead to a loss of business asset status as far as shares are concerned. The recent Special Commissioners' case of *Phillips and others (Executors of Phillips, deceased) v Revenue and Customs Commissioners* [2006] STC (SCD) 639 concerning business property relief for inheritance tax is also worth considering in this respect.

A company can hold assets and be inactive as long as the value of those assets is insignificant (Sch A1, para 11A(4)(b)). Tax Bulletin 61 states that insignificant must be given its normal dictionary meaning which it suggests is 'trifling or completely unimportant'. As guidance it suggests a figure of £1,000.

Case Study – Entitlement to BATR – Anti Avoidance Rules

Anna and Brian are 50:50 owners of a holding company (Holdco), financed by £100 of share capital and directors' loan. Anna and Brian purchased the Holdco shares and were appointed directors on 7 March

2007. The company was formed to acquire the businesses of a chain of restaurants which had gone into administration.

On 10 March 2007, Anna and Brian each paid £175,000 as a deposit to the administrator to secure the prospective purchase of the restaurant businesses by Holdco. The deposit was non-refundable, and the prices and terms of the business purchases were set at the time. Completion followed during July and August 2007 with the purchases being completed in subsidiary companies.

An offer is received for the Holdco group in April 2009. Has the two-year ownership period requirement been achieved?

Between the payment of the deposit and the completion of the purchase, the following activities took place in Holdco:

(a) a business plan, created in March 2007 when Anna and Brian first thought about acquiring the restaurants, was circulated to banks;

(b) the bank issued a facility letter;

(c) board meetings were held;

(d) solicitors were instructed to deal with lease assignments and licence applications;

(e) the directors were involved in the recruitment of key people;

(f) the directors were involved with the negotiations with suppliers to keep costs down and planning future capital expenditure.

Other matters discussed and evidenced in the board minutes included instructing auditors to apply for VAT registrations, and finding an office for the accounting function.

The major transactions of Holdco during this period were the payment of professional fees. These were initially paid personally by the directors, credited to loan accounts and reimbursed later.

The issues

There are two specific concerns:

(1) the acquisition of the businesses was not completed until several months after the acquisition of the shares, so there is a possibility that Holdco was not 'active' during that time.

(2) if the time between the acquisition of the shares and completion of the business acquisitions does count under para 11A, there is a possibility that Holdco would not count as a 'qualifying company' during that period. Given that the shares have only been held for just over two years, it is more likely that HMRC will look closely at the period of ownership.

It seems clear that Holdco was active from the signing of the contract on 10 March 2007. The directors have not only 'identified a specific business opportunity' as mentioned in the Tax Bulletin; they have exchanged contracts to buy the business. The company is either 'carrying on a business of any description' including 'holding assets and managing them' within para 11A(2)(a) and para 11A(3)(b), or it is 'preparing to' do that within para 11A(2)(b).

The directors assert that they were actively involved in pursuing the business opportunity with the administrator, and this is entirely credible given that they had handed over £175,000 to finance it.

The key question, then, is whether Holdco qualifies as a 'trading company' or the holding company 'of a trading group'.

Holdco appears capable of qualifying as a trading company in its own right under para 22A because it has a trade of making supplies of management services; the activities undertaken between March and August 2007 fall within para 22A(2)(b) or (c) as being undertaken 'for the purposes of a trade that it is preparing to carry on' or 'with a view to its acquiring or starting to carry on a trade'.

It should therefore qualify as a trading company in its own right up until the point it can be argued that holding the subsidiaries is not a 'substantial' activity until they start to trade. Holdco clearly qualifies as the holding company of a trading group under para 22B once all the subsidiaries are trading. It also appears to qualify from 10 March 2007 onwards because it falls within para 22B(1):

'(1) In this schedule, "trading group" means a group of companies–

(a)   one or more of whose members carry on trading activities, and

(b)   the activities of whose members, taken together, do not include to a substantial extent activities other than trading activities.'

From the date that the subsidiaries were incorporated, the group appears to satisfy these conditions, either Holdco is carrying on trading activities itself (including preparation for trading), or the subsidiaries are doing so.

Holdco is clearly carrying on activities which are for the purposes of a trade that a member of the group will carry on, and with a view to the group members acquiring and starting to carry on trades.

Holdco should qualify under para 22A until it incorporated a subsidiary, whereupon it should qualify under para 22B. It is an active trading company throughout the period of ownership.

Value shifting

2.12   The value shifting rules apply to close companies. The effect is to restart the relevant period of ownership from the date of the value shifting event. The paragraph is potentially wide ranging and is designed to prevent abuse of qualification for the ten-year relevant period of ownership.

Example – Value shifting

John owns 100% of South Limited which has been carrying on a modest trade for the last ten years. He also owns 100% of a newly incorporated company, North Limited, which has acquired intellectual property rights for a new related activity. A very good offer has just been received for both companies with the offer heavily weighted in favour of North Limited.

In the absence of para 12, John could have transferred the shares in North Limited, to South Limited, on a share for share exchange basis, and so have obtained maximum business asset taper relief on the sale of both companies.

Specific exclusions apply where either:

(a)   The shift in value is insignificant; or

(b)   The shift in value is not to a company with a longer qualifying holding period.

The value shifting rules are mainly relevant to non-business assets. This is because the two year business asset rate accrual period means that there will be very few circumstances in which value shifting will lead to any benefit.

Rights issues

2.13   In accordance with s 126 and *IRC v Burmah Oil Co Ltd* [1982] STC 30, a rights issue falls within the reorganisation provisions. Shares acquired on a rights issue do not form a new acquisition and fall within the existing relevant period of ownership of the original shares. At first sight, this provision opens up considerable tax planning opportunities for maximising taper relief. However, care is required in light of the value shifting rules.

If there is a rights issue by a close company and the shares are issued at below market value then there will be no value shift as long as all of the shareholders take up their rights. However, if the shares are issued for a nominal consideration and not all of the shareholders take up their rights then there will be a shift of value from those shareholders not taking up their rights to the shareholders that do take up their rights.

Example – Rights issue

Consider a private company, worth £1 million, with only three shareholders: Alan, Paul and Robert whose shareholdings are:

	000s
Alan	51
Paul	30
Robert	19
	100

If a 1:1 rights issue is made and Alan did not take up his rights then the resulting share ownership would be:

	000s
Alan	51
Paul	60
Robert	38
	149

The value of the company is only increased by £49,000 whilst Alan's shareholding has fallen from 51% to approximately 34%. Such a transaction would be caught by s 29 although s 165 hold–over relief may be available if the shares qualify as business assets. The real downside as far as taper relief is concerned is that para 12 would apply to restart the relevant period of ownership on the existing shareholdings and not just the additional rights issue shares.

Whilst para 12(4) provides a let-out for insignificant shifts of value, great care must be exercised when advising on taper relief and rights issues.

Achieving certainty on business asset status of shares

2.14   When advising a client on the sale of shares, the client is usually very anxious to have certainty that full BATR is available such that a 10% tax rate can be achieved. However, as explained above, there will often be uncertainty on the position because there is substantial non-trading activity under one or more of the criteria set out by HMRC – but not under all of the criteria. For example, a company has a substantial investment property on an asset basis but not by reference to income, profitability or management team.

To try and remove this uncertainty, Tax Bulletin 62 issued in December 2002 introduced a clearance procedure under Code of Practice 10 (COP10) but this has now been withdrawn. This enabled companies to obtain a ruling on their qualifying status from the Local Area Inspector.

There was always some dispute between advisers on whether to make an application under COP10. Where there was some uncertainty it possibly drew attention to a concern by an adviser whereas full BATR may in any case be justified by the facts. However, if the COP10 application was successful, then the certainty sought by clients could be achieved. In the absence of the COP10 ruling, what approach should now be adopted and what options are available?

(a)   Check whether a previous COP10 application was made by the client and the response received. Has anything changed since then?

(b)   Review the business in line with the HMRC guidance and consider what justifications are available if the position is queried when the self-assessment return is submitted. This should also take into account knowledge and experience on other skilled cases.

(c) Consider an application under another clearance procedure (Substantial Shareholdings Exemption (SSE), Enterprise Investment Scheme (EIS) or Enterprise Management Incentive (EMI)) which is based on similar procedures.

(d) If there is sufficient time, then consider testing the position with an earlier, smaller disposal. However, as such, the disposal would not warrant the same level of attention from HMRC and so a favourable HMRC view would not necessarily be binding.

In the end, an assessment must be made of the worst case BATR position and a taper calculation performed. The adviser must consider whether any action is possible to improve the position and the client must decide whether they are prepared to accept such a tax liability on sale (should that be the outcome).

Earnout rights

2.15 Another situation where securities are deemed to exist for tax purposes is in connection with earnouts. The taxation of earnouts is based on the decision in *Marren v Ingles* [1980] 3 All ER 95, [1980] STC 500, HL, in which it was held that the right to receive future earnout consideration must be valued at the date the shares are sold and that the sellers are taxable, at that time, on the value of that right to receive contingent monies in the future. A right to receive earnout monies is a 'chose in action' and as such is a legal right that is received at the time.

However, where the earnout consideration is satisfied solely in the form of paper (shares/loan notes) then the seller can elect under s 138A for any CGT that would have arisen on the value of that consideration to be deferred until it is encashed. When the shares are sold, part of what is received is the earnout right, which is deemed to be a security, and when the earnout is determined, this deemed security is exchanged for shares and loan notes in the purchaser. As with all such transactions, it is appropriate to obtain clearance under s 138.

The taper relief status of the deemed earnout right security will depend upon normal rules. Where the seller remains employed then business asset status should be achieved. However an earnout right security in a quoted company where there is no employment will result in non-business asset status.

Guidance issued by HMRC in 2003 following the introduction of FA 2003 and the new securities legislation in ITEPA 2003 clarified the position on whether an earnout right could be taxed as employment income. It states that the following are considered to be the key indicators in determining whether an earnout is further sale consideration rather than remuneration:

(a) The sale agreement demonstrates that the earnout is part of the valuable consideration given for the securities in the old company.

(b) The value received from the earnout reflects the value of the securities given up.

(c) Where the vendor continues to be employed in the business, the earnout is not compensation for the vendor not being fully remunerated for continuing employment with the company.

(d) Where the vendor continues to be employed, the earnout is not conditional on future employment, beyond a reasonable requirement to stay to protect the value of the business being sold.

(e) Where the vendor continues to be employed, there is no personal performance targets incorporated in the earnout.

The following factors may also be relevant:

(i) Negotiations between the seller and buyer as to the level of the earnout in relation to the value of the consideration given for securities in the old company.

(ii) Any clearance that might have been obtained under s 138 and ICTA 1988, s 707 demonstrating the bona fide nature of the transactions, and the level of the earnout linked to profitability or other key performance indicators of the business.

(iii) Evidence that future bonuses were classified or commuted into purchase consideration would indicate that the earnout was, at least partly, remuneration rather than consideration for the disposal of securities.

Position of employees

2.16   The taper relief legislation actively encourages employees to hold shares in their employing company. It enables all employees who do not have a material interest in their employer to obtain the business asset taper rate on their shares. This is the case whether or not the employing company is a trading company, or the holding company of a trading group. However, where this is the case, business asset status on quoted company shares will be lost on retirement as the individual will no longer be employed after that date. The same is true of redundancy. The impact of this change in status may well not be appreciated by the employee concerned.

The majority of employees qualifying for relief are unlikely to have sufficient personal wealth to justify a high risk investment in a single shareholding. A particular danger is that the employee loses the value of his investment and his employment at the same time.

There is no minimum level of part-time work although it is difficult to know how far this can be taken. The most extreme case is a zero hours contract which is a type that became common with certain employers (often retailers) during the last decade or so. Such a contract ties in an individual as an employee without guaranteeing any minimum amount of working hours each week. If an individual was on such a contract but had not worked even a single hour across the course of a month, would that month qualify for business asset taper relief based on the employee test?

The practical realities of life are that one would have to be able to justify the period of time being treated as employment. The documentary evidence that one would look to provide would be the contractual terms of employment showing when the employment commenced or alternatively the date of the P46 and the date of leaving would be that provided on the P45. But imagine an employee who was working, say, one night a week at a supermarket and who also occasionally worked extra shifts on request. If that employee stopped working the regular night they might continue to work shifts on request. If that individual went a couple of months without working at the supermarket but then did two or three shifts before leaving, then the P45 would probably only show the final date of leaving. In other words, it is unlikely that the payroll department would issue a P45 in the intervening period.

If the Return was under enquiry, would a contract of employment and P45 be sufficient? Presumably, if the P45 showed a very low figure for employment income then HMRC might request more details.

Example – Employed beneficiary

Sophie comes into a life interest on 7 March 2003. The fund includes 200,000 Tesco shares which have a share price of £2.00 at that time. At the time she is at tertiary college and is working part-time at Tesco two nights a week. In June 2003 she leaves college and works full-time until 7 January 2004 when she leaves to go travelling. In October 2004 she goes to university.

She works at Tesco for a month that Christmas but does not work for Tesco again until her final year at university when she starts at another Tesco store on 7 November 2007 and works part-time until 7 June 2008. The shares are sold on 7 June 2008 at £2.80 per share.

	Days	Taper rate %	Pro-rata	£
Gain (200,000 x £2.80 – £2.00)				160,000
Taper relief: (total days 1,918)				
Business asset (no of days 549)	549/ 1,918	75%	21.5%	
Non-business asset (no of days 1,369)	1,369/ 1,918	15%	10.7%	
Total taper relief			32.2%	(51,520)
Tapered gain arising on settlement				£108,480

It is interesting that an employee who holds less than 10% of the ordinary shares in a non-trading group but who holds more than 10% of another class of securities would not be able to qualify for BATR. This could happen on a share sale where the previous owners of a trading business acquire a combination of ordinary shares and loan notes eg on the sale of a construction company to a property development group with substantial property investments. It is conceivable that the additional tax cost of the lost business asset status on the shares could be greater than the value of the loan notes. In such a case, QCBs would be better than loan notes.

Prior to 6 April 2000, 'full-time working officer or employee' meant an individual who is an officer or employee of a trading company or of a trading company and one or more other trading companies with which there was a relevant connection; and who was required in that capacity to devote substantially the whole of his time to the service of that company, or to the service of those companies taken together.

The definitions of 'office', 'employment', 'commercial association', 'full-time working officer', 'group of companies', 'holding company' and 'trade' are similar to those used for retirement relief and so reference can be made to relevant case law and HMRC practice in respect of that now abolished relief. There are also similarities to the EIS legislation.

The issue was considered in the professional negligence case of *Palmer v Maloney* [1999] STC 890. At issue was the requirement to 'devote substantially the whole of his time' and what this meant. Laddie J had held in the High Court in 1998 that the existence of another unincorporated business as well as the company prevented the requirement from being fulfilled. This was overturned by the Court of Appeal although doubt was cast on HMRC's interpretation of this provision which was felt to be concessionary.

In obiter, Aldous L J said:

> 'I do not believe that ... [the word substantially] should be interpreted as widely as meaning 'in the main'. The decision as to whether the time required to be worked substantially in the appropriate capacity is a jury-type question to be decided upon the facts of each case. The level of at least three quarters of the full normal working hours referred to by the HMRC in their manual may well be appropriate as a matter of pragmatism. However, I do not believe that a person who works as a manager only 75% of the time required by his contract could be said to have worked substantially the whole time required as a manager.'

Company settlors

2.17   Schedule A1, para 17 deals with property settled by a company and takes account of the fact that trustees are entitled to taper relief but companies are not. It allows an asset to qualify only for the non-business asset taper, even if otherwise it would have qualified as a business asset. It applies to gains accruing to the trustees of a settlement if:

(a) the settlor is a company;

(b) the settlor, or an associated company, is an actual or potential beneficiary; and

(c) the settlor or any associated company is within the charge to corporation tax on chargeable gains.

Where the transfer to the trust consists of shares in the sponsoring company (eg to an Employee Benefit Trust, or a QUEST) the settlor will retain a benefit in the form of the enhanced motivation of its workers and this is supported by the accounting treatment in FRS 5 and UITF 13. Paragraph 17 will therefore apply to the new relevant period of ownership. However, as long as it is not a collective investment scheme or a unit trust, s 165 (or even s 260) hold-over relief should be available and ESC D35 would normally apply in any event such that no CGT liability would arise.

Example – Funded Unapproved Retirement Benefits Scheme (FURBS)

A FURBS is established for the directors and senior executives of a company with the funds being invested in a share portfolio including qualifying companies. The trust deed provides that any surplus not required to meet the pensions is to be returned to the company. On the sale of the shares the trustees can only qualify for the non-business rate of taper.

Paragraph 20 deals with settlements with more than one settlor which are treated as notional separate settlements for taper relief purposes. This anti-avoidance provision is designed to prevent several settlors from 'pooling' their assets in order to qualify for business asset status. Its application after 6 April 2000 is, presumably, greatly reduced because of the relaxation in the criteria for qualification for business asset status.

Assets other than shares

2.18 For assets other than shares, an asset will be a business asset if it is used wholly or partly for one of the following purposes:

(a) a trade carried on by the individual or a partnership of which he is a member;

(b) a trade of a qualifying company by reference to the individual;

(c) a trade of a group company of which group the holding company is a qualifying company by reference to the individual; or

(d) any office or employment held by an individual with a person carrying on a trade.

Letting of property

2.19 Since 6 April 2000, there is no requirement for the owner of the asset to have any interest in the shares of the company in order to qualify for BATR on a disposal of that asset. This means that for the time period since 6 April 2000 if an asset, such as land, is let to a company, and if it is being used in its trade then BATR is available.

It is important to appreciate that in order to qualify, the asset must be used for the purposes of the trade. A company must also qualify as a trading company. The position for employees is more generous but in this context, we are considering the position of third party landlords. It is therefore necessary to satisfy two conditions:

(1) the property must be used as trading premises, and

(2) the tenant must be a qualifying company or a sole trader or a trading partnership.

An even more significant relaxation applies when identifying business assets of an individual for periods commencing after 5 April 2004. This extended this concept to apply it to businesses other than companies. From 6 April 2004 it is sufficient if the trade or profession is carried on by any individual, or by a partnership of which any individual is a member. This can include an asset used by a partnership whose members include a qualifying company or group as long as the necessary conditions are satisfied.

Residential properties may meet the conditions where they are required to provide accommodation to employees of a business, eg where a property is let to a hotel for the use of its staff, or on a farm labourer's cottage or for international secondees. In each case, it will be a matter of fact.

For commercial properties, the issue is much more relevant and it is necessary to keep detailed records on let properties. A detailed description of the property should be retained on file showing the area covered by each letting unit and the usage to which the property is put. Where a firm of accountants is preparing let property accounts, then this should be an annual exercise to determine the current BATR position.

The potential tax saving is very significant and some landlords try to go further and make business asset status a condition for the tenants. In this context prior to 6 April 2004, it is necessary to consider whether businesses incorporated during the period of the tenancy and so changed status at that time. Even since April 2004, a business could be acquired by a listed company such that BATR is denied from that point in time. Early involvement of tax advisers in the sale process is also essential on large and valuable letting units.

Tainted periods of ownership are now very common as farmland qualifies since 6 April 2004 and may qualify from 6 April 2000 if the occupant was incorporated. Similar principles apply to industrial units, shops and offices. Furnished holiday letting is trading for taper relief purposes and so it is common to have tainted taper on such properties where furnished holiday letting has been undertaken for some years followed by several years of letting on assured shorthold tenancies.

Mixed use assets

2.20 A particular difficulty arises where an asset has both business asset use and non-business asset use at the same time. This is defined as a 'mixed-use period' and is by reference to the relevant period of ownership. It requires a relevant fraction to be calculated in respect of the 'non-qualifying use' but does give rise to separate notional assets.

A just and reasonable basis must be used where an apportionment is required and this is assumed to accrue evenly over time (Sch A1, para 21).

The instruction is to apportion the taper relief as to business and non-business on the basis of the actual usage of the entire asset. However, this does not create separate notional assets as in the case of roll-over relief under s 152(6) which reads as follows:

> 'If over a period of ownership ... part of a building or structure is, and part is not, used for the purposes of a trade, this section shall apply as if the part so used, with any land occupied for purposes ancillary to the occupation and use of that part of the building or structure, were a separate asset ... '

Roll-over relief requires separate calculations to be performed, which of course is needed in order to determine the proceeds for reinvestment. The taper relief legislation draftsman was unconcerned with such considerations. Taper relief still requires the asset to be looked at in totality rather than by inserting an initial logic step of creating separate assets.

The apportionment of a property between business and non-business usage has a particularly perverse result where the non-business usage is as a principal private residence, such as in an owner-occupied hotel. In that case the property must first be apportioned between the amount of gain qualifying for principal private residence relief and the amount of the gain arising on the business element. Bizarrely, the taper relief applying to only the business element must be apportioned in the same proportions as it is based on the usage of the asset and not just the gain to which it is being applied.

Where, over a period of ownership, part of a building is not used for the purposes of the trade throughout the whole, or a substantial part, of the period of ownership, the asset must be notionally divided into two parts for roll-over relief purposes, namely:

(a) one part of representing the business use; and

(b) the other part representing the non-qualifying use.

Each part will then be treated as a separate asset, with roll-over relief being limited to the chargeable gain allocated to the business use only as shown in the following example.

Example – Mixed use

John acquired a property at a cost of £400,000 on 31 October 2003. The property is sold for £800,000 on 1 November 2005.

Throughout the period 80% of the building is used for the purposes of trading.

	Total £000s	Business £000s	Non-business £000s
Proceeds	800	640	160
Cost	(400)	(320)	(80)
Gain	400	320	80

Therefore, roll-over relief is available on the business gain of £320,000 only and reinvestment of proceeds is measured by reference to the business element proceeds of £640,000. This seems fair and reasonable in order to avoid abuse.

Hold-over relief is also restricted where there is a mixed use and works in a similar way to roll–over relief. Schedule 7, para 6 has similar wording to s 152(6) and requires that 'there shall be determined the fraction of the unrelieved gain on the disposal which it is just and reasonable to apportion to the part of the asset that was so used ...' The legislation goes on to require a restriction of the amount held-over in such circumstances and would appear to be applied independently of the considerations for taper relief purposes.

If the asset in the example above is a guest house and the non-business element is the private accommodation then, in accordance with Sch A1, para 9, it is necessary to assess the business usage across the entire asset (ie the building) and restrict in line with the business proportion. As BATR as a result of the apportionment of the taper, the chargeable gain increases by £48,000 (from £80,000 to £128,000) representing 15% of the chargeable gain and at the tax rate of 40% this would amount to an additional tax liability of £19,200. The taxpayer is worse off by £11,200 because of the existence of only or main relief, as otherwise his gain would have been only £100,000 (£400,000 multiplied by the full business asset taper of 75%).

	Total £000s	Guest house £000s	Private accommodation £000s
Gain	400	320	80
Main residence exemption			(80)
Taper relief (75% x 80%)		(192)	—
Chargeable gain		128	—

But what if the non-business asset is not exempt? Eg a shop and flat above. In such a case, roll-over relief or hold-over relief would be available in full on the gain apportioned to the business element (ie the shop). Those reliefs would not be available against the non–business element (ie the flat). However, taper relief would still be available on the non–business asset even though the asset had been held for only two years and the gain relates to the non-business element. This is because taper relief is due on the mixed-use asset, but is restricted to the business use proportion (ie 80%).

	Total £000s	Shop £000s	Flat £000s
Gain	400	320	80
Rolled over or held over		(320)	—
Taper relief (75% x 80%)		—	48
Chargeable gain		—	32

Checklist

Business Asset Taper Relief	Cross Reference
Business asset status should not be assumed and the relevant conditions must be considered.	2.1
The most common issues to consider when advising on business asset taper relief are:	
• whether a company has trading asset status;	2.5
• whether employees qualify for full business asset relief;	2.16
• the position of landlords;	2.19
• the position on mixed use assets where there is both business and non-business usage at the same time.	2.20
The adviser needs to consider whether the taper status is 'tainted'.	
Specific anti-avoidance rules exist to prevent the exploitation of taper relief.	2.8
The entitlement to full business asset relief on earnout arrangements can be particularly complex and requires careful appraisal.	2.15

Chapter 3

Property Ownership (including Leases and Partnerships)

Importance of property ownership issues for capital gains tax planning

3.1 This chapter concerns planning issues in connection with property ownership. Although the main focus is land and property, the principles relate to ownership of other chargeable assets as well as land and much of the planning included in this chapter can apply to these assets in exactly the same way. It is important to determine at the outset whether the asset is subject to capital gains tax (CGT). It is not unknown for planning advice to be given that starts from the flawed assumption that the assets are capital rather than held on trading account. This issue is considered in CHAPTER 9 and also in CHAPTER 13.

It is important to establish for CGT purposes the precise legal interest in any land or property. Ownership of land, or more strictly an estate in land in England and Wales (only the Crown has the privilege of ownership), is normally held under either a freehold or a leasehold interest. This chapter will consider CGT planning involving both types of estate, under English law. Land law under Scottish law is quite different and is not considered further here.

Broadly, a person who owns a freehold owns an interest in land which lasts forever and is, in effect, an absolute owner. By contrast, a leasehold is for a finite term which can be fixed, say one month, 25 years or 999 years, or it may be periodic until either party gives notice to bring the lease to an end. There are also numerous other types of property ownership which can apply in certain circumstances.

This chapter considers transactions involving land, including sale, leasing, part disposals and options over land by individuals. Property can also be owned jointly between individuals or in partnership, and planning involving joint ownership is also considered in detail here.

There is also an important distinction between legal title and beneficial ownership. For the purposes of CGT, it is beneficial ownership that matters. The adviser must establish whether title is absolute or whether a trust arrangement exists – perhaps in the form of a constructive trust. Planning for trustees and personal representatives is considered in detail in

CHAPTER 11. Property ownership arrangements are also very important for other taxes – principally inheritance tax (IHT). The planning points covered in CHAPTER 15 may therefore also be relevant.

Throughout this chapter, all statutory references are to TCGA 1992 unless otherwise stated.

Joint ownership

3.2 Traditionally, land and property ownership is evidenced by the entry on the deeds to the property, thus the title deeds would indicate a complete ownership history, culminating in the conveyance to the present owners. Nowadays when an owner sells or gives away land, the new ownership will be registered at Her Majesty's Land Registry and it is this listing that evidences the owners of the title.

It is possible for land and property to be owned jointly, but under English law there cannot be more than four legal owners. If there are more than four (for example, partners in a partnership) the people named on the register hold the property in trust for all of the others. This is a bare trust and despite the changes to the taxation of trusts introduced in the FA 2006, for CGT purposes ownership is effectively treated as split between every individual. This creates particularly complex issues for partnerships and hence the need for Statement of Practice D12.

Ownership by more than one person can be registered in one of two ways, as joint tenants or as tenants-in-common. Property owned as joint tenants passes automatically by survivorship on the death of one of the owners, whereas a share in property owned as tenants-in-common can be left in accordance with the deceased's will or intestacy laws.

It is important to note that if a joint owner gifts their share of a property, a discount is often applicable to reduce the market value of the arithmetical share to account for joint ownership. This is because of the practical restrictions and disadvantages that come with being a joint owner as opposed to having sole control. Depending on the share involved and type of ownership, discount factors of 5–15% are usually appropriate. The actual discount to be applied in any particular case will have to be agreed with the District Valuer and it is often sensible to obtain a post transaction valuation check, with HMRC using form CG34.

The CGT issues arising from valuations are considered in more detail in CHAPTER 13.

Example – Valuation discount on joint ownership

Mr and Mrs Higgs jointly own a holiday property in Cornwall, as tenants-in-common. The property was inherited by Mr Higgs on the death of his mother on 1 May 1998 when it was worth £180,000. It was conveyed into joint names on 1 May 2000 by deed of gift. Mr and Mrs Higgs now wish to gift a ⅓ share to their daughter. The property is worth £480,000 on 1 May 2007.

The husband to wife gift on 1 May 2000 will have been a no gain/no loss transfer for CGT purposes and Mrs Higgs is deemed to have acquired a ½ share of the property on 1 May 1998. Mr and Mrs Higgs will now dispose of a ⅙th share of the property so that after the gift, it will be owned equally three ways.

A discount is appropriate in this case, as a ⅙th share being gifted will be worth less than ⅙th x £480,000 = £80,000, due to the fact that the property continues to be held jointly after the gift. A third party would not necessarily pay £80,000 for such a small share in the property, jointly owned with others.

The capital gain on the gift is calculated as follows:

	£	£
Market value at date of gift		480,000
⅙ share thereof	80,000	
Less: say 10% discount	(8,000)	
		72,000
Acquisition cost (⅙ x 180,000)		(30,000)
Gain before taper		42,000
Taper relief (35%)		(14,700)
Tapered gain		27,300

Mr and Mrs Higgs therefore each have capital gains of £27,300, which can be reduced by their individual annual exemptions if available.

It should be noted that there was no discount applied to the acquisition cost because Mr Higgs inherited the whole asset from his mother, and not a share in the asset but this is not always the case. In particular, a discount may be appropriate where a March 1982 valuation is concerned.

Valuation discounts can be very useful in terms of trying to minimise a gain particularly where a family gift is concerned. An asset can be transferred over a number of years by transferring proportionate shares. As long as the Ramsay principle (see **CHAPTER 13**) does not apply and there is no binding contract to transfer the entire asset at the outset (s 28) then the disposals will each be separate transactions taking advantage of available annual exemptions, taper relief and basic rate tax bands. Where the property being transferred to the children/grandchildren is jointly owned by a husband and wife, or civil partners, then this doubles the scope for utilising annual exemptions and lower tax bands. It also needs to be remembered that although a transaction may need to be spread over, say, three tax years to minimise CGT, that may only have to be 26 calendar months if the transactions take place in say March 2007, May 2008 and April 2009.

However, it is important that s 19 is not overlooked. This changes the valuation basis for subsequent transfers where an asset is transferred in a series of transactions. This section, together with s 20, requires the subsequent transfer to be calculated by reference to a cumulative value. As long as each subsequent transfer does not give complete ownership, then a valuation discount should still be appropriate.

However, the value of the final share of the property will be much higher because not only will no valuation discount be appropriate but it will also lead to the effective clawing back of any previous discounts.

In the example, the property is a second home. It may be that a principal private residence election is appropriate (see **CHAPTER 9**). Alternatively, if there is furnished holiday letting of the property then s 165 hold-over relief may be relevant. A final possibility would be to route any transfer via a discretionary trust. These last two options are considered in more detail in **CHAPTER 8**.

Property ownership by spouses and civil partners

3.3 Property ownership issues for CGT purposes concerning spouses and civil partners is considered in **CHAPTER 10**.

Joint ownership of property can arise in a number of other different ways. One example is where property is passed to a number of beneficiaries under a will. It is sometimes sensible planning to distribute assets to the beneficiaries to hold jointly and sell, rather than selling an asset and distributing cash. This is because beneficiaries will typically have a more beneficial tax position than the executors. This is considered further with an example in **CHAPTER 11**.

Partnerships

3.4 Tax in respect of chargeable gains accruing to partners on the disposal of jointly held partnership assets is assessed and charged to the individual partners separately. Any individual losses or claims for relief are made independently, by the respective partners. Partnership dealings in assets are treated as dealings by the individual partners, rather than by the firm. However, the CGT legislation does not deal well with partnerships and hence Statement of Practice D12 was produced to cover the various different scenarios. It is also important to remember that for CGT purposes the assets of the partnership must be considered on an item-by-item basis.

Partnerships are very flexible entities with the ability to easily vary the ownership arrangements from one year to another and to have different profit sharing or ownership interests for income than for capital. This flexibility gives tax planning opportunities. Further, partnerships are very wide ranging varying from small husband and wife partnerships to very large professional partnerships. Partnerships also feature as ownership vehicles for property ownership and development and for use in venture capital and other financial opportunities. It was this reason that special stamp duty land tax (SDLT) rules were required.

Partnerships take the following forms:

(a) 1890 unlimited partnerships;

(b) limited partnerships; and

(c) limited liability partnerships.

Limited partnerships are used particularly in the financial services industry as ownership structures for investors. They frequently involve corporate vehicles and so are taxed under corporation tax rules.

A limited liability partnership (LLP) carrying on a trade is taxed in the same way as other partnerships, unless the trade or business has permanently ceased or a liquidator is appointed or a winding up ordered by the courts. If this is the case, the LLP is instead taxed as a separate entity, in the same way as a company, with the partners treated as owning shares in the LLP based on their capital interests. If s 165 hold-over relief has been claimed on capital contributions by the partners, the gain held over crystallises at that point.

The capital gains of partners are split in the ratio in which the partners share capital profits and losses. This is usually, but not always, the same as the income profit sharing ratios, with each partner owning that fractional share of the assets. The proportion of capital contributed by the partners is irrelevant.

Partnership property is owned in trust by up to four partners on behalf of the partnership. The beneficial ownership proportions and arrangements are determined by the partnership agreement. Where the ownership arrangements are complex or unusual then it is clearly better for the terms to be documented in a formal agreement. In the absence of a formal agreement, then the terms must be implied. It is also necessary to determine whether property is partnership property or merely jointly owned. This can have implications for the valuation basis as explained above.

No discount is applied on joint ownership of assets, as partners are connected persons for capital gains tax purposes. If X and Y are equal partners, each partner's share is valued at 50% of the whole value, not a value of a 50% holding.

Is the asset a partnership asset?

3.5 It is important to establish at the outset whether an asset is a partnership asset for CGT purposes. This is particularly the case with family partnerships such as farms. There is often a lack of clarity as to the nature of the ownership particularly where there is no partnership agreement and where the partnership accounts are poorly drafted. The tax consequences could be significantly different depending on the tax position of those involved. If the asset is a partnership asset, then there will be more scope to split the gain between partners and to make use of roll-over relief.

Disposals to third parties

3.6 Where an asset is sold to a third party, or part disposal is made, each of the partners are treated as having made a sale, or part disposal of a fractional entitlement. Each partner has their own annual exemptions after taper relief is applied. This is very tax efficient and hence gives rise to planning opportunities especially where full business asset taper relief (BATR) is available. The gain on the asset is split across a number of individuals, albeit in line with their share in the ownership of the asset.

Partnership assets distributed to a partner

3.7 If a partnership asset is distributed to one or more of the partners, for example, on a dissolution, there is a deemed disposal at market value of the asset. The partners each disposing of their share of the asset will have gains or losses, based on their fractional entitlement, just like sales to third parties. However, the partner receiving the asset will not be assessed on their fractional share of the gain. Instead, their base cost to be carried forward will be the full market value at the time, reduced by the amount of the gain before taper so that, in effect, the gain is rolled over into their base cost. The same principles apply where a loss is made on the assets.

Taper relief applies as normal for the partners disposing of their fractional entitlement. The receiving partners will not obtain taper relief as the gain is rolled over. However, taper relief is not lost. This will be available on the subsequent sale of the asset as taper relief is applied on the whole gain from when the partner first has an interest in the asset.

Example – Transfer of an asset to a partner

A, B, C and D have traded in partnership from a business premises since April 2000 sharing all profits and losses equally. The property was bought for £60,000 by the partnership and transferred to C in April 2007 when it was worth £180,000.

The capital gain is calculated using the market value as partners are connected persons, with gains being calculated as follows:

	Total	Each part- ner (¼)
	£	£
Market value – April 2007	180,000	45,000
Cost – April 2000	(60,000)	(15,000)
Gain	£120,000	£30,000

Partners, A, B and D will therefore be assessed on their gains of £30,000 before taper. After 75% BATR, the gain is within their annual exemptions and no tax will be due.

Partner C is not charged on any share of the gain, instead the base cost of the premises to him becomes:

	£
Market value	180,000
Less: gain not assessed	(30,000)
Available base cost	£150,000

Looking at it another way, Partner C purchased 25% of the property in April 2000 when it was worth £60,000 and the remaining 75% in April 2007 when it was worth £180,000. Therefore C's base cost is £15,000 plus £135,000, ie £150,000.

There is limited tax planning available here, as the full gain will be assessed on ultimate sale anyway, due to the roll-over mechanism and, for example, if the receiving partner was to sell immediately in the above example, his capital gain would be the £180,000 market value, less the £150,000 available base cost, giving a gain before taper relief of £30,000, ie the same as his partners.

However, there may be scope for the receiving partner to defer their share of the gain to a later time, for example, if they have already used annual exemptions or if their anticipated tax rates will be lower. The transfer could also be tax efficient if C has significant capital losses. Full BATR can be maintained if, for example, the asset is let back to the partnership in the interim.

Changes in partnership ratios

3.8 There are often changes in partnership ratios, for example, when an existing partner leaves or a new partner joins a business. A partner who reduces their share of assets will be treated as disposing of part of the whole of those assets. Equally, a partner who increases his share, will be treated as making a similar acquisition. Where losses arise on a charge in the partnership, then it is important to consider and determine whether such losses are of restricted use as connected party losses.

The CGT treatment follows whether any consideration is paid or whether there has been a revaluation in the partnership accounts previously. It is therefore very important to review whether or not this is the case and there may be scope for planning opportunities, depending on the facts of the case.

Where there is a change in profit sharing ratios and there have been no adjustments made to the accounts for revaluation of any assets since the last change in profit sharing ratios, the disposal occurs at no gain/no loss, ie the disposal is treated as having been made for consideration equal to the disposing partner's share of the capital gains cost, plus indexation.

A partner whose share reduces will therefore carry forward a smaller proportion of the cost to set against a subsequent disposal of the asset and the receiving partner will carry forward a larger proportion of the cost, on acquisition of their fractional entitlement. Once again, capital contributions made by the partners are irrelevant in the calculation of any capital gains.

Note however that a partner joining a firm will only be entitled to taper relief for the period of ownership since acquiring their original fractional entitlement and, therefore, care should be taken where assets are sold shortly after a new partner joins, as this could result in the loss of BATR that would otherwise be available.

Where the sale of an asset is anticipated shortly after a new partner joins, this problem can easily be avoided by making a revaluation of the asset prior to the change in the partnership sharing ratios, as explained below.

Revaluation in the accounts

3.9   Where a partnership asset is revalued in the accounts, the existing partners will be credited their share of the revaluation surplus in their capital account, to account for the increase in value. This is not in itself an occasion of charge for CGT purposes, as there is no sale or disposal of the asset. However, on a subsequent reduction in their share of the partnership assets, there is a capital gain at that point. CGT is therefore charged on the fractional reduction of each partner whose share reduces for a consideration equal to the fraction of the increased value at revaluation. The acquisition cost to be carried forward for the receiving partners will be their share of the revalued cost of the asset at the time of the change in the profit sharing ratios.

The same principles apply also in the case of downward revaluation, where losses will be made.

As can be seen in the following example, it may be sensible planning to undertake revaluation in the accounts, of assets that may be sold shortly after a new partner joins, so that taper relief is not lost, as mentioned above.

Example – Revaluing an asset in the accounts

A, B, C and D are equal partners in a business, having acquired a business premises in January 1987 for £100,000. In January 2007, E joins the partnership as an equal partner. No revaluation of the premises is made in the accounts. A, B, C and D therefore each make a 5% disposal, reducing their share from 25% to 20%.

As there is no revaluation of the property, these disposals are on a no gain/no loss basis so that A, B, C and D have therefore each disposed of their 5% share for £8,130, giving a gain of £Nil as shown below:

	£	£
Proceeds		8,130
5% of original cost	5,000	
Add indexation allowance (factor 0.626)	3,130	
		(8,130)
Gain		£Nil

Partner E is treated as acquiring his 20% share in the property for the following base cost:

	£
20% of original cost	20,000
Add indexation allowance (factor 0.626)	12,520
Base cost	£32,500

On the subsequent sale in July 2007, for £420,000, the gains will be calculated as follows:

	A, B, C & D (each)	E
	£	£
Proceeds	84,000	84,000
Base cost	(20,000)	(32,520)
Indexation allowance	(12,520)	
Indexed gain	51,480	51,480
Taper relief (75% BATR)	(38,610)	—
Total	£12,870	£51,480

In this example, as the property is owned in equal shares at disposal, the gain before taper relief is the same for each partner. However, E has only owned his share in the property for six months, resulting in a loss of taper relief available.

As mentioned, this can be avoided by making a revaluation in the accounts prior to E joining the partnership, for example, if the property is re-valued at £400,000 in December 2006, each of A, B, C and D would get an additional £75,000 added to their capital accounts. In this instance, when E joined the partnership in January 2007, there is a capital gain on the fractional disposal on each of their 5% holdings, which is chargeable.

The CGT is calculated as follows:

	£
Deemed proceeds (5% x £400,000)	20,000
Less cost (5% x £100,000)	(5,000)
Indexation allowance (factor 0.626)	(3,130)
	11,870
Taper relief (75%)	8,903
Taxable gain	£2,967

In this case, each of A, B, C and D have taxable capital gains beneath their annual exemption in the 2006/07 tax year and therefore no CGT will be due.

E acquires the asset at 20% of the revalued amount, ie £80,000, so that on subsequent sale again in July 2007, the CGT computations are as follows:

	A, B, C & D (each) £	E £
Proceeds	84,000	84,000
Base cost	(20,000)	(80,000)
Indexation allowance	12,520	
Indexed gain	51,480	4,000
Taper relief	(38,610)	—
Total	£12,870	£4,000

E's share of the capital gain is therefore significantly reduced, due to the fact that the asset had been re-valued prior to his joining the partnership. The gain instead is assessed on A, B, C and D when E joined the partnership, however, they benefited from the full BATR so that the overall taxable gains are reduced.

If the intention had been for the partners to reinvest in new premises then E could alternatively have claimed roll-over relief under s 152 – see Chapter 7.

Payments outside of the accounts

3.10   There may also be payments made by new partners to buy into a partnership which are not reflected in the partnership accounts. Such payments have traditionally been made for goodwill in professional partnerships. In these cases, there is consideration received from a fractional disposal of a partnership interest, and a capital gain is therefore crystallised.

The partner making the payment will be able to deduct this in computing the gain or loss on subsequent disposal of the asset. Further, he will be able to claim a capital loss when he leaves the partnership, or when his share is reduced, if he receives a lower consideration for his share of the asset (or none).

The partners receiving payment will be able to deduct part of their acquisition cost of the assets in calculating their gain, providing the payment clearly constitutes payment for a share of the assets in the partnership accounts. Therefore, care should be taken to make sure that this is properly documented.

Example – Payment of goodwill outside of the accounts

A and B have been in partnership since 1980, sharing profits and losses equally. C joins the partnership on 1 January 2008. He acquires a 25% right to the profits and losses by making a payment of £50,000 to A. Goodwill is estimated at £20,000 at March 1982. It has not been revalued in the accounts and the partnership cost is £Nil.

A has made a disposal of 25% of the partnership, out of his 50% share of the partnership. The gain is calculated as follows:

	£
Proceeds	50,000
Less: 25% March 1982 value	(5,000)
Less: indexation allowance	(5,235)
	39,765
Taper relief (75% BATR)	(29,824)
	9,941
Annual exemption	(9,200)
Taxable gain	£741

The base cost of the 25% share of goodwill for C is £50,000.

In this example, an uplift in the value of goodwill is achieved for relatively little tax cost. The proceeds can, however, be engineered to have the benefit of having taper relief and the annual exemption, free of tax. However, this cannot be achieved if the new partner is connected in any other way to the partnership, eg the son of an existing partner, even if it is for bona fide commercial reasons.

Where no payment is made either through, or outside the accounts, a CGT charge will arise only if the transaction is not at arm's length and falls within the rules for connected persons. This treatment will also occur on a change in profit sharing ratios. Where the partners concerned are connected by another way than by partnership, the transaction will be deemed to take place at market value.

Planning is therefore limited, but a son could, for example, be brought into partnership by transferring a small partnership share to him. This share can be increased over time to crystallise latent gains, whilst benefiting from taper relief and annual exemptions. However, care should be taken to avoid such transfers being taxed as a series of transactions and this is dealt with in more detail in CHAPTER 13.

Where a transaction is treated as having taken place at market value for tax and not accounting purposes, it would be treated in the same way as payments outside of the accounts.

Partnership mergers

3.11 Where two partnerships merge to form a new partnership, the CGT treatment will follow that of a change in profit sharing ratios. If gains do arise due to a revaluation or payment outside of the accounts, it may be possible to roll over the gain of a partner continuing in the partnership, to the extent that he disposes part of his share of the assets in the old partnership and acquires the assets in the new partnership. Planning at merger stage should therefore be undertaken in order to mitigate the crystallisation of unwanted capital gains by the continuing partners.

What is the asset for CGT purposes?

3.12 It is important at the outset of any planning to determine the asset for CGT purposes. This is often an issue when advising farming clients where the asset will usually be the farm rather than the individual assets making up the farm. Similar issues arise on other properties such as a house that has been converted into flats.

When advising clients in such circumstances it is important to bear in mind both the mixed use asset rule – see CHAPTER 2 and also the part disposal rules.

Part disposal of an asset

3.13 Much of planning involving CGT on the disposal of land involves part disposals. A part disposal is a chargeable disposal for CGT purposes and includes physical disposals of part of an asset (eg sale of a three acre field from a 300 acre holding), or the disposal of a right or an interest in an asset (such as a leasehold over a freehold). Disposals of an interest in land are dealt with together with the lease arrangements later in this chapter.

In calculating the gain on a part disposal, it is necessary to apportion allowable expenditure on the part of the asset sold, and the part retained.

Where enhancement expenditure is applied specifically to one part or another, it is allocated to that part. Expenditure common to the whole asset (including initial expenditure) is apportioned using the formula a/a+b where 'a' is the proceeds on the part disposal and 'b' is the value of the part retained. This is similar to the fraction applied on the sale of rights that are paid on shareholdings, which is dealt with in CHAPTER 4.

Example – Part disposal rules

Mr Blue owns a set of three antique vases, which were inherited on the death of his mother in August 1997. There was a list value of £20,000 on them at the time. He sells one vase to a dealer for £30,000 in January 2007, at which time the remaining pair are valued at £70,000 together.

The chargeable gain is calculated as follows:

	£
Disposal proceeds	30,000
Less: cost of part sold	
$\dfrac{30,000}{30,000+70,000} \text{x} 20,000$	(6,000)
Unindexed gain	24,000
Indexation allowance (factor 0.026)	(156)
Indexed gain	23,844
Taper relief (40% – maximum non-BATR)	(9,538)
Tapered gain	£14,306

The allowable base cost of the remaining pair is reduced as follows:

	£
Original cost	20,000
Less: cost of part sold	(6,000)
Allowable expenditure	£14,000

This example shows that part disposal rules apply to the disposal of part of a set of any assets. In practice, however, part disposals occur most frequently with respect to sales of land and there are specific rules regarding small part disposals of land which give rise to tax planning opportunities. The legislation at ss 242 to 244 provides two reliefs where the disposal proceeds are small or where the proceeds exceed allowable expenditure. A third concessionary relief that relates to simplified computations may also be applied and a further concession applies to disposals of a joint interest. These are each covered in turn below.

Small disposal proceeds

3.14 If the total consideration on part disposal(s) of land in any tax year is less than £20,000, and the consideration on each disposal is less than 20% of the market value of the entire holding prior to the part disposal, a claim under s 242(1) may be made for the gain not to be chargeable. Instead, the proceeds will be deducted from the allowable cost of the land retained. The taxpayer must make a claim within the normal self-assessment time limit, being 12 months from the 31 January following the end of the tax year in which the disposal was made.

Example – Relief for small part disposal

Mr Green owns 40 acres of land which were acquired in August 1989 for £60,000. He sells six acres in February 1996 for £18,000. The market value of the entire holding was £100,000. Mr Green made no other disposals in the tax year.

The consideration received (£18,000) is less than 20% of the market value and also less than £20,000. He may therefore make a claim for relief to apply so that no tax is due. No chargeable disposal takes place in 1996/97 and the base cost of the land retained is:

	£
Cost (40 acres)	60,000
Less: proceeds on part disposal	(18,000)
Allowable expenditure	£42,000

Note that in the above example, had Mr Green sold another acre of land for £3,000 in the same tax year, then relief would not apply due to the fact that the proceeds in the tax year would have exceeded £20,000.

It should not be assumed that it is always beneficial to make a claim in these circumstances. The availability of taper relief may mean that any tax charge is insignificant so a claim would only reduce the base cost for future disposals.

Where the proceeds on a small part disposal before April 1998 were not treated as a chargeable disposal, but instead deducted from the allowable expenditure, there is a quirk in the calculation of indexation allowance on the ultimate sale of the remaining land. It is necessary to calculate indexation on the original expenditure and then add back indexation attributed to any land previously sold.

Suppose Mr Green in the above example sold the remaining 34 acres in February 2007 for £200,000. The gain is calculated as follows:

	£
Sale proceeds	200,000
Less allowable cost (as above)	(42,000)
Unindexed gain	158,000

Indexation allowance (0.404 x 60,000)	(24,240)
Indexation on small proceeds (0.078 x 18,000)	1,404
Chargeable gain before taper relief	£135,164

This deferral of a CGT charge on a small part disposal is a similar concept to that of holding over gains under s 165 or s 260. The allowable base cost of the remaining asset is reduced for subsequent sales, although in the case of a part disposal it is the proceeds received that are held-over, rather than the gain.

A similar relief is available where land is subject to compulsory purchase, under s 243(1), provided that the consideration for the part disposal is 'small' compared to the market value of the land prior to the part disposal. In practice, 'small' is taken to be the higher of 5% or £3,000. Relief under this section is available even where the proceeds of sale exceed £20,000 (Revenue Interpretation 164). However, if the vendor has taken steps to dispose of the land, eg by advertising for sale, a disposal does not meet the requirements for a compulsory purchase and therefore the relief would not be available.

Proceeds exceeding allowable expenditure

3.15   If the proceeds on a small part disposal exceed the total allowable expenditure of the whole land owned, the taxpayer may elect for the gain chargeable to be calculated on the basis of allowing the full expenditure on the whole land (s 244). Again, the election needs to be made by the normal self-assessment deadline of the first anniversary of 31 January following the end of the tax year in which the disposal was made. Claiming relief under this section also dispenses with the requirement to value the remaining land.

Relief under s 242 cannot be claimed as the base cost of the remaining land cannot be reduced by the proceeds received. This is in effect, however, an extension to that section in that the excess of the proceeds of allowable expenditure becomes immediately chargeable. The proceeds still need to be small, however, as defined above.

The gain immediately chargeable is calculated as the proceeds of the part disposal less the total allowable expenditure. This means that the base cost of the land obtained is reduced to nil and therefore, on a subsequent disposal, the only allowable deduction from the proceeds would be any incidental costs of sale and any enhancement or other costs incurred since the part disposal.

The advantage of such a claim is to increase the allowable expenditure on the part disposal of land so to reduce the capital gain. In practice, however, there is usually little advantage over the normal part disposal rules, other than to reduce the tax liability on the first disposal. There may be a slight benefit for taper relief purposes as the rate of relief on the subsequent disposal is likely to be greater and so it would be beneficial to apply this to a larger gain (particularly if the remaining land is subsequently used for business purposes). Also, it opens up planning opportunities where the income or other circumstances of the taxpayer are expected to be more beneficial in the future.

Example – Part disposal of land

Mr Orange owns four acres of land, valued at March 1982 at £2,000. He sells 1 acre on 5 April 2004 for £16,000 and the remaining land is worth £40,000 at the time. The remaining land is let to a tenant farmer at the same time and is subsequently disposed on 6 April 2007 for £60,000.

(i) Normal part disposal rules—

	£
Proceeds (5 April 2004)	16,000
March 1982 value	

$$\frac{16,000}{16,000+40,000}\text{x}2,000$$

	£
	(571)
Indexation allowance (factor 1.047)	(598)
Gain	14,831
Taper relief (25% non-BATR)	(3,708)
Tapered gain	11,123
Annual exemption	(7,900)
Taxable gain	£3,223
Tax at 40%	£1,289

On the subsequent disposal, the gain is calculated as:

		£
Proceeds (6 April 2007)		60,000
Cost (2,000 – 571)		(1,429)
Indexation allowance		(1,496)
Gain		57,075
Taper relief	(40% x 6/9 (6 years))	
	(non-BATR)	(15,220)
	(75% x 3/9 (3 years))	
	(BATR)	(14,269)
Tapered gain		27,586

Annual exemption	(9,200)
Taxable gain	£18,386
Tax at 40%	£7,354

(ii) Claiming relief under s 244—

	£
Proceeds (5 April 2004)	16,000
March 1982 value	(2,000)
Indexation allowance (factor 1.047)	(2,094)
Gain	11,906
Taper relief (25% non-BATR)	(2,977)
Tapered gain	8,929
Annual exemption	(7,900)
Taxable gain	£1,029
Tax at 40%	£412

On the subsequent disposal, the gain is calculated as:

		£
Proceeds (6 April 2007)		60,000
Cost		Nil
Gain		60,000
Taper relief	(40% x 6/9 non-BATR)	(16,000)
	(75% x 3/9 BATR)	(15,000)
Tapered gain		29,000
Annual exemption		(9,200)
Taxable gain		£19,800
Tax at 40%		£7,920

As can be seen, there is a small tax saving using this claim for relief, however, this is solely down to the increase in taper relief which is more significant in this example due to the change in the business asset status of the asset. In this case, the tax benefit of claiming the s 244 relief will increase over time because of the change in the status of the asset for taper relief purposes.

Simplified computations

3.16 The normal part disposal calculation requires a market valuation of the land retained at the time of the part disposal and in practice this may be difficult or time consuming to obtain. By concession, the gains and losses on a part disposal may instead be calculated on an alternative basis, as detailed in Statement of Practice D1.

Instead of using the part disposal rules, the land disposed of may be treated as a different asset to the land retained and the allowable expenditure apportioned between the two assets on any fair and reasonable basis. For example, where the land is all in the same use, and valued evenly, HMRC would usually accept apportionment on a fractional basis as being reasonable.

Relief for exchange of joint interests

3.17 Also by concession, where there is an exchange of interests whereby two or more joint owners of one or more holdings in land are transferred to a single individual, a form of roll-over relief is available (extra-statutory concession D26).

Gains are not charged on the exchange of interest, but instead the gain on disposal is deducted from the allowable base cost of the land in which the sole interest is retained. Where the consideration (ie the value of the land) deemed to have been received for the interest relinquished exceeds the consideration deemed to have been acquired, the amount of gain to be rolled over is restricted in the same way as the proceeds not reinvested for other roll-over relief purposes.

The concession can apply on dissolution of a partnership, or on breakdown of assets following divorce even where land is not used in the business, where previously all land has been owned jointly and afterwards the land is split between the parties so that each take a sole interest in respective parts. The concession also applies on the exchange of joint interests between two or more married couples by treating each couple as an individual.

Example – Exchange of joint interests

Andrew and Charles are brothers and jointly own a number of plots of land as follows:

	Date acquired	Cost £	Value £
Green Fields	August 1990	18,000	40,000
Brown Acre	November 1992	26,000	42,000
The Paddock	January 1998	35,000	50,000
White Lands	December 2000	20,000	35,000

After falling out, the brothers decide to split the assets so that Andrew retains Green Fields and Brown Acre and Charles keeps The Paddock and White Lands. To equalise the assets, Charles also pays £1,500 to Andrew.

Cash is not a chargeable asset and is ignored for CGT purposes and the position is as follows:

Capital gains (half shares)	£
Green Fields	
Market value	20,000
Cost	(9,000)
Indexation allowance	(2,421)
Gain	£8,579
Brown Acre	
Market value	21,000
Cost	(13,000)
Indexation allowance	(2,132)
Gain	£5,868
The Paddock	
Market value	25,000
Cost	(17,500)
Indexation allowance	(332)
Gain	£7,168
White Lands	
Market value	17,500
Cost	(10,000)
Gain	£7,500

Andrew relinquishes his half share in The Paddock and White Lands (value £42,500) and acquires Charles' half share in Green Field and Brown Acre (value £41,000).

As the interest acquired by Andrew is less than the deemed consideration relinquished, full relief is available and so the half share of The Paddock and White Lands are rolled over as follows:

		£
The Paddock		
Cost	(January 1998)	17,500
	(July 2007)	25,000
Less gain rolled over		(7,168)
Allowable base cost		£35,332

White Lands

Cost	(December 2000)	10,000
	(July 2007)	17,500
Less gain rolled over		(7,500)
Allowable base cost		£20,000

No CGT is payable.

There is a small restriction to the gain rolled over by Charles as his deemed consideration was greater than the value of the land given up, by £1,500. Effectively, this amount becomes chargeable now. In this example, this will be less than the annual exemption so that no CGT will be due, however, if this gain was much larger, Charles would look to restrict the roll-over relief available on the asset with greater taper relief. His base costs are reduced as follows:

		£
Green Fields		
Cost	(August 1990)	9,000
	(July 2007)	20,000
Less gain rolled over (8,579 – 1,500)		(7,079)
Allowable base cost		£21,921
Brown Acre		
Cost	(November 1992)	13,000
	(July 2007)	21,000
Less gain rolled over		(5,868)
Allowable base cost		£28,132
Gain charged on Green Fields		
Half share indexed gain		8,579
Less amount rolled over		(7,079)
Taxable gain		£1,500

Planning of this nature is extremely important and could avoid a significant CGT bill, for example on divorce when exchange of joint interest occurs after the end of the year of separation, where tax would otherwise be due.

Taper relief applies from the earliest date on which an interest in the asset was acquired. In the above cases, a part share of the assets was acquired originally by each party. Even though a further part share is subsequently acquired (on an exchange of joint interests), taper relief applies from the date of original acquisition. This avoids the usual pitfall of the taper clock restarting where gains are held over.

The concession only applies to joint interests in land and also any milk or potato quota exchanged with the land. If other assets are to be equalised also, it is usually sensible to do this separately from the land as the concession will not apply if, for example, one party exchanges their interest in land for the other's interest in a share portfolio.

CGT planning on the breakdown of a marriage or civil partnership is considered in CHAPTER 10 and roll-over reliefs are covered more generally in CHAPTER 7.

Receipt of compensation and insurance monies

3.18 A similar relief to that for small part disposals of land applies where a capital sum is received in respect of an asset which is not lost or destroyed. In such cases, the receipt does not amount to a disposal of the asset and is instead deducted from the base cost. This applies if:

(a) the capital sum is wholly applied in restoring the asset;

(b) the capital sum is applied in restoring the asset except for a part which is both not reasonably required and small in relation to the sum received; or

(c) the sum received is small in relation to the value of the asset.

The definition of small is again the higher of £3,000 or 5% as set out in Revenue Interpretation 164.

Capital sums derived from assets

3.19 Section 22 and numerous HMRC statements and case law decisions have tried to cover the complex issue for CGT where sums are received in respect of the ownership of an asset but where there is no disposal of the asset The most significant case law decision in this respect is *Proctor v Zim Properties Ltd* [1985] STC 90 which concerned the receipt of compensation from a firm of solicitors on the failure of a property sale to complete despite contracts having been exchanged.

The CGT treatment of such receipts is complex and a careful consideration of the facts and the different possible interpretations is required when giving any planning advice in this area. This is particularly the case when advising on compensation receipts. However, it should be noted that in accordance with Revenue Interpretation 227 a lump sum payable under Matrimonial Causes Act 1973, s 31(7B) is not a capital sum derived from an asset. Where compensation is received for temporary loss of profits, this is subject to income tax and is not a capital sum derived from an asset (Statement of Practice 8/79).

Leases

3.20   As detailed above, a lease is an interest in land which lasts for a fixed, or recurring, but not infinite period of time. There may be certain restrictive covenants placed on the lessee, governing the use of the land. The leasehold interest can usually be bought and sold in the same way as a freehold interest, however, the CGT treatment will vary depending on the term of the lease.

For CGT purposes, the duration of a lease is important. A 'long' lease is a lease with a term of 50 years or more to run, whereas a 'short' lease has less than 50 years to run and this is therefore considered to be a wasting asset, in that its value will depreciate over time. At the end of a lease, the interest in the property reverts to the freeholders and so the freeholder will also retain an interest in the land or property, which, by contrast to the lessee, will increase in value as the term of the lease expires.

The expiry date of a lease will be the first date on which the landlord has an option to terminate the lease and this will usually be defined by the contract terms. A lease will also be deemed to terminate on the first date beyond which it is unlikely to continue because of, for example, a provision that the rent will substantially increase at that time. It is important to consider this if advising on the lease terms for CGT purposes.

If a lease is renewed to follow on from an earlier lease, it is treated as the grant of a new lease, not the continuation of an old lease, and therefore the disposal of the old lease occurs. However, by extra-statutory concession D39, HMRC will not treat the grant of a lease to follow on from an existing unexpired lease, ie an extension, to be a disposal, provided that the transaction is an arm's-length deal between unconnected persons and is not part of a larger scheme. In addition, no capital must be received by the lessee, and the property and the terms of the lease must remain the same (other than duration, rent and any trivial differences).

A freeholder cannot grant a lease to himself and so it is not possible to enter into artificial arrangements to obtain any CGT advantage. This is an important issue where a property is being developed into multiple units for letting purposes. In such cases, the objective will be to create leases possibly using a company to hold the freehold. In addition, HMRC Capital Gains Manual (CG70774) states that:

> 'If a freehold or leasehold interest in land is disposed of, on terms which include the provision that the purchaser will grant a lease of the whole or part of the land in question to the vendor, that should be treated as a part-disposal by the vendor. It should not be treated as two separate disposals, one by the vendor and one by the purchaser, see *Sargaison v Roberts* (1969).'

It is possible, however, for a freeholder to be party to the lease, for example Mr Black may grant a lease to Mr and Mrs Black or a partnership of which he is a member.

CGT planning is therefore possible, but if such arrangements have little commercial merit, they may be considered to be for the purposes of obtaining a tax advantage and will be subject to anti-avoidance measures. Of course, such planning could be defended if there are legitimate commercial reasons behind the arrangement. The gain that arises on the disposal of a lease will be chargeable according to the length of the disposal.

There are four situations to consider, each of which are detailed below:

(i)   Assignment (sale) of a long lease (more than 50 years).

(ii) Assignment of a short lease.

(iii) Grant of a lease out of a freehold, or a sub-lease from a lease with more than 50 years left to run.

(iv) Grant of a lease out of a sub-lease with less than 50 years left to run.

There is an important distinction between the assignment (sale of an existing interest) and the granting (creation of a new interest) of a lease.

The disposal of a lease is the disposal of an interest in property. Where the principal private residence exemption applies to the property, it will therefore also exempt the gain on a lease over the property.

Assignment of a lease with more than 50 years to run

3.21   The assignment of a lease is the disposal of a whole asset. A long lease is not considered to be a wasting asset and so this disposal gives rise to a capital gain calculated under the normal rules for CGT.

Assignment of a short lease

3.22   As a short lease is a wasting asset, only a proportion of the allowable original expenditure on the purchase of a lease will be allowable to account for the depreciation in value. However, leases are not deemed to depreciate on a straight line basis – their value decreases more and more quickly as the term runs out. The proportion is determined by the taper of percentages in Sch 8.

The allowable proportion of the cost (or market value at 31 March 1982) is given by the formula x/y of the original cost where 'x' is the percentage for the number of years left for the lease to run on assignment and 'y' is the percentage for the number of years that the lease had to run on acquisition, or number of years the lease had to run at March 1982 if the rebased value is used at that date.

Where the duration is not an exact number of years, the relevant percentage is calculated on a linear basis for each month, ie by adding $\frac{1}{12}$th of the difference in percentages between the two years either side, for each month. Odd days of 14 or more will count as a whole month.

For example, if a ten-year lease commenced on 1 January 2000 and was assigned on 8 October 2008, the relevant percentages would be:

X (1 year 3 months) = 5.983% + 3/12 (11.629% − 5.983%) = 7.395%

Y (10 years) = 46.695%

So that the proportion of the cost allowable in calculating the CGT on assignment is 7.395% / 46.695% = 15.836%

Example – Assignment of a short lease

Mr Case acquired a ten-year lease in a shop for £40,000 on 1 January 2000. He sold the leasehold interest when he retired on 8 October 2008 for £8,000.

The allowable proportion of the expenditure is £40,000 x 15.836% = £6,334, so the capital gain is:

	£
Proceeds	8,000
Less: annual expenditure	(6,334)
Gain before taper	£1,666

In practice, due to the nature of depreciation, it is unusual to make large gains on the assignment of short leases and therefore simple planning such as utilisation of annual exemptions in tax years for which no other gains are made is often adequate.

Granting a lease out of a freehold or long lease

3.23 The granting of a lease is a part disposal for CGT purposes because the grantor retains an interest in the property (ie, the freehold or head lease). If the grantor owns the freehold, or a long lease at the time of the grant (so that it is not a depreciating asset), the gain is calculated in accordance with the normal part disposal rules.

It is therefore necessary to obtain a valuation of the remainder of the interest for the grantor. This will include the value of any rights to receive rents under the lease as granted, as well as the discounted capital value of the reversion of the property on expiry of the lease. The disposal proceeds are the premium received for the lease.

Where the lease is granted for a period of less than 50 years, part of the premium is assessable to income tax as income from land and property and this is excluded from the premium in the CGT calculation. In the a/a+b fraction, the numerator 'a' is the amount of the premium assessable to CGT and 'a' in the denominator is the value of the whole premium.

The amount assessed to income tax is 2% x (n − 1) x premium, where 'n' is the number of years of the term of the lease.

Example – Granting a short lease out of a freehold

Mr Lloyd acquired a freehold property in January 1987 for £40,000 which he used in his business. In March 2008, he granted a 25-year lease for a premium of £25,000. The market value for the reversion, including the right to receive rents, was £95,000. The tax position on the grant of the lease is as follows:

Income tax	£
Premium	25,000
Less 2% x (25 – 1) x 25,000	(12,000)
Amount assessable to income tax	£13,000

The balance of the premium is charged to CGT.

Capital gains tax	£
Balance of premium	12,000
Less cost of a part disposal	(4,000)

$$\frac{12,000}{25,000+95,000} \text{ x } 40,000$$

Indexation allowance (factor 0.626)	(2,504)
Indexed gain	£5,496

Planning may be appropriate in determining the lease premium to be charged in order to take best advantage of the available taper relief and any exemptions. However, a proportion will still be charged to income tax and this needs to be borne in mind when considering such an approach. The shorter the term of the lease, the more of the premium will be charged to income tax rather than CGT, significantly reducing the scope of planning available.

There is more opportunity for CGT planning when granting a long lease, as none of the premium is assessable to income tax. For example, in the above example, if the term of the lease was 50 years, the optimum premium to be charged would be £62,646 so that the CGT is as follows:

	£
Premium	62,646
Less part disposal	

$$\frac{62,646}{62,646+95,000} \text{ x } 40,000$$

	(15,895)
Indexation allowance (factor 0.626)	(9,951)
Indexed gain	36,800
Taper relief (75% BATR)	(27,600)

Tapered gain	9,200
Annual exemption	(9,200)
Taxable gain	£Nil

The scope for planning is dependent upon the value of such a lease but if there is an ability to adjust the premium by varying, for example, the rents payable, then this can present a planning opportunity from a CGT perspective.

Granting a sub-lease out of a lease with less than 50 years to run

3.24 This situation is more complicated because there is a part disposal of a wasting asset and part of the premium is assessable to income tax. In addition, part of the costs of the head lease will have been assessed to income tax.

The fact that the head lease is a wasting asset is dealt with by using the same percentage table found at Sch 8, with the formula $(x-z)/y$ of the original cost or market value at 1982 where:

x   is the percentage corresponding to the number of years the head lease has to run at the time of granting the sub-lease.

z   is the percentage corresponding to the number of years remaining on the head lease at expiry of the sub-lease.

y   is the percentage for the length of the head lease on acquisition (or remaining at March 1982 if appropriate).

It is not possible to grant a sub-lease to extend beyond the term of the head lease.

The chargeable gain is calculated by deducting an allowable proportion of the cost from the full premium and this is reduced by depreciation. From this, the actual amount assessed to income tax is deducted, however, this cannot create or increase an allowable capital loss.

Example – Granting a sub-lease out of a short lease

On 1 January 1984 a 30-year lease was acquired for £12,000. On 1 January 2000, a sub-lease was granted for five years for £20,000.

On the grant of the original lease in January 1984, of the £12,000 premium paid, £6,960 (2% x (30 – 1) x £12,000) is assessable to CGT and the remainder, £5,040, is assessable to income tax.

On the grant of the sub-lease, the amount subject to income tax is calculated as follows:

	£	£
Premium received		20,000
Less allowable for reduction		
2% x (5 − 1) x £20,000		(1,600)
		18,400
Less allowance proportion		
Payment for head lease	12,000	
Less 2% x (30 − 1) x 12,000	(6,960)	
	5,040	
5/30ths thereof		(840)
Amount assessable to income tax		£17,560

The CGT is calculated by deducting the allowable cost from the full premium and then deducting the amount assessable to income tax as follows:

x14 years 58.971%

z9 years 43.154%

y30 years 87.330%

Depreciated cost is (58.971 − 43.154)/87.330 x 12,000 = £2,173

The CGT computation is therefore:

	£
Premium received (full)	20,000
Depreciated cost	(2,173)
Indexation allowance (factor 0.872)	(1,895)
	15,932
Less amount assessable to income tax	(17,560)
Indexed gain	£Nil

A loss cannot arise by deducting the amount assessable to income tax and therefore in this example, no amount of the premium is charged to CGT.

If a loss arises on the grant of the sub-lease before deducting the amount assessable to income tax, it is reduced by the amount of tax relief given against letting income that is calculated by working out the amount assessable to income tax.

The shorter the period of the sub-lease, the greater the amount of premium is subject to income tax, meaning that the amount assessable to CGT will be smaller and possibly covered by taper relief and annual exemptions.

However, the calculations are complicated and often give unexpected results, so it would be very sensible to advise clients of the tax position prior to entering into arrangements. What at first may seem to be a capital disposal may be more of an unexpected issue for income tax purposes and if this is the case, it severely restricts any planning available through the use of losses or tax efficient investments, for example.

In considering the tax consequences and any planning available, it is essential to ascertain whether the transaction involves an assignment of an existing lease or the granting of a new leasehold interest and also the length of the leases involved. It is very important that the position is fully understood and all the necessary details obtained.

Options

3.25 Another form of wasting assets are options to buy or sell an asset. This can be the right to buy or sell any asset, but typically it will be over shares or land. This chapter primarily concerns land and as with leasehold interests, the CGT implications and planning should be an integral part to any transactions involving options.

Options to buy or sell land typically have a fixed term, for example, a farmer may grant a property developer an option to buy his agricultural land for £x before a certain fixed date. Typically, a premium will be paid for the option and the developer can then later decide on when and if he will buy the land, considering factors such as whether planning permission may be granted, etc.

Because such options will expire at a certain date, they are usually deemed to be wasting assets and the allowable expenditure is deemed to waste away to nothing over the lifetime of the option, on a straight line basis. An option is a right to buy or sell, and this right is a capital asset.

The grant of an option is a disposal of a new asset and not a part disposal of the asset over which the option is created. The allowable expenditure is therefore only the incidental costs of the grant; there is no element of the underlying asset attached to the option. If the option is exercised, the treatment changes.

Where an option is exercised, the grant and the exercise (ie the subsequent disposal of the underlying asset) are treated as a single transaction taking place when the option is exercised. Proceeds from the grant and sale are aggregated and costs are deducted. Where tax has already been paid on the grant of the option, a credit is available against the tax payable on the exercise of the option.

For taper relief purposes, the exercise of an option determines the end of a period of ownership for the person disposing of the underlying asset. The business status of the asset is determined by reference to the use of the underlying asset. Therefore, the business asset status of the asset during the period of the lease remains very important. If there is an option in place in such a way that the asset is not exposed to fluctuations in value, taper relief will be denied – see CHAPTER 2.

Example – Grant of an option

Mr Johnson owns a plot of land which he bought for £8,000 on 1 January 1987. He grants an option on 1 January 1997 to a property developer where by he will sell the land for £250,000 at any time before 31 December 2007, as the property developer chooses. The developer pays £15,000 for this option and this is exercised on 31 December 2005.

There is a chargeable gain on the grant of the option in 1997 as follows:

	£
Proceeds	15,000
Less: annual exemption	(6,300)
Taxable gain	£8,700
Tax at, say, 40%	£3,480

At the exercise of the option, the gain is as follows:

	£
Proceeds (250,000 + 15,000)	265,000
Cost	(8,000)
Indexation allowance (factor 0.626)	(5,008)
Indexed gain	251,992
Taper relief (75% business)	(188,994)
Gain after taper	£62,998
Tax at, say, 40%	25,199
Less tax paid on the grant	(3,480)
Liability due	£21,719

If the option is abandoned, the grantor made a chargeable disposal at the time of the grant, but no further tax is due. The grantee acquired a chargeable asset at the grant of the option, however, there is no subsequent disposal. No capital loss can arise, when dealing with options over land, unless the option is to acquire assets for the purpose of a trade.

In practice, the CGT issues concerning the granting of options relate to BATR issues, base cost issues and the underlying ownership arrangements. These are dealt with elsewhere in this chapter.

Chattels exemption

3.26 Section 262 provides an exemption from CGT on the disposal of tangible moveable property where the value of this asset (proceeds or market value on a connected party transfer) is £6,000 or less. This exemption enables assets to be sold or given away free of CGT and so should not be overlooked. It is particularly relevant where a property is disposed of together with contents.

There is a further relief that caps the maximum gain on sale at ⅗rds of the excess of proceeds over £6,000. This further relief cannot apply if the proceeds are £15,000 or more.

Example – Chattels exemption

James purchased an antique chair in June 1985 for £800. He sold the chair at auction in July 2007 for £7,650 net of the auctioneer's 10% commission.

	£
Gross proceeds	8,500
Less: incidental costs of sale (10%)	(850)
Net proceeds	7,650
Less: cost	(800)
Unindexed gain	6,850
Less: indexation allowance to April 1998 (factor 0.704)	(563)
	£6,287
Restricted to a maximum of 5/3 x £(8,500 – 6,000)	£4,167
Gain after taper relief = £4,167 @ 60% (Maximum non-BATR)	£2,500

Chattels are dealt with on an item-by-item basis unless they form part of a set. It is also important to make sure that only chargeable assets are considered. Motor cars are ignored for CGT purposes (s 263) as are decorations for valour (s 268) unless acquired by money or money's worth.

As ever, this exemption raises valuation issues and it is important that appropriate experts are involved. From a planning perspective it is important to enquire into the assets being disposed of and to break down the contract consideration as appropriate between exempt and non-exempt items. However, it is still important to consider the IHT position, especially if the assets qualify for exemption from IHT.

Conclusion

3.27 The property ownership arrangements for chargeable assets are an essential part of CGT planning. As well as common ownership structuring issues, there are a number of fairly unusual CGT reliefs that can be taken advantage of if the circumstances permit. However, the first stage of any CGT planning is to fully explore the ownership structure in order that unwise assumptions are avoided.

Checklist

Property Ownership	Cross Reference
It is important that the legal ownership of any asset is fully researched and assessed before advising on planning to mitigate CGT.	3.1
Particularly complex and practical considerations arise in respect of partnerships. These are, in the main, addressed in SPD12.	3.4
Tax planning opportunities can arise where there is a part disposal of an asset and it is important that the adviser considers and assesses the 'asset' concerned.	3.13
Where a client is exchanging land with a joint owner, then relief from CGT may be available.	3.17
Computations in respect of leases are complex and careful consideration of the nature and terms of any lease is required.	3.20
It is important the proceeds from the sale of chattels are separately identified and exemption from CGT claimed where appropriate.	3.26

Chapter 4

Shares and Securities

Overview of tax planning opportunities

4.1 Whilst there is much that can be written about the calculation of gains on shares and securities, this book is concerned with planning to mitigate capital gains tax (CGT) rather than explaining the rules of calculation. Many of the planning opportunities are in fact covered elsewhere in this book and what is covered here are issues that are specific to shares and securities – although even in that context, there is still considerable overlap with CHAPTER 2 and CHAPTER 5.

This chapter considers:

(a)   the nature and definition of shares and securities;

(b)   matching rules;

(c)   investment wrappers and ownership structures;

(d)   a purchase of own shares;

(e)   the structuring of private equity investment;

(f)   issues for employees; and

(g)   potential liabilities under warranty and indemnity claims.

All statutory references in this chapter are to TCGA 1992 unless otherwise stated.

Meaning of 'security'

4.2 Securities are chargeable assets for CGT purposes. The adviser therefore needs to be aware of what constitutes a security in order to properly advise clients. Government loan stock (gilts) are not securities for CGT purposes and a corporate bond is not a security if it meets the conditions of s 116 and hence constitutes a Qualifying Corporate Bond (QCB). The distinction between a QCB and a non-QCB is considered in CHAPTER 5.

The CGT legislation does not contain a universal definition of security. It is not the case that any debenture will qualify as a security. The HMRC Capital Gains Manual at CG17930 includes some commentary on the definition of a security and states that a company debenture possessing the characteristics of 'the debt on a security' is a security prior to 6 April 2001 before the definition was clarified in Sch A1. Considerable guidance is

---

included in the HMRC Capital Gains Manual (CG534000 onwards) on what is deemed to be a simple debt and what is deemed to be a security. Section 21 provides that all debts are chargeable assets but not all debts are securities.

The fact that gilts are not chargeable assets can be helpful when looking to realise cash from an investment portfolio. If the portfolio is full of shares and securities that are heavily pregnant with gains, then the only option may be to sell the gilts and then review the other shares to maximise the use of the annual exemption and taper relief and sell those shares that can provide the necessary cash. However, investment considerations must not be forgotten as what may be the most beneficial outcome from a CGT perspective may not be in the best overall financial interest of the client.

Identification rules for individuals, trustees and personal representatives

4.3 The major problem with computing a capital gain arising on the disposal of shares or securities is the identification of what has actually been disposed of. If shares or securities that comprise one holding have been bought or otherwise acquired on several occasions at different prices, rules are required to match disposals with particular acquisitions.

Example – Requirement for matching rules

Larry acquires shares in ABC plc over a number of years, as shown below:

Date	Transaction	No of shares
28/07/1979	Purchased	500
19/08/1985	Purchased	1,000
14/10/1991	Inherited	7,500
20/12/1999	Purchased	1,800
18/04/2006	Reinvested dividend	40
18/10/2006	Reinvested dividend	45
Total holding		10,885

If Larry sells 4,000 of the shares on, say, 31 July 2006, it is necessary to ascertain which of the 10,885 shares he has actually sold.

The rules in s 104 onwards provide that disposals of securities made by individuals, trustees and personal representatives are matched in the following order:

(a) With acquisitions on the same day (if more than one then pooled). Special rules apply for shares acquired on the same day by an individual under different employee share schemes. The individual can elect to match shares with smaller inbuilt gains before those with larger gains, instead of matching with the pool.

(b) With acquisitions during the following 30 days on a first in/first out basis (FIFO). These are with effect from 17 March 1998.

(c) With acquisitions between 6 April 1998 and disposal on a last in/first out basis (LIFO).

(d) With the shares in the FA 1985 pool.

(e) With the shares in the frozen 1982 pool.

(f) With acquisitions made before 6 April 1965 on a last in/first out basis (LIFO).

In Larry's case above therefore, he would have sold the 40 shares acquired on 18/04/2006, the 1,800 shares acquired on 20/12/1999 and 2,160 of the shares in the FA 1985 pool (comprising the two holdings acquired on 19/08/1985 and 14/10/1991). Larry would therefore have retained the following shares:

Frozen 1982 pool	500
FA 1985 pool	6,340
18/10/2006	45
Total	6,885

Had the reinvestment of the dividend on 18 October 2006 been before 30 August 2006 (within 30 days after the sale) then they would have been the first shares matched with the sale instead.

The identification rules can also be a key component to certain tax planning schemes and so it is important that they are fully understood. As will be clear from the above, the rules have changed on several occasions since CGT was introduced.

The introduction of taper relief meant that pooling of shares had to cease for acquisitions on or after 6 April 1998. This was necessary so that the time of each acquisition could be recorded and retained and each treated separately from other acquisitions. Shares acquired in the period from 17 March to 5 April 1998 which are shares of the same class as shares already held on 16 March 1998 and in the same company, are treated for this purpose as acquired before 17 March 1998.

Securities falling within the same class retained on 6 April 1985 but acquired before 6 April 1982 comprise a single asset (the frozen 1982 pool) which cannot grow by the addition of further securities but may decline as disposals are made out of the pool. It is possible to submit an election for securities held at 6 April 1965 to be brought within the pool if no election has previously been made. In the absence of an election, such securities comprise separate assets which are not included in the 1982 pool. Where a disposal of securities is identified as being extracted from the 1982 pool the indexation allowance will be calculated by reference to a partial disposal of a single asset. The gain or loss arising on disposals will be determined on a similar basis. The pool will usually be treated as acquired for a consideration representing market value at 31 March 1982. Adjustments to that value will be required to recognise any part disposal made before 5 April 1988.

For securities of the same class acquired after 5 April 1982 and retained on 6 April 1985 a second pool is created (the FA 1985 pool) and these are identified by applying the pre-1985 rules. The pool is treated as a single asset. It follows that each disposal made from the pool represents the part disposal of an asset. This pool contains acquisitions made up to and including 5 April 1998 with the indexation allowance calculated to the month of April 1998 and then frozen.

Apart from the 30-day rule and the continuing application of s 105, each acquisition of securities taking place after 5 April 1998 involves a separate asset which does not enter into any 'pool'. It is important that details of these acquisitions are fully recorded as some may easily be overlooked. For example, many public companies encourage shareholders to use stock dividend options or dividend reinvestment plans (DRIPs). The exercise of each option will reflect the acquisition of a new asset.

Reinvestment of dividends

4.4 Prior to 5 April 1998, stock dividends were treated as being acquired on the same date as the original holding and so increased the original holding by the number of additional shares acquired through the stock dividend and increased the base costs by the amount of dividend reinvested. The indexation allowance was calculated with effect from the original date of acquisition of the holding. From 6 April 1998, stock dividends are treated as separate acquisitions for the purposes of the matching rules and taper relief.

Unfortunately, where shares were acquired many years ago and dividends reinvested over a long period of time, the capital gains calculation can become rather complex. Particular care is needed if the shareholding is ex-dividend as it is possible that a further acquisition of shares can take place within 30 days of the disposal when the dividend arising is paid and then reinvested under the stock dividend scheme. This can potentially cause problems in tax planning. For example, you may carefully calculate a loss arising on a particular shareholding to offset a gain on another shareholding during the year but failure to take account of any dividends that may be reinvested within 30 days of the sale of shares can potentially ruin the tax planning and, even worse, crystallise a further capital gain.

Example – Reinvestment of dividends

Mark acquired shares in Oak plc as follows:

Date		Quantity	Cost
		No	£
31/03/2001	Bought	10,000	20,000
01/05/2003	DRIP	50	50
01/11/2003	DRIP	75	100
01/05/2004	DRIP	60	90
01/11/2004	DRIP	85	120
01/05/2005	DRIP	70	150
01/11/2005	DRIP	100	220
01/05/2006	DRIP	75	190
01/11/2006	DRIP	110	300
		10,625	£21,220

The shares were valued on 3 April 2007 at £1.50 per share, which would potentially give rise to a capital loss as follows:

		£
Proceeds	(10,625 @ £1.50)	15,938
Less: total cost		(21,220)
Loss available		£5,282

As Mark had already realised a gain in 2006/07 (a sizeable gain with no taper relief available) he sold the 10,625 shares in Oak plc on 3 April 2007 to crystallise the loss in order to offset the gain.

Unfortunately for Mark, he had failed to take into account the fact that the shares became ex-dividend on 31 March 2007 and he received a special dividend of 50p per share on 1 May 2007 of £5,312 (10,625 x 50p). The share price had fallen to 80p a share and so the dividend was used to acquire 6,640 new shares in Oak plc on 1 May 2007. This acquisition is therefore matched with the sale of shares made on 3 April 2007, as it is within 30 days of their disposal.

The revised position is then as follows:

Acquisition date		Quantity sold	Cost	Proceeds	Gain / (loss)
		No	£	£	
31/03/2001	Bought	3,360	6,720	5,040	(1,680)
01/05/2003	DRIP	50	50	75	25
01/11/2003	DRIP	75	100	112	12
01/05/2004	DRIP	60	90	90	—
01/11/2004	DRIP	85	120	129	9
01/05/2005	DRIP	70	150	105	(45)
01/11/2005	DRIP	100	220	150	(70)
01/05/2006	DRIP	75	190	112	(78)
01/11/2006	DRIP	110	300	165	(135)
01/05/2007	DRIP	6,640	5,312	9,960	4,648
		10,625	£13,252	£15,938	£2,686

Mark retains 6,640 from the shares acquired on 31 March 2001. The loss of £5,282 he had expected is in fact a gain of £2,686. Incidentally, the price of Oak plc recovered to over £2 per share quite quickly after the sale. This was particularly frustrating for Mark, because he only made the sale due to the CGT saving available due to the apparent losses.

A further illustration concerns units issued by some unit trusts where dividends are not distributed, but applied to acquire new units. Here also, the acquisition of each new unit must be carefully recorded as representing a separate asset.

Matching rules and spouse transfers

4.5 The matching rules present CGT planning opportunities and one such opportunity involves utilising inter–spouse (or inter-civil partner) transfers.

It is common CGT practice to realise losses on shares and securities in a tax year where there is a capital gain arising in excess of the annual exemption. Often, it will seem that there are no losses available to be crystallised in a tax year.

However, by careful use of the inter-spouse transfer and by making use of the matching rules, there could still be losses available after all.

Although inter-spouse transfers are treated as being at no gain/no loss, the transfers of shares from one spouse to another are still subject to the usual share matching rules. It may sometimes be possible to gift shares in a holding that were at a lower base cost than the current value to the spouse or civil partner, whilst retaining shares acquired at a higher value which have been acquired at an earlier date.

Example – Matching rules and spouse transfers

George owned shares in A plc and B plc. The A plc shares were subject to a compulsory takeover in 2006/07 causing a capital gain to arise of £20,800. There was no taper relief available. George had no other gains or losses up until that point during 2006/07, nor did he have any losses brought forward. George is a higher-rate taxpayer.

George held 20,000 shares in B plc, valued at £2.50 per share (value of holding £50,000).

The shares in B plc were acquired as follows:

01/03/00 – 8,000 at £4.00 per share = £32,000

19/06/03 –12,000 at £1.25 per share = £15,000

George had a record that the base cost of his 20,000 shares in B plc was £47,000, so initially assumed he was sitting on a £3,000 gain for these shares. However, as inter-spouse transfers are subject to the usual matching rules, despite being deemed to be transferred at no gain/no loss, George was able to transfer 12,000 shares in B plc to his wife Jean, leaving George with 8,000 shares. The base cost of George's 8,000 shares was therefore £32,000. On 31 March 2007 George sold his 8,000 shares in B plc, realising a loss as follows:

	£
Proceeds: (8,000 @ £2.50)	20,000
Less: base cost	(32,000)
Loss	£12,000

This loss was then offset against the capital gain on the A plc shares and George's capital gain was below his annual exemption for 2006/07, saving CGT of £4,800 (£20,800 – £8,800 = £12,000 @ 40% = £4,800).

In the above example, George's wife, Jean, would be left with 12,000 shares with a pregnant gain of £15,000. If they wish to sell the shares in B plc, then Jean could have sold some before 5 April 2007 and some after, or alternatively at a later date transferred some back to George. Extreme care would be needed in this case to ensure that the shares are not gifted back to George within 30 days of him selling his shares in B plc as his disposal would then be matched to the shares transferred back to him by his wife rather than the shares acquired on 1 March 2000.

Consideration of the new targeted anti-avoidance rules (TAAR) is required before advising on such loss planning. The TAAR is discussed in CHAPTER 12. The extent to which HMRC will apply the TAAR is currently uncertain.

Bed and breakfast transactions

4.6 Prior to 1998 it was a common tax planning technique for an individual to contemplate bed and breakfast transactions. The main feature of these transactions involved the sale of securities and the reacquisition of those securities the following day, usually in an attempt to produce an allowable loss on disposal or perhaps to identify a gain that could absorb the annual exemption or losses.

Example – Traditional bed and breakfast approach

Adam acquired 1,000 shares in Mouse plc on 17 June 1993 for £3,000. In 1996/97 the share price had increased to £9 per share, although Adam was confident that the shares were still very much undervalued. He sold the shares at that point to crystallise a gain of £6,000 (ignoring indexation and costs of sale) so as to utilise his annual exemption. He then bought the shares back the next day at £9 per share. His base cost was then £9,000 (ignoring transaction costs).

However, the use of bed and breakfast transactions was effectively removed by the 30-day rule, which applies to the disposal of securities taking place on or after 17 March 1998. This rule requires that a disposal of shares must be matched with an acquisition of similar shares taking place in the following 30-day period. Disregarding brokerage and fees, and assuming the market price remains constant, this matching will eliminate the creation of a gain or loss. Therefore, the use of bed and breakfast transactions by an individual no longer achieves the desired tax advantage.

The tax adviser should be aware of the need to check whether any bed and breakfasting has taken place when advising on CGT. This can be a problem when taking on a new client who may have owned shares, on the face of it for a number of years, when in actual fact bed and breakfasting had taken place in the years after the original acquisition.

The history is relevant as the idea remains and has been adopted since 1998 to take advantage of other repurchasing approaches. One solution may involve the sale of securities by one individual and the immediate repurchase of similar securities by a second individual, perhaps a husband or wife, so called 'bed and spousing'. Other possibilities include repurchasing the shares through another vehicle, such as a Self Invested Personal Pension (SIPP) or selling shares in, say, Royal Dutch Shell and purchasing new shares in BP ie in the same industry sector. Another method is to 'bed and ISA' whereby a shareholding is sold in order to utilise the individual's CGT annual exemption and is then repurchased within a tax free ISA.

Example – Modern bed and breakfast approach

Hilda acquired 10,000 shares in Plinth plc in 1999 for £1,000. In 2006/07 they were worth £9,800 and Hilda sold the shares to realise a gain of £8,800 to make use of her annual exemption. On the same day, Hilda's civil partner, Doris, acquired 10,000 shares in Plinth plc.

By the same token, it may also be appropriate for Doris to sell some of her own shares to make use of her annual exemption and Hilda could then reacquire them.

Timings of gains and losses

4.7 Gains and losses arising in a year of assessment must be merged and only the tapered net gains remaining can be reduced by the exempt amount. An individual who has realised modest chargeable gains in a year of assessment should therefore avoid, if possible, any additional transaction later in the same year which is expected to produce a loss. It may be advisable to defer the loss-making transaction until a date falling after 5 April, thereby enabling the chargeable gains to obtain the full benefit of the annual exemption.

Example – Loss timing

Steve has already realised chargeable gains of £8,000 in the early part of 2007/08 and anticipates an allowable loss of around £7,500 from a disposal later in the year. This will give net gains of £500, leaving a substantial part of his annual exemption unrelieved. If the loss-making disposal is postponed until 2008/09, liability to CGT may well be avoided on the gains of £8,000, with the possibility that the expected loss of £7,500 will reduce subsequent liabilities.

Where allowable losses exceed chargeable gains, those losses may be carried forward to the following year and offset against net gains arising in that year. However, losses carried forward in this manner must not reduce the net gains for the following year below the exempt amount. Should a balance of unrelieved losses remain, the balance is then carried forward to future years. Ensuring that the untapered net gains for a future year do not exceed the exempt amount may preserve the full benefit of allowable losses brought forward. It is therefore possible to have net gains equal to the exempt amount for a year of assessment and so incur no liability whilst leaving brought forward losses undisturbed. Loss planning is considered further in CHAPTER 12.

Where one spouse/civil partner has losses and the other does not, then the ownership of an asset could be transferred from one spouse to the other, thereby enabling the transferee to undertake a disposal to an outside party and offset chargeable gains against allowable losses. In this manner losses incurred by one party to a marriage/partnership can be indirectly set against gains of the other party. Again the implications of the new TAAR need to be considered and reference should be made to CHAPTER 12.

Rights issues

4.8 Rights issues raise particularly complex issues for CGT because they have always been deemed to be acquired as part of the original holding. This gives rise to particular issues for taper relief and this point is considered in CHAPTER 2. There are also issues for Enterprise Investment Scheme (EIS) investments and for Enterprise Management Incentives (EMI). More generally, the normal computational rules for CGT in s 122 will apply on a rights issue including the rules on small capital distributions. This is because s 123 treats the sale of rights as a capital distribution. If s 122(2) would apply to the deemed capital distribution because it is small the value of the capital distribution should be deducted from the allowable base cost. This point is covered in Revenue Interpretation 34.

It is not uncommon for taxpayers to take up part of their entitlement to a rights issue and sell the balance of the rights nil paid. They may well sell the rights nil paid to help finance the acquisition of the new shares. The value of the property not disposed of in the part-disposal formula, B in s 42, depends upon when the taxpayer accepts the allotment of the shares they propose to take up. If it is a sale of rights before allotment is accepted then B is the market value of the rights they will retain and the market value of the original shareholding. If a sale of rights is made after allotment is accepted, then B is the market value of the new shares and the market value of the original shareholding.

Investment wrappers and ownership structuring

4.9   The major downside with the share matching rules is that each acquisition is treated as a separate asset for taper relief purposes. Most quoted shares will be non-business assets for taper relief purposes with the result that CGT is likely to be due on gains at rates close to 40%. However, this is on the basis that the annual exemption has already been utilised. In truth, many portfolio investors will be able to manage their CGT rate down by maximising the use of the annual exemption each year. For investors with large share portfolios, the benefit of the annual exemption will be minimal. This is even more of an issue when planning a large new investment in a share portfolio – such as from the proceeds of a business sale.

The ideal is to invest through an investment wrapper such that taper relief accrues on the wrapper rather than the underlying investments. This allows the fund to buy and sell shares without having to treat each acquisition as a separate holding for taper relief purposes. Whilst the concept is straightforward, the difficulty is to arrive at a tax-favoured investment vehicle. Otherwise, the unfavourable taper relief position is simply passed onto the fund.

The favoured investment wrapper is a unit trust or more usually now, an OEIC (Open Ended Investment Company). Certain providers will set up a personal OEIC for the investor through which the portfolio is then held. Current minimum investment levels are around £1 million although over time this limit will probably fall as such planning becomes more commonplace. The planning is most appropriate to those looking to invest a substantial cash sum as such investors are not limited by existing inbuilt gains. Such products can also be structured to be favourable from an investment perspective.

For smaller scale investors, the best approach is to follow an overall investment policy that seeks to minimise CGT including investment into the following:

(a) ISAs;

(b) pensions;

(c) venture capital trusts (VCTs);

(d) EIS investments; and

(e) investment bonds.

Gilts and corporate bonds are not subject to CGT and so can be used as part of a portfolio. However, the best way to otherwise maximise non-BATR is to invest into collective funds such as unit trusts and investment trusts. For those investors looking to maximise the use of their annual exemption, then investment in zero coupon preference shares can be attractive. Such shares yield no income but their value will rise over time as the redemption date approaches. They represent structured products with a certain capital gain built in.

It is important that the adviser raises the CGT planning issues for portfolio investments with their clients and works closely with the clients' other financial advisers to make sure that tax liabilities are minimised.

Purchase of own shares

4.10   An investor in a private company may wish to sell their shareholding but be unable to because there is no market for such shares. The other shareholders may be interested in acquiring the shares but be unable to because they have insufficient funds. In such cases, advisers should consider that a possible purchaser is the company.

If the company has sufficient distributable reserves it may be possible for the company to acquire the shares of the exiting shareholder. Further it may be possible for that payment to be treated as a capital distribution in the hands of the recipient as opposed to being treated as income (see below). The capital distribution treatment can be extremely tax advantageous when the exiting shareholder is entitled to full BATR as this could mean that they achieve an effective tax rate of 10% as opposed to 25% (which would be the case on a distribution). Issues relating to the entitlement to BATR are considered in CHAPTER 2.

Historically, companies were not allowed to purchase their own shares under company law and the position only changed at the beginning of the 1980s. For tax purposes, any such repurchase of own shares would be a distribution, but it was decided to allow capital distribution treatment in certain cases in order that the vendor could be in a comparable position to that of an independent party on an arm's-length sale. At that point in time, the CGT rate was significantly lower than the income tax rate.

In 1988, Nigel Lawson cut the income tax rate and increased the CGT rate such that it became more attractive for individuals to have income tax treatment, rather than have the distribution taxed as a capital gain. This did depend upon the circumstances as if retirement relief was available then clearly capital distribution treatment was likely to be better. It also depended upon the March 1982 base cost value. However, by the mid 1990s it was becoming more common for income distribution to be preferred and transactions were being structured such that the conditions for capital treatment were deliberately breached. However, the introduction of taper relief has now taken us back to the position when capital distribution treatment on purchase of own shares was originally introduced and it is often more desirable. This is in general terms though and the specific circumstances still need to be considered in each case.

On a purchase of own shares there is no acquisition by the company corresponding to the disposal by the shareholder because the shares are cancelled. As a result none of the legislation which requires an acquisition and a disposal can apply. This means that the connected persons provision in s 18 does not apply and so an Inspector should not refer the valuation to Shares Valuation Division on the grounds that the company and the shareholders were connected persons. A valuation will only be necessary if the Inspector believes the purchase is not a bargain made at arm's length within s 17.

In order for capital distribution treatment to apply the purchase must be for the benefit of the trade or to settle an inheritance tax (IHT) liability. Where it is for the benefit of the trade under ICTA 1988, s 219(1)(a) then the exiting shareholder must satisfy the conditions within ICTA 1988, ss 220–224 which in broad terms are as follows:

(a) the transaction must not be part of a scheme to avoid tax;

(b) the vendor must be UK resident;

(c) the vendor must have owned the shares for five years;

(d) the vendor must reduce his interest in the company to 75% or less of his percentage shareholding before the purchase of shares by the company; and

(e) that there will be no continuing connection between the vendor and the company.

Trade benefit test

4.11 Usually advice in connection with a purchase of own shares relates to a transaction within ICTA 1988, s 219(1)(a). Often one of the biggest hurdles in achieving capital distribution status for such a payment will be the satisfaction of the 'trade benefit test'. The approach will usually be that this is satisfied because there is disagreement amongst the shareholders and Statement of Practice 2/82 offers some helpful comments by HMRC in this respect. In particular it states that:

'If there is a disagreement between the shareholders over the management of the company and that disagreement is having or is expected to have an adverse effect on the company's trade, then the purchase will be regarded as satisfying the trade benefit test provided the effect of the transaction is to remove the dissenting shareholder entirely. Similarly, if the purpose is to ensure that an unwilling shareholder who wishes to end their association with the company does not sell their shares to someone who might not be acceptable to the other shareholders, the purchase will normally be regarded as benefiting the company's trade.

Examples of unwilling shareholders are as follows:

- an outside shareholder who has provided equity finance (whether or not with the expectation of redemption or sale to the company) and who wishes to withdraw that finance,

- a controlling shareholder who is retiring as a director and wishes to make way for new management,

- personal representatives of a deceased shareholder, where they wish to realise the value of the shares,

- a legatee of a deceased shareholder, where he does not wish to hold shares in the company.'

As can be seen, this gives considerable flexibility.

Example – Capital distribution treatment

A manufacturing company has reached capacity on its current site and is considering a £20 million expansion of facilities. The main shareholders and directors are two brothers; Chris (45) and Edward (55). Edward does not support the expansion plans, feeling that at this stage of life he does not have the energy to push through the operational changes, and so it has been agreed that he should not continue as a director or a shareholder.

Edward's 30% share of the company is worth £300,000. Assuming Edward is a higher-rate taxpayer and the shares were acquired for £30 on incorporation, eight years ago, the position would be as follows:

(a) If the £300,000 is taxed as income (ie, as a distribution) then the tax payable would be circa £75,000 (effective rate 25%).

(b) As a capital distribution, the tax liability would be:

	£
Proceeds	300,000
Less: selling costs	(2,500)
Less: cost	(30)
	297,470
Taper relief at 75% (maximum BATR)	(223,103)
Chargeable gain	74,367
Less: annual exemption	(9,200)
Chargeable gain	£65,167

91

For Edward as a higher-rate taxpayer the CGT will be £26,069. Therefore, there is a tax saving of £48,931 (75,000 – 26,069) if the payment can be treated as a capital distribution.

Substantial reduction in vendor's interest

4.12   In accordance with ICTA 1988, s 221 in order to achieve CGT treatment on a purchase of own shares then one of the conditions is that the 'vendor's interest as a shareholder must be substantially reduced'. Section 221 sets out the basis of calculation of this test in subsections (3) to (7) as follows:

'(3)   The question whether the combined interests as shareholders of the vendor and his associates are substantially reduced shall be determined in the same way as is (under the following subsections) the question whether a vendor's interest as a shareholder is substantially reduced, except that the vendor shall be assumed to have the interests of his associates as well as his own.

(4)   Subject to subsection (5) below, the vendor's interest as a shareholder shall be taken to be substantially reduced if and only if the total nominal value of the shares owned by him immediately after the purchase, expressed as a fraction of the issued share capital of the company at that time, does not exceed 75 per cent of the corresponding fraction immediately before the purchase.

(5)   The vendor's interest as a shareholder shall not be taken to be substantially reduced where—

(a)   he would, if the company distributed all its profits available for distribution immediately after the purchase, be entitled to a share of those profits, and

(b)   that share, expressed as a fraction of the total of those profits, exceeds 75 per cent of the corresponding fraction immediately before the purchase.

(6)   In determining for the purposes of subsection (5) above the division of profits among the persons entitled to them, a person entitled to periodic distributions calculated by reference to fixed rates or amounts shall be regarded as entitled to a distribution of the amount or maximum amount to which he would be entitled for a year.

(7)   In subsection (5) above 'profits available for distribution' has the same meaning as it has for the purposes of Part VIII of the Companies Act 1985, except that for the purposes of that subsection the amount of the profits available for distribution (whether immediately before or immediately after the purchase) shall be treated as increased—

(a)   in the case of every company, by £100, and

(b)   in the case of a company from which any person is entitled to periodic distributions of the kind mentioned in subsection (6) above, by a further amount equal to that required to make the distribution to which he is entitled in accordance with that subsection.'

The legislation therefore requires two tests, a 'nominal value' test and a 'distributable profits' test. In both cases, the vendor's interest must be reduced by 25% or more. The nominal value test is the one usually necessary and as a result the distributable profits test can often be overlooked. This second test is likely to pose a problem and consideration will therefore be required where the company has preference shares in issue.

Example – Substantial reduction in shareholder's interest (simple test)

Linda owns 260,115 £1 ordinary shares in Bouncy Castle Limited. Linda's brother Matthew and sister Lucinda own the remaining shares. The total issued share capital of Bouncy Castle Limited is 800,000 £1 ordinary shares. As such, Linda's total interest in the company represents a 32.5% shareholding.

In order to qualify for CGT treatment, due to the substantial reduction in interest condition, the minimum number of shares that Linda must dispose of is calculated as follows:

	No of shares
Linda's current interest required	260,115
Linda's required interest offer the purchase of own shares	(174,114)
Minimum share disposal	£86,001

Before the transaction Linda owns 260,115 shares, Linda's interest must be reduced to, at the most, a 24.4% interest (being 75% of Linda's current interest). The shares acquired by Bouncy Castle Limited will be cancelled. If Linda disposes of 86,001 shares, her interest will be reduced to 24.4% because Linda's revised total interest will be 174,114 shares of a total 713,999 (800,000 – 86,001) issued shares.

Example – Substantial reduction in shareholder's interest (both tests)

Josie owns 50 shares out of an issued share capital of 100. To achieve a substantial reduction (ie, 25%) in the nominal value, the company has to repurchase 20 shares. Supposing the company has distributable profits of £15,000 as well as 10,000 10% £1 preference shares, all of which are held by Josie, then would the test be met?

	£
Distributable profits	15,000
Statutory addition – s 221(7)	100
Preference dividend – s 221(7)	1,000
	£16,100

Josie's entitlement prior to the repurchase is:

	£	
Preference dividend	1,000	
50% of balance of £15,100	7,550	
	£8,550	*(53.11% of the total)*

After the repurchase Josie's entitlement would be:

	£	
Preference dividend	1,000	
37.5% (75% of 50%) of balance of £15,100	5,663	
	£6,663	*(41.39% of the total)*

This only amounts to a reduction of 22.07% and as a result the substantial reduction test for distributable profits is not met.

The continuing connection test

4.13   One practical aspect that can sometimes cause HMRC to refuse or rescind capital distribution treatment is the financing of the transaction. This is because ICTA 1988, s 228 defines a person as being connected with the company:

'if he directly or indirectly possesses or is entitled to acquire more than 30 per cent of:

- the issued ordinary share capital of the company, or

- the loan capital and issued share capital of the company, or

- the voting power in the company.'

The continuing connection issue can pose a problem where the company cannot fund the cash proceeds without additional financing. It is possible to obtain clearance even where the proceeds will effectively be loaned back by the spouse or a family member. This was demonstrated in the case *Preston Meats Ltd and another v Hammond (Inspector of Taxes)* [2005] STC (SCD) 90. The specific circumstances of this case are quite complex but essentially at the same time that a payment of £150,000 was made to the exiting director and his wife for their ordinary shares, the company issued 130,000 £1 redeemable interest bearing preference shares, carrying no voting rights.

The clearance application made reference to the issue of the redeemable preference shares but stated that a high percentage of them would be issued to the exiting shareholders' daughter (who, as she was aged over 18, would not be regarded as an associate). In the event the shares were registered in the name of the exiting director and he had accounted for all interest received on the shares on his own tax return. They contended that the arrangements fell within s 219 because in reality the exiting director acquired 30,000 shares for his own benefit and the remaining 100,000 for the benefit of his daughter. Further the Special Commissioner found, based on the evidence given by the exiting director, he did not contemplate that his daughter would have 100,000 of the shares to do with as she pleased. The treatment of the preference shares as being issued to the exiting shareholder meant that his interest in the company had not been sufficiently reduced to satisfy the relevant condition. Therefore, treatment of the payment of £150,000 as a capital distribution was rejected.

Income distribution versus capital distribution

4.14   Where the taper relief period is tainted, or the company is not a trading company, such that full BATR is not available, then it may well be that the income tax treatment is preferable to the CGT rate that would otherwise be payable. This is particularly likely to be the case where trusts are involved. In such cases, there are technical issues as to whether or not the re-purchase of shares represents capital or income in the hands of the trustees, but on the basis that it is distributed as income, then it will be necessary for the trustees to make an additional payment of tax in order to be able to make the tax payable on the income distribution fully recoverable. For higher-rate taxpayers who can then not recover that additional tax, this can amount to an effective tax rate on the income distribution to the trust of 40%. In such cases, therefore, trustees are always likely to prefer a repurchase of shares to the receipt of a substantial dividend, or equally to a capital distribution on the winding up, as considered in **CHAPTER 5**.

One of the issues is that of differing objectives between the parties, such that a repurchase of shares from trustees could be an attractive option for removing such tensions. This may be the case, for instance, where the trust concerned is an accumulation and maintenance settlement. Following the FA 2006 changes, it may be that if the trustees have decided to change the trust deed, such that absolute entitlement is achieved at age 18 or otherwise to forward in the age 18–25 trust regime, that the family would prefer a slightly different approach and may now prefer not to have a potentially tax-inefficient approach whilst the trustees hold the shares in a family company. The IHT points are considered further in **CHAPTER 15**.

A clearance procedure is available where a purchase of own shares is being considered and details are included in Statement of Practice 2/82. It is possible to apply for clearance on either capital or income distribution treatment. Clearance should also be applied for under ITA 2007, s 701 that the transactions in securities rules will not be invoked. As ever, it is important that the anti-avoidance provisions are fully considered and a separate disclosure made in any clearance application. Such points are considered further in **CHAPTER 13**.

Limited partnership structures

4.15 The British Venture Capital Association (BVCA) issued guidelines on 26 May 1987 following discussions with the then Inland Revenue regarding the tax treatment of partnerships established under the Limited Partnerships Act 1907 and used as vehicles for raising funds wholly or partly for equity investment in unquoted companies. This memorandum is reproduced in the Company Tax Manual at paragraph 36580. A further memorandum was issued in 2003 following the changes introduced by FA 2003, Sch 22 and this can be found in HMRC's Employment Related Securities Manual at paragraph 30520.

A limited partnership established for the purpose of raising funds for investment into companies will be regarded as carrying on a business and will represent a partnership within the definition in s 1 of the Partnership Act 1890 for the purposes of UK taxation. Where a venture capital fund is run through the medium of a limited partnership and it purchases shares and securities with the intention of holding them as investments, any profits or losses on disposal of those shares and securities will not be treated as trading income. Where the general partner provides management assistance to the companies in which investments are held by the partnership, such assistance would not, of itself, cause the limited partnership to be treated as trading. This approach seems somewhat surprising in view of s 37(1) which gives income tax primacy over CGT.

The income and capital gains arising within the partnership are subject to tax upon receipt by the partnership as the income and gains of the partners who are entitled to them and gains are taxed in accordance with Statement of Practice D12. This does not extend to circumstances where the partnership is carrying on a business of lending money and the acquisition of shares and securities is ancillary to that business.

Share owning structures involving limited partnerships and providing returns to investors structured as 'carried interest' are very topical at the time of writing this chapter. This is due to the widespread press criticism of the entitlement by the private equity industry to BATR on their investments. As a result a change to the BVCA guidelines is possible. Announcements could be made in the 2007 Pre-Budget Report and any changes are likely to impact on CGT planning possibilities. In this context, concern over tax-motivated incorporation and the defeat for HMRC in *Jones v Garnett (Inspector of Taxes)* [2007] UKHL 35, [2007] 1 WLR 2030 should also be borne in mind. Any changes could go wider than what is commonly termed the 'private equity industry'. It may also be helpful to provide some further explanation on carried interest.

Example – Carried interest for a private equity investment

In a typical private equity fund established as a limited liability partnership, the investment managers would be employees or directors of the general partner. Consequently, the carried interest acquired by the investment managers is, for tax purposes, an employment-related security and therefore potentially within the income tax regime. The general partner would manage the fund and would charge a management fee (usually a percentage of the fund commitments). The investors would contribute a small amount of capital and would provide the remaining funding by way of interest-free loans available to draw down on demand (a typical ratio of capital to loans would be: 0.01:99.99). The investment managers typically contribute an amount that equals 20% of the total capital contribution.

Returns on investment would commonly be distributed as follows:

(a) first, repayment to the investors of loans;

(b) next, a return to investors of a preferred return (typically 8% of the monies lent);

(c) next, to the investment managers a 'catch up' (typically 25% of the preferred return); and

(d) the balance would be allocated 80:20 in line with the capital contributions.

If the conditions of the safe harbour are complied with then these returns are subject to CGT rather than income tax. The safe harbour does require that investment managers are paid market rate remuneration for their work and that the returns received by managers must relate to the performance of the fund and not to any individual performance targets. The terms of the arrangement must be negotiated between the investors on an arm's-length basis and the managers must pay the same price for their partnership share as the investors (and therefore risk the loss of that investment if the fund is not successful).

The approach set out in these memoranda is a safe harbour. They do not affect the right of any taxpayer to argue that a different interpretation should apply to a taxpayer's specific circumstances. Also HMRC will not be bound by the memoranda if the main purpose, or a significant purpose, of the arrangements is avoidance of liability to tax or National Insurance.

If the profit sharing ratios vary during the life of a limited partnership without consideration passing outside the partnership then paragraph 4 of Statement of Practice D12 applies. As long as no revaluation or adjustment is made through the partnership accounts then the disposal between the partners will be treated as made on a no gain/no loss basis. Where, as a result of the application of paragraph 4 certain limited partners are deemed to have acquired a proportion of costs financed by other partners, the limited partnership may adjust the amounts payable to members of the partnership on its termination. If this is expressed as not being in consideration of a change in the profit sharing ratio then it will not be treated as consideration for the purposes of paragraph 6. The CGT treatment of partnerships including planning opportunities arising from Statement of Practice D12 generally are considered in Chapter 3.

Issues for employees

4.16 One of the issues considered throughout this book (such as in CHAPTER 1 and CHAPTER 3) is whether a disposal is subject to CGT or otherwise assessable to income tax perhaps as a trading transaction or because of an anti-avoidance provision. Another possibility is that a disposal is deemed to be an employment income receipt and taxed accordingly.

The definition of securities in ITEPA 2003, s 420 for the purposes of employment-related securities is more exhaustive than the definition of securities used in TCGA 1992. For example it includes government loan stock, but the great majority of employment-related securities will nevertheless be chargeable assets. The definition of 'employment-related securities' is set out in ITEPA 2003, s 421B(8). Where shares and securities are taxable as employment income then a charge to income tax will arise on:

(a) the increase in value of such shares and securities after they are acquired;

(b) gains on exercise of share options; and

(c) when the risk of forfeiture is lifted from shares previously subject to such a risk or on disposal of such shares.

The assessment to income tax is in priority to CGT. Section 120 sets out the rules on how any sums paid as income tax can be deducted as additional expenditure within s 38.

The rules on the treatment of securities in relation to employment income are deliberately widely drawn. In particular, it is important to appreciate that ITEPA 2003, s 421B(3) states that:

'a right or opportunity to acquire securities or an interest in securities made available by a person's employer or by a person connected with a person's employer, is to be regarded ... as available by reason of any employment of that person unless–

(a) the person by whom the right opportunity is made available is an individual, and

(b) the right or opportunity is made available in the normal course of the domestic family or personal relationships of that person.'

Therefore, the gain on shares acquired whilst employed may constitute part of the employee's income when sold unless there is a specific provision confirming assessment to CGT or because the securities were acquired at market value. From a CGT planning perspective the most favoured employee share arrangement is EMI which is considered separately below.

A gift of shares by a shareholder to an otherwise unconnected employee will have income tax consequences regardless of the submission of a s 165 hold-over claim. If the offer is for a transfer of existing shares to an employee then there will be a disposal of shares by the person transferring them to the employee. The transfer will be in connection with the employment so s 17(1)(b) will apply and the disposal will be at market value.

Management buy-outs and employment related securities

4.17 The tax adviser should take particular care when advising clients in management buy-out (MBO) transactions. Prior to the introduction of ITEPA 2003, Pt 7 it was often the case that where a management team invested in a new company, which was then used to acquire a target company, the shares would not be treated as acquired by reason of employment. However, that is no longer the case. Where an MBO team invest in a new company and that company then purchases a target company, the new company shares acquired by the management fall within the definition of employment-related securities in that the shares were made available by virtue of the manager's previous employment. In such cases advisers therefore need to consider the full implications of ITEPA 2003, Pt 7.

The BVCA memoranda of understanding deal with certain tax issues for managers of a company that is financed by a venture capital/private equity provider such as those involved in an MBO. HMRC accepts that the ratchet arrangements on managers' shares will not of themselves result in any charge under ITEPA 2003, Pt 7, Chs 1 to 5 if they conform to all of the following:

(a) They are such that the participation of different holders of ordinary capital in the company might vary accordingly to the performance of the company but not according to the personal individual perform- ance of any particular holder.

(b) They are in existence at the time the venture capital or private equity investor acquires its ordinary capital.

(c) The managers pay an open market price for their shares in the ordinary capital at the time of acquisition.

A detailed consideration of the treatment of employment-related securities within ITEPA 2003, s 421B on an MBO is outside the scope of this book.

Enterprise Management Incentives (EMI)

4.18 It has been widely recognised that one of the main limitations for small company growth is the difficulty of recruiting and keeping key personnel. The government has sought to address this through tax- advantaged share incentives which are designed to encourage skilled personnel to move to smaller enterprises. The most appropriate scheme for granting share options to employees will often be under the EMI scheme. The relevant conditions for an EMI scheme are set out in ITEPA 2003, Sch 5 and Sch 7D, Pt 4.

In broad terms, tax-advantaged share options with a market value of up to £100,000 may be granted to a qualifying employee of a qualifying company, subject to total share value of £3 million under EMI options to all employees. The shares must be in an independent trading company (the company must not be under the control of another company) that has gross assets of no more than £30 million. The company must also carry on a qualifying trade. The criteria here is largely drawn from the EIS criteria and as a broad brush approach advisers can assume that if a company carries out a qualifying trade for EIS purposes it will also qualify for EMI.

From an income tax perspective, assuming the grant of the option is at market value, there will be no income tax or National Insurance contributions (NICs) payable. However, advisers are no doubt aware that one of the key benefits of EMI share options is the CGT treatment. For share options granted under EMI, the taper relief period runs from the date that the share options are granted (Sch 7D, para 15) rather than the exercise date. This can mean that two years after the grant of the option, an individual can achieve an effective CGT rate of 10%, because of BATR.

There is a requirement that the company or at least one company within a group must exist wholly for the purpose of carrying on a qualifying trade. HMRC's guidance on what constitutes a trading company is set out in their Venture Capital Scheme Manual (VCM 15070). Where advisers are uncertain whether a company will be qualifying for EMI purposes, there is a clearance procedure in place. Clearance procedures are dealt with in further detail in CHAPTER 13. Specifically EMI clearances are dealt with by the Small Company Enterprise Centres.

All options granted under an EMI scheme must be registered with HMRC within 92 days of the date that the option is granted. An EMI1 form must be completed and supplied to HMRC. There is no requirement to submit the option agreement or any other legal documentation in relation to the grant. This 92-day deadline is crucial. If the option is not registered with HMRC it will be treated as an unapproved share option and the potential tax advantages lost. Advisers should therefore make note of the dates of grant, 92 days post grant and exercise of any share options on their permanent file records.

Sections 127 to 130 do not operate where there is a share reorganisation and the employee makes a payment for further shares, for example on a rights issue. This stops the further shares being treated as the same asset as the qualifying shares and being treated as acquired at the same time as the qualifying shares.

Sale of EMI shares

4.19 It may well be the case that EMI share options have been granted in the past and subsequently an offer is received to sell the company. The owner/manager may often wish to grant further options before completion to satisfy past commitments to employees. In such a case (assuming the conditions outlined above and in ITEPA 2003, Sch 5 are met), clients should be advised to grant EMI options which become exercisable immediately before completion.

Advisers should be wary, however, of the company independence condition and issues that may affect the share valuation. Where possible, clients should endeavour to grant any further options prior to the signing of any Heads of Terms. Where an offer for the company share capital has already been received, the valuation process will also be delicate. To ensure that no income tax charge or NICs arise on the grant of the option it must be at market value. Clients would be well advised to avoid getting into the finer details of negotiation before further share options have been granted.

Where clients wish to grant options immediately prior to completion or where options have been granted within the past year so that full BATR does not apply, the purchaser may be prepared to offer loan notes (specifically non-qualifying corporate bonds) to key option holders rather than cash. This can allow BATR to continue to run however care needs to be taken here as the taper relief clock is restarted from the date of the issue of the loan notes. Paper for paper treatment should be available for the exchange of option shares for loan notes.

One benefit of an EMI scheme is that the taper relief period runs from the date that the share options are granted rather than from the exercise date, which is normally the case for options. However, if the shares are exchanged for loan notes then a problem can arise as Sch 7D, para 15 refers only to 'a disposal of qualifying shares' when providing for the taper relief period to run from the date that an option is granted. As loan notes are not 'qualifying shares' (Sch 7D, para 14(3)), the taper relief period will only run from the actual date of acquisition, ie the exercise date.

Example – Quick Sale Limited

Alice was granted an EMI option on 9 August 2006 over 1,000 shares in Quick Sale Limited. The option was exercised on 10 August 2007 and six months later an offer is received for all the shares in the company. As only 18 months BATR is available, the advice may be to exchange the shares for non-QCBs in order to extend the taper relief period so that maximum BATR can be achieved. If this is suggested then it is important for the adviser to explain that the taper relief period will be reduced by 12 months. This could be detrimental if future BATR status on the non-QCBs is uncertain.

As explained above, BATR runs from the date the option is granted, so where options have been granted and subsequently the shares in the company are sold, individuals will receive BATR according to how long has passed since the grant of that option assuming they receive cash in consideration of their shares.

Advisers should also consider whether employees should endeavour to take some of their initial consideration in cash to utilise annual exemptions. An individual could also consider the availability of a spouse/civil partner's annual exemption. The option holder could transfer some of their option shares to their spouse/civil partner immediately after exercise, but before a company is sold. This would then allow the transferee spouse to sell some of the option shares to the purchaser to utilise their annual exemption.

The share pooling rules are considered earlier in this chapter, but advisers should always consider these where an option holder is selling their shares. If the individual has several EMI options which qualify for different rates of BATR it is possible to identify which of the option shares are being sold and which are perhaps being exchanged for loan notes say. In such circumstances, option holders will want to sell the option shares which qualify for the most favourable rate of BATR relief and exchange the ones that do not for non-qualifying corporate bonds.

Warranties and indemnities

4.20 In terms of the sale of a significant shareholding in a private company, then it is a normal part of the sales process for the vendor to give warranties and indemnities.

(a) A warranty is an assurance or promise in the acquisition agreement, the breach of which may give rise to a claim for damages.

(b) An indemnity is an undertaking by one person to meet a specific potential legal liability of another. An indemnity entitles the person indemnified to a payment if the event giving rise to the indemnity takes place. Unlike a claim for breach of warranty, there is no need for the indemnified party to establish that he has suffered loss.

One quite simple piece of tax planning that can easily be overlooked in the process of a business sale is to ensure that any claim for warranties or indemnities is treated as being a deduction of consideration received by the seller otherwise HMRC could argue that such a payment is a separate capital loss arising in a subsequent tax year.

An example of possible wording to be included in the Share Purchase Agreement is:

> 'All payments by the vendors under the warranties or indemnities in this agreement will be treated as repayments by the vendors of the consideration paid for the shares pursuant to this agreement.'

Where there are several vendors and all are jointly and severally liable under the sale and purchase agreement then there may be a separate deed between the warrantors apportioning responsibility in relation to owner-ship. The position on a deduction can be especially complex in such circumstances and careful consideration of the position is required as part of the sale planning.

Example – Impact of 'repayments clause'

Darren disposed of his 100% shareholding in a limited company in March 2007 for £500,000. In May 2008 Darren agrees and settles an indemnity claim for £100,000. In the absence of a clause in the Share Purchase Agreement for the sum to be treated as a repayment of consideration, then HMRC could maintain the position is as follows:

	2006/07 £
Proceeds	500,000
Less: cost	(1)
	499,999
Taper relief @ 75%	(374,999)
Chargeable gain	125,000
Less: annual exemption	(8,800)
	£116,200

In 2007/08 Darren would have a capital loss of £100,000. If Darren has no capital gains in that year this loss would be carried forward.

If the appropriate clause is made in the agreement, then the 2006/07 computation would be revisited when the indemnity claim is settled as follows:

	2006/07 £
Proceeds (£500,000 – £100,000)	400,000
Less: cost	(1)
	399,999
Taper relief @ 75%	(299,999)
Chargeable gain	100,000
Less: annual exemption	(8,800)
	£ 91,200

Conclusion

4.21   There are plenty of CGT planning points relating to shares and securities and what is appropriate will depend upon the specific client situation. However, the two very important principles to bear in mind are that it should not be assumed that CGT treatment is the only possible or even best, tax treatment that can apply and that it is long-term structuring and planning that is most important to get the best result for the client.

Checklist

Shares and Securities	*Cross Reference*
Planning involving shares and securities is relevant to private investors, entrepreneurs and employees.	
In order to be able to advise on planning ideas involving shares and securities it is necessary to consider the legislative rules on definition of securities and share matching.	**4.2**
Opportunities arise to minimise CGT through pre-sale spouse transfers.	**4.5**
Long-term planning is essential to minimise CGT and this involves consideration of the ownership structure.	**4.9**
Extraction of value from a company by means of a purchase of own shares can be very attractive.	**4.10**
It is essential that taxation of gains as income is considered and this is relevant when structuring arrangements especially for private equity investors.	**4.15**
The CGT treatment of arrangements involving EMI can be particularly complex and should be carefully considered.	**4.18**

Chapter 5

Company Reorganisation and Incorporation

Introduction

5.1   The decision to proceed with a reorganisation has to be evaluated in terms of the benefits outweighing the costs, and capital gains tax (CGT) will be one of the costs that should be considered. It is also important to consider how an individual should best invest in a commercial venture in order to minimise CGT in the long term. The crucial point for advisers is that the CGT position of a shareholder needs to be considered even when the individual's affairs are not necessarily the focus of the work in hand. This will often be the case where a business is looking to incorporate, consolidate or even de-merge.

While this book is aimed at individuals and trustees, inevitably this chapter has to stray into the tax position of companies. This is, however, with a view to outlining the impact on the shareholders rather than the business itself. Detailed consideration of the tax position on reconstructions and reorganisations is outside the scope of this text.

In terms of eventually realising a profit or loss on an investment, this is likely to be a capital receipt and as such subject to CGT. Whether or not a transaction is subject to CGT is considered in CHAPTER 1 and CHAPTER 13. To the extent that an activity is undertaken through a partnership, including a limited liability partnership (LLP) carrying on a trade, reference should be made to CHAPTER 3.

In this chapter all statutory references are to TCGA 1992 unless otherwise stated.

Incorporation

5.2   When the business of a sole trader or partnership incorporates, the individuals concerned are treated as having disposed of their business to the new limited company. As such, a potential CGT charge arises in relation to the disposal. However, it is possible to plan to optimise the CGT position on incorporation and there are two forms of relief to avoid a CGT charge on incorporation:

(1)   s 162 incorporation relief; and

(2)   an approach taking advantage of s 165 hold-over relief.

The s 162 approach is a long-standing relief and is an automatic relief that applies where the conditions are satisfied. However, as will be clear from the following explanation, the s 165 hold-over relief approach is the one that is most commonly used as it is more flexible in terms of allowing a tax-efficient extraction of future profits from the company. Despite this, incorporation under s 162 has two potential advantages:

(1) It is much more advantageous in terms of business property relief (BPR) for inheritance tax (IHT) purposes as the new shares represent replacement property for BPR such that a new two-year qualification period is not invoked.

(2) It is a way of achieving deferral of CGT where an unincorporated business is to be sold for consideration in the form of shares in the purchaser. This was the approach typically used when corporate groups were buying estate agency partnerships in the late 1980s. However, the impact of business asset taper relief (BATR) means that this approach would not be attractive now. That said, where a partnership is to be sold to a corporate entity with some of the consideration to be deferred, a pre-sale incorporation should still be explored, perhaps with a combination of the planning ideas that follow.

Mechanics of s 162 relief

5.3 Where a transfer of the entire assets of a business is made to a company in exchange for the issue of shares, it is likely that s 162 will apply. In broad terms, this provision means that the chargeable gain or gains arising on the transfer of assets will be rolled over and subtracted from the cost of acquiring the shares. Subsequently, the gain is deferred until the shares are disposed of. Provided a number of conditions are met, this treatment will automatically apply whenever the business of a sole trader or partnership is transferred to a company. The conditions are as follows:

(a) the business must be transferred as a going concern;

(b) all of the assets of the business except cash are transferred; and

(c) the consideration for the transfer must be wholly or partly in exchange for shares in the company.

Relief under s 162 is calculated by working out the gain arising on each asset transferred and then applying a fraction to the aggregate net gain. This fraction is the market value of the shares (ie the market value of the assets transferred) divided by the market value of the whole consideration received in exchange for the business. The effect of this is to then defer the element of the gain which relates to the assets other than cash.

The meaning of business is considered in HMRC Capital Gains Manual at CG65712. This confirms the normal position that the term 'business' goes much wider than 'trade' and so allows for the possibility of incorporating an investment business activity and still being eligible for s 162 relief. The alternative approach to incorporate under s 165, which is considered below, is only available for trading assets.

Example – Section 162 incorporation relief

Donald commenced trading in June 1978. On 20 August 2007 he transferred his business to an existing company in exchange for 10,000 ordinary £1 shares in the company and £20,000 in cash. The assets and liabilities transferred were as follows:

	Market value 31.03.82 £	Market value 20.08.06 £
Freehold buildings	11,000	60,000
Furniture and equipment	5,500	3,000
Trading stock	3,000	6,000
Goodwill	1,000	50,000
Debtors	600	11,000
Creditors	(200)	(10,000)
	£20,900	£120,000

The market value of the shares received is £100,000 since the total consideration for the transfer is £120,000 and £20,000 was received in cash. The chargeable gains arising are as follows:

	Based on market value 31.03.82 £
Freehold buildings	60,000
Less: MV 31.03.82	(11,000)
Unindexed gains	49,000
Less: indexation allowance (factor 1.047)	(11,517)
	£37,483

	Based on market value 31.03.82 £
Goodwill	50,000
Less: MV 31.03.82	(1,000)
Unindexed gains	49,000
Less: indexation allowance (factor 1.047)	(1,047)
	£47,953

The furniture and equipment are chattels valued below £6,000 and so are exempt from CGT.

Summary of total chargeable gains

	£
Indexed gains (37,483 + 47,953)	85,436
Less gain deferred based on market value of the shares received	
100,000/120,000 x £85,436	(71,197)
Gain after incorporation relief	£14,239

The deemed acquisition cost of the 10,000 ordinary shares is £28,803 (£100,000 – £71,197) and taper relief starts to run on the shares from 20 August 2007 (the date of transfer).

The gain after incorporation relief will be subject to CGT after the deduction of taper relief. Assuming that Donald has no other chargeable gains in the year then he has lost an element of his annual exemption and available taper relief as the capital gain is lower than his annual exempt amount (£9,200 – 2007/08). This can be shown as follows:

	£
Gains after incorporation relief	14,239
Taper relief at 75%	(10,679)
Gain before annual exemption	£3,560

Whilst there is no CGT liability on incorporation, a different approach would have better utilised taper relief and the annual exemption. Incorporation relief itself cannot be restricted to ensure that any losses brought forward, taper relief entitlement or the annual exemption are utilised. However, the tax adviser should be aware that from a planning perspective it is possible to ensure that the element of consideration received not in shares, is equal to the amount remaining chargeable before taper relief plus the annual exemption.

In the example above, if Donald had received cash or a loan balance of £51,688 then the market value of the shares would be £68,312 (£120,000 – £51,688). No CGT would have arisen and Donald would have made the most of his taper relief entitlement and annual exemption. This can be shown as follows:

Example – Maximising taper relief and annual exemption on incorporation

	£
Indexed gains (as above)	85,436
Less: gain deferred	
$\dfrac{\pounds 68,312 \times \pounds 85,436}{\pounds 120,000}$	(48,638)
Gain after incorporation relief	36,798
Taper relief at 75%	(27,699)
	9,200
Less: annual exemption	(9,200)
	£Nil

Section 162 relief? No thanks! – Election under s 162A

5.4   Where the taxpayer meets the conditions explained above, s 162 incorporation relief will automatically apply. Following the introduction of BATR it became clear that s 162 relief could penalise the taxpayer instead of being advantageous. This is because although the share issue assumes a continuity of the business through the roll-over, it does restart the taper relief period. As such, a sale in the two-year period following incorporation is denied maximum BATR even where a business has been trading for many years.

After much lobbying, this was recognised by the insertion of s 162A, which applies to transfers taking place on or after 6 April 2002. This enables an election to be made for the purpose of disapplying s 162. Where the election is made, chargeable gains arising on the transfer of assets to a company will not be rolled over but will remain assessable to CGT. This has no effect on the period of share ownership by the transferor but gains arising on the disposal of shares will not then be swollen by rolled-over gains.

Example – Disapplying s 162

On 1 December 2005, Alan transfers his long-established business to a company in exchange for shares. Relief under s 162 automatically applies. At the time the business is worth £175,000 and this is satisfied by the issue of

175,000 shares. The chargeable gain before taper relief rolled over on incorporation is £60,000. Alan's shares have a base cost of £115,000.

In May 2006, Alan receives an unexpected offer for his shares of £200,000. As the shares have only been held for five months, there is no entitlement to taper relief and his chargeable gain would be £85,000, calculated as follows:

	On disposal of shares 2006/07 £
Proceeds	200,000
Base cost	(115,000)
Chargeable gain (pre-taper)	85,000
Taper relief	—
Chargeable gains before annual exemption	£85,000

However, by electing to disapply s 162 Alan could benefit from full BATR at the time of incorporation such that his assessable gains for 2005/06 and 2006/07 become as follows:

	On incor-poration 2005/06 £	On disposal of shares 2006/07 £
Proceeds		200,000
Base cost (value at incorporation)		(175,000)
Chargeable gain (pre-taper)	60,000	25,000
Taper relief @ 75%	(45,000)	—
Chargeable gains before annual exemption	£15,000	£25,000

In addition to being of assistance when there is an unexpected offer to buy the business shortly after incorporation, the flexibility afforded by being able to disapply s 162 can also be beneficial where an individual has incorporated as part of a sale of the business but the sale subsequently falls through. Previously, a well-advised taxpayer would have structured the deal so as to fall out of incorporation relief in order to maximise his taper entitlement and would then be faced with an immediate tax charge. One of the planning opportunities presented by s 162A is that an individual can go ahead and structure the sale transaction so as to obtain relief under s 162 but opt out of the relief if the sale goes ahead as planned.

The time limits for making the election under s 162A are as follows:

(a) If the shares acquired at the time of the incorporation have been disposed of by the end of the tax year following that in which the transfer of the business took place, the election must be made no later than the first anniversary of the 31 January next following the tax year in which that transfer took place.

(b) If the shares acquired at the time of the incorporation have not all been disposed of by the end of the tax year following that in which the transfer of the business took place, the deadline for the election is extended by one year.

Any transfer of shares under s 58 will not be treated as a disposal for the purpose of triggering the shorter time limit.

Restriction of gain deferred under s 162

5.5 Under s 162 the proportion of the gain deferred is restricted by reference to the market value of the share consideration. Therefore, for a significant element of the gain to be deferred the share consideration must be a substantial proportion of the overall market value of the assets being transferred. This effectively reduces the scope for part of the consideration to be in the form of a loan account which could then be drawn down (tax free) over a period of time. An alternative option is the possibility of issuing redeemable preference shares, however advisers should be wary that the restrictions of company law do not give preference shares the same flexibility as a loan account. Further, in view of the wide scope of the legislation governing transactions in securities (see, for example, ITA 2007, s 689), it will be prudent to apply for clearance under ITA 2007, s 701 against the possibility of those rules being invoked.

Advisers could also then bear in mind that extra-statutory concession (ESC) D32 does offer a means of increasing the loan balance. This states that when third party business liabilities are taken over by a company on the transfer of an unincorporated business, these liabilities are not treated as non-share consideration. HMRC's Capital Gains Manual (CG65749) provides guidance in this respect and says that the concession applies only for the purpose of establishing the extent of 'other consideration'. It does not operate in the computation of the net cost of the shares.

Care is required here. Where there are substantial personal liabilities in the unincorporated business, if that is refinanced with borrowing in the company it will represent non-share consideration as the company is taking on a personal liability of the sole trader. Advisers will need to make sure that a significant tax liability is not caused by what may seem at first sight reasonable and straightforward financing arrangements. As ever, clear and proper documentation will help avoid such difficulties.

Example – Section 162 incorporation with personal liabilities

Amy has a business and is considering incorporation. The balance sheet position is as follows:

	£
Freehold property	900,000
Fixtures and fittings	45,000
Stock	45,000
	990,00
Personal mortgage	(500,000)
	490,000
Financed by capital	£490,000

The property originally cost £300,000 and there is also goodwill valued at £180,000. The market value of the shares on incorporation is £670,000 (£490,000 + £180,000) and this is the amount that can be rolled over under s 162. Despite the availability of incorporation relief Amy will still incur CGT on incorporation due to her financing arrangements. The gain is calculated as follows:

	£
Gain on property (£900,000 – £300,000)	600,000
Gain on goodwill (no base cost)	180,000
Total chargeable gains	780,000
Less: gain rolled over under s 162	(670,000)
Chargeable gain	£110,000

The position is more complex if there is a mixture of business and personal liabilities. In such cases, advisers should consider whether refinancing is appropriate prior to incorporation.

Specific issues in relation to the incorporation of professional partnerships were covered in ICAEW Tax Representation 7/95 which considers the assumption of annuities payable to retired partners. HMRC accept that these do not represent consideration on incorporation under s 162. This is likely to be less of an issue now, both because of the introduction of LLPs and the less common use of annuity arrangements. However, the principle and the reasoning set out by HMRC may be relevant when considering other scenarios.

Treatment of property and goodwill on incorporation

5.6 If a decision is made to incorporate, then it is fairly clear cut that the ownership of the day to day trading assets must be transferred to the company. These are unlikely to be chargeable assets and so this is not significant from a CGT perspective. However, careful consideration should be given to the treatment of property assets and goodwill.

As far as properties are concerned, there are various tax issues to consider including any Stamp Duty Land Tax (SDLT) charge on incorporation and the possible means of extracting profits from the company by charging a rent. However, from a CGT planning point of view, the key difference is between qualifying for BATR if the property is retained in personal ownership as opposed to a double tax charge if the property has been sold by a company and then the net proceeds are extracted by the shareholder(s). If it is intended that the property will continue to be used in the business in the long term, then sale issues are less relevant and in any case roll-over relief should be available. Further, if the property is held outside of the company then a lower rate of BPR will apply so IHT also needs to be carefully considered.

For s 162 to apply there is a prerequisite that all of the assets are transferred to the company with the exception of cash. It may be possible to mitigate the impact of these conditions whilst operating within the requirements of s 162. For example, it may be commercially feasible to create a lease out of the freehold prior to incorporation and this would necessarily involve the removal of the property from the business. Having done this the property can be leased to the business for a commercial rent and it is the lease that is transferred on incorporation rather than the freehold. However, it may be more appropriate to incorporate utilising s 165 hold-over relief instead. This is considered below.

Goodwill and intellectual property raises similar issues. BATR may be available on the shares in the new company but would a purchaser be prepared to acquire the shares? The adviser should consider retaining the goodwill in the personal name of the owner and licensing it to the company. This does depend upon putting appropriate legal documentation in place. A final point to consider is that commencing trading through a limited company at the outset is probably unwise from a CGT planning perspective. This is because at that point in time, there will be no goodwill value and possibly only a minimal intellectual property value. If there is a period of trading prior to incorporation, such that a goodwill value can be developed then this could subsequently be transferred to the company for a capital sum. From a CGT point of view, in terms of planning for a future disposal, it is far better to obtain limited liability by trading through an LLP than a limited company.

Incorporation utilising s 165 hold-over relief

5.7   It is possible to defer the CGT that would otherwise arise on incorporation as long as s 165 hold-over relief is available. This can be achieved where a sole trader establishes a limited company with, say, £2 of nominal share capital and then transfers individual chargeable assets to that company at an undervalue. This relief is considered in detail in CHAPTER 8. In the context of incorporation, the chargeable gains (based on the market value of the chargeable assets transferred) can be held over under s 165 where:

(a) the disposal is made otherwise than at arm's length;

(b) the transferee is UK resident or UK ordinarily resident;

(c) the transferor and transferee claim the relief; and

(d) the assets transferred fall within the following categories:

    (i) an asset used in a trade carried on by the trustees or by a beneficiary who had an interest in possession in it immediately before the disposal;

    (ii) shares or securities of a trading company or the holding company of a trading group where either:
- the shares are not listed on a recognised stock exchange;
- the trustees control not less than 25% of the voting rights;

or

    (iii) agricultural property which would qualify for IHT agricultural property relief.

The gain held over is that calculated before taper relief. In effect, therefore, the company takes over the transferor's allowable expenditure and indexation allowance on the individual assets transferred and the gain is deferred until the company sells that asset.

Example – Incorporation under s 165

Gerald commenced trading in June 1978. During the summer 2007, Gerald is contemplating incorporating the business and the following market values are determined:

	Market value
Freehold buildings	300,000
Furniture and equipment	3,000
Trading stock	6,000
Goodwill	200,000
Debtors	11,000
Creditors	(10,000)
	£510,000

The balance sheet, were Gerald to incorporate under s 162 or s 165, is as follows:

	Incorporation s 162	Incorporation s 165 with goodwill at undervalue	Incorporation s 165 with goodwill at market value
	£	£	£
Freehold buildings	300,000	—	—
Furniture and equipment	3,000	3,000	3,000
Trading stock	6,000	6,000	6,000
Goodwill	200,000	30,000	200,000
Cash		2	2
Debtors	11,000	—	—
Creditors	(10,000)	—	—
Director's loan	—	(39,000)	(209,000)
	£510,000	£2	£2

By incorporating using s 165:

(a) Gerald can retain the freehold in his own name, and therefore avoid paying SDLT (under s 162, the SDLT would have been £9,000 (3% x £300,000)).

(b) Also, the debtors can be collected by the sole trader business and used to satisfy the trade creditors of that business with the excess cash collected either retained by Gerald or introduced into the company by way of a further loan.

If the goodwill is transferred at £30,000, a level at which the chargeable gain post taper relief would be covered by Gerald's annual exemption, Gerald would have also created a directors' loan account of £39,000 that can be drawn down by him tax free. Alternatively, Gerald could transfer the goodwill at full market value and pay the CGT which would be calculated as follows:

	£
Market value	200,000
Less: MV 31.3.82	(1,000)
Unindexed gains	199,000
Indexation allowance (factor 1.047)	(1,047)
	197,953
Taper relief @ 75%	(148,465)
	49,488
Less: annual exemption	(9,200)
Chargeable gain	£40,288

Thus, Gerald could pay CGT on a gain of £40,288 to obtain an additional director's loan of £170,000. This can be repaid by the company, tax free, over the next few years instead of the extraction of funds as salary or dividends, either of which would be taxable at much higher rates than the effective CGT rate shown above. The issue of the valuation of goodwill and the potential CGT planning is considered further in Chapter 13.

In some cases, neither ss 162 or 165 will be available because of the nature of activities and the deal structure. In cases where neither relief is available it is important to note that on incorporation, Enterprise Investment Scheme (EIS) deferral relief may be available (see CHAPTER 6).

Incorporation between 1 April 1982 and 5 April 1988

5.8 If an unincorporated business which was trading on 31 March 1982 was incorporated between 1 April 1982 and 5 April 1988, Sch 4 provides that any rolled-over or held-over gain with a pre-31 March 1982 element can be halved in the event of a subsequent disposal of shares or assets. This is subject to the taxpayer making a claim to this effect.

Liquidation of a company

5.9 Sections 162 and 165 are available to roll-over or hold-over gains arising on the incorporation of a business. Unfortunately, there are no equivalent provisions to deal with the liabilities on disincorporation. The chargeable gains on disincorporation may be substantial, taking into account both the development of the business inside the company and the fact that the underlying assets may have a low base cost because of the deferred gains when the company was originally incorporated.

The transfer of chargeable assets from the company to the proprietor will be a connected party transaction, requiring the use of market value to compute the gains. However, in the absence of a third party sale, there will be no proceeds with which to pay the tax. Alternatively, if the company has enough cash to settle its tax liabilities the assets will be distributed in specie to the shareholders. There is still a double charge as the company has a liability on its gains and the shareholder has an income tax liability on the receipt. A liquidation with the receipt of a capital distribution is likely to be better from a CGT perspective. Distributions made in the course of dissolving or winding up the company are treated as capital distributions and are therefore chargeable to CGT by virtue of s 122.

Where a private company is dissolved under Companies Act 2006, s 1003 without going through a formal winding-up procedure, any pre-dissolution distribution is, strictly speaking, an income tax matter. Nevertheless, by virtue of ESC C16, HMRC will, in practice, treat such a distribution as a capital receipt if the taxpayer wishes. Certain assurances must be given to the Inspector beforehand. Normally, the Inspector will require that any remaining tax liabilities are paid and confirmation that, once the assets have been distributed, the company will request the Registrar of Companies to strike the company off the register. Although ESC C16 merely requires the company and its shareholders to agree to pay any corporation tax, in practice, HMRC insist that it is actually paid otherwise they will object to the 'striking off' application.

Example – ESC C16

Jim and Jackie are equal shareholders in End of the Road Limited, a company which has traded for many years. The profit and loss account balance is £250,000 and there is minimal share capital. Jim and Jackie have no capital losses and no other gains in the year. Both Jim and Jackie are higher-rate taxpayers. A decision is made to strike the company off the register in Summer 2007.

	Jim £	Jackie £
Distribution	125,000	125,000
Taper relief – 75%	(93,750)	(93,750)
Maximum BATR	31,250	31,250
Less: annual exemption	(9,200)	(9,200)
	£22,050	£22,050

On this basis, Jackie and Jim have a CGT liability of £17,640 (£44,100 x 40%) as opposed to a higher-rate income tax liability on a dividend of £62,500 (£250,000 x 25%). On the grounds of case law, there is potential scope for a challenge by HMRC on the basis of the transactions in securities legislation. This is considered in Chapter 13. The position is more defensible if the company is formally liquidated. Also there are legal differences between a striking off and a liquidation and advice should be taken from a Licensed Insolvency Practitioner. Care is also required that assets do not pass to the Crown through the principal of Bona Vacantia. In this context the repayment of share capital of up to £4,000 will be permitted.

Planning capital distributions

5.10 The above example assumes maximum BATR is available. This is unlikely to be the case as once the company ceases to trade, the shares become non-business and their taper period is tainted. It is possible that the company could instead be treated as inactive within Sch A1, para 11.

The winding up of the affairs of a company would be regarded as an activity but where a company is in liquidation with no winding up activities that will be an inactive period as set out in HMRC Tax Bulletin 61 (October 2002). However, where the company's activities and assets are being formally wound-up under the Insolvency Act 1986, this is generally regarded as a non-trading activity. Reference should be made to CHAPTER 2.

As a general rule, the earlier the capital distribution, the less tainting so the sooner the winding up can be completed, the better. However, this is no substitute for preparing detailed calculations. A further option is to at least make an immediate initial distribution. Where substantial delays are anticipated in the making of capital distributions, a shareholder may find it would be beneficial to transfer his shares to a settlor-interest trust. This would trigger a capital gain based on the market value of the shares.

If a shareholder received more than one capital distribution, all but the last one will be treated as a part disposal in respect of the shares. The normal part disposal formula in s 42 will be used to apportion the base cost of the shares where:

A = the amount of the interim capital distribution; and

B = the residual share value at the date of the interim distribution.

Depending on the amounts involved, it may be beneficial to phase the timing of the capital distributions over several tax years. This will enable the shareholders to benefit from more than one annual exemption. It may be possible to pay capital distributions over three separate tax years without dragging the liquidation out too long by paying distributions on, say, 5 April 2008, 5 September 2008 and 6 April 2009. Where there are a number of shareholders, the benefits of using multiple annual exemptions may be considerable.

In accordance with s 122, small interim distributions are deducted against the shareholder's base cost, thus effectively postponing any gain. HMRC Tax Bulletin 27 (February 1997) explains that HMRC do not insist on deducting the small proceeds against the cost. Part disposals and the issues relating to small distributions are considered further in CHAPTER 3. Statement of Practice D3 allows for a practical approach to the need for share valuations at the time of each interim distribution.

Pre-liquidation dividends are only likely to be preferred where, for one reason or another, the shareholders cannot benefit from maximum BATR. This may well be the case where a company has acquired substantial property assets, such that BATR status has been lost. The position may be particularly complex where there have been changes in the family owner-ship of the shares such that holding periods and taper relief varies and where trusts are involved. The optimum income dividend/capital distribu-tion mix will depend on the shareholder's indexed-based cost and taper relief position.

Particular care is required where there are ongoing activities as the liquidation and arrangements to carry on the activity could amount to a transaction in securities. This anti-avoidance provision could apply where a company (with retained profits) is liquidated with its business being sold to another company under the same or substantially similar ownership.

This is broadly what happened in *CIR v Joiner* [1975] 1 All ER 755. However, in that case, the House of Lords held that the arrangement was only caught because of an agreement which varied the shareholders' rights to a capital distribution on a winding up.

However, the *Joiner* case also concluded that simply putting a company into liquidation was not sufficient in itself to be a transaction in securities. HMRC are very likely to argue that where a business is transferred to another commonly controlled company in the course of a winding up that this would be challenged as a transaction in securities. The only exception to this would be where the businesses are being transferred as part of a genuine reconstruction operation within ss 136 and 139 using s 110 of the Insolvency Act 1986.

Group formation – Share for share exchange

5.11 It is often the case that an individual owns 100% of the share capital of a number of limited companies, each originally set up for a different purpose. It may become the case that the individual and corporate entities would be best served if the business activities were 'consolidated'. Most likely, the decision will be driven by commercial factors and perhaps corporation tax and income tax issues. It may be part of a merger with another organisation or as part of packaging the business activities for an ultimate sale. However, often advisers will be acting on behalf of the individual and not necessarily the company, and the CGT position of the shareholders should be considered. It is still necessary to overcome the CGT liability that would otherwise arise on such a reorganisation.

Relief from CGT is available under s 127 where new shares or securities are received in exchange for the existing shares or securities. This is known as paper for paper relief and is considered in CHAPTER 4.

Example – Share for share exchange

Tim owns two companies with the following assets and liabilities at market value (with base cost indicated in brackets):

	Company A £	Company B £
Freehold property (base cost £50,000)		100,000
Intellectual property (base cost £20,000)	200,000	
Goodwill pre-1 April 2002 (base cost £Nil)		100,000
Trading stock		6,000
Debtors		11,000
Creditors		(10,000)
Bank loan		(50,000)

Director's loan		(50,000)
Deferred gain	£200,000	£107,000
Share capital	2	2
Retained earnings and revaluation reserve	199,998	106,998
	£200,000	£107,000

Tim could sell his shares in Company B to Company A such that Company A is a holding company and Company B is a 100% subsidiary. Following the formation of the new group, the freehold property could be transferred into Company A; affording it some protection against trading risk of Company B. The sale of shares in Company B would be subject to CGT and even if Tim's shareholding qualified for 75% BATR, the chargeable gain would be calculated as follows:

	£
Deemed proceeds	107,000
Less: cost, say	(2)
	106,998
Taper relief @ 75%	(80,248)
Chargeable gain before annual exemption	26,750
Less: annual exemption	(9,200)
Chargeable gain	£17,550

This could be an acceptable tax liability especially if the annual exemption is available. However, a much more significant liability would arise if maximum BATR is not available. Also, this assumes that the transaction would be within CGT rather than a transaction in securities. This is debateable, bearing in mind the case of *CIR v Cleary* [1967] 2 All ER 48 which is discussed further in Chapter 13.

An alternative is for Tim to exchange his shares in Company B for shares in Company A. This is a type of corporate restructuring that is not treated as a disposal for CGT purposes as it comes within s 136, hence there should be no chargeable gain.

Variations of the share for share exchange in the above example are possible where share ownership is different for both companies concerned but in these cases:

(a) care would be required to ensure that shares are correctly valued ie, that share ownership in the holding company correctly reflects the respective value of the two companies being brought together; and

(b) stamp duty may be payable if ownership of the two companies pre and post share for share is not mirrored.

Advance clearance should be sought under s 38 to confirm that the relief is available and also under ITA 2007, s 701. In order to meet the requirements of ss 136 or 139, it is necessary for the reorganisation of shares and securities or of businesses to amount to a 'scheme of reconstruction'. A 'scheme of reconstruction' is defined in Sch 5AA to mean a scheme of de-merger, division or other restructuring that meets the first and second, and either the third or the fourth of the following conditions:

(i) The scheme involves the issue of ordinary share capital of a company to holders of ordinary share capital of another company.

(ii) The entitlement of any person to acquire shares is the same as any other person with shares of that class.

(iii) That the business or substantially the whole of the business carried on by the company is carried on by the successor companies.

(iv) The scheme is carried out in pursuance of a compromise or arrangement with members under the Companies Act (power of a company to compromise with creditors and members).

To obtain clearance, the taxpayer or their adviser must apply in writing to HMRC giving details of the proposed transaction. HMRC is obliged to notify its decision within 30 days of receiving the application, or within 30 days of receiving any additional information which has been requested. If HMRC has requested further information but this is not supplied, the application lapses.

The application must provide the following information:

(a) tax reference numbers of the parties to the transaction;

(b) full details of the transaction (including any preparatory transactions or reorganisations already effected);

(c) the purpose of the transaction and the commercial reasons for it; and

(d) copies of the latest accounts and memoranda of association of information of each company involved in the transaction.

Where clearance is given by HMRC, it is only valid in relation to the particular transaction for which clearance was applied for and only if it has been carried out within any time limit set out within the application. If full details had not been given to HMRC when the clearance was obtained, or the details were inaccurate or misleading, the clearance will be invalid. This is considered further in CHAPTER 13.

Deferred consideration

5.12 CHAPTER 4 considers the sale of shares and the potential for CGT in general whilst this chapter is concerned with issues specific to reorganisations. However, one particular issue which is relevant to both is where part of the consideration for the sale of the shares is to be deferred. This deferred consideration could take the form of:

(a) shares in the purchaser;

(b) an earnout arrangement; or

(c) simple payment at a later date.

In accordance with s 28 the consideration is taxable in the year of assessment in which the contract is entered into regardless of the date of payment. Therefore, the vendor will be taxable on monies that have not been received (and may never be received). The role of the tax adviser in such cases is to explain this issue and to consider alternative methods of structuring the transaction. This is likely to involve issuing paper in exchange for the shares as well as cash and in replacement for the deferred element. This paper will either be a security such that it qualifies for relief under ss 127 to 130 or under s 116 where the paper is a Qualifying Corporate Bond (QCB).

In general terms a loan note is a document issued by a company detailing the terms and conditions of the loan, including dates of redemption etc. These can be qualifying or non-qualifying corporate bonds. The distinction between qualifying and non-qualifying is based on the terms and conditions of the loan notes, ie for a particular transaction it is possible to construct either qualifying or non-qualifying QCBs. Clearance cannot be obtained for reconstructions involving QCBs as s 136 is only concerned with the issue of securities.

In recent years, the decision as to whether or not the transaction is structured with QCBs or non-QCBs has been prompted by taper relief considerations. Where a vendor already qualifies for maximum BATR then QCBs are the most attractive. Where the taper period is tainted, or the maximum period has not been obtained, then non-QCBs will be attractive if the vendor believes that he can improve his taper position.

Obtaining non-QCB status

5.13 In general, unless specific clauses are inserted into the loan documentation, then the outcome will be a QCB. In order to obtain non-QCB status, the loan note documentation can:

(a) be denominated in a foreign currency;

(b) have provision made for redemption in a foreign currency (so that the condition in s 117(1)(b) is not satisfied);

(c) give the right to the holder to subscribe for further loan notes (so that the condition in s 117(1)(a) is not satisfied); or

(d) provide for interest tied to profits so that the loan note is non-commercial (so that the condition in s 117(1)(a) is not satisfied).

There are a number of other possibilities but the second option remains the most common and the foreign currency is normally US dollars.

Advisers should be wary that care is required that the loan note does not become a deeply discounted security within ITTOIA 2005, Pt 4, Ch 8, as in that case it will automatically be a QCB. If the loan stock is issued for less than 15 years and the discount is greater than 0.5% times the number of years to redemption then the loan note will be a deeply discounted security. If a floating rate is used then this will not give rise to a deeply discounted security issue other than on the redemption in a foreign currency. The danger is that the re-designation or redemption in the foreign currency could cause the loan note to become a deeply discounted security. The normal approach is to limit the foreign currency equivalent to between 99.5% and 100.5% of the amount of the foreign currency if the sterling amount was converted at the spot rate on redemption. HMRC could argue that the lower and upper limits make the possibility of redeeming in a foreign currency unrealistic and as such the inserted provisions have no commercial purpose.

The non-QCB must be a security although as it is likely to be issued as part of a reorganisation, the s 251(6) relaxation should remove this problem in most cases. However, in order to achieve the commercial justification it is prudent to try and ensure that the criteria are achieved. In *Taylor Clark International Ltd v Lewis (Inspector of Taxes)* [1998] STC 1259, Robert Walker J stated that a 'debt on a security' must:

(i) be capable of assignment;

(ii) carry interest; and

(iii) have a structure of permanence ie, have a fixed term and not be capable of being repaid early without a penalty.

Section 251(6) was introduced to block avoidance of CGT by taking debentures on reorganisations that did not qualify as a 'debt on a security'. Section 251(6) is therefore somewhat of a sweep-up clause and deems a debenture issued by any company to be a security:

'(a) it is issued on a reorganisation (as defined in section 126(1)) or in pursuance of its allotment on any such reorganisation;

(b) it is issued in exchange for shares in or debentures of another company and in a case to which section 135 applies and which is unaffected by section 137(1);

(c) it is issued under any such arrangement as is mentioned in subsection (1)(a) of section 136 and in the case unaffected by section 137 where section 136 requires shares or debentures in another company to be treated as exchanged for, or for anything that includes, that debenture; or

(d) it is issued in pursuance of rights attached to any debenture issued on or after 16 March 1993 and falling within paragraph (a), (b) or (c) above, and any debenture which results from a conversion of securities within the meaning of section 132, or is issued in pursuance of rights attached to such debenture, shall be deemed for the purposes of this section to be a security (as defined in that section).'

The distinctions in terms of the CGT treatment between a simple loan or debt, QCB and non-QCB are summarised below.

Type of deferred consideration	Taxation implications
Debt (s 21)	The whole of the proceeds from the sale including the amount left as deferred consideration are subject to CGT in the year of assessment in which contracts are exchanged.
QCBs (s 117)	The element of the proceeds relating to the qualifying QCBs is not taxed until receipt – the CGT computations are prepared for the entire disposal but the element relating to the QCBs is deferred. A disadvantage with a QCB is that no loss relief is available if the acquiring company is unable to redeem it. Therefore, when the QCBs are redeemed (albeit for no value) the original deferred gain is taxed in full. In such cases it is usual to gift the QCB to a charity.
Non-QCBs (s 127)	The element of the proceeds satisfied by the issue of non-QCBs is not treated as a disposal at completion but will be taxed on the redemption of the loan note. The non-QCB is a security and paper for paper relief applies. Consequently, if the acquiring company is unable to redeem the security automatic loss relief is available as it will be the proceeds on redemption that are used in the computation of the gain. While taper relief will continue to accrue following the exchange of the shares for the non-QCBs it should be borne in mind that the loan notes will not necessarily be classified as a business asset ie, despite the continued availability of taper relief the business asset element could be increasingly diluted post-takeover, the longer the non-QCBs are held prior to their redemption.

Example – Structuring deferred consideration

Zat and Liam are equal shareholders in Defence Limited. The company is very young having only been incorporated three years ago. Therefore, Zat will qualify for BATR at 75% and Liam will not qualify for any BATR. Zat has been a shareholder for three years but Liam has been a shareholder for less than a year. Zat's base cost for his share is £1 whilst Liam has a base cost of £100,000.

The purchaser, Big Four plc, has offered £10 million for the shares of which £2 million is payable on completion and £8 million over the next five years.

If the consideration is simply left as outstanding the CGT position will be as follows:

	Total	Zat	Liam
	£	£	£
Proceeds	10,000,000	5,000,000	5,000,000
Base cost		(1)	(100,000)
		4,999,999	4,900,000
Taper relief		(3,749,999)	—
		1,250,000	4,900,000
Annual exemption		(9,200)	(9,200)
Chargeable gain		£1,240,800	£4,890,800
CGT @ 40%		£496,320	£1,956,320

In the absence of any structuring then Zat has to pay nearly half his cash consideration in CGT and Liam is unlikely to have the funds to pay his CGT liability.

If the deferred consideration is structured as QCBs then only 1/5 of the gain is chargeable now and the balance is deferred.

	Zat	Liam
	£	£
Assessable gain (2007/08)	£250,000	£980,000
Deferred gain	£1,250,000	£3,920,000

As can be seen, Liam is still in a much worse position than Zat but the ability to accrue taper relief (preferably BATR) will greatly reduce his tax liability.

A tax scheme has been promoted based on the promise that a non-QCB could be converted into a QCB such that the inbuilt gain on the security dropped out at that point in time. This approach was considered in *Harding v Revenue and Customs Commissioners* (2007) SpC 608. The Special Commissioner held that the attempted conversion from non-QCBs to QCBs was ineffective and that the loan notes continued to represent securities.

Both QCBs and non-QCBs can be transferred under s 58 without crystallising a CGT liability although the taper relief position for non-QCBs could be changed by such a transfer. However, such planning enables maximum advantage to be taken of annual exemptions and basic rate tax bands. Such transfers can be undertaken after the sale of shares has been concluded, subject to the terms of any sale agreement.

Reconstruction of mutual companies

5.14   Schedule A1, para 18 provides rules for assets acquired in the reconstruction of mutual business and it is a special provision to deal with the ownership period for taper relief. When a company with mutual status transfers its business to a company which issues shares to the members of the mutual company, members of the mutual body may be able to qualify for s 127 treatment upon receiving the shares in the new company by virtue of s 136(5) which extends the rules of ss 135 and 136 to any interests in a company in which no share capital is possessed by members of the company. The CGT treatment of this type of de-mutualisation depends on its precise terms.

Where it has been agreed that s 136(5) applies, then the period of ownership for taper relief will start from the time the shares are issued on the de-mutualisation rather than at any earlier time. Where s 217 (de-mutualisation of building societies) applies, no gain arises on the de-mutualisation and the qualifying holding period for taper relief will begin when the shares are issued.

Reconstructions involving de-mergers

5.15   For a two (or more) shareholder company undertaking more than one trade there is the possibility that the individuals concerned may wish to go their separate ways, each focusing on a specific activity. Whilst a separation of ownership could be achieved by the transfer of specified trade and assets and liabilities to a new company or companies under distinct ownership of each individual, this can have significant tax implications as the trade and assets will need to be disposed of by the company.

Example – De-merger of a company

Paul and Kim own 50% each of PK Limited. The company activities include two distinct trades. Paul and Kim have decided that their personal objectives and the objectives of both businesses would be best served if the activities were separated. Paul wishes to continue with the website activities and Kim wishes to focus on search engine maximisation.

The businesses are both worth £500,000 each and both have chargeable assets which are principally pre-2002 goodwill and the property used for trading. These assets would give rise to chargeable gains of £200,000 on disposal. The company will have in excess of £650,000 distributable reserves when the trade and assets are transferred (at market value).

Statutory de-merger

5.16   There is scope within the tax legislation for individuals, operating through limited companies, to reorganise their affairs. The de-merger provisions are largely contained in ICTA 1988, ss 213 to 218 and aim to make it easier to divide and put into separate ownership the trading activities of a company. This does offer a convenient procedure for a company to split, however, the de-merger provisions are hedged in by a number of conditions which frequently prevent the application of the exemption. Where a distribution qualifies as a statutory de-merger, it is treated as exempt and hence not treated as income in the hands of the recipient. No chargeable gain arises on a shareholder on a statutory de-merger as the new shares inherit the base cost of the old shares. A clearance procedure is available and Statement of Practice 13/80 provides a helpful summary of the position and HMRC's approach to the relief.

To achieve the statutory de-merger two new companies are set up and the assets of the company to be demerged (the distributing company), are distributed to the new companies in exchange for an issue of shares by those companies to all or any of the members of the distributing company. There are three specific scenarios where a statutory de-merger could be used. These are as follows:

(a)   a distribution directly to all or any of the members of a company of shares in a 75% subsidiary;

(b)   a distribution of the assets of a trade to one or more companies in exchange for an issue of shares by those companies to all or any of the members of the distributing company; and

(c)   a distribution of the shares in one or more 75% subsidiaries to one or more companies in exchange for an issue of shares by those companies to all or any of the members of the distributing company.

Example – Statutory de-merger

In the scenario outlined in the example above, two new companies are set up and the trade and assets of PK Limited are distributed to two new companies in exchange for an issue of shares by those companies to Kim and Paul respectively.

One of the essential features of a statutory de-merger is that both distributing and demerged companies must be trading. This route is not therefore appropriate for splitting a company that consists of trade and investment activities.

Non-statutory de-merger

5.17   An alternative reconstruction mechanism to the statutory de-merger is a liquidation partition under the Insolvency Act 1986, s 110.

This works by liquidating the original company and distributing the assets as a capital distribution on liquidation. The distribution is not liable to income tax because it is made on the winding up of a company.

A distribution of shares in a subsidiary company as part of the reconstruction will not be a distribution for income tax purposes because it is made on a winding up. There is no gain or loss on the disposal of a business by the company because s 139 will apply. Also, there is no CGT charge on the disposal of the shares in the company in exchange for shares in the new companies because s 136 will apply and so treat the transaction as a reorganisation within s 126.

Example – Non-statutory de-merger

The process to achieve a s 110 de-merger can be outlined, using the example above (featuring Kim and Paul), as follows:

(a) in the first instance, two new companies are created; Newco A and Newco B;

(b) Kim will form Newco A (to take over the trade and assets of search engine maximisation) and Paul will form Newco B (to take over the website activities);

(c) PK Limited is formally liquidated by the shareholders passing a special resolution;

(d) under s 110, a scheme of reconstruction takes place, under which the liquidator transfers the respective trades to Kim and Paul's new companies, which in turn issue shares to Kim and Paul as consideration.

Whilst the example of PK Limited involves two trades, this has only been used so that it can cover all the various possible approaches. The main attraction of a s 110 is the ability to separate out two businesses rather than two trades. Therefore, where a company has, over time, developed an investment business in addition to it's trading activity, it is possible to separate out the activities into two new companies. From a CGT planning perspective, the attraction is to be able to remove a tainting of the BATR position on a trading company. This may be the case if the aim is to sell the trading activity in the future but to retain the investment business.

Case Study – s 110 de-merger

This case study is considered in CHAPTER 2 and CHAPTER 8. For ease of reference the background facts to the scenario are repeated here.

Trendy Fashion Shops Limited has been incorporated for 29 years. It originally had a single shop (Homestore) but then expanded to have a chain of five shops. Following a strategic review in 2004, a decision was made to cease trading from two of the shops (Old Town and New Town) which were then let to tenants. The trading shops are now Homestore, High Street and Retail Village. The company owns all of the shops with the exception of Retail Village which is leasehold.

The directors and shareholders are:

	No of shares (£1 ordinary)	
Alan and Barbara Hazel (husband and wife)	4,500	(45%)
Thomas Hazel (son)	5,500	(55%)
	10,000	

The directors have obtained planning permission to redevelop the top two floors of the Old Town shop and also to extend the property. This will create five apartments in addition to the letting shop. Alan Hazel intends to occupy one of the apartments.

The intention is to convert the New Town shop into two luxury apartments. No decision has yet been made as to whether these apartments are to be let or sold.

Alan and Barbara Hazel have no desire to continue with the trade, preferring to focus their efforts on enhancing a property portfolio. Thomas, meanwhile, has big plans for growing the retail activities and was frustrated in 2004 by the decision to retract. The directors have asked for advice as to how they can 'split' the activities of Trendy Fashion Shops Limited so that Thomas can pursue his retail growth strategy whilst Alan and Barbara concentrate on the property portfolio.

The balance sheet of Trendy Fashion Shops Limited is as follows:

Trendy Fashion Shops Limited
Balance Sheet as at 30 June 2007

	£000s
Fixed assets:	
Homestore	1,250
High Street	750
Old Town	500
New Town	400
Goodwill	500
Fixtures and fittings	100
	3,500
Working capital	(250)
Long-term bank loans	(600)
	£2,650

Represented by:

Share capital	10
Profit and loss account	2,390
Revaluation reserve	250
	£2,650

After redevelopment, the Old Town property will be worth £1 million and £700,000 for New Town. The conversion costs are £250,000 for Old Town and £150,000 for New Town. The conversion costs are to be funded by additional bank debt. The apartment to be occupied by Alan Hazel will be worth £200,000.

Profitability of the trade is currently declining such that the goodwill value may fall although Thomas believes that he can reverse that trend.

Forecast Position after Redevelopment

	Total	Alan Hazel's apartment	Re-mainder of Old Town	New Town	Trading Assets
	£000s	£000s	£000s	£000s	£000s
Homestore	1,250				1,250
High Street	750				750
Old Town	1,000	200	800		—
New Town	700			700	—
Goodwill	500				500
Fixtures and fittings	100				100
					2,600
Working capital	(250)				(250)
	4,050	£200	£800	£700	£2,350
Long-term bank loans	(1,000)				
	£3,050				

The separation under s 110 could be carried out as follows:

(a) Thomas will form Newco A (to acquire the trade) and Alan and Barbara will form Newco B (to take over the investment properties);

(b) the debt is apportioned between the two Newcos so that market value equates to Thomas and his parents' percentage ownerships of Trendy Fashion Shops Limited:

	Trade	Investment	Total
	£000s	£000s	£000s
Before debt apportionment	2,350	1,700	4,050
Debt	(673)	(327)	(1,000)
Market value of assets	£1,677	£1,373	£3,050
	55%	45%	100%

(c) the existing company is formally liquidated by the shareholders passing a special resolution;

(d) a scheme of reconstruction takes place under which the liquidator transfers the respective trade/investment business to Thomas's and Alan and Barbara's new companies, which in turn issue shares to Thomas and Alan and Barbara.

It is important to note that for a s 110 de-merger to be implemented, under s 139(1)(a) there is a requirement that what is distributed is 'the whole or part of the company's business'. This point was considered in *Baytrust Holdings v CIR* [1971] 3 All ER 76.

As such, any parts of a company transferred to Newco A and Newco B must constitute a 'business'. In this instance a 'business' requires a degree of activity and commercial organisation as opposed to say a single investment property. In the case of Trendy Fashion Shops Limited, this condition would appear to be satisfied as the investment business consists of more than one property. Where there is any doubt it may be necessary to augment the investment business activities prior to implementing the s 110 reconstruction.

Going forward, Thomas has a company that is solely a trading company and so should qualify for maximum BATR. However, the BATR position for IHT purposes has almost certainly been worsened by the reconstruction and this point is considered further in CHAPTER 15.

A s 110 reorganisation can therefore be a very powerful tool in achieving a CGT efficient structure where the BATR position is currently tainted. It can be achieved without a tax charge other than in respect of stamp duty. However, it is not a cheap operation as apart from the tax adviser's costs there will also be significant legal fees and the cost of a liquidator and the necessary liquidation disbursements including the required financial bond which is calculated by reference to the asset worth of the company being liquidated.

An alternative approach for Trendy Fashion Shops Limited could be a purchase of own shares as discussed in CHAPTER 4. This would be with payment for the shares repurchased in specie or otherwise the purchase of own shares would have to be accompanied by a buyout of the assets of the company to be taken by the exiting shareholder. However in that case there would be a tax charge in the company on the disposal of assets at a gain, an SDLT charge payable by the recipient of the assets and more particularly the vendor of the shares will have to suffer a CGT charge on their shares based on the tainted taper position. These issues do not make this an attractive option.

Conclusion

5.18 CGT planning for individuals in the context of company reorganisation and incorporation is a diverse area, which often interacts with corporation tax and other taxes. Incorporation should be considered carefully in each case to determine whether s 162 relief is appropriate or whether the client would be better advised to transfer assets to the new company using s 165 hold-over relief. At this point in time, advisers should also be considering the longer-term CGT position for the client.

In all cases the responsibility of the adviser will depend upon the terms of engagement in place but for those advising private clients, it is necessary to consider the implications of any corporate restructuring on the shareholder's CGT position.

Checklist

	Cross Reference
Company Reorganisation and Incorporation	
There are some significant CGT planning opportunities in connection with incorporation. Two routes are available – s 162 and s 1265.	5.2
The treatment of goodwill on incorporation gives rise to planning opportunities.	5.6
Planning opportunities are available in respect of capital distributions on a liquidation.	5.9
It is possible to avoid CGT on the formation of a group.	5.11
It is possible to plan deferred consideration on a sale through the use of loan notes and earnout arrangements.	5.12
Reliefs are available to prevent CGT liabilities arising on a de-merger.	5.15

Chapter 6

Enterprise Investment Scheme (EIS) and Tax Efficient Investing for Capital Gains Tax

Investing to mitigate capital gains tax

6.1   One of the objections to capital gains tax (CGT) prior to its introduction had been the fact that it would deplete capital available for investment and so damage a capitalist economy. If capital is eroded then so is investment and future economic growth. There has been considerable research, both in the UK and the USA, to try and establish the damage done by CGT in terms of discouraging an entrepreneurial society. The main conclusions from this have been that the extent to which CGT erodes the capital base will depend upon the rate of CGT being charged. This has influenced policymaking on CGT rates and the introduction of taper relief.

The potential for damage to business investment became particularly acute in the decade from 1988 to 1998 when CGT was being levied at 40% on all gains. As a result, a number of reliefs were introduced to enable reinvestment of gains. However, this position changed with the introduction of taper relief and in particular, business asset taper relief (BATR). As such, reinvestment of gains has become less important for entrepreneurs than it was during the 1990s and of the CGT reinvestment reliefs, the only one currently available is deferral relief under Sch 5B which is connected with a claim under the Enterprise Investment Scheme (EIS) provisions of ITA 2007. All statutory references in this chapter are to TCGA 1992 unless otherwise stated.

Whilst the position on business assets has improved, reinvestment of capital gains is still important to private investors who may be making gains on shares or property that are subject to a rate of CGT of 40% or not much less. The particular attraction for this group is that Alternative Investment Market (AIM) company shares can qualify for EIS because AIM is treated as unlisted for these purposes. As such, private investors can invest in EIS shares which do have an exit route.

It is therefore appropriate to categorise tax efficient investing to minimise CGT between two distinct areas:

(1) entrepreneurs or business angels; and

(2) private investors.

Whilst much of the rules are relevant to both categories, the emphasis used in the tax planning relevant to each, differs between them. Most entrepreneurs, if they qualify for full BATR, will be happy to accept a CGT liability of 10% or less and will not wish to complicate their affairs by seeking to enter into reinvestment arrangements which will force them to commit the proceeds in a certain way. It is also the case that the restrictive nature of the EIS rules is more of a problem to commercial business arrangements than it is for those investing into a marketed and structured product.

Private investors tend to be interested in reinvesting to defer CGT for two particular reasons:

(1) to spread forward a gain over several years, such that advantage can be taken of annual exemptions and basic rate tax bands; or

(2) as part of an inheritance tax (IHT) strategy where the CGT liability is a barrier to making gifts.

Before considering the planning ideas in detail it is helpful to summarise the background to the current relief.

Background to the current EIS regime

6.2 EIS is both a very generous tax relief scheme and a very complex one. The scheme is a successor to the old Business Expansion Scheme (BES) and Reinvestment Relief. The complications in the EIS legislation derive from anti-avoidance legislation introduced to counteract abuses of those former schemes. It is important to appreciate the background to the current EIS regime in order to understand the different scenarios that clients may present. Specifically, an ongoing knowledge of the now defunct reinvestment relief is still required.

As a result of Nigel Lawson's Budget of 1988, all gains were taxed as income. It did not take long for the economic disincentive effect of these changes to demonstrate itself. Norman Lamont acknowledged the issue as early as 1993 in his Budget Statement when he said:

'Many business people claim that existing capital gains tax reliefs leave them with large tax liabilities when they sell their businesses. They claim that this prevents them from starting new businesses or from investing their capital, and with it their experience, in other businesses.'

With this, he announced the introduction of reinvestment relief and from 1 January 1994 there was the withdrawal of the BES and the introduction of EIS. This was followed by the new Venture Capital Trusts (VCTs) which included CGT deferral relief as part of the tax incentive package. VCTs were introduced in 1995 and announced in a press release, which said that:

'The Chancellor's intention is to put in place an effective set of measures to generate investment in the unquoted trading company sector. The aim, in particular, is to help provide more funds where they are most needed, among dynamic, innovative growing businesses.'

Reinvestment relief was a very important and very complex relief from CGT during the mid to late 1990s. The aim of reinvestment relief was to extend roll-over relief to investment in qualifying private companies. This, by definition, acknowledged the extent to which capital was otherwise being reduced. As an alleged simplification, reinvestment relief was merged into the EIS in 1998 and so created the two strands of EIS relief – full income tax relief and CGT deferral relief.

The amounts invested in EIS and VCT investments grew probably more or less consistently, as the level of capital gains grew on the stock market and as the economy recovered from the recession of the early 1990s. However, in April 2003 'Research into the Enterprise Investment Scheme and Venture Capital Trusts' prepared by PACEC for the Inland Revenue attempted to identify the characteristics of EIS and VCT investors. It 'found that there are two distinct types of EIS investors, and that the two types have different investment patterns from one another. "Deferral-only" EIS investors (ie those attracted into the scheme mainly or solely to access the opportunity to defer their liabilities on other capital gains) tend to invest significantly more than "mainstream" EIS investors (who are attracted into the scheme for a variety of tax and non-tax reasons)'.

Prior to April 2004 it was possible to defer gains by investing in a VCT but, following on from this research and subsequent consultation, the Treasury decided to restructure the VCT regime to make it an income tax incentive investment only. This is because it was concluded that VCT investors differed from EIS investors although there is considerable overlap.

New restrictions on EIS – FA 2006 and FA 2007

6.3 In June 2006 research was undertaken for HMRC by Ipsos MORI in respect of the 'Evaluation of the Changes to Capital Gains Tax since 1998' and this provided further evidence of the effectiveness of the EIS scheme. Whilst knowledge of EIS was quite low amongst the CGT payers surveyed, the research did conclude that:

'the benefits of EIS were clear to users, with four in five (79%) saying that they would not have made their investment if EIS had not been available.'

This research goes on to conclude that it is the ability to defer CGT that encourages investment in EIS companies. This enables a group of serial entrepreneurs to put money made from business transactions back into new younger companies in order to make a return. Whilst the majority of EIS investments are fairly modest (less than £100,000), there are also a number of larger investments.

Despite this strong support for the EIS, FA 2006 contained a new restriction of the EIS relief by substantially reducing the asset test limit on investment. For shares issued on or after 6 April 2006 the gross assets must not exceed £7 million immediately before the issue and must not exceed £8 million immediately afterwards (ICTA 1988, s 293). Whilst this is unlikely to be a stumbling block for a business angel investor, it has restricted investment into AIM companies.

FA 2007, Sch 16 has now introduced two new restrictions for qualifying companies:

(1) a restriction of the total funds raised in any 12-month period to £2 million in respect of any tax advantaged schemes (EIS, VCT and Corporate Venturing Scheme); and

(2) a restriction to a maximum number of 50 full-time employee posts at the time of investment.

The 2007 Budget Report stated that these restrictions are being introduced following the publication of the new 'State Aid for Risk Capital Guidelines' by the European Commission and that the government is required to make the necessary changes to the schemes.

The' State Aid for Risk Capital Guidelines' provide for an annual limit of €1.5 million or such higher figure as can be justified. The Treasury believes that the highest figure that can be justified is £2 million on the basis of the PACEC research referred to above. The 50-employees limit has been adopted as it is the employee numbers limit used for the small company EU definition and will therefore satisfy the guidelines.

The threshold of £2 million is likely to be a problem in terms of the AIM market. This is because most new share issues will exceed £2 million because of the fixed cost of a flotation and ongoing listing expenses. As such this fundraising limit will prevent new issues on AIM qualifying for EIS. On the OFEX market share issues tend to be smaller than on AIM but even so, there are share issues in excess of £2 million.

The likelihood is that most EIS work will continue to qualify as it is undertaken for business angels involved in new start-ups or those investing in early stage businesses. However, the cumulative impact of both the FA 2006 and FA 2007 changes is likely to severely limit EIS portfolio services investing into AIM and OFEX shares.

Types of EIS relief and possible client scenarios

6.4 It is important to appreciate that there are two types of EIS relief:

(1) The 'full EIS relief' which includes exemption from CGT on any gain, the potential for CGT deferral relief and a 20% income tax credit. The maximum up front tax relief under this relief is 60%. In order to qualify for this relief, the maximum ownership of the shares and loan stock by the new investor is limited to 30%. Understandably there are

also a large number of further restrictions that can apply. The maximum subscription in any one tax year is £200,000.

(2) The more limited form of EIS which is a CGT only relief and is referred to as 'deferral relief'. It is not necessary for the shares acquired to be subject to the EIS income tax relief. Under this relief, there is no restriction as to the percentage ownership of the shares and loan stock but there are still a number of complex restrictions to consider. The maximum tax benefit is 40% of the investment although the tax relief percentage is typically lower because of the likelihood of taper relief being available on the original gain. There is no maximum subscription.

Although an investor must not be 'connected with' the share-issuing company if full EIS relief is to be obtained, this condition does not extend to deferral relief. Deferral relief is not confined to individuals and a restricted range of trustees can also take advantage of the relief. Residency issues in connection with EIS are considered in CHAPTER 14.

In advising clients on CGT planning, the tax adviser needs to be aware of the following client scenarios:

(a) a base cost of shares which has been reduced by a rolled-over gain by virtue of reinvestment relief;

(b) a shareholding with a deferred gain under EIS;

(c) a shareholding with EIS which is exempt from CGT;

(d) a VCT investment with a deferred gain; and

(e) possible clawback situations that could occur to give rise to a CGT liability.

It is important to identify the potential CGT liabilities that could arise under each of these scenarios which may be part of an unpleasant legacy from a different era of CGT planning.

Deferral relief

6.5 As far as CGT is concerned, the tax benefits of EIS are that a deferral relief under Sch 5B is available for a qualifying investor to defer a chargeable gain arising:

(a) on the disposal of an asset;

(b) on the occasion of certain events withdrawing reinvestment relief;

(c) on a chargeable event arising under Sch 5B itself; or

(d) on a chargeable event affecting VCT investments under the deferral provisions of Sch 5C.

In order to qualify for CGT deferral relief under EIS, the following requirements need to be satisfied in relation to the investor:

(i) eligible shares in a company for which the investor has subscribed wholly in cash are issued to him or her at a qualifying time;

(ii) that the company is an active qualifying company (namely an unquoted or AIM listed company carrying on a qualifying trade);

(iii) that the shares are fully paid up;

(iv) that the shares are both subscribed for and issued for bona fide commercial purposes, and not as part of arrangements the main purpose, or one of the main purposes, of which is the avoidance of tax; and

(v) that all the shares comprised in the issue are issued in order to raise money for the purpose of a qualifying business activity and that the money raised by the issue is employed for the purpose of the business activity within specified time limits.

It is necessary for the issue of shares to take place at a qualifying time, which is identified as any time in the period commencing one year before and ending three years after the date of the disposal or other event. HMRC may grant an extension to this period. The relevant time periods have varied in the past.

It is possible to specify any amount of gain to defer and this is a useful tax planning tool which can be used to leave a reduced chargeable gain, which can be absorbed by an individual's annual exemption. It may also enable the tax efficient utilisation of CGT losses.

Example – Planning the amount to defer

Fred is a higher-rate taxpayer who has a capital gain of £50,000 on a property sale on which taper relief of 15% is available. He crystallises losses of £1,200 from the sale of some shares standing at a loss. He invests £50,000 in qualifying shares for deferral relief purposes. He does not have to defer the full £50,000 invested. The best outcome will be to only defer part of the total invested amount and this is shown as follows:

	£
Capital gain	50,000
Amount deferred under EIS	(37,977)
	12,023
Less: capital losses	(1,200)
	10,823
Taper relief at 15%	(1,623)
	9,200
Annual exemption	(9,200)
	£Nil

A number of provisions exist to prevent undue exploitation of deferral relief. The broad effect of these provisions is to disqualify shares from being treated as eligible shares. This will either prevent a claim for deferral relief being made or create a chargeable event leading to the termination of deferral relief previously granted. The main events that may create this result are the following:

(a)   the existence of a pre-arranged exit scheme;

(b)   the existence of put and call options. This can often be an issue with shareholder agreements;

(c)   the receipt of value from the company, either by the investor or by some other person who has obtained deferral relief;

(d)   the making of investment-linked loans. This prevents loan interest relief being claimed for income tax purposes in such circumstances; or

(e)   failure by the company to apply the proceeds of a share issue for a qualifying purpose.

The receipt of any value from the company within a period commencing one year before the share issue date and ending three years after that date or, if later, three years after the date trading commenced, will disqualify the status of eligible shares. This can be avoided if the receipt is of 'insignificant value' (usually an amount not exceeding £1,000) or where full restitution is immediately made to the company.

EIS qualifying status for companies

6.6   In order to benefit from EIS relief, the company must be a qualifying company. Similar qualification criteria apply to the Enterprise Management Incentives (EMI) and Corporate Venture Schemes. A number of businesses that are considered to be asset rich, and therefore less risky, are excluded from qualifying. The most common are farming, property development, hiring of assets and hotels but there are also a number of other restricted trades that do not qualify for EIS. Non-qualifying activities can be carried on by the company as long as those activities are not significant. In this context 'significant' means more than 20% of the activities.

To achieve qualifying company status, and therefore to establish the existence of an active company, either the share-issuing company or a subsidiary of that company must carry on a qualifying trade or trades. The list of activities which must be avoided if a qualifying trade is to be identified is considerable. The general effect is to disqualify activities that have interests in land and those, which do not, apparently, incur the required measure of commercial risk.

Advance clearance

6.7   To assist the investor (and the company concerned) a clearance procedure is available from HMRC. This is available through the Small Company Enterprise Centre at Llanishen, Cardiff to establish whether a trade is a qualifying one.

Clearance should be sought but it will only be valid as long as all matters are fully disclosed in the clearance application. For instance, it is important to disclose future expansion plans especially if these could include non-qualifying activities or overseas expansion or even the acquisition of subsidiary companies. Clearance can only be obtained to say that the company's trade qualifies for the EIS relief on the basis of the facts disclosed to HMRC. HMRC will not confirm that the specific investment will qualify for the relief. Only unlisted companies, including companies whose shares are dealt on the AIM, can be treated as qualifying companies.

As part of the reforms made in 1998 the definition of a qualifying trade was restricted. Previously, property development as well as woodlands had been included but these have now been removed and are restricted by ss 297 and 298. Particular care is therefore required to establish whether reinvestment relief or EIS was claimed even though the trade may not appear to be a qualifying one. Otherwise, when advising a client actions may be taken that cause a deferred gain to crystallise so generating an unexpected CGT liability.

A particular problem area is where the company just meets the requirements to qualify as an EIS company at the time of the share issue but where there is a danger that future expansion in a specific direction could cause that qualification to be lost and the EIS relief to be clawed back. In this respect, an EIS investment could potentially limit the commercial development of a business.

Procedure for claiming EIS relief

6.8   After the investment is made, a form EIS1 needs to be submitted by the company to HMRC to claim the EIS relief. This can be a claim either for the full relief or for deferral relief. The latest date for a claim to be made is 31 January nearly six years after the end of the tax in which the gain arose.

If HMRC are satisfied that the relief qualifies, then the Inspector will issue form EIS2 which will enable the company to issue the EIS3 certificate to the investor. This will show the period for which restrictions apply to the shares in the company in order to avoid any clawback of the EIS relief. These restrictions relate to the company's trading activities and prevent diversification into areas that could mean that it ceases to be qualifying for EIS purposes. Restrictions also apply to the percentage shareholding the investor may hold and financial arrangements between the investor and the company. The period for which the restrictions apply is usually three years from the date of the share issue.

Deferral of CGT is possible in respect of gains made in the three years prior to the investment in the shares or in the following 12 months. Therefore, where the gain has been made in a previous tax year, a tax repayment could be obtained as soon as the EIS3 certificate is issued by the company to the investor.

That part of the chargeable gain which is included in the claim for deferral relief will not be treated as arising at the time of the disposal or other event. That part must be deferred until the occasion of some future chargeable event. It must be emphasised that, unlike some other forms of roll-over relief, (see CHAPTER 7) the amount of deferral relief claimed is not subtracted from the disposal proceeds or from the cost of acquiring a replacement asset. The cost of the shares remains unaffected.

Example – Contrasting reinvestment relief with EIS

Alan has invested £2,000,000 in shares in an unquoted trading company as follows:

	£
1 January 1998	1,000,000
1 January 1999	1,000,000
	£2,000,000

Reinvestment relief was claimed against the original investment on 1 January 1998. A gain of £1,000,000 was reinvested into this shareholding. Deferral relief under EIS was claimed against the share subscription on 1 January 1999 for a gain of £1,000,000 on which there was no entitlement to taper relief.

On a sale of the shares, the original holding has a CGT base cost of £Nil. The shares acquired on 1 January 1999 have a CGT base cost of £1,000,000 but the deferred gain will crystallise on the sale of the shares.

Assuming a sale of the entire shareholding on 1 January 2006 for £6,000,000, the CGT position is as follows:

	Original investment	Further subscription	Total
	£	£	£
Proceeds	3,000,000	3,000,000	6,000,000
Base cost	—	(1,000,000)	(1,000,000)
Untapered gain	3,000,000	2,000,000	5,000,000
Taper relief at 75%	(2,250,000)	(1,500,000)	(3,750,000)
	750,000	500,000	1,250,000

Deferred gain	—	1,000,000	1,000,000
Chargeable gains	£750,000	£1,500,000	£2,250,000

Clawback events

6.9 EIS qualifying status is very complex and can be denied or clawed back if certain events take place within the relevant time period. The clawback event could either be as a result of the company failing to qualify for EIS status or otherwise as a result of the investor losing his/her qualifying status.

In particular, events that fall into the following two categories can cause problems:

(1) reorganisations of the business, operating companies or financing and share capital arrangements, and

(2) transactions with the shareholder benefiting from EIS relief (or with members of his/her immediate family).

When a chargeable event occurs in relation to qualifying shares the deferred gain will crystallise and become chargeable to CGT. Transfers within marriage are considered in CHAPTER 10 whilst the position for those becoming non-resident is considered in CHAPTER 14.

CGT planning for different types of investor

6.10 Having set out the background to the CGT deferral rules and having reviewed the general principles, it is now sensible to consider the planning opportunities for the two different types of investors.

Business angel investor

6.11 Tax advice will be required by the business angel investor in respect of both the initial investment and in respect of the steps required to avoid a clawback of relief. EIS advice to business angel investors is now one of the highest risk areas of tax advice for many firms. Anecdotal evidence suggests that many EIS claims fail at the outset because of inadequate structuring regardless of any subsequent clawback issues and this is due to receipt of value by the investor.

There are both upsides and downsides in terms of claiming EIS relief in respect of an investment. In the past venture capitalists have been known to resist investing in companies where EIS relief applies. This is because the rules may interfere with commercial decisions that would otherwise be made. The complications and restrictions should not be underestimated, but against this, the benefit of the tax relief substantially reduces the after-tax cost of the investment. Unfortunately EIS planning is often done on the cheap at the outset with adverse consequences later on. This is particularly the case for business angel investors who need to be prepared to pay for good advice prior to any involvement with the company in order to make sure that qualifying conditions are not breached.

Some points to watch out for on share issues are as follows:

(a) The shares must be subscribed for in cash. The investor must not purchase the shares from an existing shareholder. The shares must not be issued in exchange for services or assets transferred to the company. If this is the arrangement then the company must acquire the service or asset as a separate transaction on arm's-length terms.

(b) The shares must be fully paid. It is important that formal company secretarial procedures are complied with and that monies are properly paid as set out in the subscription letter.

(c) The shares must be ordinary shares. The investor can not receive shares on terms that are preferential to other shareholders.

Where the full EIS relief is being claimed then it is important that the existing connection tests concerning previous employment are fully complied with. It is also important that the percentage control tests are strictly complied with. In this context it is important to consider all the tests of control and to refer to any arrangements set out in a shareholders' agreement.

For the business angel investor, it is very important that he does not become connected with the company such that the EIS requirements are not met. Specifically, this has implications for:

(i) the size of the shareholding. This must be less than 30% of the equity. The combined loan and equity interest must also be less than 30% of the total;

(ii) the point at which any paid employment is taken on;

(iii) the terms of any shareholders' agreement; and

(iv) the prevention of a claim for loan interest relief.

When structuring an investment, reference should be made to the online guidance at www.hmrc.gov.uk/eis

In advising a business angel investor, it is important that all the EIS qualifying conditions are fully considered. It is prudent to run through the form EIS1 in detail with the directors and the investor (if different) to make sure that matters are fully understood. In particular, attention should be paid to the requirements as to a correct and valid share issue and with regard to receipt of value (covered in Note 10 to the form).

Details of any value received from the company since the shares were issued must also be entered on the form EIS1. In this context the 'insignificant amount' is £1,000 and so is not proportionate in any way to the amount of deferral relief claimed. A receipt of value in excess of £1,000 will cause all the tax benefits to be denied. Sch 5B, para 13(2) defines receipt of value as including:

- repayment of share capital, etc;

- the company setting a personal debt on the investor's behalf or releasing him from a liability to another person;

- making a loan or advancing money to the investor;

- providing a benefit or facility to the investor;

- disposing of an asset to the investor for no consideration or for a consideration below market value; and

- acquiring an asset from the investor in excess of its market value.

The language is very wide ranging. In completing the form EIS1, the directors must consider these points and bear them in mind for the future. If such an event does occur, then the directors are required to notify HMRC within 60 days. There is a potential penalty of up to £3,000 for incorrect completion of form EIS1.

The opening balance on any director's loan account must be entered on the form EIS1 together with any changes to the company's issued share capital and loan capital since each share issue. A particular problem is where the individual concerned receives a loan from the company. If this does occur then the loan must be repaid immediately if there is to be any chance of protecting the tax relief.

Example – Overdrawn director's loan account

Albert invests £500,000 in a small private company. CGT of £200,000 is deferred. As a result of poor payroll procedures, Albert's director's loan to the company becomes overdrawn by £5,000. This is not identified and rectified at the time such that the loan account remains overdrawn. The CGT deferred of £200,000 becomes payable as a result of the overdrawn loan account.

Private portfolio investors

6.12 EIS investments provide an opportunity to diversify portfolios and so reduce risk. The reason why these investments are possible options is because of the ability to defer CGT. In addition, any income tax relief available can be reinvested into low-risk investments to further reduce the risk exposure of the overall portfolio. Private investors can acquire shares listed on AIM or OFEX without having to make use of the services of a specialist stockbroker. Equally, many generalist stockbrokers will feel able to acquire such shares for their clients. Another option is an Approved EIS Investment Fund.

However, there are specialist stockbrokers and investment houses who concentrate on providing such services and that employ stockbrokers and analysts who are only concerned with shares that will qualify for EIS and IHT business property relief (BPR). Such stockbrokers include Singer & Friedlander, Brewin Dolphin and Christows. These stockbrokers have minimum portfolio sizes in terms of the de minimis amount an individual can invest and the current minimum is around £30,000. It will of course vary between stockbrokers. A further development in recent years has been the move by the VCT houses and other specialist investment boutiques into the provision of EIS portfolios and products. This is because they have specialist knowledge of this area as a result of their work in providing VCTs and with the reduction in the VCT market, are now concentrating far more on EIS.

It is possible to mitigate gains by investing in approved EIS funds which make use of pre-approval of their investments. These have been less common because they have more restrictive investment periods and are more similar in nature to unit trusts or a VCT. However, investment levels can start from as low as £3,000.

Example – Spreading forward a gain

Martin and Harry are brothers who inherited a run down residential property divided into several bedsits. They have now sold the property at a large gain to a developer, who was keen to acquire the property for a luxury apartment development. Both Martin and Harry are basic rate taxpayers, who do not utilise their annual exemptions each year.

The property has only been owned for less than four years and, therefore, minimal taper relief is available. However, by each brother investing a significant proportion of their proceeds in an EIS portfolio with a specialist stockbroker, it is possible to defer the gain and then look to realise shares each subsequent tax year over time such that the annual exemption is utilised and the balance of any basic rate band. However, there is an investment risk for Martin and Harry to consider.

Example – EIS deferral and IHT planning

Mark is very elderly and is not spending all of his income. He has a quoted share portfolio with significant gains on some of the shares. He has considered gifting, but as he does not expect to survive seven years, he is concerned about the double charge to CGT and then IHT. However, by disposing of quoted shareholdings and reinvesting into AIM, he could defer the capital gains which would be wiped clear on his death by rebasing and could qualify for BPR after two years.

There is therefore considerable flexibility and opportunity involving investment opportunities available to clients looking to shelter capital gains. However, it must be remembered that there are very important investment considerations with any such planning and the tax adviser can only point out the tax benefits of using such a scheme. The investment advice can only be provided by someone suitably regulated and authorised by the FSA for giving the appropriate advice.

EIS investments are invariably referred to as high-risk. However, risk is a relative concept and this is sometimes overlooked. The marketing of such investments concentrates on the tax breaks, but investors will not put money in what they perceive to be bad investments regardless of tax relief as attitudes to pensions testify. EIS investments must therefore withstand scrutiny as investment opportunities on their own merits. EIS investments should be regarded as medium to long-term investments.

What needs to be appreciated is that there is a risk in all equity investments. The skill of the investor (and his advisers) is to manage that risk. This is achieved by balancing risk and reward, spreading investments over different timescales and spreading investments over a number of investments (and sectors). Portfolio theory studies have demonstrated that 15 to 20 holdings are all that is required to achieve close to maximum risk minimisation.

Many clients already have a very high-risk exposure and EIS investments can be used to reduce that exposure. Specifically, clients with very large holdings in a single company such as:

(a) former employees, who have taken advantage of share options;

(b) former shareholders of companies that have been sold to listed companies in exchange for shares in the purchaser; and

(c) inherited shareholdings.

In each of the above cases it is likely that the shareholding is heavily pregnant with gain and the high-risk position is maintained because of the potential impact of CGT. As tax advisers we will often be asked to advise clients on strategies to reduce CGT and these will typically involve advice to realise the shareholding over a period of time to take advantage of taper relief, annual exemptions and the basic rate tax band. Such planning tends to unrealistically assume a constant share price and so is a high-risk investment strategy for the client.

Case Study – Diversifying risk

Mr and Mrs Smith have equal shareholdings in a single quoted company, X plc, valued at £600,000 in total. The base cost is negligible. There is no entitlement as Mr and Mrs Smith have never worked for X plc. The shares were acquired by Mr and Mrs Smith when they were appointed out of a discretionary trust to them just over two years ago when hold-over relief was claimed under s 260.

Mr Smith has an income of £80,000 (mainly salary) and Mrs Smith has an income of £10,000. The only other shareholdings are privatisation and de-mutualisation holdings which are worth about £10,000.

A possible investment strategy is as follows:

(1)March 2007

Mr Smith sells £110,000 worth of stock in X plc and invests £100,000 into an EIS portfolio. The gain will be deferred and Mr Smith will benefit from an income tax rebate of £20,000.

Mrs Smith sells £90,000 worth of stock in X plc.

(2)April 2007

Mr Smith sells £110,000 worth of stock in X plc and invests £100,000 into the EIS portfolio. The gain will be deferred and Mr Smith will benefit from an income tax rebate of £20,000.

Mrs Smith sells £90,000 worth of stock in X plc.

The remaining shareholding in X plc is worth £200,000.

In the next 12 months or so Mrs Smith reinvests £100,000 in EIS deferral investments (potential for income tax relief is ignored) leaving gains of £40,000 (approximately) in each tax year. The CGT arising is assumed to be £15,000 in total for the purpose of this case study.

Mr Smith has a minimal CGT liability in each tax year and so this is ignored for the purposes of this case study.

As a result of this diversification there is a net tax refund of £25,000 due to Mr and Mrs Smith which is receivable over the next two years. This can be invested along with the other share proceeds into lower risk or diversified investments in due course, or even retained as cash.

The impact on the portfolio is as follows:

	Before		*After*	
	£000s	*%*	*£000s*	*%*
X plc	600	98.4	200	31.5
Other shares	10	1.6	10	1.5
AIM/OFEX shares	—	—	300	47.3
Cash for reinvestment	—	—	125	19.7
Totals	610	100	635	100

The tax planning strategy of realising gains over a period of time can then be pursued.

There are two major limitations to this approach:

(1) the availability of suitable investment opportunities; and

(2) the ability to realise any investment.

Liquidity is a problem with smaller listed companies generally because there are fewer trades in their shares. This position has been made much worse since the abolition of reinvestment relief as EIS CGT deferral relief only applies on new share issues with the inevitable impact on the sale and purchase of shares in the secondhand market. In some cases share repurchases have been used to try to increase liquidity.

Example – Sheltering a gain through investment products

Mr and Mrs Jones sell a property for £300,000 after costs. The property was acquired in March 1997 for £100,000 and there is therefore a capital gain on the sale. After taper relief, the capital gain on sale is £120,000. Mr and Mrs Jones are higher-rate taxpayers but do each have their annual exemptions available to them?

In addition to EIS CGT deferral relief through investment into an AIM portfolio, some other investment ideas to consider are as follows:

(a) Personal pension contributions – it is possible to make a pension contribution to reduce the income subject to higher rate tax and so bring the capital gain down within the basic rate band. For taxpayers that are over 50 this could be by way of a contribution into an immediately vesting personal pension. Tax-free cash of 25% of the contribution could be drawn immediately. The balance would be taken as an annuity or possibly by way of drawdown on the fund.

If Mr and Mrs Jones are into higher rates because of earned income then significant pension contributions may be a possible option. However, if the income is non-taxable then they will be restricted to a contribution of only £3,600 each. This can still be appropriate on small gains but will not have much impact on a gain of this size.

If Mr and Mrs Jones will cease to be higher-rate taxpayers in the near future then planning involving pension contributions may be attractive.

(b) Film partnership or other tax loss partnership schemes – these types of schemes make use of trading loses which are then utilised against gains. This tax planning approach is considered in detail in Chapter 12. The position for Mr and Mrs Jones will again depend upon their wider investment objectives. As with pension planning it enables income to be reduced so mitigating CGT at the higher rate. However, the added benefit here is that the loss can be offset directly against the gain. As maximum non-BATR the trading loss will be more efficiently set against income taxed at 40% or 41% in priority to setting it against the capital gain.

The key question to raise with Mr and Mrs Jones is their intentions with regards to the sale proceeds. If the aim is to reinvest the proceeds then the use of investment products including EIS may be appropriate. The desire to also obtain BPR for IHT purposes will also be relevant when investment planning. As is the case so often with CGT planning, IHT considerations are interlocked. This is considered further in Chapter 15.

Outlooks for EIS planning to mitigate CGT

6.13   The significant reduction in effective CGT rates brought about by BATR, and now that many non-business assets at least qualify for maximum non-BATR together with the restriction to AIM and OFEX-based investments because of the FA 2006 and FA 2007 changes, have substantially reduced the need and scope for EIS tax planning. As a result, many of the issues covered in this chapter are less important for planning advice now – although the principles are still relevant.

However, should effective CGT rates increase then the position could change. For now, EIS planning for private investors is mainly connected with BPR planning for IHT.

Checklist

	Cross Reference
Enterprise Investment Schemes and Tax-efficient Investing for CGT	
For many years there have been reliefs available to defer CGT where monies are reinvested in certain tax-efficient structures. Relief from CGT is available through the EIS.	
The EIS regime has developed over many years and currently has two strands:	6.4
• full EIS relief, and	
• deferral relief.	
The planning approaches vary depending upon whether the client is a business angel investor or a private portfolio investor.	6.11

Chapter 7

Roll-Over Relief

Introduction

7.1 As far as individuals are concerned, the roll-over relief legislation at its core remains much the same as that introduced in 1965. Over the years the relatively brief statutory rules have been supplemented by other provisions and there has been considerable case law to clarify matters but the legislation itself remains complex and at times, woolly. As a result, HMRC have issued a number of concessions and so the taxpayer and adviser alike need to carefully consider all these rules if they are to make the most of the tax planning opportunities available.

Roll-over relief extends to gains arising on the disposal of qualifying business assets and gains from the transfer of an interest in land to authorities and others able to exercise compulsory purchase powers. In addition, claims are available to effectively roll over gains attributable to the receipt of capital sums derived from assets. All in all, the provisions are a key component of the taxpayer's armoury and can enable individuals to shelter gains from the ravages of capital gains tax (CGT).

That said, many individuals will be unable to satisfy the strict requirements which enable the several forms of roll-over relief to be obtained and must therefore look elsewhere for an efficient shelter. This chapter endeavours to explain the principles underpinning roll-over relief as well as these specific requirements, and to identify the planning opportunities and pitfalls surrounding the legislation.

Roll-over relief may be available in the following circumstances:

(a) for qualifying business assets;

(b) for certain land and buildings where a sale is forced on the ownership; and

(c) where compensation is received.

Where roll-over relief is available, then an asset can be disposed of without a liability to CGT arising although many restrictions can apply.

Replacement of business assets

7.2 The longstanding roll-over relief for business assets is outlined in s 152. All statutory references in this chapter are to TCGA 1992, unless otherwise stated.

Section 152 is a provision designed to prevent CGT having to be paid where a business sells a chargeable asset and reinvests the proceeds in a new qualifying business asset. One of the key requirements of the legislation is that it is the disposal proceeds that require reinvestment, not the chargeable gain itself.

It is a further requirement that the new business asset is acquired within a 12-month period prior to the date of the disposal or within a 36-month period after. Careful planning is required to ensure that the proceeds are utilised within the prescribed timescale otherwise the benefit of sheltering the chargeable gain can be lost. While the time limits can be extended at the discretion of HMRC, this is by no means a straightforward procedure. In broad terms the taxpayer is required to show:

(a) that he/she had a firm intention to acquire the new asset within the four-year time limit;

(b) that he/she was prevented from doing so by something beyond his/her control; and

(c) that the asset was acquired as soon as possible thereafter.

In practice it may be very difficult to satisfy all three of these conditions. That said, where the time limits have been exceeded and there is a genuine reason for the delay, it may still be worth approaching HMRC to see if they are willing to extend the 36-month post-disposal window.

When interpreting these time limits, the taxpayer should be wary of one of the most common pitfalls within the legislation; to qualify for roll-over relief it is a requirement that the new asset is brought into use on acquisition. This is considered further later in this chapter.

The effect of making a roll-over relief claim means that the asset disposed of is treated as being sold for consideration that gives rise to neither a chargeable gain nor loss and the acquisition cost of the new asset is reduced by the amount of the chargeable gain.

Example – Notional cost of replacement asset

Emma purchased shop premises for £20,000 from which to run her floristry business. She sold the shop for £28,000 which, ignoring costs, gave rise to a chargeable gain of £8,000. Within 18 months of selling the old shop, Emma bought a new flower shop for £35,000.

Emma is entitled to claim roll-over relief. The consideration received for the original shop is notionally reduced to £20,000 giving rise to neither a chargeable gain nor loss. The notional cost of the new shop is then reduced to £27,000, being the actual consideration paid less the chargeable gain rolled over.

Clearly, this provides a welcome opportunity for individuals to defer the payment of CGT and with some careful planning can be relatively easily achieved. However, in addition to the restrictive four-year acquisition window, the taxpayer must meet a number of further requirements in order to qualify for the relief.

The qualifying asset, both for the purposes of disposal and acquisition, must be one included within a relevant class as set out in the legislation. A complete list of the relevant classes can be found in s 155 (the Treasury has the power to add to these by Statutory Instrument). In terms of the most common assets, this list includes the following:

(i) land and buildings occupied and used for the purpose of the taxpayer's trade;

(ii) fixed plant or fixed machinery which does not form part of a building; and

(iii) goodwill.

In terms of tax planning it is worth noting that the old asset and the new asset need not fall within the same relevant class. For example, proceeds from the sale of goodwill may be reinvested in, say, fixed plant and machinery and (assuming the other requirements are met) roll-over relief would still be available.

However, while the relevant class requirement is fairly easy to satisfy, the taxpayer will often fall foul of the further requirement that, for periods after 31 March 1982, both the old and new assets must also be used either in:

• a trade carried on by the taxpayer; or

• a trade carried on by the taxpayer's personal company.

It is therefore crucial in ascertaining eligibility for roll-over relief to understand what HMRC deem to constitute 'a trade' and what constitutes a 'personal company'.

Definition of the term 'trade'

7.3   It is a basic requirement of the legislation that the asset disposed of must be used for the purpose of a trade. 'Trade' is defined in ICTA 1988, s 832(1) and includes 'every trade, manufacture, adventure or concern in the nature of trade'. Where profits are chargeable to income or corporation tax this will often provide a good indication as to whether a trade exists.

However a trade and a business are not necessarily one and the same. Specifically, the letting of a residential property does not constitute a trade for roll-over relief purposes. The letting of furnished holiday accommodation on the other hand does. This can provide significant planning opportunities for the taxpayer.

Furnished holiday lets can be an attractive option for a retiring taxpayer, say, looking to reinvest proceeds from the disposal of business assets. The new property must be taken into business use on acquisition but there is no claw back if it ceases to be used in a business in the future. A furnished holiday let property could therefore subsequently be let on assured shorthold tenancies at a future date and the roll-over relief claimed on the original acquisition would not be withdrawn.

The legislation also provides for a number of other activities which are treated as a 'trade' for roll-over relief purposes. These include professions, vocations, offices and employments. The provisions are also extended to the discharge of functions of a public authority, the occupation of commercial woodlands with a view to the realisation of profits, trade bodies and non-profit making bodies such as sports clubs.

It is also worth noting that where two trades are carried on at the same time they are treated as a single trade for roll-over relief purposes. Similarly, where two trades are carried on successively, they are treated as a single trade. For example, a butcher who sells his business and reinvests in a flower shop may claim roll-over relief for qualifying assets sold and acquired. For the purpose of this section of the legislation 'successively' is defined as an interval of no longer than three years between the two trades. This provides significant scope for the deferral of tax where an individual chooses to explore a new business venture albeit as a result of the cessation of a previous trade or at the same time.

Personal company

7.4 Roll-over relief may also be claimed where a qualifying asset is owned by an individual but the trade in question is carried on not by themselves but rather by the taxpayer's 'personal company'. A personal company is defined in s 157 and is one where the taxpayer exercises not less than 5% of the voting rights in that company. The definition is the same as that used for s 165 hold-over relief (see CHAPTER 8) and was that previously applying for retirement relief purposes. Interestingly whether the individual works full time or not at all is not relevant here.

While on first reading this may seem like a generous provision, this section of the legislation is in fact very restrictive because the company must be the individual's same personal company both at the date of disposal and at the date of acquisition. Particular care is required where a disposal and reinvestment is proposed for a sole trader who is intending to incorporate. While the new asset may be used in the trade of the taxpayer's personal company, the old asset will not have been. Incorporation is considered in detail in CHAPTER 5.

However, there is no requirement for the company to be a personal company during the period between the time of disposal and the time of acquisition. As such, while it might not always be commercially appropriate, it could be wise to plan any changes in share ownership around the dates of disposal and acquisition where significant chargeable gains could arise.

If an individual's voting rights were 5% at the date of disposal, say, but have since fallen to less than 5%, the company shareholdings could be adjusted prior to the acquisition of a new qualifying asset to ensure that the individual once again owns 5% or more of the voting rights at that date. There is no claw back if the taxpayer's shareholding subsequently falls to less than 5% of the voting rights post-acquisition of the new qualifying asset.

Care should also be exercised where the taxpayer owns shares in a company which form part of a group and the taxpayer's asset is used by one of the group companies. Where an asset is used by a company which is 100% owned by a holding company in which the taxpayer has greater than a 5% interest, the 'personal company' provisions are unlikely to apply. This was demonstrated in the case of *Boparan v HMRC* [2007] SSCD 297.

Example – Interpretation of 'use by a personal company'

Mr and Mrs Smith own a company, Smith Limited. Mr Smith owns 55% of the shares in the company and Mrs Smith owns 45% of the shares. Smith Limited owns 100% of the share capital in Jones Limited. Mr and Mrs Smith sold some buildings that they let to Smith Limited and acquired some buildings which they then let to Jones Limited.

Roll-over relief is not available to Mr Smith. This is because Jones Limited is not deemed to be a personal company within s 157 and therefore the asset is not a qualifying asset used in a trade carried on by Mr Smith's personal company. It is HMRC's view that this would be far too wide a construction of the expression 'voting rights which are exercised in a company' because the rights are only exercised by a two-stage process.

Inter-spouse transfers

7.5 Inter-spouse transfers are considered in detail in CHAPTER 10. A no gain/no loss transfer does not give rise to a clawback of roll-over relief even if the asset is no longer in business use. It is important that the same spouse owner(s) of the original asset becomes the owner(s) of the new asset as otherwise roll-over relief could be wholly or partially denied.

Subsequently, the asset can be transferred within marriage if a different ownership arrangement is desired.

Sale proceeds wholly reinvested

7.6 Any chargeable gain arising on the disposal of a qualifying asset is reduced to nil provided the whole of the disposal proceeds are reinvested in a new qualifying asset. Indexation allowance is calculated on the old asset in accordance with the usual rules and so reduces the gain rolled over. Indexation allowance (if any) is calculated on the cost of the new asset after deducting the rolled-over gain. Taper relief does not apply to the rolled-over gain.

Taper relief only applies to the new asset from the date of acquisition, not from the date the old asset is disposed of. Taper relief on the old asset is therefore lost. Particular care needs to be taken where assets that have been owned for more than two years are disposed of, especially if it is possible that the new asset could be sold within two years of acquisition.

While the payment of tax is deferred, rolling over the proceeds from the old asset may mean that the generous 75% taper relief which is applied to business assets held for two years or more may be lost. For further explanation of business asset taper relief (BATR), see CHAPTER 2.

Example – Interaction of roll-over relief and taper relief

Dave bought a hotel to run as a business for £80,000 on 1 August 1986. Dave sold the hotel for £500,000 on 1 January 2006. The disposal costs were £4,500. Dave had also bought a new hotel on 1 September 2005 for £550,000. The new hotel was sold for £800,000 on 1 January 2007.

Roll-over relief is fully available because the new hotel was bought less than a year before the old hotel was sold and the whole of the disposal proceeds were reinvested. If Dave were to make a roll-over relief claim his tax returns for the tax years 2005/06 and 2006/07 would include the following:

Old asset (computation for 2005/06)

	£	£
Disposal proceeds		500,000
Less:cost	(80,000)	
disposal costs	(4,500)	
		(84,500)
Unindexed gain		415,500
Less: indexation allowance to April 1998		(53,360)
Rolled-over gain		£362,140

No taper relief is available to reduce this gain

New asset (computation for 2006/07)

	£	£
Disposal proceeds		800,000
Less:cost	550,000	
Less: gain rolled-over	(362,140)	
		(187,860)
Unindexed gain @ 50%		612,140
Taper relief (1 September 2005 – 1 January = 1 year)		(306,070)
Chargeable gain		£306,070

However, in this example for BATR purposes, Dave owned the old hotel for longer than two years but the new hotel for only one year.

If Dave had not made a roll-over relief claim the computations would have been as follows:

Old asset (computation for 2005/06)

	£	£
Disposal proceeds		500,000
Less: cost	(80,000)	
disposal costs	(4,500)	
		(84,500)
Unindexed gain		415,500
Less: indexation allowance to April 1998		(53,360)
		362,140
Taper relief @ 75%		(271,605)
Chargeable gain		£90,535

New asset (computation for 2006/07)

	£
Disposal proceeds	800,000
Less: cost	(550,000)
	250,000
Taper relief @ 50%	125,000
Chargeable gain	£125,000

If roll-over relief is claimed then the total chargeable gain is £306,070 whereas if roll-over relief is not claimed, the combined chargeable gain on both assets is only £215,535. There is therefore a significant CGT saving even before considering the potential benefit of the combined gain being spread over more than one tax year.

The interaction of roll-over relief and BATR was particularly severe on the terms of the original taper relief legislation when first introduced in 1998. It was a significant factor in the decision to reduce the maximum BATR qualification period to two years and as a result the interaction is now less of an issue – especially as there is a time limit of five years and ten months after the end of the year of assessment for claiming roll-over relief. The safest approach is therefore to make a provisional claim for roll-over relief in the first instance.

Provisional claims for roll-over relief

7.7   The individual will often not know how long they intend to retain the replacement business asset for before selling. Where a person carrying on a trade disposes of an old asset, the taxpayer may make a declaration in his self-assessment return for the period in which the disposal takes place that the whole or any part of the consideration will be reinvested in a newly qualifying asset within the relevant period.

Roll-over relief is provisionally given as if the intended acquisition had actually taken place. This declaration ceases to have effect if it is withdrawn by the taxpayer, if the taxpayer no longer intends to make the investment, or if it is superseded by valid claims for the actual acquisition of a qualifying new asset.

A specific time limit is set for such a provisional claim based on the roll-over relief time limits. If the declaration is not superseded or withdrawn, it expires on the relevant day which is the 3rd anniversary of the normal filing date. On the declaration ceasing to have effect, any adjustments necessary are made to the appropriate CGT self-assessment.

It will often be beneficial therefore for the taxpayer to make a provisional claim and to then calculate the tax payable after disposal (in light of the known taper relief position) to see whether it is beneficial to make the actual roll-over relief claim or not.

The provisional claim is made on a form IR290. Eventually either a substantive claim will be made where a replacement asset is acquired or the provisional claim must be withdrawn. The taxpayer should not submit provisional claims of this nature unless there is a real intention to acquire a replacement asset. Should a provisional claim eventually exceed the amount, if any, of roll-over relief due, any CGT on the excess will become payable plus interest from the original payment date. Surcharges could also be applied. This can therefore be a very costly process if the reinvestment deadline is overlooked by the taxpayer or if the proceeds are not reinvested.

Partial reinvestment of proceeds

7.8   If only part of the proceeds received on the disposal of an old qualifying asset are reinvested, then only part of the gain may be rolled over into the new qualifying asset. Relief is only available where the amount reinvested exceeds the allowable expenditure on the old asset plus indexation allowance; there is no relief unless at least the unindexed base cost is reinvested.

Example – Partial reinvestment

Michael purchased a qualifying business asset for £12,400. The asset was sold for £16,000, realising a gain of £3,600. Michael then bought a replacement asset for £14,000. Only some of the disposal proceeds were reinvested. The difference between the cost of the new asset and the proceeds received for the old asset was £2,000 (£16,000 – £14,000). This is less than the £3,600 gain Michael realised on the disposal of the old asset and therefore not all of the gain can be rolled over. '

The amount not reinvested (£2,000) is immediately chargeable to CGT. Roll-over relief can be claimed on the balance of £1,600 (£3,600 – £2,000). This amount is deducted from the cost of the new asset.

The chargeable gain is therefore the smaller of the proceeds not reinvested and the gain on the old asset. Taper relief applies to the gain remaining chargeable but does not apply to the rolled-over gain.

If, due to the availability of an exemption, only part of the gain arising is chargeable, the amount available for roll-over is reduced accordingly. For instance, if in the example above only 50% of the gain was chargeable then only £1,000 would become immediately chargeable, being half of the amount not reinvested – £800 could then be rolled over and deducted from the cost of the new machinery.

Further, where the taxpayer sells or realises part of an asset and makes a chargeable gain, the gain cannot be deferred by rolling over the gain to reduce the cost of the part of the asset which is retained as this does not constitute a new asset, see *Watton v Tippett* [1997] STC 893.

It is also worth noting, however, that if an asset is sold and then reacquired for commercial reasons, roll-over relief can be claimed by virtue of ESC D16.

This concession can provide planning opportunities to tidy up the legal ownership of family assets where the land is in joint names. This may be the case where properties have been inherited by siblings who now wish to partition the assets between them.

Example – Part disposal

Steve owns a hotel which is used solely for the purpose of the trade. Steve sells part of the hotel to realise some of the equity tied up in the property. Roll-over relief is not available against the part of the hotel that Steve retains. The remaining part is not a new asset separate from the part disposed of.

Non-business use

7.9   Given the strict requirement that both the old and new assets are used for the purpose of the trade, it is inevitable that the taxpayer will often be faced with a chargeable gain arising on a mixed-use asset, namely one that is used for both business and non-business purposes.

Where part of an asset is used for the purpose of the trade and the other part is not, the asset must be notionally divided into two parts for the purpose of roll-over relief; one part representing the business use and the other representing the non-business use.

Each part is then treated as a separate asset and roll-over relief is limited to the chargeable gain allocated to the part used for business purposes only.

Example – Mixed-use asset and apportionment of proceeds

John acquired a property which consisted of two offices at a cost of £500,000 on 31 October 2004. The property was sold for £900,000 on 1 November 2006.

During the period of ownership John used one of the offices for the purpose of his trade and the other was let to a charity. Based on floor space, only 80% of the building was used by John for the purpose of his trade. As such the £900,000 proceeds should be apportioned between the business and non-business parts of the asset.

	Total	80% business part	20% non-business part
	£000s	£000s	£000s
Proceeds	900	720	180
Cost of acquisition	(500)	(400)	(100)
Unindexed gains	£400	£320	£80

Roll-over relief is available in relation to the business part of the gain only, ie £320,000. As such the proceeds relating to the business element only should be reinvested if John intends to claim roll-over relief. Therefore, John must reinvest £720,000 (ignoring any unused annual exemption) to maximise his entitlement to roll-over relief. The gain of £320,000 would then reduce the cost of the new qualifying business asset.

This requirement to apportion the asset according to the business usage also applies to the acquired asset. Where two persons are jointly purchasing such an asset and where one individual only has a gain to roll over, the business part of the building should be acquired by the person with the gain to roll over.

Mixed usage can provide good planning opportunities where the taxpayer does not wish to fully reinvest the proceeds and depending on the taper relief status of the asset, see CHAPTER 2.

Example – Roll-over relief claim for a mixed-use asset

A solicitor sold part of the goodwill of his practice for £200,000. Six months later he entered into a partnership with his brother and they jointly purchased freehold premises which comprised a shop and flat for £300,000. The property was purchased in joint names, 75% of it belonging to the solicitor and 25% to his brother. The partnership retail business was carried on from the shop which occupied 75% of the space, and 25% of the space was used for non-business purposes.

The solicitor reinvested the whole of the £200,000 proceeds he received for the sale of goodwill in the freehold premises. However, since the new property was used 75% for business purposes and 25% for other purposes, roll-over relief is limited to 75% of the solicitor's share of the property. Roll-over relief is therefore restricted to £168,750, being the business part (75%) of the solicitor's share (75%) of the £300,000 cost of the new property.

If the solicitor had owned the whole of the beneficial interest in that part of the building used for business purposes, rather than just 75%, roll-over relief of up to £225,000 (£300,000 x 75%) would have been available. As such, the legal contracts could have been drafted so that the solicitor acquired the business part of the property and his brother acquired the non-business part.

Further, if the solicitor had entered into a partnership with his wife, maintaining the same 75/25 split, the solicitor could have acquired the entire freehold premises and then gifted 25% of the property to his wife. In this way up to £300,000 would have been available for the solicitor to roll over the proceeds from the disposal of the goodwill.

This concession can provide planning opportunities to tidy up the legal ownership of family assets where the land is in joint names. This may be the case where properties have been inherited by siblings who now wish to partition the assets between them.

Apportionment is also required if the asset has been used for both business and non-business purposes during the period of ownership or for a substantial part of it. Where an asset is used for business purposes, say, for the first two years of ownership and then ceases to be used for the purpose of the trade for a year but after this time the taxpayer once again reverts to its original use, apportionment to reflect the non-business usage is required. Effectively the period when the asset was used for non-business purposes is treated as a separate asset.

Two important considerations apply:

(1) It is important to fully establish the usage of the asset over the period of ownership to make sure that no restriction of the roll-over relief claim is missed.

(2) Such a restriction may even be beneficial if it is not intended to fully reinvest the proceeds.

Asset brought in to use

7.10 Within the legislation there is also a strict requirement that the new asset is used for the purpose of the trade before it is disposed of. If a piece of land was purchased by the taxpayer with the intention of building an industrial warehouse but the land was then disposed of before the warehouse was built, the land would not qualify for roll-over relief.

The new asset must be taken into use for the taxpayer's trade on acquisition.

Example – 'Taken in to use on acquisition'

The freehold interest in a factory, occupied by tenants, is acquired by the taxpayer. The taxpayer is unable to occupy the factory until the current tenants have vacated the premises, which, according to their tenancy agreement, will be nine months after the freehold is acquired. In light of this nine-month delay between the date of acquisition and the date when the factory is first used for the purpose of the trade, any proceeds from the previous disposal of a qualifying asset cannot be rolled over into the freehold interest. This is because the taxpayer has failed to bring the asset into use on acquisition.

Careful planning is therefore required where an individual is looking to acquire an asset but restrictions dictate when the asset can be used for the purpose of the taxpayer's trade. HMRC's manual provides further guidance to supplement the legislation and says that the 'acquisition and taking into use must be reasonably proximate to one another'. While this would suggest that HMRC may accept some delay and that there is no requirement for the asset to be taken into use immediately, the taxpayer should be careful not to place too much reliance on this.

If the taxpayer is able to demonstrate that there is some link between the acquisition date and when the asset is brought into use, roll-over relief may still be available. However, where there is no demonstrable link between these two events roll-over relief will be denied. In the example above, the date of acquisition and the date when the asset was brought into use were clearly not proximate to one another given the nine-month period where occupation was prohibited.

Further, it is unlikely to be acceptable to acquire a property with the intention of carrying out one trade and then at a later date bringing the asset into use for the purpose of a different trade.

Some relief is provided by ESC D24 which permits roll-over relief where an asset is acquired but not immediately brought into use by the trade. The concession is granted providing the taxpayer proposes, and commences, work of a capital nature on the asset and when complete, the asset is then used for the purpose of the trade.

The taxpayer should also take particular care with regards to the dates of exchange and completion. Where disposal proceeds are being reinvested in new land or buildings especially, the case of *Campbell Connelly & Co Ltd v Barnett (Inspector of Taxes)* [1992] STC 316 illustrated that it is the completion date rather than the date that contracts are exchanged that is relevant. This differs from the general principle underpinning CGT which dictates that it is the date of exchange that is the chargeable event when calculating any gain or loss. This gives rise to some difficult conflicts between the CGT legislation generally and the roll-over relief provisions.

Where the taxpayer is looking to claim roll-over relief, he should try and ensure that the completion date falls within 36 months of the date of disposal and he should endeavour to bring the newly acquired asset into use immediately.

Improvement expenditure

7.11   Where the taxpayer incurs improvement expenditure to enhance the value of an asset he already owns, there is an extra-statutory concession ('ESC') D22 that allows the improvement costs to be treated as incurred when acquiring a new asset. This could therefore apply to the construction of a building on land already owned by the taxpayer. This enables gains arising on the disposal of another business asset to be rolled over against the improvement expenditure.

Some other ESCs that may be relevant when considering the acquisition of a new asset are:

(a)   ESC D23 enables land (and other qualifying assets) acquired on the dissolution of a partnership to be treated as new assets. As such roll-over relief can be claimed.

(b)   ESC D25 enables the extension of a leasehold or the acquisition of a further interest in an asset already used for business purposes to be eligible for the purposes of claiming roll-over relief. This may be the case where the taxpayer holds the leasehold interest in a property and then acquired the freehold reversionary interest.

Depreciating assets

7.12   Where roll-over applies and the new asset acquired is a depreciating asset, the treatment for roll-over relief purposes is different. The gain arising on the old asset is not rolled over into the new asset completely. Instead the gain is deferred until the first of the following three events arises:

(1)   the new asset in disposed of;

(2)   the new asset ceases to be used for the purpose of the taxpayer's trade; or

(3)   ten years after the acquisition of the new asset.

Therefore if the asset is not disposed of and continues to be used for the purpose of the trade, after ten years the gain on the old asset becomes chargeable. (It is worth noting that ESC D45 provides that the death of the taxpayer is not treated as an occasion for a charge to arise.)

Taper relief is then available for the period for which the old asset was held but no further relief is available to reflect the period of ownership of the new asset. This is because the gain is deferred rather than being rolled over.

A depreciating asset is defined as any item which is a wasting asset, or will become a wasting asset, within ten years. A wasting asset is an asset that has a predictable life not exceeding 50 years.

Example – Roll-over relief for depreciating assets

In November 2004, Marjory purchased a property from which to run her hairdressing salon for £80,000. In September 2006, Marjory sold the shop for £95,000. Later that year, in November 2006, Marjory acquired the lease for a new property for £98,000. The lease had 48 years left to run. On 1 March 2007, for health reasons, Marjory ceased to trade and the lease was sold.

The chargeable gain arising on the disposal of the first shop is calculated as follows:

	£
Disposal proceeds	95,000
Cost of acquisition	(80,000)
Gain	£15,000

This gain would be treated as not chargeable until the lease on the shop was sold or ceased to be used or, if neither of these events occurred, after ten years. In this case, the asset ceased to be used for the purpose of the trade on 1 March 2007 and this is the date at which the gain on the first shop becomes chargeable.

If Marjory had purchased a further qualifying asset before 1 March 2007, the gain could have been rolled over into the new asset. Where the proceeds of an old asset are reinvested in a new depreciating asset and the gain is rolled over, the rolled-over gain can be transferred if a new non-depreciating asset is then purchased before the gain becomes chargeable.

For the purpose of identifying where a depreciating asset exists, the following key principles are relevant:

(a) freehold land, whatever its nature, will not comprise a wasting asset nor any building or works on it;

(b) plant and machinery must in every case be regarded as having a predictable life of less than 50 years;

(c) 'life' in relation to any tangible moveable property means useful life.

A building on leasehold land where the lease has less than 60 years to run is a depreciating asset. HMRC also take the view that where plant or machinery has become an integral part of a freehold building it will be treated as such for roll-over relief purposes.

Compulsory purchase of land

7.13 There are specific provisions within the legislation that provide for roll-over relief in circumstances where a disposal of land or buildings arises as the result of a compulsory purchase order, or land is disposed of to a body having such powers. Relief is provided under s 247 and only extends to the disposal and acquisition of 'land' and not to the other relevant classes of asset for which business asset roll-over relief may be available. The term 'land' is defined in s 247 as including 'any interest in or right over land'. Later in the act, the section which deals with interpretation defines land to include 'messages, tenements and heriditaments, houses and buildings of any tenure'.

Once again, the application of this section of the legislation is uncertain and there are a number of planning opportunities involving the definitions and application of the principles outlined in the act. However, this section does provide significant scope for tax planning given that the new qualifying asset can be any land unless it is the individual's principal private residence ('PPR'). PPR is considered in detail in CHAPTER 9.

Where the taxpayer disposes of an asset under the provisions of this section, it is possible that the chargeable gain could be deferred through the reinvestment of the proceeds in property. However, it is difficult to see that expenditure incurred on the construction of a new building on land already owned by the taxpayer could be argued as using the disposal proceeds in acquiring other land for the purpose of this section. Buildings and land are not deemed to be separate assets.

The issue of what constitutes a body or authority is also important and based on this definition there are many more planning opportunities than the taxpayer will often recognise. This section is not merely restricted to public authorities. Commercial organisations such as water companies or gas works may also have the power to exercise compulsory acquisition. Perhaps more crucially the definition also includes situations where a tenant exercises their statutory right to acquire the freehold reversionary interest or perhaps a new leasehold interest from their landlord under the Leasehold Reform Acts. Such transactions are common in certain parts of the country. Further, a tenant exercising their rights under 'right to buy legislation' under the Housing Acts 1985 to 1996 will also qualify.

Section 247 gives rise to a number of planning opportunities that are not otherwise generally available. Apart from council houses, right to buy legislation is most commonly encountered with clients owning significant longstanding property portfolios. In particular, many London properties are leasehold with lease extension rights. Where a tenant exercises his right to extend the lease or purchase the freehold then the owner can reinvest the proceeds in a new buy-to-let property with full roll-over relief being available. Given that many clients will ask their advisers whether or not let property gains can be reinvested, the opportunity presented by s 247 is a very valuable one.

It is vital that advisers carefully question their clients about the nature of property disposals to check whether any of them qualify for relief. It is also important to remember that s 152 roll-over relief is available on furnished holiday let (FHL) accommodation and so there are wider roll-over relief opportunities for residential property than are often appreciated. The ability to average FHL status across several properties should also not be overlooked.

The ability to reinvest under s 247 into commercial property, farmland etc also enables a subsequent disposal of such a property to qualify for BATR so allowing an improved taper relief position to be achieved as a result of the roll over.

Relief under this section can be claimed even if the disposal is not the result of an actual compulsory purchase order. The legislation provides that the disposal must be to an authority exercising or having compulsory powers. It would seem that the legislation has been drafted to avoid having to go through the process itself. Given that a compulsory order is not necessarily required, the fact that a number of bodies that could potentially be included within the definition of 'a body having compulsory acquisition powers' means that there are a number of scenarios, often overlooked, where roll-over relief could still be claimed.

That said, it does not suffice that a body or authority simply has compulsory powers. For example, an organisation may have the power to purchase land for the construction of, say, an airport runway, but this does not mean that if such a body purchased an office building for their own occupation, the provisions of this section would apply.

Another important component of the legislation which must not be overlooked is the requirement that, prior to the disposal, the taxpayer has not taken any steps to dispose of the land. 'Steps taken' is deemed to include active marketing or advertising, or the communication of the intention to sell. However, where the intention to sell has been communicated to the vendor's advisers, this does not necessarily mean that roll-over relief is prohibited. The issue is whether the intention has been communicated to third parties.

Where the taxpayer has previously marketed land, it is still possible to plan the transaction so that relief under this section is still available. While the legislation does not specify any time period within which previous marketing or communication is deemed to be demonstrating 'willingness to sell'. It would seem to be the case that any activity that falls foul of this section, is to be disregarded if it took place more than three years before the compulsory acquisition in question, (see CCAB TR 477).

Compulsory acquisition and principal private residence relief

7.14 For the purposes of s 247 roll-over relief, new land does not include land where on the subsequent disposal, the whole or part of the land would be covered by the PPR exemption. Specifically, new land is excluded where:

(a) it is a dwelling house, or part of a dwelling house, or an interest in, or right over, a dwelling house, and

(b) by virtue of, or of any claim under any provision of ss 222 to 226, the whole or any part of a gain accruing on a disposal of it by the landowner at a material time would not be a chargeable gain.

A subsequent disposal is deemed to be within six years of acquisition. Therefore the taxpayer could reinvest the proceeds in a further property so long as he does not elect for that property to be his principal private residence within six years of acquisition. This can be a powerful planning tool if the individual owns a number of homes, see CHAPTER 9. However if the new property acquired is the individual's only PPR, there would be no ability to choose whether to elect or not and roll-over would be denied.

Exchange of interests in land

7.15   ESC D26 specifies that where interests in land which are in joint beneficial ownership of two or more persons are exchanged and as a result of the exchange each joint owner becomes sole owner of part of the land formerly owned jointly, a roll-over relief along the lines of s 247 may be claimed.

Previous roll-over relief claims and rebasing

7.16   When advising clients, it is important to closely question the history of the ownership of the asset and whether any previous roll-over claims were made in order that the base cost is not mistakenly overstated. This is particularly important as the events may relate to events many years before. In the same way, it is important that good records are kept of all roll-over relief claims made by a client and that permanent files are kept up to date.

Disposal after 5 April 1988 of assets which were held on 31 March 1982 by the person making the disposal are re-based by reference to the market value of the assets on 31 March 1982. The unindexed gain is calculated on the assumption that the person making the disposal had sold and immediately reacquired the asset on 31 March 1982, at its then market value.

For the purposes of roll-over relief, if the original asset was acquired before 31 March 1982 and the new asset was acquired between that date and 5 April 1988 (and the new asset was disposed of on or after 6 April 1988), a transitional relief applies (see FA1992, Sch 4) which gives a one half reduction in the rolled-over gain.

A claim must be made within one year of 31 January following the tax year in which the gain arises. If the new asset was acquired before 31 March 1982, rebasing will effectively eliminate the rolled-over gain.

Damaged, lost or destroyed

7.17   A form of roll-over relief is also available where an asset is lost, damaged or destroyed. Where this arises and a capital sum is received by an individual this will give rise to a capital gain. This will often be the case where proceeds are received as the result of an insurance claim or where some sort of compensatory payment is received. If the asset is then restored or replaced in whole or part, a form of roll-over relief is available.

Where an asset is merely damaged but not destroyed, the receipt of a capital sum is treated as a part disposal using the fraction A/A + B where A is the capital sum and B is the unrestored value of the asset.

However on receipt of a capital sum, the taxpayer can make a claim for it to not be treated as a part disposal if any of the three circumstances below arise:

(1) the capital sum is wholly applied in restoring the asset;

(2) the capital sum is partly applied in restoring the asset and the part not applied is small compared with the whole capital sum; or

(3) the amount of the capital sum is small, as compared with the value of the asset. 'Small' means the higher of 5% of the capital sum received, or £3,000.

In each case, the part disposal proceeds are rolled over by deducting them from allowable expenditure on a later disposal of the asset.

Restricting the claim for roll-over relief

7.18 It is important to consider the availability of the annual exemption before the claim for roll-over relief is made. Often it is beneficial to restrict the claim in order to preserve the individual's unused annual exemption. This is demonstrated in the following case study.

Case Study – Restricting the claim for roll-over relief

Julian acquired a block of flats in Cornwall in May 1996. The flats were acquired by the tenants under right to buy legislation such that roll-over relief is available under s 247. Proceeds of £42,206 were received by Julian on 21 September 2004 for Flat 1. On 2 June 2005 Julian received £117,214 for Flat 2 and on 5 January 2006 Julian received £51,535 for Flat 3.

On 29 September 2005, Julian also disposed of some shares he had acquired before April 1998 and made a chargeable gain of £7,906.

Julian was a higher-rate taxpayer for the years 2004/05 and 2005/06.

The proceeds Julian received can be summarised as follows:

Tax year	Flat 1	Flat 2	Flat 3
	£	£	£
2004/05	42,206		
2005/06		117,214	51,535

In the tax year 2004/05, Julian should restrict his claim for roll-over relief to utilise his annual exemption of £8,200. Julian has owned the shares for six complete years since April 1998 and is entitled to the bonus year such that taper relief at 25% is available. As such, the taxable gain on the shares is as follows:

	£
Chargeable gain on disposal of shares	7,906
Less taper relief at 25%	(1,976)
Taxable gain	£5,930

Julian therefore has £2,270 (£8,200 − £5,930) of his annual exemption available for the tax year 2004/05. Taper relief at the same rate will also apply to the gain arising on Flat 1. Therefore, to preserve Julian's annual exemption, his roll–over relief claim should be restricted as follows:

£2,270 x 100/75 = £3,026

In the tax year 2004/05, a roll-over claim of £39,180 (£42,206 − £3,026) should be made. Julian will need to reinvest £39,180 of the net proceeds received for Flat 1 by 21 September 2007, which is 36 months after the disposal proceeds were received.

In the tax year 2005/06, Julian should also restrict his claim for roll-over relief to utilise his annual exemption. In 2005/06 the exemption increased to £8,500. Julian made no gains in that tax year other than on the disposal of Flats 2 and 3.

Taper relief at 30% will apply to these gains. This is because Julian has owned the flats for seven complete years (plus the bonus year) since April 1998.

The roll-over relief claim for 2005/06 should be restricted as follows:

£8,500 x 100/70 = £12,143

In the tax year 2005/06 Julian could restrict his roll-over relief claim for either Flat 2 or Flat 3. If he restricts his claim for Flat 2, he will need to reinvest £105,071 (£117,214 − £12,143) by 2 June 2008, which is 36 months after the disposal. Julian would then need to reinvest £51,535 (all of the proceeds for Flat 3) by 5 January 2009, which is 36 months after the disposal.

If Julian restricts his claim in respect of Flat 3, he will need to reinvest £117,214 (all of the net proceeds received for Flat 2) by 2 June 2008 and £39,392 (£51,535 − £12,143) by 5 January 2009.

Julian's roll-over relief claims can be summarised as follows:

Tax year	Uninvested proceeds	Amount of restriction	Amount required to be invested
	£	£	£
2004/05	42,206	(3,026)	39,180
2005/06	168,749	(12,143)	156,606

Conclusion

7.19 Roll-over relief is a complicated aspect of the legislation applying to CGT but it can provide a powerful tool in terms of tax planning.

As part of any tax planning exercise, the key areas to consider are the preservation of the taxpayer's annual exemption by restricting the claim for roll-over relief and the interaction of roll-over relief and taper relief. All too often these areas are overlooked by advisers and the annual exemption is lost or a claim for roll-over relief is made where it would be more beneficial for the taxpayer to make the most of the availability of BATR.

However, where roll-over relief is used effectively and the pitfalls and planning opportunities are understood, it can provide an excellent shelter from the ravages of CGT.

Checklist

	Cross Reference
Roll-Over Relief	
Roll-over relief enables a CGT liability to be avoided where the proceeds from sale are reinvested in qualifying assets.	
The main roll-over relief is for business assets (s 152).	7.2
Roll-over relief is also available where property is disposed of under a compulsory purchase or right to buy legislation (s 247).	7.13
Further roll-over reliefs are available where an asset is damaged, lost or destroyed and the monies are reinvested in the asset.	7.17

Chapter 8

Relief from Capital Gains Tax on Gifts and Sales at an Undervalue

Capital gains tax reliefs available for gifts, etc

8.1   A gift is a disposal for capital gains tax (CGT) purposes such that CGT will be payable in the absence of any relief. Further, where a sale takes place at an undervalue, then if the parties are connected, the market value of the asset must be used for the purposes of the CGT calculation. The meaning of 'connected persons' is as set out in TCGA 1992, s 286 and broadly covers family relations, related trusts, business partners, related companies and certain shareholdings in those related companies. All statutory reference in this chapter are to TCGA 1992 unless otherwise stated.

Gifts and sales at an undervalue mainly take place in connection with succession planning for family property assets and business assets as part of a strategy to reduce exposure to inheritance tax (IHT) and in connection with giving to charity and other public bodies.

In considering potential CGT planning, opportunities are available for the following types of gifts:

(a)   gifts of land and buildings and shares and securities to charity, etc;

(b)   transfers into or out of most trusts;

(c)   gifts of business assets and;

(d)   gifts of agricultural property even if not comprised within a business undertaken by the donor.

However, if none of the above reliefs are available, then the CGT payable should be able to be settled by ten annual instalments where an election is made under s 281. This facility is not available if a hold-over relief claim was capable of being made unless or to the extent that the held-over gain was less than the chargeable gain otherwise arising on the disposal. All outstanding instalments will fall due for payment if the asset is sold.

The instalment facility is available on gifts of the following types of assets:

(i)   land or an estate or interest in land;

(ii)   shares or securities of a company, which, immediately before the disposal, provide the transferor with control; and

(iii) shares or securities not listed on a recognised stock exchange.

Planning in the area of gifts is particularly important as in such cases there will not be cash funds available to settle the tax liability arising. The planning also needs to take into account other tax issues including income tax and IHT.

Gifts of securities and real property to charity

8.2 It is appropriate to first consider gifts to charity as the available relief in such a case is an outright exemption from CGT.

Relief is available from CGT under s 257 which combined with a special form of gift aid relief under ITA 2007, s 431 (formerly ICTA 1988, s 587B) is extended to provide exemption from CGT on gifts to charity of shares, securities, land and buildings and other real property.

Where a disposal is made to a charity or certain public bodies by way of gift or at an undervalue for a consideration, in excess of the base cost and costs of disposal, then the transaction is treated as taking place at no gain/no loss. This means that a liability to CGT is avoided on the gift. However, gift aid relief should still be available under ITA 2007, s 431. As a result, gifts of shares and real property can be a very tax effective way of charitable giving.

Gift aiding of shares and real property is treated differently to cash gifts which are deemed to have been made net of basic rate tax. For gifts of real property, the value of the gift is deducted from total income in the year of the gift and tax worked out accordingly.

If a charity is unable to accept the gift because it does not maintain a share portfolio then the gift could be structured through the Charities Aid Foundation (CAF) or another such organisation. The issue of valuation is also important in tax planning for gifts of land and buildings or unquoted shares. Appropriate valuations should be obtained and a formal certificate obtained from the charity. The issue of valuations is considered further in CHAPTER 13.

Example – Gifting of shares to charity

John wishes to give £10,000 of quoted shares to a registered charity in December 2007. The shares have a negligible base cost and John will already utilise his annual exemption for 2007/08 as a result of other share disposals. John has annual employment income of £50,000 and minimal investment income.

As a result of the gift, John's income tax liability for the year will be reduced by £4,000.

Careful planning of income tax on sources of income is required to maximise the benefit of gift aid under ITA 2007, s 431, in particular where there is dividend income or if pension contributions are being made.

Payments on account will also be reduced (if appropriate). It may also be beneficial to spread gifts over several years.

HMRC have also confirmed in Revenue Interpretation 23 in May 1992 that s 257 exempts the deferred gain on Qualifying Corporate Bonds (QCBs) such that no CGT liability arises on either the donor or the charity on a subsequent disposal.

Sections 258 and 259 provide further exemptions from CGT on certain gifts of works of art to public bodies and gifts of land to housing associations and registered social landlords.

Background to hold-over relief

8.3 If the gift is not to a charity then no exemption from CGT is available. The next avenue to explore is whether a hold-over relief is available. This transfers the asset on a no gain/no loss basis such that the recipient inherits the base cost of the donor and so stands in his or her shoes. It acknowledges that cash is not being generated to settle the CGT liability arising and so prevents a crystallisation of that tax liability until disposal on an arm's-length sale.

Hold-over relief was first introduced in 1978 and in its original form it applied to a narrow range of business assets and built upon the retirement relief legislation. Both used what became Sch 6 which is why the definition for hold-over relief had to change when retirement relief was abolished. Also, by 1978 capital transfer tax had been introduced and the purpose of the relief was to avoid a double tax charge on gifts.

The original business asset hold-over relief was largely superseded in 1980 by the introduction of a general hold-over relief which was not limited by reference to particular classes of assets. The widespread use of this general hold-over relief ended with its withdrawal for disposals after 13 March 1989. In his Budget Statement that year Nigel Lawson justified the change by saying that this relief:

> 'was introduced by my predecessor in 1980, when there was still capital transfer tax on lifetime gifts, in order to avoid a form of double taxation. But the tax on lifetime giving has since been abolished, and the relief is increasingly used as a simple form of tax avoidance.'

This meant that hold-over relief could from then on only be claimed for either business assets (s 165) or where the gift was immediately chargeable to IHT (s 260). These 1989 changes were again poorly drafted and left open the opportunity for planning as whilst s 260 hold-over relief was designed to alleviate double taxation, it is available even where no IHT is payable (because of the nil rate band). During the 1990s hold-over relief became a central tool in the mechanics of avoiding CGT and has therefore led to specific anti-avoidance rules being introduced. A good understanding of the hold-over relief rules is therefore essential when advising on CGT planning.

Before considering entitlement to hold-over relief, the first stage is to calculate the tax liability that would otherwise arise. This enables the worst case position to be assessed and provides a benchmark for the benefits and disadvantages of any hold-over relief claim to be judged against. The main issues to consider are the re-starting of the taper relief period and the loss of certain potential future CGT reliefs.

It should not be assumed that a s 165 hold-over claim would invariably be beneficial where assets are transferred by way of gift. For example, the chargeable gains arising to the transferor may be eliminated by taper relief and the annual exemption, or perhaps by allowable losses.

It is also appropriate to consider s 260 hold-over in priority to s 165 as there is no asset class restriction for s 260 although it is dependent upon the involvement as one party to the gift of a relevant property trust. Prior to FA 2006, a relevant property trust more or less meant a UK resident discretionary trust. However, since the FA 2006 changes, the breadth of s 260 hold-over relief has been expanded.

Section 260 hold-over relief

8.4   Section 260 hold-over relief is available where the transferee is either a UK resident individual or the trustees of a UK resident settlement and the disposal is one of the following made otherwise than by way of bargain at arm's length:

(a)   A chargeable transfer of relevant property for IHT purposes, or one which would be so chargeable but for the annual £3,000 exemption. This may be particularly attractive where the value transferred for IHT purposes falls within the nil rate band. Transfers of relevant property are considered further below.

(b)   Exempt transfers for IHT purposes made to political parties, to maintenance funds for historic buildings, or comprising exempt transfers of designated property and transfers of settled property to maintenance funds for historic buildings.

(c)   Property held on accumulation and maintenance (A&M) trusts where a beneficiary, not previously having acquired an interest in possession, obtains a vested interest and the property simultaneously ceases to be held on those trusts. This type of disposal is becoming of less importance because of the phasing out of A&M trusts.

Transfers of works of art that do not incur an immediate charge to IHT.

Residency implications are considered in CHAPTER 14.

Relevant property trusts

8.5   The extension of the relevant property rules to a larger number of trusts extends the availability of hold-over relief and has implications for

CGT planning. Broadly, trusts created after 22 March 2006 will now, with two exceptions, be subject to the special 'relevant property' rules in IHTA 1984, Ch 3 that were previously restricted to only discretionary trusts. The two exceptions are trusts where there is an 'immediate post–death interest' (IPDI) or a disabled person's trust. For existing trusts, there are transitional provisions. The purpose of the IPDI rules is to largely exempt will trusts from the special relevant property tax rules.

Dawn Primarolo explained that the purpose of the FA 2006, Sch 20 changes is to prevent the use of non-discretionary trusts for IHT planning purposes. She gave the following specific example of planning that the government regarded as unacceptable:

> 'Grandparents put £1m into an A&M trust in the name of their new born grandchild. No IHT is paid when the trust is set up and once the grandparents survive seven years, any potential IHT liability is wiped out. The trust is set to operate in accordance with the grandparent's wishes, even after they have died. The trust is set up ostensibly to pay for the grandchildren's education, but the child's parents also have substantial wealth, so in practice, the contents of the trust are barely touched. At 25, the A&M trust, now worth £2m having been actively invested in, transforms into an IIP trust for the grandchild. No IHT is paid at that point. Trustees will follow the grandparent's wishes in deciding how the now adult grandchild will benefit from it. The grandchild might eventually receive it outright, or alternatively the trustees might decide to give the trust to someone else entirely.'

The main thrust of these changes is to attack lifetime trust tax planning and will impact on CGT because of the way it interacts with IHT – specifically in respect of hold-over relief. A number of financial products and tax planning schemes made use of interest in possession trusts (IIP) with flexible powers of appointment. These were effectively discretionary trusts but did not have to be treated as representing relevant property.

The availability of 100% business property relief (BPR) or agricultural property relief (APR) means that the types of planning condemned by Dawn Primarolo are still available on business and agricultural assets. Hold-over relief can then be dealt with under either s 165 or s 260. This leaves open the possibility of combining traditional planning with AIM and/or other off market share portfolios although care is required to ensure that the BPR qualification criteria are achieved and maintained. However, trusts are far less efficient for income tax purposes following the withdrawal of repayable tax credits and the increase in income tax rates. For a period of time this was not such an issue because of the brought forward balance on the tax pool but these are by now typically exhausted.

Accumulation and maintenance trusts

8.6 The dust continues to settle on the impact of FA 2006, Sch 20 which brought almost all trusts within the existing discretionary trust tax regime for IHT. This also has knock-on implications for CGT because of entitlement to s 260 hold-over relief. One particular issue to consider is the position of existing A&M trusts. This is because Sch 20 contained transitional provisions to allow changes to trust deeds to be made prior to 6 April 2008.

A&M trusts are a creation of the IHT legislation in that they are effectively a discretionary trust with tax advantages because they are not subject to the ten-year anniversary charge. These advantages were increased when the potentially exempt transfer regime for IHT was introduced in 1986.

The effect of the 1988 Budget which introduced the 40% tax rate for CGT together with 40% IHT encouraged the use of A&M trusts to hold shares in family companies. This was particularly good planning where a newly incorporated company was being set up and there was a grandparent who could then settle newly issued shares onto an A&M trust in favour of the grandchildren. The grandchildren would then become entitled to the shares at age 25, possibly with an interest in possession applying from age 18.

On the termination of the settlement, there would be a CGT liability as a result of s 71. This could be held over if s 165 hold-over relief applies if the shares concerned are business assets. This would re-start the clock for taper relief purposes and if historically there is any tainting of the taper, then this could be a good thing. However, where the shares concerned do not qualify for s 165 hold-over relief because the assets are not business assets within the taper relief legislation, then one had to rely upon the potential for hold-over relief under s 260(2)(d). This is not available if an interest in possession already existed at 22 March 2006.

The options for amending A&M trusts prior to 6 April 2008 depend upon the drafting of the existing trust deed. The advice will be different if the deed provides for the beneficiaries to become absolutely entitled at some stage rather than simply becoming entitled to an interest in possession with no absolute entitlement at any point. If the beneficiaries become absolutely entitled at age 18 then no action is required. However, many trust deeds provide for absolute entitlement at age 25.

Subject to meeting the necessary conditions, an A&M trust that gives absolute entitlement at age 25 will become a new '18–25 trust' at 6 April 2008 provided that no further additions are made to it. This '18–25' regime is slightly more favourable than the historic discretionary trust regime. An 18–25 trust will continue to be treated as an A&M trust until the beneficiaries become 18. After that point, there will be IHT charges on any advancement of property from the trust and also when the beneficiaries become aged 25. However, the maximum rate of tax will be restricted to 4.2% of the amount distributed and in all likelihood, may actually be 0%. This depends on the size of the gifts made by the settlor and the nil rate band at the time that the property is vested in the name of the beneficiaries.

The legislation appears to say that the class of beneficiaries needs to be closed at 6 April 2008, meaning that no further grandchildren, if any, can benefit. Where the trust terms either only provide for a life interest or for absolute entitlement at an age older than 25 then it is necessary to consider whether it is worth amending the trust deed prior to 6 April 2008. Such trusts need to be considered on a case-by-case basis. The s 260 hold-over position needs to be very carefully assessed for such trusts.

Example – Hold-over relief on an A&M trust

On 8 May 1991, Len Endacott settled 15% of the shares in Len Endacott Limited on an A&M settlement for his grandchildren. The trust beneficiaries are Sophie (born 7 March 1991), Josie (born 22 November 1993) and Katie (born 24 December 1996). Beneficiaries become entitled to an interest in possession at age 25. Len Endacott Limited has since sold its trade and is now an investment company.

The A&M trust will cease to qualify as such on 6 April 2008 unless the terms are changed. The trust cannot qualify as an 18–25 trust as the beneficiaries only receive an interest in possession rather than absolute entitlement to capital. Therefore, in April 2008 the trust will become discretionary and entitlement to hold-over relief will continue even after the beneficiaries become entitled to an interest in possession.

Routing the gift of the asset via a trust

8.7 The attraction of s 260 hold-over relief is that it enables any asset to be transferred without a CGT liability arising as long as it is routed via a trust – normally a discretionary trust. In order for s 260 hold-over relief to apply, the transfer must be chargeable for IHT purposes. As far as the transfer out of the trust is concerned, this requires a delay of at least three months between the transfer into the trust and the appointment out. This is in order for the appointment out to be a chargeable transfer.

It is also important to bear in mind that if the value of the gift exceeds the balance of the available nil rate band for IHT, then a tax liability will arise at 20% (lifetime rate) on the chargeable value of the transfer. For a husband and wife (or civil partners) it is possible to transfer an asset by this method up to a value of £600,000 (twice the nil rate band). However, careful consideration of all the planning issues is vital. A larger amount is possible if there is any entitlement to BPR or APR.

The option of routing via a trust does mean that hold-over is effectively available for all assets subject to the donor and recipient being prepared to involve the use of a trust. This is especially so since it is better for the trust to have some existence in its own right and not to be only an inserted step that can be ignored by the Ramsay principle, see CHAPTER 13.

Interaction of hold-over relief and principal private residence relief

8.8 Whilst s 260 hold-over relief is available on any asset type, there is an anti-avoidance provision to prevent exploitation of principal private residence (PPR) relief. Sections 226A and 226B prevent PPR relief where the gain represents a gain that has been postponed by hold-over relief under s 260. It applies where there is the disposal of, or of an interest in, a private residence by an individual or the trustees of a settlement and that disposal takes place on or after 10 December 2003. It must also be shown that all or part of the gain arising on disposal would be exempt by the private residence provisions of s 223 and that the allowable expenditure entering into the calculation of gain was reduced following an earlier disposal, or disposals, for which a s 260 hold-over relief claim was directly or indirectly made. In this situation no PPR will be available in relation to the later disposal. This does not prevent the making of a claim for hold-over relief, but restricts or eliminates PPR relief where a claim has been made.

An example of the arrangements being attacked was where an individual had a second home, which did not qualify for PPR relief. That individual transferred ownership of the property to a discretionary settlement that was not settlor-interested and made a claim under s 260. Acting in accordance with the settlement deed, the trustees allowed a beneficiary, probably a close relative of the transferor, to occupy the property as a qualifying residence. When the occupation terminated, the property would have been sold. As throughout the period of ownership by the trustees the property qualifies as a private residence, the entire gain arising on disposal, including that held over by the earlier s 260 claim, would have been exempt from tax.

Transitional relief is available where the matching earlier disposal, or all such disposals, occurred before 10 December 2003. The prohibition from obtaining PPR relief is then confined to that part of the period commencing on 10 December 2003 and ending at the time of the later disposal. This will, of course, only be significant if the requirements for the application of s 223 were satisfied before 10 December 2003. For the purposes of this time apportionment calculation the deemed final 36 months of ownership in s 223 is disapplied. In assessing the benefit of any transitional relief, the longer the period from the original s 260 claim to 10 December 2003 the better.

It must be emphasised that s 226A does not preclude the availability of a hold-over relief claim under s 260 where the requirements of that section are satisfied and no settlor-interested settlement is involved. However, the trustees need to carefully consider whether the claim is beneficial.

If no s 260 claim is made, CGT will be calculated in the normal manner. The alternative is to make a claim under s 260, thereby denying the transferee any PPR relief in the future. Careful calculations and sensitivity analysis needs to be done to assess whether this is worthwhile. It will depend on the future intentions with regard to the property. It may also be worth appointing a property out of the trust to the beneficiary in order to make maximum use of the transitional relief. Whilst this may require some tax to be paid by the trustees, this may be the best approach in the long term. Claiming s 260 hold-over would also restart the taper clock and so any accrued taper to date would be lost. Given that the asset will be a non-business asset, it is likely to be many years before the current taper relief position is regained.

Example – Interaction of s 260 hold-over and PPR

Robert transfers a house to a discretionary trust on 16 November 1998 and claims hold-over relief under s 260. The house is valued at £60,000 at the time with a deferred gain of £27,000. The house is tenanted until 1 May 1999 when Josie takes up occupation. The property is extended and then on 10 September 2003, the trustees decide to appoint the property to Josie. It was intended that the gain arising would be held over under s 260.

	£	£
Valuation		500,000
Transfer value	60,000	
Less: held-over gain	(27,000)	
		(33,000)
Enhanced expenditure		(115,000)
		352,000
Less PPR relief (1,593 days out of 1,758 days)		(319,000)
Untapered gain		£33,000

The untapered gain of £33,000 could be held over, but, if so, then Josie will only be entitled to PPR relief for the two-month period up to 10 December under the transitional rules. Even though Josie has no intention of ever selling the property, it is probably better to suffer the tax on the appointment.

Business asset hold-over relief

8.9 A trust does not need to be involved where a gift is of a qualifying business asset. However, it is important that unfounded assumptions are not made on the status of a perceived business asset. The position needs to be carefully assessed especially where there has been a period of non-business use of an asset or where investment activities are carried on. As such, even where at first sight a qualifying business asset is involved it may be safer to fall back on the s 260 hold-over route.

Section 165 hold-over applies where an individual makes the disposal of a qualifying asset otherwise than under a bargain at arm's length. The transfer may be made to any person including an individual, a company or trustees administering settled property. A bargain not at arm's length includes a gift and sales at an undervalue. Whilst the side note to s 165 reads 'Relief for gifts of business assets', it is not only outright gratuitous transfers which are brought within its scope.

Example – Sale at an undervalue

On 30 November 2005, Andrew sells a business property to his brother Paul for £200,000. The market value of the property at the time was £500,000. The indexed base cost is £180,000.

The held-over gain is calculated as follows:

	£	£
Market value		500,000
Less: indexed base cost		(180,000)
Unrelieved gain		320,000
Actual consideration	200,000	
Less: allowable deductions	(180,000)	
		(20,000)
Held-over gain		£300,000

The ability to receive some consideration without crystallising a significant CGT liability is an important feature of the hold-over relief legislation (both ss 165 and 260). With careful planning, it can enable the passing of consideration across for an asset whilst at the same time making use of the taper relief and the annual exemption to minimise CGT. This can often be beneficial as part of a restructuring of family ownership arrangements.

Business assets

8.10 The qualifying business assets for which s 165 hold-over can be claimed are as follows:

(a) An asset, or an interest in an asset, used for the purposes of a trade, profession or vocation carried on by the transferor or by the transferor's personal company, or by a member of a trading group of which the holding company is the transferor's personal company.

(b) Shares or securities of a trading company, or of the holding company of a trading group, where the shares or securities are not listed on a recognised stock exchange. There is no minimum shareholding requirement.

(c) Shares or securities of a trading company, or of the holding company of a trading group, where the assets are listed on a recognised stock exchange but the trading company or holding company is the transferor's personal company.

'Trade' includes the occupation of woodlands managed on a commercial basis with a view to profit and also the commercial letting of furnished holiday accommodation. The Alternative Investment Market (AIM) is not a recognised stock exchange.

'Personal company', 'holding company', 'trading group' and 'trading company' originally adopted the meanings used for retirement relief purposes but following the repeal of that relief on 5 April 2003 new definitions have been introduced. This does not affect the definition of 'personal company', which remains unaltered but now appears in s 165 itself. Significant changes have, however, affected the three remaining expressions, which now adopt the meanings used for taper relief purposes (Sch A1, para 22). This identifies a holding company as a company that has one or more 51% subsidiaries. A group of companies comprises a 'trading group' if one or more members carry on trading activities and the activities of all members, taken together, do not include to a substantial extent activities other than trading activities. A 'trading company' is a company carrying on trading activities whose activities do not include to a substantial extent activities other than trading activities.

Whilst these changes of definition may seem minor and technical they in fact have very wide reaching implications. Prior to the change s 165 hold-over relief was available where a company was wholly or mainly a trading company (ie 50% or more). Now it is necessary to satisfy the much more demanding requirements of the taper relief legislation see CHAPTER 2. It should not be assumed that because s 165 hold-over relief has been claimed in the past that it continues to be available.

Section 165 is extended to include two further groups of assets:

(a) Agricultural property that qualifies for APR for IHT purposes.

(b) Trust assets including:

  (i) An asset, or an interest in an asset, used for the purposes of a trade, profession or vocation carried on by the trustees making the disposal or by a beneficiary who had an interest in possession in the settled property immediately before the disposal.
  (ii) Shares or securities of a trading company, or of the holding company of a trading group, where the shares or securities are not listed on a recognised stock exchange.
  (iii) Shares or securities of any other trading company, or of the holding company of a trading group, where not less than 25% of the voting rights exercisable by shareholders in general meeting are exercisable by the trustees at the time of the disposal.
  (iv) Agricultural property qualifying for APR for IHT purposes.

Agricultural property

8.11 It is important to appreciate the extension of s 165 hold-over relief to agricultural property as this is often overlooked. Hold-over relief is extended by Sch 7 where the asset qualifies as agricultural property under Chapter II of Part V of the Inheritance Tax Act 1984. Importantly, whilst the IHT relief is restricted to the agricultural value, this is not the case with hold-over relief. As such, hold-over relief is available on agricultural land where there is development potential. This is confirmed in Revenue Interpretation 8 issued in November 1991.

However, the extent of assets qualifying for APR is probably diminishing. For example, some farm buildings have been converted to industrial units or perhaps offices. In addition, activities previously undertaken on agricultural land may now bear little relationship to agriculture. Indeed, an increasing number of cases taken on appeal before Special Commissioners now question whether land and buildings have relinquished or retained their former 'agricultural' nature. This has become even more of an issue with the change to farming subsidies and the introduction of the Single Farm Payment. HMRC have attempted to give some guidance on their view on this issue in a special edition of a Tax Bulletin issued in June 2005.

Gift of shares to company

8.12 To counter alleged tax avoidance the application of s 165 hold-over relief was removed for disposals on or after 9 November 1999 where a disposal of shares was made to a company. This removal was unintentionally withdrawn on 5 April 2003 following the repeal of other legislation. It was then reinstated for disposals taking place on or after 21 October 2003. Seemingly the disposal of qualifying shares to a company between 6 April 2003 and 20 October 2003 could confer entitlement to hold-over relief.

Use of settler-interested trusts

8.13 A particular planning technique using s 165 hold-over relief involved a settler-interested interest in possession trust. Settlor-interested trusts were widely used to crystallise entitlement to retirement relief during the phasing out of that relief. Subsequently, they were used in combination with hold-over relief to re-start the taper clock at the time when many vendors of business assets had tainted taper.

They still have planning possibilities where the aim is to 'bank' entitlement to a relief. Examples could include to ensure entitlement to PPR relief on the former garden where the house is to be sold first, or to crystallise a disposal within 12 months of reinvestment to ensure roll-over relief. Whilst such planning is still possible, such lifetime trusts may now give rise to an immediate IHT liability as opposed to just a potentially exempt transfer. However, where the transfer is covered by BPR and APR or the amount is within the available nil rate band then such planning may still be attractive.

There can be no entitlement to hold-over relief (either ss 165 or 260) on the transfer of assets to the trustees of a settlement if there is a settlor who retains an interest in that settlement, or where arrangements exist whereby the settlor can obtain such an interest (s 169B). This approach is not limited to disposals made by individuals but extends to disposals undertaken by trustees, if of course a qualifying gain would arise. The prohibition may also apply to the disposal of assets to the trustees of a settlor-interested settlement if there has been some earlier disposal, which may have taken place before, on, or after 10 December 2003, and made by an individual who immediately following the transaction retains an interest in the settlement, or arrangements exist whereby such an interest can be acquired.

It is possible that at the time of a disposal to trustees none of the conditions preventing the application of hold-over relief exist. However, these conditions may commence to apply at a later date falling within the 'clawback period'. This period commences at the time of the disposal to the trustees and ends six years following the end of the year of assessment in which that disposal takes place. If at the time the disqualifying condition commences to apply no claim for hold-over relief has been made, there can simply be no claim. However, where a claim has previously been made, the chargeable gain held over will be treated as arising when the disqualifying condition first emerges. The calculation of taper relief, if any, will be based on a period ending at the date of the original disposal.

A person is a settlor in relation to a settlement if:

(a) he is an individual; and

(b) the settled property consists of, or includes, property originating from him.

This is a very wide definition and could include the simple payment of expenses on behalf of the trust. It is important to note that the transferor does not have to be interested in the settlement. If another person causes the settlement to become settlor-interested, the hold-over relief will either be denied or clawed back. This could be caused by something very minor such as a beneficiary settling accountancy fees on behalf of the trust. This point was confirmed by HMRC at the time of the Finance Bill in 2004.

Another possibility is that a beneficiary providing unpaid services to a company owned by the trust could cause a problem. It is quite conceivable that in such circumstances the shares may have been placed into trust in conjunction with a hold-over claim. This is a concern for those making gifts to settlements and relying upon hold-over relief, and presumably some kind of undertaking from the trustees will be required. It is also a point for the trust lawyers to consider when drafting new deeds.

The clawback provisions apply in respect of transfers made to settlements after these new rules come into effect. Hold-over relief is not clawed back if a trust becomes settlor interested after 10 December 2003 as long as the original transfer was prior to that date.

Overall these new rules mean that considerable care needs to be taken in advising on hold-over claims on transfers to settlements. On a procedural level, ongoing monitoring is required with appropriate deadlines marked on files and diary systems for the clawback period in a similar way to Enterprise Investment Scheme (EIS) relief.

Example – Clawback of hold-over relief

Peggy acquired a significant shareholding over many years in A plc, with a negligible base cost.

In January 2005, Peggy transferred 30,000 shares in A plc into a new non-settlor interested trust, the Holmes Discretionary Trust. The shares were worth £180,000 (£6 per share), and had an indexed base cost of just £3,000. Peggy claims s 260 relief and a gain of £177,000 is held over. The base cost for the trustees is £3,000 (10p per share).

Within two months, the share price in A plc has fallen to £4 per share. The trustees sell 25,000 shares in A plc in March 2005 as follows:

	£
Proceeds of sale	100,000
Less: base cost (25,000 x 10p)	(2,500)
Trust exemption	(4,100)
Capital gain	£93,400

The trustees pay the CGT of £37,360 on 31 January 2006.

In March 2006, the Holmes Discretionary Trust becomes inadvertently settlor-interested. A chargeable gain equal in amount to the held-over gain of £177,000 (before taper relief) becomes chargeable on Peggy for the tax year 2005/06. She can benefit from 25% taper relief that would have applied if the gain had arisen on her disposal in January 2005. CGT of £49,700 is payable on 31 January 2007.

The trustees' gain on disposal of the shares is recomputed on the basis that s 260 relief was not due on Peggy's transfer of the shares to the trust. So the chargeable gain arising to the trustees is reduced to nil and they now have capital losses of £50,000. The CGT of £37,360 is repaid to them.

Trading status and restriction of held-over gains for non-trading

8.14 Where an asset has not been used for a qualifying purpose throughout the period of ownership the amount held-over is restricted. A similar restriction may apply where a building or structure has been only partly used for a qualifying purpose during the ownership period. The held-over gain arising on the disposal of shares or securities issued by a company may require restriction if not all chargeable assets of the company are also used for business purposes. This latter restriction is limited to the disposal by a transferor who either retained 5% or more of the voting rights or could treat the company as his or her personal company at any time within 12 months preceding the disposal date. These restrictions are contained in Sch 7.

Schedule 7 contains two types of restrictions for hold-over relief.

(1) For asset disposals there is a restriction by reference to business usage of A/B where A is the number of days of business usage during the period of ownership and B is the total number of days in the period of ownership. It is important to remember that the asset must be a business asset at the time of transfer in order to qualify for hold-over in the first place.

(2) For share disposals there is the same restriction which used to feature in the retirement relief legislation of CBA/CA where CBA is Chargeable Business Assets and CA is Chargeable Assets. Despite the introduction of the Intangible Assets Regime, goodwill continues to be a chargeable business asset for these purposes.

Case Study – Trendy Fashion Shops Limited and hold-over relief

This case study is considered in CHAPTER 2. For ease of reference the scenario is again repeated here.

Trendy Fashion Shops Limited has been incorporated for 29 years. It originally had a single shop (Homestore) but then expanded to have a chain of five shops. Following a strategic review in 2004, a decision was made to cease trading from two of the shops (Old Town and New Town) which were then let to tenants. The trading shops are now Homestore, High Street and Retail Village. The company owns all of the shops with the exception of Retail Village which is leasehold.

The directors and shareholders are:

	No of shares (£1 ordinary)
Alan and Barbara Hazel (husband and wife)	4,500
Thomas Hazel (son)	5,500
	10,000

The directors have obtained planning permission to redevelop the top two floors of the Old Town shop and also to extend the property. This will create five apartments in addition to the letting shop. Alan Hazel intends to occupy one of the apartments.

The intention is to convert the New Town shop into two luxury apartments. No decision has yet been made as to whether these apartments are to be let or sold.

On a turnover basis, and by reference to the management time, the company is clearly a trading business. What is the position on the asset basis?

Trendy Fashion Shops Limited
Balance Sheet as at 30 June 2007

	£000s
Fixed assets:	
Homestore	1,250
High Street	750
Old Town	500
New Town	400
Goodwill	500
Fixtures and fittings	100
	3,500
Working capital	(250)
Long-term bank loans	(600)
	£2,650
Represented by:	
Share capital	10
Profit and loss account	2,390
Revaluation reserve	250
	£2,650

After redevelopment, the Old Town property will be worth £1 million and £700,000 for New Town. The conversion costs are £250,000 for Old Town and £150,000 for New Town. The conversion costs are to be funded by additional bank debt. The apartment to be occupied by Alan Hazel will be worth £200,000.

Profitability of the trade is declining such that the goodwill value may fall.

Forecast Position
after
Redevelopment

	Total	Alan Hazel's apart-ment	Re-mainder of Old Town	New Town	Trading Assets
	£000s	£000s	£000s	£000s	£000s
Homestore	1,250				1,250
High Street	750				750
Old Town	1,000	200	800		—
New Town	700			700	—
Goodwill	500				500
Fixtures and fittings	100				100
					2,600
Working capital	(250)				(250)
	4,050	£200	£800	£700	£2,350
Long-term bank loans	(1,000)				
	£3,050				

The pure trading assets represent £2,350,000 out of gross assets of £4,050,000 – 58%. Depending on the allocation of the bank loans, the proportion of trading to investment assets could vary. However, the intention is to use the rental income to repay the bank borrowing and so the bank debt should reduce over time in any event.

If the usage of the apartment by Alan Hazel is part of his remuneration arrangements, then it could be considered to be part of the trading assets of the business.

If the letting of the Old Town shop is only temporary and it could be brought back within the trade at a later date, then it could be a trading asset. A sale of the New Town apartments with reinvestment of the proceeds in the trade would increase the proportion of trading assets.

Overall the conclusion must be that there is potential tainting of the Business Asset Taper Relief (BATR) position. For BATR purposes it is necessary to look at the position over the period of ownership such that a short period of tainting may not be disastrous to the tax position. Further, on a sale there will be at least cash proceeds and the seller of the shares may well be prepared to accept the risk of tainting in order to conclude the deal. Different considerations apply to a family gift of shares. The client will want to be assured that hold-over relief will be available before the gift is made.

Possible Gift of Shares by Alan and Barbara Hazel on 31 October 2007

Number of shares	4,500
% shareholding	45%
	£
Valuation (assumed to be the same for both CGT and IHT purposes)	600,000
Less base cost (31/03/82)	(82,000)
	518,000
Less: gain held-over under s 165	(383,320)
Untapered gain	134,680
Taper relief at 75%	(101,010)
	£33,670

The claim to hold-over relief is restricted as there are non-trading assets. The current restriction could be calculated as follows:

	£000s	
Homestore	1,250	Business asset
High Street	750	Business asset
Old Town	500	
New Town	400	
Goodwill	500	Business asset
Homestore	£3,400	

Hold-over relief is available but will be restricted to:

CBA = chargeable business assets – £2,500

CA = all chargeable assets – £3,400

CBA/CA = 74%

On the above basis, there would be a restriction to the hold-over relief claim but this assumes that the company qualifies as a trading company for BATR at the time of the gift. There is clearly a risk that it does not. If it ceased to qualify as a trading company at, say, 30 June 2004, then no hold-over relief will be available and the chargeable gain would then increase as follows:

	£
Gain pre hold-over and taper relief	518,000
Taper relief	
06.04.98 – 30.06.04 – 75% (2,277 days)	
01.07.04 – 31.10.07 – 40% (1,218 days)	
Total days 3,495	
Overall taper rate 62%	(325,304)
Chargeable gain	£192,696

If the shares are transferred into a discretionary trust then no CGT liability should arise. This is because CGT can be avoided on the transfer to the trust by claiming hold-over relief under s 260 (which is definitely available). As well as considering the CGT position, it is necessary to ensure that the value of the shares transferred into the trust does not exceed the nil rate band (£300,000) for IHT purposes. Based on our current valuation, the value of a 45% shareholding is £600,000. However, BPR should also be available to restrict the chargeable transfer of value for IHT purposes.

Therefore, a transfer routed via a discretionary trust or trusts can be made without a tax liability arising as long as the trust is not settlor-interested. Care is required that there is no reservation of benefit and so it is also important to ensure that if Alan and Barbara are to remain as directors that their remuneration arrangements are wholly commercial. If Thomas has children then such a discretionary trust could in any case be tax efficient for school fees planning purposes.

As already mentioned in respect of a sale at an undervalue, a limitation to the held-over gain may be necessary where the transferee provides 'actual consideration' for the disposal. To calculate this limitation two factors will be used, namely:

(a) the amount of the actual consideration; and

(b) the allowable expenditure available to the transferor when calculating the gain.

Actual consideration provided by a transferee would usually reflect the price payable on transfer but it may take some other form. For example, if A gives assets to B and B gives assets to A, difficulties may be experienced in demonstrating that one alleged 'gift' was not consideration for the other. It is advisable to leave a reasonable period of time between the respective gifts to ensure that they cannot be linked with each other. Caution may also be necessary where the transferee enters into some undertaking or obligation in return for the alleged gift of an asset as this may demonstrate the provision of actual consideration.

If the actual consideration exceeds the allowable expenditure the excess must be subtracted from the held-over gain (see example below). This may produce some balance of chargeable gain accruing to the transferor and increase the effective cost of acquisition by the transferee. This can be a useful planning approach with an aim of keeping the tapered gain within the annual exemption.

Interaction with inheritance tax

8.15 The transfer of an asset may create, or subsequently prove to be, a chargeable transfer for IHT purposes. If IHT becomes payable by reason of the transfer, and a hold-over claim is made, some relief is given to the transferee. When calculating chargeable gains arising on the future disposal of the asset the transferee may subtract the smaller of:

(a) the IHT attributable to the value of the asset, and

(b) the amount of the chargeable gain, which would otherwise accrue to the transferee, calculated by ignoring any IHT on the original transfer.

It is unlikely that lifetime gifts incurring an immediate liability to IHT will lead to a claim under s 165 as the alternative claim made available by s 260 must receive priority. However, most lifetime gifts made by an individual will comprise potentially exempt transfers which only become chargeable should the transferor die within a period of seven years from the date of the gift.

Hold-over relief under s 165 can provide a substantial shelter from liability to CGT. It is possible to contemplate the near indefinite retention of business assets within the ownership of a family without incurring CGT liability by arranging successive gifts to different generations matched by suitable claims.

No liability to CGT currently arises on the value of assets retained at the time of an individual's death. It may therefore be advisable for a potential transferor to contemplate the retention of assets during his lifetime, leaving those assets to be distributed as a testamentary disposition on death. This should reduce, perhaps substantially, the chargeable gain accruing to the potential transferee or legatee from a future disposal. Such planning is likely to depend upon the availability of BPR and APR for IHT purposes.

Interaction with CGT taper relief

8.16 Where the chargeable gain on a transfer of assets is eliminated by a claim for hold-over relief no taper relief will be available to the transferor. The commencement of ownership by the transferee will date from the time of disposal and that person cannot adopt the period of ownership by the transferor. This re-starting of the taper clock can be very useful as long as the asset will be a business asset after the transfer. As such the hold-over claim washes out any previous tainting and after one year a 50% taper rate will be achieved and the maximum 75% after two years. However, the danger with such short periods of business usage is that any loss of business asset status for even a short period of time will significantly reduce the taper rate.

Where an asset already qualifies for maximum BATR on a transfer of an asset, then a careful review of the position should be made before a claim for hold-over relief is made. As the CGT payable may well be less than 10% of the chargeable gain arising, it may be better to settle the tax falling due.

Example – Re-starting the taper clock

John has owned some tenanted farmland for many years. From 6 April 1998 to 5 April 2004 it was a non-business asset. On 6 April 2004, John transferred the land to his son as part of some estate planning and because the land may be sold in the future.

The land will now qualify for the maximum business asset taper rate on 6 April 2006 rather than on 6 April 2014 as would otherwise have been the case.

Married couples and divorce

8.17 Section 165 hold-over relief cannot apply where a married couple or civil partnership are living together as man and wife such that the no gain/no loss transfer rules apply. However, hold–over relief is relevant where the couple are separated and this issue is considered in CHAPTER 10.

Non-residency

8.18 Residency is relevant to hold-over relief claims and in particular consideration must be given to the future residency position of the transferee. This is considered in CHAPTER 14.

Valuation issues

8.19 One of the difficulties with trying to assess the need for a hold-over relief claim is establishing the potential CGT otherwise payable. This is a particular problem with unquoted shares or land where the tax position depends on a valuation of the asset concerned. The problem is especially significant where the asset concerned is a minority shareholding of unquoted shares.

There are also different valuation principles applying for CGT and IHT. Both valuations will need to be considered if the asset is to be subject to a s 260 hold-over claim.

The issue of tax planning and valuations for CGT is considered in CHAPTER 13.

Partial claims for relief

8.20 Neither s 165 nor s 260 enable a partial claim for hold-over relief to be made. Either the full eligible gain will be held over or a claim must be withheld. However, it is important to remember that hold-over relief claims need to be considered on an asset-by-asset basis.

Example – Hold-over relief planning for shareholdings

Stanley and Enid Porridge are included within the class of beneficiaries of the Erica Settlement. The trustees of the Erica Settlement have agreed to appoint out the following investment holdings to Stanley and Enid in their joint names:

	Indexed cost	Proceeds	Un-tapered gain	Tapered gain
	£	£	£	£
5,125 European Fund	9,211	66,420	57,209	34,325
2,941 Opportunities Fund	2,123	8,599	6,476	3,886
453 Global Fund	1,432	8,104	6,672	4,003
1,191 Special Situations Fund	3,766	22,415	18,649	11,189
	£16,532	£105,538	£89,006	£53,403

It has been proposed that hold-over claims will be signed by the trustees and the beneficiaries of the shares. No IHT exit charge arises on the appointment out of the trust.

Stanley Porridge is a higher-rate taxpayer but his CGT annual exemption is available in full each year. Enid Porridge (Stanley's wife) works part-time and has an income of about £5,000. Enid's CGT annual exemption is available in full each year.

If hold-over relief is claimed then a substantial entitlement to taper relief will be lost. Stanley and Enid are keen to sell the shares as soon as possible in order to reduce their personal mortgage.

Hold-over relief could be claimed on the 5,125 units in the European Fund, the 2,941 units in the Opportunities Fund and the 453 units in the Global Fund. As such, the only capital gain that would arise on the trustees would be on the 1,191 units in the Special Situations Fund. The value of that holding at the date of appointment was £22,415 and this would be subject to an effective tax rate of 24% in the hands of the trustees, giving rise to a tax liability of £4,476.

The holdings of the units in the Opportunities Fund and the Global Fund should be appointed into Enid's name. Of the 5,125 units in the European Fund, 1,650 units should be appointed to Stanley and 3,475 units to Enid.

Stanley would sell 825 units in the European Fund which should more or less give proceeds of his annual exemption such that there is no CGT liability. Enid would sell 2,650 units giving proceeds of just over £45,000. Both retain 825 units to be sold in 2008/09.

Enid would also sell the entire holdings of the units in the Opportunities Fund and the Global Fund. These would generate proceeds of around £16,700.

Stanley and Enid would receive total proceeds in their personal names of around £61,700 and have a tax liability of approximately £6,700. Overall, Stanley and Enid would receive net proceeds from the trustees of £18,000 and proceeds in their own names of £61,700, making a total of £79,700. The retained 1,650 units in the European Fund would enable Stanley and Enid to realise proceeds of a bit over £18,000 next year with no CGT liability.

Previous hold-over relief claims

8.21   When advising clients on CGT, it is important to correctly identify any previous claims that should be reflected in the base cost of the asset. In the main this applies where gains have previously been rolled over or held over against the acquisition cost or March 1982 value. In doing this, it needs to be borne in mind that the rules for hold-over relief have not always been the same and as mentioned above, hold-over was available on a wider class of assets from 1980 to 1989.

A particular issue is where a claim for hold-over relief was made in the period 1 April 1982 to 5 April 1988, ie during the period of partial rebasing. In such cases, a claim for transitional relief is possible under Sch 4. This provides that where the gain held-over related to an asset at 31 March 1982 and the new asset was acquired prior to the introduction of full rebasing then the held-over claim can be halved.

Example – Schedule 4 transitional relief

Mrs Handel gifted an asset that she had held for many years to her son in December 1982. At the time, the asset was worth £10,000 and the held-over gain was £2,000. The unindexed base cost for the son was therefore £8,000.

The son now intends to sell the asset for £100,000. As a result of a claim under Sch 4, the held-over gain is reduced by £1,000 giving an unindexed base cost of £9,000.

Claiming hold-over relief

8.22   A claim for hold-over relief must be submitted on form IR295. The claim must be made jointly by the transferor and the transferee, unless the transferees are trustees of a settlement when the transferor only need make the claim. Claims submitted by trustees must also be made on a joint basis, unless the transferees are a second body of trustees when the transferor trustees only are required to comply.

No time limit is specified for making a claim, which may therefore be submitted within the normal extended period of five years and ten months after the end of the year of assessment in which the transaction occurred. It should be noted that it is a claim for hold-over relief and not an election. Elections can be revoked whereas claims can only be amended or withdrawn within the enquiry window. Therefore, whilst the time period is five years and ten months for the submission of the claim, a final decision needs to be taken earlier unless the transferor is prepared to pay the tax in the meantime.

The frequent need to submit a joint claim should not be overlooked, particularly when making a gift of assets. Once the transferee has obtained the ownership of assets he or she has no legal obligation to enter into the claim and no financial incentive to do so – quite the reverse. It is therefore advisable to obtain the donee's signature to a joint claim simultaneously with the making of a gift, although caution must be exercised to ensure that this action does not demonstrate the provision of 'consideration' by the donee.

Checklist

	Cross Reference
Relief from CGT	
A number of CGT reliefs are available where an asset is gifted or sold at an undervalue. These reliefs provide useful planning opportunities especially where there is:	
• A gift of securities or real property to charity.	8.2
• A transfer to a trust.	8.5
• A disposal of a business asset at an undervalue.	8.9
• A gift of agricultural property.	
Particular care is required on the interaction with taper relief and inheritance tax.	8.15

Chapter 9

Principal Private Residence Relief

Introduction

9.1   The capital gains tax (CGT) treatment of an individual's only or main residence is one of the most commonly dealt with areas of the CGT legislation. Given that an exemption exists for gains arising on an individual's principal private residence (known as 'PPR' relief), it is an area that provides significant scope for tax planning. As such an understanding of these planning opportunities and the common pitfalls is helpful for individuals and tax advisers alike.

When James Callaghan, the then Chancellor of the Exchequer, announced the government's intention to introduce CGT in 1964 he said that gains on the 'only or principal residence' would be exempt. Since its introduction in 1965 there have been very few attempts to remove the exemption or suggestions that its removal is politically desirable or likely. The PPR rules, and their application, have developed from both legislation and subsequent case law and interpretations.

This chapter considers the background to PPR relief and sets out the relevant legislation and interpretations following important case law. Some of the key planning areas are considered, such as when the owner has periods of absence, where the property has been let or had an element of business usage and where the owner has more than one residence. Whilst it is assumed that the reader has a certain level of background knowledge on PPR relief, it is important to outline here some of the key principles and concepts underpinning the relief. Unless stated otherwise, all statutory references in this chapter are to TCGA 1992.

In broad terms, the specific topics covered in this chapter are as follows:

- Definition of a 'dwelling house'.

- Important relevant case law.

- The disposal of the house before the garden.

- Property that has also been let.

- Property with an element of business usage.

- More than one property owned – including elections.

- Job-related accommodation.

- Dependant Relative Relief.

- Rights deriving from a main residence.

- Tax planning from the breaking of the PPR rules.

The position of trustees and personal representatives is considered in CHAPTER 11.

What is a dwelling house?

9.2 One of the key principles underpinning PPR is what defines a dwelling house. The taxpayer and adviser must have a firm understanding of HMRC's interpretation in order to plan effectively for the disposal of any property.

Further to relevant case law such as *Batey v Wakefield* [1982] 1 All ER 61 the definition of a 'dwelling house' is deemed to comprise of the main building and also the relevant buildings adjoining it, for example, a garage or even a separate building occupied by staff. The individual's interest may be either a whole or part interest in a property.

The PPR exemption also extends to gardens and grounds of up to half a hectare in size (just under 1¼ acres) surrounding the dwelling itself. Prior to March 1991, the permitted area was just one acre but this was increased to the nearest metric equivalent of half a hectare in 1991.

Importantly, whilst the area of gardens is quantified, this is not entirely prescriptive and the area may be increased to such an area as may be required for the 'reasonable enjoyment' of the property given the size and the character of the dwelling house. The permitted area includes the 'footprint' of the dwelling house.

In broad terms this means a larger house would generally need a larger area of gardens and grounds compared to a smaller house in order to achieve its full market value. That said, this can be a very grey area for the taxpayer as the character of a house is, of course, rather subjective.

Where an individual is looking to dispose of their main residence and the surrounding land does exceed half a hectare, the following three areas should be considered in terms of assessing whether the character of the dwelling warrants larger grounds:

(1) the period and style of the house. For example, an historic building may have been built specifically because of its setting and would be worth substantially less without part of the accompanying land;

(2) the proximity of other amenities. For example, if the property was within the immediate proximity of a train track, it would be reasonable for that dwelling to have a larger piece of land separating the property from the track; and

(3) the locality of the dwelling. For example, it is perhaps to be expected

that a large stately house in the Cotswolds, say, would require generous grounds compared to a large town house in central London which may have little or no grounds given its urban location.

The Special Commissioners case of *Henke and another v Revenue & Customs Commissioners* [2006] STC (SCD) 561 is concerned with the extent of the permitted area. The case is topical as it has become common for parts of gardens to be sold off for development as a result of both rising property values, the demand for building plots and the trend towards smaller gardens with houses.

In 1982, Mr and Mrs Henke purchased a 2.66 acre plot of land with planning permission for one dwelling. Work did not commence on construction of the property (Oak House) until February 1991 and was not completed until June 1993. It was a very large property.

In July 1995, Mr and Mrs Henke obtained planning permission for two separate dwellings to be built on part of the garden and grounds of Oak House. Each sub-plot comprised 0.54 acres and the plots were sold in 1999 and 2001. Prior to the sale of each plot, the land had been maintained as part of the garden and grounds of Oak House.

There were two issues in the case:

(1) that PPR relief can only commence from 1993 when the house was completed. Prior to that time, the land could not be garden and grounds of the house. ESC D49 provides some limited extension to the relief where the property is constructed within 12 months of acquiring the land. However, that was not the case for Mr and Mrs Henke; and

(2) whether or not a 2.66 acre plot represented the permitted area for Oak House. The legislation provides that the permitted area is half a hectare or such larger area as is required for the 'reasonable enjoyment' of the property having regard to the size and character of the dwelling house.

It was held that the permitted area should be 0.82 of a hectare or 2.03 acres. It was also held that the restriction was required under s 223(1) in respect of the period prior to the construction of the dwelling house.

Conditions for PPR

9.3 Capital gains arising on a dwelling house are exempt from CGT if the following two conditions are satisfied:

(1) the dwelling house was an individual's only or main residence throughout the period of ownership; and

(2) the dwelling house, or part of it, was not acquired for the purpose of realising a gain on the disposal.

In practice, HMRC has said that it would only apply the second condition (which is set out in s 224(3)) where the primary purpose of the acquisition was an *early* disposal at a profit. Where this is the case, it is likely that income tax would be charged on the disposal as a trading activity instead of CGT.

Individuals should be wary that PPR relief can also be potentially restricted where expenditure is incurred on the property wholly, or partly, for the purpose of realising a gain from the eventual disposal. In practice, HMRC is more likely to apply this restriction than the second condition outlined above. Examples here would include barn conversions, the conversion of a property into flats or the acquisition by a leaseholder of the freehold of a property. It should be noted, though, that PPR relief should not be restricted where the individual has only obtained planning permission, or removed any restrictive covenants, but has not actually carried out any further work.

It is worth pointing out that the period of ownership does not include any period prior to 31 March 1982, so such periods are ignored. Naturally, as capital gains on a main residence are exempt, any losses arising are not allowable for capital gains purposes. For more information on losses, see CHAPTER 12.

In order to qualify for relief, the gain must arise on a residence. Therefore, where somebody acquires a property but does not reside in it for any period of time then no PPR relief can be available. It is also important to establish that the surplus on disposal of the property is a gain and not a trading transaction and there is a considerable body of longstanding case law on this point. Unsurprisingly, there has also been a great deal of case law and HMRC interpretation surrounding the PPR legislation and it is worth summarising the important cases to provide an overview of some of the pitfalls and planning opportunities available.

Is there a trade?

9.4 The large gains on residential property in recent years together with the fashion to be a property developer, have led HMRC to argue a trading motive in cases when there is a succession of gains on residences. The investigating Inspector will cite the following badges of trade:

(a) whether the motive was one of realizing a profit;

(b) the nature of the assets and the way in which they were acquired;

(c) the number of transactions;

(d) whether any modifications, enhancements or improvements took place;

(e) the intervals between purchase and sale;

(f) the method of financing the transactions; and

(g) the existence of trading activity in the same field, ie whether the owner is a builder or otherwise engaged in the construction or property development field.

The last point derives from the fact that the old case law mainly covers builders who, having constructed properties and retained them for a period of time (perhaps many years), attempted to argue that the transactions were capital gains rather than trading activities. These cases relate to a time before the introduction of CGT and the courts were generally unsympathetic to the traders concerned.

In return, it is worth the adviser stressing that whether or not a sale of property is a trading transaction is fundamentally a matter of intention at the time. This is based upon the following case law decisions on property development transactions:

1   *Marson v Morton* [1986] STC 463 – In the High Court, Sir Nicholas Browne-Wilkinson, the Vice Chancellor said:

    'What were the purchaser's intentions as to resale at the time of purchase? If there was an intention to hold the object indefinitely, albeit with an intention to make a capital profit at the end of the day, that is a pointer towards a pure investment as opposed to a trading deal.'

2   *Turner v Last (Inspector of Taxes)* (1965) 42 Tax Cas 517 – In the High Court, Justice Cross said:

    '... the mere fact that when you buy a property, as well as intending to use and enjoy it, you also have in your mind the possibility that it will appreciate in value, and that a time may come when you may want to sell it and make a profit on it, does not of itself make you a trader.'

3   *Taylor v Good (Inspector of Taxes)* [1974] 1 All ER 1137 – In the Court of Appeal, Lord Justice Russell reiterated the view of Justice Cross and set out the requirement to consider the intention on acquisition of a property. At that point, there is either a trading motive or there is not.

    Therefore, the case law clearly establishes that the only issue when considering whether a transaction is on capital or revenue account is the intention at the time. If there is an intention to own a property for personal enjoyment, or to generate investment income, then it is held on capital account and so subject to CGT – regardless of whether or not the plans on acquisition come to fruition.

The difficulty is proving intention and there is often limited evidence available, one way or the other. Where the property is financed by debt, then the nature of the borrowing is important – an overdraft arrangement is symptomatic of a trading arrangement whereas a fixed-rate mortgage with redemption penalties is indicative of a long-term intention to retain a property. Living in the property does not prevent the activity from being a trade.

Particular care is therefore required when advising those who are connected with a property trade. It is important that a premature assumption is not made that CGT treatment applies.

Facilities and services

9.5 Where there is any concern that a residence may not constitute a dwelling, the importance of facilities and services should be carefully considered in an attempt to assess the availability of PPR relief.

In the case of *Makins v Elson* [1977] 1 All ER 572, the taxpayer owned a caravan and it was unclear whether this would constitute his PPR. The caravan had water, electricity and a telephone line and although the caravan had wheels, it was off the ground resting on supports. On the facts, it was held that the caravan was in fact the taxpayer's dwelling house and also his only and main residence. The caravan therefore qualified for PPR relief.

However, in a similar case, *Moore v Thompson (Inspector of Taxes)* [1986] STC 170, the taxpayer owned a caravan that was jacked up on breeze blocks but it lacked facilities such as the supply of a telephone line, electricity and water. In this case, PPR relief was not available due to the lack of facilities.

Other buildings sited with the main residence

9.6 Another key area which can often require consideration prior to any disposal is where the site of the main residence also includes other buildings. This may arise if, say, a coachman's cottage is situated within the grounds of a larger property.

In *Batey v Wakefield* [1982] 1 All ER 61, Mr Wakefield owned 1.1 acres in Wiltshire and he built a house on the land. He used the house for weekends and holidays, but elected to treat the house as his only or main residence (elections are considered later in this chapter). There were burglaries in the area and Mr Wakefield subsequently decided to also build a chalet bungalow on the 1.1 acre site. The chalet bungalow had separate access from the road and it was separated from the main house by a tennis court and yew trees. In return for gardening, caretaking and housekeeping services a married couple lived in the chalet bungalow rent free. When Mr Wakefield retired, he moved to his Wiltshire home and subsequently sold the chalet bungalow.

The resulting capital gain was held to be exempt under s 222. It followed that an individual's residence includes not only the main building, but also some other buildings which are occupied for the purpose of the main residence, for example a staff bungalow (as was the case for Mr Wakefield). This could also then include, say, a detached garage, a garden shed or a summer house.

However, in *Markey v Sanders* [1987] STC 256, a bungalow which was occupied by a gardener and housekeeper but was sited about 130 metres from the main house, at the end of a driveway, was not deemed to form part of the taxpayers' residence. It was the size of the other building that was relevant here; there were as many bedrooms in the bungalow as there were in the main house. It is therefore important to consider the relative size of all buildings on any one site when determining the availability of PPR relief.

In *Williams v Merrylees* [1987] STC 445, the staff lodge had its own access and was 200 metres from the main house. It was sold with the remaining land three years after the main house and part of the land were disposed of. In this case, however, the staff lodge was a modest residence and PPR relief was available as it was held to be part of the taxpayer's only or main residence up to the date of the sale of the main house.

Disposal of house before garden

9.7   In terms of CGT planning it is important to avoid disposing of land after the main residence has already been sold. In the case of *Varty v Lynes* [1976] 3 All ER 447, the taxpayer sold part of the land with his main residence in 1971 and then in 1972 sold the remainder of the land. He was not granted exemption under s 222(1)(b) on the part of the land sold in 1972, as this was not 'land which he had for his own occupation and enjoyment with that residence'.

Careful thought needs to be given to cases where some of the garden is to be sold at a different time to the property. If possible, it should be sold before the house or at the same time.

This is notwithstanding the fact that some of the land may exceed the permitted area for PPR purposes.

It may be worth making a disposal of the garden prior to the sale of the main house in order to take advantage of the available PPR. This could be by way of a transfer to a limited company or a trust – perhaps a settler-interested life interest trust. There may be other tax issues to consider, such as stamp duty land tax (SDLT) on a transfer to a company or IHT on a transfer into trust.

Another issue can arise where the garden is not contiguous, ie adjacent to the main house. It is common for some gardens to be across a road from the main house, and this should not give rise to a dispute. However, where a garden is acquired and is some distance from the house then HMRC is likely to contest the claim for PPR relief. The point is expanded upon in

Revenue Interpretation 119 which also makes reference to the further case of *Wakeling v Pearce* [1995] STC (SCD) 96.

Periods of absence deemed to be periods of occupation

9.8 In circumstances where a dwelling house has not been occupied by the taxpayer for the full period of ownership, part of the capital gain arising will be chargeable and part will be exempt. The element of the gain that is exempt under the PPR rules is pro-rated depending on the actual and the deemed occupation divided by the period of ownership. An important point to note is that it is only periods of occupation since 31 March 1982 that are included in the calculation.

However, there are certain periods of absence which are deemed to be periods of occupation for the purpose of PPR relief and this can provide significant scope for tax planning opportunities. The periods of absence detailed below are deemed to be periods of occupation, provided that the dwelling house was actually occupied for a period of time both before and after the period of absence, and on the basis that no other residence qualified for relief during that period of absence. It is worth noting that occupation prior to 31 March 1982 *would* qualify as actual occupation in this case.

The three circumstances that are deemed to be periods of occupation are set out in s 223 as follows:

(1) any periods of absence, no matter how long, during which the owner or his/her spouse (or civil partner) was employed abroad;

(2) any periods of absence which do not in total amount to more than three years; and

(3) any period or periods of absence totalling not more than four years, where the owner or his spouse (or civil partner) was unable to occupy the dwelling house by virtue of the location of his place of work, or because his employer required him to live elsewhere in order to do his job properly.

In determining whether a dwelling house is the owner's PPR, no minimum period of occupation has been set out in the legislation. It is generally regarded to be a question of the quality of occupation, rather than the length of the occupation period itself.

Extra-statutory concession (ESC) D4 waives the requirement to occupy the house after a period of absence in the case of an individual who has worked abroad, or elsewhere in the UK, and is unable to resume occupation of the property because the terms of his employment require him to work elsewhere.

The final 36 months of ownership are always treated as a period of occupation. It is this deemed period of occupation that is commonly utilised in tax planning where an individual has more than one residence. This is considered in further detail later in this chapter.

Where an individual either buys land and builds a dwelling house on it, or arranges alterations or redecoration to an existing dwelling, then he or she is regarded as being in occupation. Importantly this is provided that the work is completed within 12 months of purchase although in certain exceptional cases, this period may be extended to two years. Relief is not given if the dwelling house is not occupied after the works are completed (ESC D49).

Example – Deemed occupation

Roger purchased a property in Coventry on 1 February 1982 for £48,000. He then spent the next six months renovating the house and moved in on 1 August 1982. He lived in the house until 31 July 1987, when he took up a two-year contract of employment in Paris.

On returning to the UK on 1 August 1989 he took up employment as a restaurant manager in Ipswich and was required to live in the flat above the restaurant. He subsequently changed jobs and returned to live in the house in Coventry on 1 August 1994. On 1 August 1995 he moved in with an elderly relative. The relative died and Roger sold his house in Coventry on 1 May 2006 for £275,000.

The market value of the house in Coventry at 31 March 1982 was £50,000. The capital gain arising (ignoring any improvement expenditure and costs of sale) is calculated below:

The periods of actual, deemed occupation and non-occupation are as follows:

Period	Notes	Exempt (months)	Charge-able (months)
1.2.82 – 31.3.82	Ignore as before 31 March 1982	—	—
1.4.82 – 31.7.82	Deemed occupation (ESC D49 ie period of occupation)	4	—
1.8.82 – 31.7.87	Actual occupation	60	—
1.8.87 – 31.7.89	Deemed occupation as employed abroad	24	—
1.8.89 – 31.7.94	Deemed occupation – 4 years working away from home in the UK plus 1 year for any purpose	60	—
1.8.94 – 31.7.95	Actual occupation	12	—
1.8.95 – 30.4.03	Non-occupation (not followed by period of actual residence)	—	93

1.5.03 – 30.4.06	Deemed occupation (final 36 months)	36	—
	Totals (289 months)	196	93

The capital gain arising is calculated as follows:

			£
Disposal proceeds			275,000
Less:	Market value 31 March 1982	50,000	
	Indexation allowance @ 1.047	52,350	
			(102,350)
	Indexed gain		172,650
	Less PPR exemption		
	$\dfrac{196}{289}$ x £172,650		
			(117,091)
	Capital gain before reliefs and annual exemption		£55,559

The tapered capital gain arising is 65% x
£55,559 = £36,113.

Roger should be questioned as to the actual usage of the property during the times of non–occupation. Specifically, whether the property was let at any time, even if only informally, as this may enable let property relief to be available. Also there was an opportunity for Roger to elect for the Coventry property to have remained as his main residence but that was not done.

The rules for deemed periods of occupancy provide scope for some very generous tax relief. In particular, once a property has qualified as a PPR then the final 36 months of ownership are automatically exempt for CGT purposes.

Therefore, if two residences are available to the same person and both at some stage qualified as an individual's PPR then the final 36 months of ownership for both properties will be exempt. In the same way it is possible that the same person may have owned three or more properties, each of which at some stage has been their main residence, and therefore each will qualify for PPR relief for the final 36 months of ownership and so on. It is important that individuals and their advisers identify the potential for taxpayers to occupy a second property in order to become eligible for the very generous 36-month exemption period. This can often require planning well in advance of any intention to dispose of the property.

Given that it is the 'quality' as opposed to the 'quantity' that determines occupation, a relatively short period of occupancy, say two to three months, would seem to be acceptable. This could then provide eligibility for the final 36 months of ownership of that property to be exempt from CGT. This remains one of the more generous CGT reliefs and with house prices increasing and with property investment continuing to prove popular it would perhaps not be surprising if it is limited or removed in due course.

The letting of the main residence

9.9   There is a further relief available against CGT arising on the sale of an individual's PPR known as let property relief. This is available where the dwelling house or any part of it has been let as residential accommodation at any time during the period of ownership. In this situation the capital gain arising attributable to the period of letting is chargeable only to the extent that it exceeds the lower of:

(a)   the exempt amount due to PPR relief;

(b)   the capital gain arising during the let period; and

(c)   £40,000.

The application of the let property relief cannot give rise to an allowable loss. The limit of £40,000 is available to each property owner so a husband and wife owning a property jointly could claim a maximum amount of £40,000.

The definition of residential accommodation was examined in *Owen v Elliott (Inspector of Taxes)* [1990] STC 469. In this case Mr Owen owned a private hotel and his wife did the cooking, housekeeping and so on. During the summer season visitors stayed for short periods, but in the winter they often stayed for several months. In the summer, Mr Owen and his family lived in an annex, but in the winter they occupied the whole hotel. On the disposal of the property, Mr Owen agreed with the Inspector of Taxes that one third of the gain on disposal was exempt under the PPR rules. Mr Owen then claimed further relief under the let property exemption, because he argued he had provided residential accommodation in his private residence for the guests. HMRC argued that, in their view, providing accommodation for hotel guests was not letting the property as residential accommodation. This is set out in Statement of Practice 14/80.

It was, however, held that the let property exemption applied where property was 'let ... as residential accommodation'. The phrase did not merely refer to premises let which were likely to be occupied as a home. Thus the lettings were within the definition of 'residential accommodation' and further relief under s 223(4) was available.

Where a lodger shares living accommodation with a house owner and their family, and has meals with them, then there is no chargeable gain in respect of the letting. Similarly, no chargeable gain arises in respect of accommodation let under the income tax 'rent a room relief' rules.

Example – Let property relief

Chris makes an indexed capital gain of £50,000 on the disposal of his house on 31 July 2006. He purchased the house on 1 August 1995. He lived in the property from acquisition to 31 July 1997, let it as residential accommodation for the period 1 August 1997 to 31 July 2003 and from 1 August 2003 to the date of sale the property was not occupied or let.

The capital gain is calculated as follows:

	£
Indexed capital gain	50,000
Less: PPR relief for first 24 months plus final 36 months (60/132 x £50,000)	(22,727)
	27,273
Less: let property relief – lower of:	
(i) PPR relief £22,727 (as above)	
(ii) Gain in let period £27,273 (as above)	
(iii) £40,000	
	(22,727)
Capital gain before other reliefs and annual exemption	£4,546

Note that the tapered gain will be 65% x £4,546 = £2,955

Example – Partial occupation of let property

If in the example above Chris only let a quarter of the property as residential accommodation and he occupied the other three quarters during that period, the position would be as follows:

	£	£
Indexed capital gain		50,000
Less: PPR relief for first 24 months plus final 36 months		
60/132 x £50,000	22,727	
Less: PPR relief for period where ¾ of the property was occupied		
72/132 x 3/4 x £50,000	20,455	
		(43,182)
		6,818
Less let property relief – lower of:		
(i) PPR relief £43,182		
(ii) Gain in let period £6,818 (72/132 x 1/4 x £50,000)		
(iii) £40,000		
		(6,818)
Capital gain		£Nil

Example – Increasing the let property relief

Owain disposed of a property in 2006/07, which for part of the period of ownership had been his PPR and had also been let for 12 months. This property had been owned for a total of 120 months.

The total capital gain was £20,000 and the PPR relief was calculated to be £9,000.

The calculation of the let property relief can be somewhat contentious here.

Section 223(4) is constructed on the basis of what is chargeable to CGT rather than what is exempt. It states that you need to determine the chargeable gain relating to the actual period of letting which is then compared with the lower of the gain already covered by PPR relief and £40,000. The excess is then chargeable to CGT.

In Owain's case, it is only a very small part of the gain that relates to the let period, 12/120 x £20,000 = £2,000. In this interpretation, £2,000 is not therefore chargeable to CGT which would leave a balance of £9,000 chargeable (£20,000 – PPR relief of £9,000 – let property relief of £2,000).

However, HMRC's statement in their Capital Gains Manual (CG64721) states 'the gain relieved under s 223(4) is only the gain arising by reason of the letting. In a similar case in which a dwelling house has only been used either as the owner's only or main residence, or has been let as residential accommodation, it may be accepted that the gain remaining after PPR relief is the gain arising by reason of the letting. That gain may be relieved to the extent of the limit set out in CG64714 to CG64715'.

One could therefore take the view that in Owain's case, the house was used only as a main residence, or for residential letting, assuming that at all other times the property was unused rather than being used for, say, a business purpose. On the basis of CG64721 it could be argued that the lettings relief should actually be £9,000 (equivalent to the PPR relief) and not £2,000. This would leave £2,000 chargeable to CGT (£20,000 – £9,000 PPR – £9,000 let property relief).

This example is included to show that the legislation surrounding let property relief is grey and its treatment can be contentious. It also demonstrates that in some cases there could be some argument for claiming a seemingly higher exemption for let property relief and placing reliance on CG64721.

Dwelling house used for business purposes

9.10 Where part of a property is used *exclusively* for the purposes of a business, then the capital gain is apportioned and the part that is attributable to the business use is a chargeable capital gain. The apportionment is made with reference to an appropriate basis, for example, the floor area used for business and private purposes respectively, or the proportion of household expenses charged as a business expense.

Where a dwelling is used for both business and non-business use, there is no relief on the business element for the final 36 months of ownership.

HMRC's view of what is and what is not deemed to be 'exclusive use' is a matter of fact to be decided on a case-by-case basis. For example, a business woman working occasionally at her dining room table clearly does not have exclusive business use of her dining room, but a professional photographer who has a room at home set aside for use as his studio probably does have exclusive use of that room for business purposes only.

However, in such a case the claim for business expenditure for income tax purposes should be considered in the light of the potential impact on entitlement to PPR relief on a future sale of the house. There may be personal use of the studio.

Example – Dwelling used for business purposes (non-exclusive use)

Simon is a partner in a firm of solicitors. He regularly works from home and he uses his study for this purpose. Simon also uses the study in his capacity as secretary to a local investment club. His children use the study to do their homework and his wife also uses the study for dealing with the household paperwork.

Simon is able to show that no part of the house is exclusively used for the purpose of his business and therefore no restriction on PPR relief should arise on its sale. Any income tax claim for business use of residence would need to be consistent with this. It is usually unwise to ever claim 100% of costs for income tax purposes.

Example – Interpretation of 'exclusive use'

Ceinwen runs a bed and breakfast business from home. The bed and breakfast activities are contained within three rooms in the upstairs rear section of the property. These comprise a large bedroom, a small breakfast room and a bathroom. There is a door at the end of the corridor, closing the bed and breakfast suite of three rooms from the rest of the property. The guests are able to access the three rooms either by the main stairs through the house or via a door that opens directly into the garden.

When the rooms are not in use for bed and breakfast, they are available for the use of the whole family and are frequently used. The remainder of the property is used exclusively by Ceinwen's family.

For the purpose of deciding whether PPR is available in full, it is important that the part of the building used for bed and breakfast is only exclusive to the extent that members of the public are in residence. For the rest of the time, the rooms are available to Ceinwen and her family for their use.

As there is no exclusive use of any of the property for business purposes, then there should be no restriction to the PPR relief available on a subsequent sale of the property.

For taper relief purposes, the chargeable gain remaining after the PPR exemption is then apportioned according to the extent of business use and the taper relief calculated. This is considered further in respect of mixed use assets in Chapter 2.

Example – Part of dwelling used exclusively for business purposes

Stephen owned a dwelling and used a room exclusively as an office for business use. The floor area of the office amounted to one tenth of the total floor area of the property. The rest of the property was occupied as his PPR and the office was used for business use only throughout the period of ownership.

The property was acquired for £100,000 on 31 January 1999 and was sold on 31 January 2007 for £200,000.

The capital gain arising (ignoring costs of purchase and sale) is calculated as follows:

	£
Proceeds of sale	200,000
Cost	(100,000)
	100,000
Less: PPR relief (9/10ths)	(90,000)
Gain before taper relief	£10,000

This gain then needs to be apportioned between the business and non-business use for taper relief purposes as it is a mixed use asset.

	Business asset 1/10	Non-business asset 9/10	Total
	£	£	£
Gain before taper relief	1,000	9,000	10,000
Tapered gain @ 25%/70%	250	6,300	7,900

In terms of tax planning, it would be beneficial to avoid exclusive use of part of a dwelling for business purposes to protect the PPR relief. If a study is used by the taxpayer for the purpose of his/her trade, it would be advisable for him to allow family use of this room at other times.

Position of trusts and personal representatives

9.11　There are some particular issues as far as a claim for PPR relief by trustees in respect of a property occupied by a beneficiary and these are considered in CHAPTER 11.

One of the issues to consider is whether the arrangements could amount to a constructive or implied trust. Such an arrangement can arise where a property is provided rent free for life or for some other set period. This scenario is explored further in a case study in CHAPTER 15.

Divorce and PPR

9.12   This particular issue in connection with the availability of PPR on arrangements arising under a divorce is considered in CHAPTER 10.

More than one property

9.13   An increasingly common area requiring tax planning in connection with the main residence is where more than one property is owned. This may be because a holiday home has been acquired, property has been inherited or investment property has been purchased. It may also be the case that there is a second residence due to the location of an individual's employment.

The PPR election – Section 223

9.14   Married couples or civil partners that live together can only have one residence that qualifies as their main residence for PPR purposes. This is outlined in s 222(6). This can be overlooked and can cause difficulties especially where each spouse owns their own property. However, it should be remembered that the final 36 months of ownership are automatically exempt in all cases.

Where a taxpayer has more than one residence, he or she needs to nominate which is to be regarded as the main residence for PPR purposes. This should be done in writing to HMRC within two years of acquiring the second residence. This election may then be varied at a later date, which can provide some very useful tax planning opportunities. Once the election is in place, the variation can be made without the need for the actual occupancy of the properties to change.

However, in order for the election to be made it is necessary that the taxpayer has actually resided in both residencies, at least from time to time. HMRC do not regard a residence which is occupied by license (which includes living with relatives), occupying a hotel room or some job-related residence as being a residence for the purposes of s 222(5). Therefore, if somebody owns a house which they use at the weekend, but they live with their parents during the week, then there is no need for them to make an election. HMRC will treat them as only having one residence, being the house that they actually own.

On the occasion when a marriage or civil partnership has broken down and one of the partners owns or has an interest in the family home, but ceases to occupy the property, then the departing partner may continue to be treated as resident for CGT purposes. This only applies provided that the remaining partner has continued to reside in the home and that the departing partner has not elected that a different house be treated as their main residence. This concession (ESC D26) does not apply on a disposal to a third party, only where the interest in the property is transferred to the remaining partner.

Where an individual acquires a second residence, he should exercise his entitlement to submit to HMRC an election to treat one of the two (or more) as his PPR, under s 223. The occupation of a property under a tenancy, although not a license, will make it a residence for these purposes. Even if the election is to be made in favour of the property which is as a matter of fact the main residence, the advantage of making an election is that it can be subsequently varied.

If an election has not been made within two years, then the option ceases to be available until a new combination of residences is acquired. However, once an election has been made, then an election can take effect within any time during the two years preceding the variation.

There is no statutory form that the election should take. It is common for HMRC to acknowledge receipt of the election; however, this does not confirm that they have accepted it. It has been becoming increasingly common for HMRC to enquire into subsequent disposals where elections have been made.

A point that is often overlooked is that the legislation is concerned with having two or more residences – not the ownership of two or more properties. Therefore, where an individual both owns a house and rents a flat, he does have two residences. Where someone has a main residence and a tenanted property, then there is only one residence available. If the tenant vacates the let property and it becomes a second home, then it is at that point that two residences become available.

Example – Election for PPR

Neil inherited Maisie Cottage in November 1996. The probate value was £120,000.

Between 1 January 1996 and 31 January 1997, Neil lived in the property for short periods to keep the property in a reasonable and habitable condition. The property was subsequently let from 1 February 1997 to 28 February 2003.

The property was left in a poor state by the tenant. Significant repair work was undertaken by Neil and during the repair work he lived in the property from time to time.

Neil also owned Sheba House, since 1990, where he lived throughout when not living in Maisie Cottage.

An election nominating Maisie Cottage to be the PPR was filed on 18 February 2005. This is within two years of 28 February 2003 when Neil once again acquired a second residence, when Maisie Cottage became vacant. Whilst Maisie Cottage was let, he only had Sheba House available to him as a residence.

Maisie Cottage was sold on 31 October 2006 for £170,000 (net of costs of sale).

The CGT calculation is as follows:

	£	£
Proceeds of sale		170,000
Less: probate valuation – November 1996	120,000	
Indexation allowance to 5 April 1998	6,840	
		(126,840)
		43,160
PPR relief (final 3 years of ownership)		
36/119 x £43,160		(13,057)
Let property relief (TCGA 1992, s 223(4))		
Restricted to lesser of gain in let period, £40,000 or		
PPR relief		(13,057)
		17,046
Less taper relief @ 35%		(5,966)
		11,080
Annual exemption		(8,800)
Taxable gain		£2,280

In the absence of an election the gain would have been as follows:

	£
Capital gain	43,160
Less taper relief @ 35%	(15,106)
	28,054
Annual exemption	(8,800)
Taxable gain	£19,254

This is £16,974 higher than with the election, potentially £6,790 of CGT if the entire gain is taxed at 40%.

Which property is the main residence?

9.15   In HMRC's Capital Gains Manual at CG64552, there is a list of criteria to determine which of two or more residences, is a person's main residence for the purpose of PPR. The list is not exhaustive and is far from providing a definitive guide, however, it is a useful starting point.

The list includes looking at the address shown on tax returns, the address shown on third party correspondence (for example dividend counterfoils), how each property is furnished, where the property owner is registered to vote, where the property is in relation to the person's place of work and where the owner's family stays. The Capital Gains Manual does say that the relative extent to which each residence is occupied as a residence is not a material factor.

An example would be where a person has a house in the country, but works in the city. They own a second residence in the city to live in during the week, although his family lives in the country house. In this case it is most likely that HMRC would treat the country property as the main residence as a question of fact despite the likelihood that the taxpayer actually spends more time at the city abode.

The tests that are applied for council tax purposes are also a useful way of attempting to determine which property is a person's main residence. These can be segregated under four distinct headings:

1   Occupation rights

    (a)   At each residence review whether the individual is an owner, a tenant (and the nature of any tenancy), or a lodger of any accommodation provided with employment.

    (b)   What is his/her right to occupy a property?

    (c)   Is residence conditional? For example, dependant on holding a work permit.

2   Personal connections

    (a)   At which residence is the individual registered with a doctor or dentist?

    (b)   Where are the majority of his or her possessions kept?

    (c)   Where does he or she return to during periods of leave or at the end of employment?

    (d)   What are the long-term intentions?

    (e)   Where is the individual registered to vote?

    (f)   Consider the membership of clubs and other social activities.

    (g)   Which address is used as the usual postal address?

    (h)   Which property does he or she regard as the main residence?

    (i)   How is time split between the residences?

3   Family connections

    (a)   At which residence does the spouse and dependent(s) live?

    (b)   From which residence do any children attend school?

    (c)   At which residence does the individual spend time with the family?

4   Other sundry issues

    (a)   Merchant seamen; such individuals are not considered to be resident on a ship.

    (b)   Services personnel; these are considered as mainly resident in accommodation, provided privately, rather than any service accommodation.

In the event that an election has not been made and a second property has not been sold, even though, on the face of it, it is not the main residence, it is worth looking at the overall facts underpinning the properties to determine whether or not there is scope to claim the second property has at some stage been the main residence, so that at least some exemption (not least in respect of the final 36 months) may apply. In some cases, it is certainly not clear that there is a definitive main residence and care should be taken to ensure that the ability to claim relief is not overlooked or denied unnecessarily.

An election will only have effect as long as it remains necessary to determine which of two properties is the main residence. In other words, an election remains effective only as long as the taxpayer has more than one residence.

Although it is commonly thought that a main residence election must be made whilst the two properties are owned, HMRC's Capital Gains Manual gives an example at CG64512 of a case where a residence election was made after the sale of a property, which the manual clearly indicates is acceptable.

The fact that the final 36 months of ownership are always eligible for PPR relief once a property has qualified as a main residence, potentially allows two or more properties to qualify for PPR relief concurrently throughout the entire period of ownership.

How long must a property be the main residence?

9.16   Returning to the issue of how long a property needs to be a main residence to qualify for PPR relief, HMRC's Capital Gains Manual at CG64512 contains an example where an election for a one-week period is shown as being acceptable. The tax case (*Goodwin v Curtis (Inspector of Taxes)* [1998] STC 475, CA) held that occupation of the property for only five weeks did not constitute residence for the purpose of PPR relief. It would seem therefore that a minimum period of at least two to three months would be safer.

Example – Election for PPR where property inherited

Melanie lived for many years in her only residence, in the Lake District. Melanie then inherited her mother's property in Devon on 30 September 2001, when her mother died. On the advice of her accountants, Melanie filed a PPR election with HMRC for her Lake District property to be her PPR with effect from 30 September 2001 when she acquired a second potential residence.

Melanie had business interests in Devon and regularly stayed with her mother prior to her death. Following the death of Melanie's mother, it was also necessary for Melanie to spend several weeks at a time in Devon administering her mother's estate and also looking after her own interests.

The main residence election in respect of the Lake District property was filed on 10 September 2003 (within two years of acquiring the Devon property). The election was subsequently varied so that the Devon property was the elected main residence with effect from 1 March 2004.

The Devon property was subsequently sold on 31 October 2004. As the property already qualified as the main residence, the final 36 months of ownership were automatically exempt from CGT leaving only one month out of the 37 months of ownership chargeable to CGT. This was covered by the annual capital gains exemption for the year of disposal.

It is not uncommon for taxpayers to acquire a second residence on the death of an elderly relative and, as shown in this example, by a careful review of the facts and utilising the ability to file a main residence election, it is possible to significantly reduce or even eliminate capital gains arising on the sale of the inherited property.

Validity of elections

9.17 As HMRC do not comment on the validity of elections filed, care should be taken to ensure that any elections filed do not state, for example, that the property is elected for a fixed period after which the election automatically reverts to property B. The legislation gives the right to vary a notice by means of 'a further notice' and therefore the example above does not comply strictly with these conditions.

It would be better to file separate elections for property A and property B to minimise the risk of HMRC later rejecting the election. This may seem like a relatively minor point, but an increasing number of enquiries into PPR elections serves to demonstrate that HMRC are taking more interest in these and care will need to be taken with the wording of the election itself.

Late elections

9.18 ESC D21 allows for late elections to be made with regard to rented property constituting a residence. The two-year election period is extended if the interest in a second property used as a residence has negligible value and the taxpayer is unaware of the need to elect. Once he becomes aware of the need to elect, then the election must be made within a reasonable time period.

Job-related accommodation

9.19 The rules relating to multiple residences are relaxed for self-employed and employed people living in job-related accommodation. This would include the tenant of a public house, or a vicar living in a vicarage. These people will be treated as occupying any second dwelling house that they own, provided only that they intend in due course to occupy the dwelling house as their only or main residence. For example, on retirement they may intend to reside in their second property. In these cases, it is not necessary to actually establish residency, although it is necessary for an individual to nominate the second property as their main residence.

Residence occupied by a dependent relative

9.20   Before 6 April 1988 where somebody owned a house which was let rent free as the sole residence to their dependent relation or that of their spouse or civil partner, they could claim exemption for that house as well as their own main residence.

However, where an individual owned two or more such properties then he/she could only make a claim in respect of one of them.

A dependent relative means any relative of the taxpayer or his/her spouse or civil partner who is unable to maintain him or herself due to old age or infirmity or a widowed, divorced or separated mother of the taxpayer or his spouse or civil partner.

HMRC have clarified the requirement that the dependent relative actually occupy the property rent free. This condition will be satisfied even when the dependent relative pays all or part of the council tax and the costs of repairs attributable to normal wear and tear in the property (ESC D20).

This exemption will no longer apply if the property was first occupied by the dependent relative after 5 April 1988. However, the exemption continues to apply where the property was first occupied by the dependent relative before that date.

In cases where a taxpayer disposes of a property that has been occupied by a dependent relative, it is important to determine when that relative first occupied the property.

If the property ceases to be the dependent relative's sole residence, then any later period of residence by that or another dependent relative beginning after 6 April 1988 will be disregarded when calculating dependent relative relief. The capital gain arising will be apportioned on a time basis.

This relief can still be relevant to certain client situations but the terms are restrictive and care is required. It may be that a safer tax planning approach is to rely upon the trust exemption for beneficiaries under either a formal deed or a constructive/implied trust. This is considered further in CHAPTER 11 and in CHAPTER 15.

Rights deriving from main residence

9.21   A practice has developed of assisting employees relocating to a different area by using a relocation company to buy an employee's house on terms where he can share in any excess proceeds should the house eventually be sold for a higher amount. HMRC accept that this right to receive a capital sum will generally be exempt to the same extent as the gain on the home, provided the right is not held for more than three years. This concessional relief also applies to other joint owners of the property as well as the employee.

This concession also applies where the employer buys the house as well as where the relocation business is carried on as an unincorporated business, rather than a company.

PPR? No thanks! – Breaking the PPR rules

9.22 PPR relief is a powerful exemption that ensures that a capital gain arising on the disposal of somebody's residence is not chargeable to CGT, subject to meeting the relevant statutory conditions.

However, it is also true that if a loss is made on the property then that loss would not be available to offset other capital gains arising on other assets. In order to ensure that a loss is allowable it would be necessary to break the PPR rules.

In cases where large taxable gains have arisen on other assets, or are anticipated at some point in the near future, then it may be sensible to consider whether or not the rules which normally allow PPR relief to apply can be broken so that at least some of the loss on the dwelling property will be allowable. This is in essence a case of using the previous planning points in reverse.

Excessive land

9.23 As explained earlier in this chapter, the PPR exemption extends to gardens and grounds of up to half a hectare in size or such an area as may be required for the reasonable enjoyment of the property, given the size and character of the dwelling house.

Where there is a sale of a large plot at a loss, such that the total land disposed of with the property exceeds half a hectare, it would be sensible to restrict the permitted area to the basic half a hectare. It would appear to be acceptable that a taxpayer could quite legitimately decline to argue that a larger area is required for the reasonable enjoyment of the property. The excess of land would therefore not qualify for PPR relief and an allowable loss could be claimed on it.

However, it would remain possible for the Inspector of Taxes to appeal to the Commissioners to rule that a larger area is required. It would then be down to the taxpayer to argue for the smaller area. This is, of course, a complete reversal of the normal procedure of trying to claim as much land as possible as being exempt under PPR relief.

Example – Restricting grounds to utilise a loss

Brian acquired Dibly Cottage in Suffolk in 2002 for £300,000. The property was sold in 2007/08 for £250,000. Having taken the advice of a professional valuer, it was concluded that £20,000 of this loss related to an area of 0.3 hectares of land which was in excess of the permitted 0.5 hectares normally allowable.

Whilst it was a fairly large cottage and Brian could probably have comfortably argued that the full 0.8 hectares of land were in keeping with the property given the size and character of it, he declined to claim that the full area of land was necessary. The capital loss of £20,000 was offset against large capital gains made through his stocks and shares portfolio during the same tax year.

It is assumed in this case that HMRC could potentially refer the case to the Commissioners to argue that the larger area was required and that PPR should cover the full disposal.

In the case of Brian in the above example, he could potentially have disposed of the house and some of the land in a separate contract to the disposal of the rest of the land at a later date. In the case of *Varty v Lynes* [1976] 3 All ER 447, considered above, the taxpayer sold part of the land with this main residence in 1971 and then sold the remainder of the land in 1972. He was not granted PPR exemption for part of the land sold in the later year. It would therefore seem to follow that by selling the house and some land before the sale of the rest of the land Brian would trigger a capital loss on the sale of the second part of the land in this case.

Withdrawals of PPR elections

9.24   An election for a property to be a residence for PPR purposes can be varied by further notice in writing in respect of any period not earlier than two years prior to the date of the further notice. This could be useful if the elected main residence could be sold at a loss. This may not always be useful as the final 36 months of ownership of a PPR are automatically exempt, whereas the election can only be withdrawn up to a maximum of two years before.

Example – Withdrawal of PPR election

George has two properties, a house which he inherited from his parents in 2000 and a flat which he purchased closer to his place of work on 6 April 2005. George thought that the flat would grow substantially in value, given its location, and he also did not consider that it was likely that he would sell the house that he inherited.

However, in 2006, George changed jobs and decided to sell the flat, which had actually reduced in value since acquisition. Before 5 April 2007, George varied the original PPR election with effect from 6 April 2005 that the house was the main residence for PPR purposes, having the effect that the flat never qualified for PPR relief.

The varying of the election had completely set aside the original election. The flat was subsequently sold and the loss arising was available to carry forward and offset future capital gains. An important point here is that, if George had not varied the election within two years of acquiring the flat, there may have been a small period of time when it qualified as a PPR and therefore the final 36 months of ownership would have been exempted under the PPR rules. In this case, the loss arising would not be allowable.

Periods of absence

9.25   To ensure that the periods of absence set out in s 223(3) are ignored for PPR relief purposes, there must be a period of time both before and after the absence, when the property was the main residence. In a case where it is likely that a loss would result on a sale, then the taxpayer could simply fail to reoccupy the property at all after a period of absence before the sale. The loss in this case would be allowable as the period of absence would be denied for PPR purposes.

Example – Failure to occupy residence

Ronnie acquired 147 Break Street on 1 February 2002 for £225,000. On 1 February 2004 he moved out and spent the next few years travelling around and staying in various hotels, camping or staying with relatives. The property was left empty, although he let various members of his family stay there if they were in the area. In late 2006, he had the property valued and calculated he would receive no more than £175,000 after costs. This would mean selling at a loss of £50,000. Ronnie anticipated making a large capital gain on some shares in the next few years and a carried forward capital loss would be extremely useful. He realised that the property would undoubtedly take a few months to sell, as it was not in a particularly desirable area.

He had the option at that time to either move back into the property, or to move in with his sister for the short term. The final 36 months of ownership are automatically covered by PPR relief. Without reoccupation, then a sale on 1 August 2007 would mean that the period 1 February 2002 to 31 January 2004 and the period 1 August 2004 to 1 August 2007 would be exempt, leaving the period 1 February 2004 to 31 July 2004 taxable, creating an allowable loss as follows:

	£
Loss	50,000
Less PPR relief of 5/5.5 x £50,000	(45,455)
Allowable loss	£4,545

However, if he had reoccupied the property then the period that he was away, up to a maximum of three years, would also be covered by PPR relief and so no allowable loss would arise.

Disclosure of gains on tax returns

9.26   The issue of disclosure is considered in CHAPTER 13. As will be apparent from many of the examples above, there is plenty of scope for dispute with HMRC in relation to the interpretation of entitlement to PPR relief. It is, therefore very important that the basis of computation and the essential facts are fully disclosed on the appropriate return. This should be considered when the planning advice is being given to the client and their attention drawn to the relevant question(s) on the tax return form. Particular care and thought is required as to the best approach where one of the property owners is not in receipt of a self-assessment return. In such a case, disclosure may need to be by way of letter, but it may be preferable to ensure that the individual concerned does receive a self-assessment return for the year of the disposal.

Conclusion

9.27   PPR relief continues to be one of the most generous reliefs available to shelter the taxpayer from liability to CGT. That said, in order to make the most of the tax planning opportunities available, there are a number of grey areas surrounding the legislation that require consideration on a case-by-case basis. Such issues include the extent to which grounds are covered by PPR relief, periods of absence during ownership and where the taxpayer owns more than one property. Perhaps the key to effective tax planning in this area is to be forewarned and, where possible, the taxpayer and adviser alike are advised to consider the planning opportunities available well in advance of the intention to sell. It is also important that CGT is considered when advising on other tax issues in respect of the property, such as tax relief for income tax purposes.

Checklist

	Cross Reference
PPR Relief	
Principal private residence relief is a very generous CGT relief. As part of any planning to maximise the relief, it is necessary to consider in the main the following:	
• Is there a dwelling house?	9.2
• Is it a trading transaction?	9.4
• Physical extent of the relief and order of disposals	9.6
• Periods of occupation of the property as a residence	9.8
• Availability of let property relief	9.9
• More than one residence	9.14
• Whether a property has been occupied by a dependant relative	9.20

Chapter 10

Marriage and Divorce (including Civil Partnerships)

Introduction

10.1 When capital gains tax (CGT) was introduced in 1965, the legislation was drafted such that transactions between married couples were ignored. The transfer is treated as being on a no gain/no loss basis as with transfers between group companies. However, even though at that time husbands and wives were jointly taxed, CGT has always been on the basis of independent taxation. This approach gives rise to both pitfalls and tax benefits which in turn present tax planning opportunities.

As far as married couples and civil partners are concerned, the CGT issues to consider relate to the ownership of assets between the couple. As such, much of the planning is by nature very long term. The CGT issues to consider in the event of divorce derive from the need to divide up those same marital assets between the two parties.

This chapter considers the basic rules and complications which apply to both married couples and civil partners which advisers need to watch out for. It then covers some particular issues for business assets including taper relief and hold-over relief, tax planning in terms of ownership arrangements between spouses and concludes by considering the position on a divorce. All statutory references are to TCGA 1992 unless otherwise stated.

Capital gains tax issues for married couples and civil partnerships

10.2 The specific CGT issues for married couples and civil partners are as follows:

(a) Beneficial asset transfer rules.

(b) Extended connected party rules and the broadening of many anti-avoidance rules to include spouses/civil partners such as the settlor interest provisions for trusts.

(c) Restricting the entitlement of married couples/civil partners to only one principal private residence (PPR) between them.

However, married couples are not treated as a single unit for CGT purposes. Disposals by each spouse have to be separately calculated and returned and the tax rates applying are dependent upon the individual income level of the spouse concerned. It is unnecessary to consider the taxable income of the other spouse, although this is relevant when planning ownership proportions.

In addition, there are issues arising from the interaction with other taxes – principally income tax and inheritance tax (IHT). The split of assets between a married couple can lead to very different income tax liabilities and is particularly important in terms of will planning in order to ensure that the nil rate tax bands for IHT are fully utilised by each spouse. This is considered further in CHAPTER 14.

Basic rules on transfers of assets

10.3   Transfers of capital assets between spouses and civil partners who are living together are on a no gain/no loss basis, and thus do not attract an immediate CGT charge. Assets not subject to CGT, such as trading stock, cannot be transferred on a no gain/no loss basis.

Spouses and civil partners remain 'connected persons' until one party to the marriage dies or a divorce decree becomes absolute. As connected persons the parties will still be subject to the market value rule on any transfer of assets. However, it remains possible to transfer assets between a husband and wife or civil partners 'living together' without creating chargeable gains or allowable losses (s 58). For this purpose a husband and wife or civil partners are treated as 'living together' unless:

(a)   they are separated under a court order or by a deed of separation; or

(b)   they are separated in such circumstances that the separation is likely to be permanent.

The position on separation is complicated by the fact that s 58 refers to 'living together in any year of assessment'. By concession, HMRC will allow transfers between a husband and wife or civil partners to take place on a no gain/no loss basis up to 5 April following the date of separation.

It is often beneficial for spouses/civil partners to transfer assets between them for CGT purposes. As already mentioned, this is to ensure that full advantage is taken of both annual exemptions, lower income tax rate bands and capital losses. However, it is important to bear in mind that this advice is from a tax perspective only. There are wider legal issues to consider.

Example – Planning to utilise losses

Mr and Mrs Brown have jointly owned a property as tenants-in-common since 1980. In March 1982, the property was worth £25,000. It was sold in May 2007 for £225,000 making an indexed gain of £173,825.

Mr Brown has losses brought forward on a share portfolio of £75,000 and has no income. Mrs Brown is a higher-rate taxpayer. No PPR relief is available.

A sale of the property in equal proportions gives rise to the following liability:

	Mr Brown	Mrs Brown	Total
	£	£	£
Indexed gain	86,913	86,912	173,825
Losses brought forward	(75,000)		(75,000)
	11,913	86,912	98,825
Taper relief (40%)	(4,765)	(34,765)	(39,530)
	7,148	52,147	£59,295
Annual exemption	(9,200)	(9,200)	
Taxable gain	£Nil	£42,947	
CGT payable @ 40%		£17,179	

However, it can be seen that much of the losses brought forward have been wasted, as have Mr Brown's lower rate tax bands.

By transferring a larger share of the property to Mr Brown, these losses can be better used and also take advantage of his lower tax rates. In this case, varying the ratio of ownership 6:1 so that Mr Brown owns 6/7ths and Mrs Brown 1/7th on disposal.

The tax computation becomes as follows:

	Mr Brown	Mrs Brown	Total
	£	£	£
Indexed gain	148,993	24,832	173,825
Losses brought forward	(75,000)		(75,000)
	73,993	24,832	98,825
Taper relief (40%)	(29,597)	(9,933)	(39,530)
	44,396	14,899	£59,295
Annual exemption	(9,200)	(9,200)	
Taxable gain	35,196	5,699	
CGT payable			
£2,230 x 10% =	223		
£32,370 x 20% =	6,474		
£596 x 40% =	238		
£5,699 x 40% =		2,280	
	£6,935	£2,280	
Total tax liability		£9,215	

The saving of approximately £8,000 is generated using Mr Brown's lower and basic rate tax bands, rather than all of the tax being payable at 40% due to the use of losses. Mr Brown's annual exemption is also fully utilised. However, it is important to consider the individual circumstances first, for example, such a transfer may not be appropriate where the receiving spouse has used their annual exemption and pays higher rate tax.

Inter-spousal transfers can also be advantageous in conjunction with loss relief, both to use up losses brought forward or to preserve them where they would otherwise be wasted due to the availability of taper relief. This is subject to targeted anti-avoidance rules contained in FA 2007, and this is detailed further in CHAPTER 12. The CGT issues in respect of pre-sale transfers are considered later in this chapter.

In this example, a change in the ownership proportions is fairly straightforward as it is only a case of amending the deed of trust. In other cases, a formal conveyance may be necessary. If significant legal work is required then the legal fees concerned may negate the benefit or make any alteration unachievable in the time available. As such, forward thinking and long-term planning is the best approach.

Ownership arrangements for assets between spouses/civil partners

10.4 Ownership arrangements for CGT purposes are considered in detail in CHAPTER 3. However, there are particular CGT planning issues for the ownership of assets for married couples and civil partnerships which arise from the desire to maximise the special tax benefits available.

For income tax planning purposes, it is common for assets to be owned jointly between spouses and civil partners. This ownership may be achieved either by putting the legal ownership into joint names or alternatively by effecting a declaration of trust to transfer the beneficial ownership.

A decision then needs to be made whether the properties are to be owned as joint tenants or as tenants-in-common. If the ownership proportions are to be anything other than 50:50, then the property must be owned as tenants-in-common. However, ownership as tenants-in-common does have will drafting implications and at the same time as purchasing a property, it is sensible to make sure that up to date wills are in place.

The income tax legislation treats joint assets as being owned equally unless a declaration is made to the contrary. The declaration under ITA 2007, s 837 (formerly ICTA 1988, s 282) is to have income tax assessed on the actual beneficial ownership proportions. As CGT is assessed on the beneficial interest in an asset it will be calculated using the same proportions.

Example – Joint ownership of property

Simon and Elizabeth own a garage which is let for £2,000 per year. As Simon is a higher-rate taxpayer, and Elizabeth is a non-taxpayer, the ownership proportions were varied such that the garage is owned 99% as to Elizabeth and 1% as to Simon.

Simon and Elizabeth agree to sell the garage for £35,000. The indexed base cost is only £4,000. The legal fees on sale are £300. The garage has been owned since 1995.

	Total (100%)	Elizabeth (99%)	Simon (1%)
	£	£	£
Sale proceeds	35,000	34,650	350
Less legal fees	(300)	(297)	(3)
Indexed base cost	(4,000)	(3,960)	(40)
	30,700	30,393	307
Taper relief – 40%	(12,280)	(12,157)	(123)
	18,420	18,236	184
Annual exemption	(9,384)	(9,200)	(184)*
Taxable gain	£9,036	£9,036	£Nil

* restricted

Simon and Elizabeth may have expected the gain of £18,420 on this jointly-owned asset to be fully covered by their annual exemptions but this is not the case. However, a transfer back into equal ownership prior to the sale would have enabled both annual exemptions to be fully utilised and so almost entirely extinguish the gain. However, as explained further below, this must be a genuine transfer of beneficial ownership in order for it to be effective.

Ownership of business assets between spouses/civil partners

10.5 The ownership arrangements for business assets between spouses/ civil partners are particularly important because of the importance of business asset taper relief (BATR) on the disposal of such assets – see CHAPTER 2. There are also implications for other tax planning and this is considered further in CHAPTER 14.

For BATR, the holding period usually commences when an asset is acquired by an individual. However, an exception arises where the asset was acquired from a spouse/civil partner at a time when the parties were 'living together'. A husband and wife/civil partner are then effectively treated as a 'single person' and this enables the transferee to adopt the transferor's period of ownership.

Where a business asset used for the purposes of a business carried on by the transferor is transferred to a spouse not involved in the business the taper entitlement could become tainted. Since the widening of entitlement to BATR on 6 April 2004, this is less of an issue – however, it is still relevant where employment is concerned and in respect of potential tainting.

For BATR purposes, inter-spouse transfers are an unintended area of complexity due to poor drafting of the legislation. The explanatory notes to the 1998 Finance Bill suggested that if a spouse transferred an asset to the other spouse, then the latter spouse would inherit the former spouse's acquisition date. Thus, the combined period of ownership would be taken into account for taper relief purposes. In addition, the status of that asset during the former spouse's period of ownership would be judged by reference to that former spouse. However, this is not what the legislation says. Further, the position is different depending on whether shares or other assets are being considered.

For periods before an inter-spouse transfer, the question of whether an asset qualifies as a business asset can be considered by looking at the use to which the asset is put by either spouse.

Example – Availability of BATR on property asset

John is the sole proprietor of a retail business operating from a shop which he has owned personally since before March 1998. He transfers ownership of the shop to his wife on 1 April 2000.

The shop is used for 'the purposes of a trade carried on at that time by [an] individual' during the relevant period of ownership but this in itself does not mean that BATR applied. It is nevertheless necessary to consider when the shop does actually qualify as a business asset for periods prior to April 2004.

Time	Owner	Who must carry on trade?	Business asset?
06.04.98 – 31.03.00	John	Either spouse	Yes
01.04.00 – 05.04.04	John's wife	Spouse making disposal	No

However, if the ownership arrangements had been reversed, ie originally owned by John's wife and then transferred to John, then full BATR would be available.

Whilst the position on multiple transfers is not entirely clear cut, it is widely accepted that BATR can be revived by an inter-spouse transfer before the eventual disposal.

Therefore, if John's wife transfers the shop back to him on 31 March 2004 the position will be as follows:

Time	Owner	Who must carry on trade?	Business asset?
06.04.98 – 31.03.00	John	Either spouse	Yes
01.04.00 – 01.03.04	John's wife	Either spouse	Yes
01.04.04 – 05.04.04	John	Spouse making disposal	Yes

This example is of more historic interest because after 6 April 2004, the shop would qualify for BATR in the hands of John's wife. However, ownership of such assets should still be reviewed to identify potential tainting.

For shares, the legislation is silent as far as inter-spouse transfers are concerned. So when shares are transferred between spouses/civil partners, the issue of whether the shares constitute a business asset or not are wholly dependent on the status of the shares with respect to the spouse who finally disposes of them.

Example – Listed company employer

Paul owned shares in his employer, a listed trading company which he acquired in 1997. He gave them to his wife on 1 December 1999 and she sells them on 1 September 2007.

Time	Owner	Status depends on whom?	Business asset?
06.04.98 – 30.11.99	Paul	Paul's wife	No
01.12.99 – 01.09.07	Paul's wife	Paul's wife	No

However, the business asset status can be revived by a pre-disposal transfer back to Paul.

There are some further complications and anomalies in the drafting of the taper relief rules for married couples and civil partnerships. However, one particular issue to bear in mind is that whilst the deemed spouse share transfer date will apply for taper relief purposes, it will not apply for the purposes of the share identification matching rules (see Revenue Interpretation 233).

Example – Shareholding matching rules

John buys 100 shares in X plc on 11 February 2002. Peg buys 150 shares in X plc on 12 December 2003. On 20 March 2005, John gives his shares in X plc to Peg. On 30 November 2006, Peg sells 100 shares.

For the purposes of calculating any gain or loss on Peg's disposal, Peg is treated as disposing of the shares she had received from John (being the later of her two acquisition dates). This is notwithstanding the fact that, for taper relief purposes, those shares have an ownership period dating back to February 2002.

229

As a result of the significant change in qualification for BATR on shareholdings on 6 April 2000, particular care needs to be taken where there were transfers between spouses/civil partners prior to that date.

Example – Pre-6 April 2006 status of shares

Adam and Eve owned equally between them 8% of the shares of a trading company. For periods before 6 April 2000, both individuals were full-time officers or employees of the company.

If one spouse owned 5% or more of the shares, then the company would be a qualifying company by reference to that spouse, but not the other. Otherwise, the company would, in respect of the period before 6 April 2000, not be a qualifying company by reference to either spouse.

It is sometimes suggested that transferring shares now would retrospectively enable the 5% (or, where appropriate 25%) threshold to be passed. The apparent justification of that viewpoint is that Sch A1, para 15 treats the transferee spouse as having acquired the transferred shares when the transferor spouse actually acquired the shares. If a spouse originally held 4% of the shareholding and is deemed to have acquired a further 1% at some stage on or before 6 April 1998, then it is thought that the 5% condition is satisfied throughout the first two years of the taper relief regime.

However, Sch A1, para 15 is drafted restrictively and does not work in such a way. It only applies for the purposes of Sch A1, para 2 and does not have any effect on paragraphs Sch A1, paras 6 and 6A. Therefore, if a company was not a qualifying company by reference to an individual on a particular date, a subsequent inter-spouse transfer of shares will have only a prospective effect on the status of the company (and its shares) by reference to that individual.

Example – Material interest in non-trading company

Henry and Herbert are colleagues (otherwise unconnected) working for an investment company, Big Returns Limited. Each has a 6% stake in the company which they acquired in May 2000. Neither has a material interest in the company which is a qualifying company by reference to both of them. Henry and Herbert enter into a civil partnership on 1 July 2007. On the same day, Henry transfers his shareholding to Herbert who subsequently sells the shares on 31 July 2007.

When Herbert sells the shares, he has a material interest in the company so that the company cannot be a qualifying company by reference to him at that time. However, prior to 1 July 2007 the shares did qualify as business assets and this is not altered retrospectively by the transfer of the shares between the civil partners.

Shares qualifying under the Enterprise Investment Scheme

10.6 Where a spouse/civil partner owns shares that have qualified for relief under the Enterprise Investment Scheme (EIS), it is possible to transfer some or all of the shares to the other spouse/civil partner without a clawback of EIS relief. However, whilst such a transfer is beneficially treated for tax purposes, it is typically of limited benefit. This is because the EIS shares concerned typically generate a nil or minimal dividend so denying much income tax benefit. For CGT purposes, the shares will be exempt from tax if full EIS relief has been claimed. For IHT purposes, business property relief (BPR) should be available such that there is limited estate planning possibilities.

Therefore, a transfer of EIS shares is only likely to be appropriate for shares in a family company on which EIS deferral relief has been claimed. Such a transfer may be appropriate for income tax planning purposes in connection with the extraction of profits by way of dividends jointly between a couple. EIS is considered in detail in CHAPTER 6.

Residency issues

10.7 The decision in *Gubay v Kington (Inspector of Taxes)* [1984] 1 All ER 513, [1984] 1 WLR 163, [1984] STC 99, 57 TC 601, HL confirms that there is no barrier to a no gain/no loss transfer from a UK resident spouse/civil partner to a non-resident spouse/civil partner. It may be that the couple in such a situation are separate but there should be no presumption that this is the case. Residency and CGT issues are considered further in CHAPTER 14.

Pre-sale transfer between spouses

10.8 Where an asset owned by one spouse is standing at a gain and is about to be sold, then a possible piece of planning is to transfer the asset into joint ownership to take advantage of annual exemptions, lower tax bands, losses, etc. This is a fairly straightforward procedure for shares as completion of a stock transfer form will suffice. For other assets, it may require legal conveyance although transfer of beneficial ownership by a declaration of trust should be adequate. However, one particular concern is how close to any third party sale can a spouse transfer take place?

HMRC will normally accept that a transfer is effective even if it is just prior to the eventual sale. HMRC will only seek to challenge a transfer where it amounts to a gift of sale proceeds rather than a gift of the underlying asset itself. Therefore, there must be actual beneficial ownership of the asset itself prior to sale and it must not be a 'done deal' at the time of the spouse transfer.

Example – Pre-sale transfer – Simple scenario

Mr Good has acquired 10,000 shares in his quoted employer as a result of participation in company share option schemes. Mr and Mrs Good wish to sell these shares to reduce their mortgage. The shares are worth £6 per share. The base cost is £1 per share.

Both Mr and Mrs Good have their annual exemptions available. Mr Good is also entitled to full BATR. Mrs Good has no entitlements to taper relief as the shares have been owned for less than three years. Mr Good is a higher-rate taxpayer whilst Mrs Good only works part-time and has an income of £10,000.

Mr Good could transfer 2,640 shares to Mrs Good prior to sale.

	Total £	Mr Good £	Mrs Good £
Untapered gain	50,000	36,800	13,200
Taper relief @ 75%		(27,600)	—
		9,200	13,200
Annual exemption		9,200	9,200
Taxable gain		£Nil	£4,000
Capital gains tax @ 20%			£800

If Mr Good had sold the shares the liability would have been £1,320. The pre-sale transfer achieves a tax saving of £520.

Where capital losses are involved, then reference should be made to the new anti-avoidance provisions in FA 2007, s 27 which are considered in CHAPTER 12. The Ramsay principle could also be applied to such planning and the implications of that are considered in CHAPTER 13.

However, the position can be much more complex and involve reliefs (such as PPR) and tainted taper. The approach should always be to prepare detailed calculations and to ask the necessary questions up front to determine the best approach. There will usually be uncertainties as to the likely timing of disposals (especially, where properties are concerned) and also as to the likely level of taxable income in the year of disposal. It may be that the tax savings are too small in relation to the professional fees and grief involved in making any transfer.

Example – Pre-sale transfer planning – More complex scenario

Mr and Mrs Best are going to sell two properties. One property is a furnished holiday let, qualifying as a business property that they have owned for three years, which has made a gain of £100,000. The other is a flat in London, a non-business property which has made a gain of £120,000 over six years. Each are owned jointly as tenants-in-common. Mr and Mrs Best are both higher-rate taxpayers and Mr Best has losses brought forward of £100,000.

The CGT position is as follows:

	Mr Best £	Mrs Best £
Holiday let	50,000	50,000
London flat	60,000	60,000
	110,000	110,000
Losses brought forward	(100,000)	
	10,000	110,000
Taper relief (75% BATR)	(7,500)	(37,500)
(20% non-BATR)	—	(12,000)
	2,500	60,500
Annual exemption	(9,200)	(9,200)
Taxable gain	£Nil	£51,300
CGT payable @ 40%		£20,520

If, however, the properties are transferred prior to sale, so that Mr Best sells the London flat and Mrs Best sells the furnished holiday let, this will make much better use of the losses brought forward.

The CGT position would then be as follows:

	Mr Best £	Mrs Best £
Holiday let	—	100,000
London flat	120,000	—
	120,000	100,000
Losses brought forward	(100,000)	—
	20,000	100,000
Taper relief (75% BATR)	—	(75,000)
(20% non-BATR)	(4,000)	—
	16,000	25,000
Annual exemption	(9,200)	(9,200)
Taxable gain	£6,800	£15,800
CGT payable @ 40%	£2,720	£6,320
Total tax liability		£9,040

However, the position could be different if both properties are not sold in the same year of assessment. It would appear that the furnished holiday let has only been used as such but the usage of the London flat is not clear. The issue therefore is whether it has ever qualified as a PPR and, if so, for both of them – or for only one of them pre-marriage. If PPR relief is available then let property relief may also apply. In this case, if Mrs Best occupied the flat for six months as her PPR (maybe with some element of doubt as to whether it was a main residence on the facts) then a sale of that property by Mr Best would not be the best result. This is because in that case there would be PPR relief of 42 months (six months plus final 36 months) as well as let property relief.

Instead, it would be better for Mrs Best to dispose of all of the London flat as follows:

		Mr Best	Mrs Best
		£	£
Holiday let		100,000	—
London flat		—	120,000
		100,000	120,000
Less: losses		(91,800)	
PPR 42/72 months		—	(70,000)
Let property relief		—	(40,000)
		9,200	10,000
Taper relief	(75% bus)	(6,900)	
	(20% non-bus)		(2,000)
		2,300	8,000
Annual exemption		(9,200)	(9,200)
Taxable gain		£Nil	£Nil

If this was the outcome, then no CGT would be payable and losses of £9,200 would still be preserved to carry forward. If a higher-rate taxpayer, with losses brought forward, makes a capital gain on the sale of a business asset, the relief on losses may be as low as 10%, when only 1/4 of the gain on a business asset is chargeable. In addition, it is not possible to restrict the use of losses brought forward to preserve taper relief before applying the annual exemption. It may therefore be beneficial to transfer business property to a spouse and allow a tax liability to become chargeable, in order to preserve losses brought forward if these will be utilised in a more beneficial manner in the future.

In the above case, the PPR relief arises from a period prior to the marriage. Pre-sale transfers may be extremely straightforward and clearly beneficial but care is required that it is not automatically assumed to be in the best interests of the couple from a tax perspective.

Marriage and civil partnership breakdown

10.9 Where a couple has substantial assets, then it will be necessary to allocate these between the couple in the event of a divorce.

Where possible, substantial transfers of assets (particularly chargeable assets) between the parties should take place before the end of the tax year in which separation occurs. If this is not possible, for example where the couple separate towards the end of the tax year, the choice of assets to be transferred should be considered carefully having regard to the CGT consequences either for the transferor, where there is an immediate liability, or for the transferee, where a future disposition is being contemplated. The tax base cost of the asset should be obtained and documented in any event. It may be less readily forthcoming if requested later. Suitable assets to transfer on which little or no CGT should arise include the matrimonial home (assuming it qualifies for PPR relief), personal property subject to the chattels exemption, government gilts, assets showing losses which can offset against gains and those where the gains are less than the annual exemption, assets qualifying for substantial amounts of taper relief and those eligible for s 165 hold-over relief.

Where the transfer in question will give rise to a CGT liability the usual consideration of timing and splitting may reduce the total tax liability by allowing the realised gains to fall into different tax years, so permitting advantage to be taken of two annual exemptions. If the transferor's spouse/civil partner's CGT rate is likely to be lower in one tax year than another (for example due to their not working, studying or retiring), accelerating or delaying a transfer of assets could improve the CGT position.

Whilst it is clear that the time of disposal and acquisition is the time of the making of the agreement between the parties where disposal is by agreement (s 28), the position under a transfer pursuant to a court order is more complex. The disposal cannot be treated as taking place earlier than the date of the order, but if the order precedes the decree absolute, it only takes effect later on decree absolute by reason of the Matrimonial Causes Act 1973. There is therefore scope for adjusting the timing either by mutual agreement between the parties to accelerate some or all of the transfer or by mutually requesting that the court hearing is adjourned into a new tax year. In some cases, a favourable result can be achieved by asking the court to make an order for some assets and adjourning the hearing for the others.

Example – Timing of decree absolute

Assume a court order for the transfer of property late in a tax year with a decree absolute only due early in the following tax year – where a tax benefit would follow from making the disposal in the earlier tax year. The parties could achieve that benefit by agreeing to affect the transfer forthwith without waiting for the order to take effect. Indeed if the order related to two buy to let properties – Town Flat and City Flat, then it might be beneficial to accelerate the disposal of one property and not the other.

The reverse position can also apply where it is tax beneficial to push back the date of disposal.

HMRC's view as set out in Capital Gains Manual CG22403–22426 is that assets are disposed of for CGT purposes as follows:

(a) a court order following decree absolute/final dissolution order – the date of the court order;

(b) a consent order before decree absolute/final dissolution order – HMRC accepts the parties' agreement on the date of disposal if the tax at stake is small. They require supporting information and documentation where larger amounts of tax are involved;

(c) other court orders before the decree absolute/final dissolution order – the date of court order; or

(d) a contract – the date of contract.

HMRC consider that the exchange of property should be treated for CGT purposes as the acquisition by each spouse/civil partner of a new, exclusive beneficial interest in that part of the land which is allotted to them in exchange for the disposal. Under extra-statutory concession D26 roll-over relief under s 246 may be available if the land received does not include a dwelling house which is, or becomes, used as an only or main residence. Where the exchange of interests is unequal, only one spouse/civil partner will be able to claim complete deferral of the gain. The spouse/civil partner who is deemed not to have fully reinvested the payment in the new interest will have a chargeable gain. He or she may then require the other spouse/civil partner to pay them further compensation for the immediately chargeable gain. This issue is considered in more detail in CHAPTER 7.

Meaning of separation

10.10 It is not always easy to define the date of separation. It may be that the date has already been established by the solicitors advising the parties, however, often there is some doubt – especially if the break up is near the end of the tax year. Particular problems can arise where the couple own more than one property, say a country house and a city flat. The husband works in the city and he increasingly stays in the city at the weekend. In such a case, the date of separation may be open to doubt. A further point is that couples may often separate and then get back together again only for the relationship to eventually fail.

The tax adviser needs to be wary of being bullied into a position where advice is given on a marriage breakdown based upon a debatable date of separation. In such a case, it is safer to pursue a strategy that does not rely upon the couple 'living together as man and wife' for the purposes of s 58. The HMRC Relief Instructions Manual provides guidance on HMRC's view as to what constitutes reconciliation after a separation. This notes that 'it is possible for there to be a reconciliation without the couple moving back in together' (paragraph 1080).

Example – Property transfer on divorce

Pete and Kate have been married for several years. Their assets include two properties in Fore Street. One is let on an assured shorthold tenancy and the other is let as a furnished holiday let. Both properties are owned jointly as joint tenants.

Pete and Kate separated on 15 February 2005. After 6 April 2005, a transfer of their interest in the properties will be a disposal for CGT purposes. Hold-over relief under s 165 on divorce in respect of a furnished holiday let is considered below.

CGT planning issues on divorce

10.11 Tax planning in the event of a divorce is typically concerned with how best to partition the assets between the couple without a liability to CGT. The point is that there is no third party sale from which proceeds will be received to settle any tax payable and liability to CGT will only seek to limit the funds available to split between the parties to the divorce. Typically, the parties' objectives are not in conflict (ie both want to avoid a liability to CGT) and the adviser will therefore be jointly instructed as an independent expert to advise how best this can be achieved.

For business assets, there are options available although there can be complications. The most common CGT issues on divorce now arise on buy to let portfolios although other assets such as share portfolios could be involved.

Historically, the marital home was exempt due to PPR relief because of the generous exemption of the final 36 months in any event and also because of certain concessionary practices on the part of HMRC. However, as a result of FA 2006, Sch 20, there are now IHT issues where Mesher orders are involved which in turn have CGT complications.

Valuation Issues

10.12 It is important to ensure that the correct valuations are obtained when advising on divorce matters. Frequently valuations are provided for the entirety of properties rather than for a part share on which a discount would apply. Valuation issues are concerned in detail in CHAPTER 13 and the issue of the valuation discount is considered in CHAPTER 3.

Mesher orders

10.13 Section 225 provides for PPR relief to be extended to a gain accruing to the trustees of a settlement on a disposal of settled property where during the period of ownership the dwelling house was the only or main residence of a person entitled to occupy it under the terms of the settlement.

The HMRC Capital Gains Manual (CG65365) defines a Mesher order as 'an order by the Courts that a spouse holding an interest in the matrimonial home should hold it on trust for a limited period, for example, until remarriage of the other spouse or death of the other spouse or the 18th birthday of the youngest child of the marriage and entitling the other spouse to occupy the home for the trust period'.

The manual goes on to explain that this amounts to a trust arrangement and confirms that s 225 relief is available.

There is no exclusion in FA 2006, Sch 20 from the lifetime IHT charge for settlement created as part of a divorce settlement. An attempt to get some exclusion for divorce settlements during the Finance Bill Committee Stage was not successful. For CGT purposes, s 225 will continue to be available for such a Mesher order. However, as this will be a lifetime settlement, it will represent relevant property and so if the value of the house exceeds the nil rate band, there will be an immediate charge to IHT at the time of the divorce order. Depending on the age of the children, it could be in trust for quite a while. The likely planning will now be to try and avoid having a Mesher order because of the IHT consequences. If that is the case, then the benefit of PPR relief under s 225 will also have to be sacrificed. However, a lifetime settlement will open up the possibility of a future claim for hold-over relief under s 260 although it is difficult to see what benefit it provides. In addition, a future claim for PPR is prevented where a s 260 hold-over claim is made (see CHAPTER 8).

Hold-over relief under s 165

10.14 The possible existence of actual consideration frequently gives rise to difficulty where assets are transferred. If the transfer takes place during the tax year of separation then no claim for s 165 hold-over relief is required. However, a later transfer of assets may well be made in exchange for the transferee giving up or surrendering the right to receive financial provision.

For many years HMRC maintained that, whether the transfer was made as the result of a court order, by consent after a divorce decree had become absolute or without recourse to the courts, the value of the right surrendered would comprise 'actual consideration'. Comments made by Coleridge J in G v G [2002] EWHC 1339, in a judgment made available on 31 July 2002 caused HMRC to change their approach. In the absence of recourse to the courts, no change in the earlier approach was required. Where there is such recourse, and a court makes an order for ancillary relief under the Matrimonial Causes Act 1973 resulting in a transfer of assets from one spouse to another, or makes an order formally ratifying an agreement reached by the divorcing parties dealing with the transfer of assets, a different approach is required. In this situation it is now the view of HMRC that the spouse to whom the assets are transferred does not give 'actual consideration' in the form of surrendered rights as the order reflects the exercise by the courts of independent statutory jurisdiction.

This change in direction also applies to similar orders made under the Family Law (Scotland) Act 1985. The revised approach, which was made available in August 2003, extends to new claims for hold-over relief made on or after 31 July 2002 and also to outstanding claims which remained unsettled on that date. Therefore, with appropriate planning and documentation, there is considerable scope to take advantage of s 165 hold-over relief on a divorce.

Conclusions

10.15   Tax planning opportunities arise from the ability to transfer assets between spouses/civil partners on a no gain/no loss basis without restarting the period of ownership and whilst still qualifying for certain CGT reliefs. Marriage and civil partnerships have what can only be described as a strange half-way house status within the CGT code, with a mixture of joint taxation and separate assessment. This peculiar status can give rise to both tax planning approaches as well as potential pitfalls for the uninformed.

Checklist

	Cross Reference
Marriage and Divorce (including Civil Partnerships)	
Capital gains cannot arise on transfers between spouses or civil partners living together as man and wife because of s 58. The position changes if the spouses or civil partners separate.	
Whilst in general terms marriage and civil partnerships are very useful in terms of tax planning, such arrangements can be restrictive such as in respect of the limitation on only one principal private residence.	
There are long-term planning issues to consider in terms of the ownership of assets between spouses and civil partners.	10.4
Where transfer between spouses or civil partners take place in a tax year after the year of separation, then careful CGT planning is required.	10.11

Chapter 11

Trusts and Estates Planning

Background to planning involving trusts and estates

11.1   The motives for settling money on trust are primarily non-tax, such as to provide for a widow where there are children from a former marriage or to provide a home for a mentally incapacitated child. However, there are also tax planning advantages in establishing trusts and even those trusts set up to provide security for loved-ones will have tax implications for the individuals involved.

Where the motives are tax orientated, it is now fairly unusual for capital gains tax (CGT) to be the driving force. Instead, the desire to make a gift into trust will normally be fuelled by inheritance tax (IHT) objectives. If there was no tax on the death estate, then many potential settlors would simply retain their wealth until they died. (That said, the set up of some trusts is prompted by the desire to save income tax – usually as part of funding school fees, etc.)

However, even if CGT is not the driving force, advisers still need to take care when a trust is established. Section 70 provides that a CGT charge arises when assets are transferred into settlement and as such, planning is required to avoid this charge. This will invariably involve utilising hold-over relief under s 260. This is considered in CHAPTER 8. Bespoke planning in relation to the types of asset most commonly transferred into trust; land and buildings, unquoted shares in family companies and quoted securities, is also considered elsewhere in this book.

Further, CGT has also historically been a barrier to the winding up of a trust and so should also be considered as part of any type of trust reorganisation exercise. It is within this context then that the adviser requires a broad awareness of the complex legislation that applies to trusts. Whilst this chapter is far from exhaustive it endeavours to provide a basic framework of the key CGT issues relevant to trust and estate planning.

All statutory references in this chapter are to TCGA 1992 unless otherwise stated.

Estates and deeds of variation

11.2   A transfer of assets to a beneficiary under a will is not a chargeable disposal for CGT purposes as the beneficiaries of the estate inherit the assets at probate value and are deemed to acquire them at the date of death. Significant tax planning opportunities are presented by deeds of variation under IHTA 1984, s 142. It may be possible to vary an estate to benefit taxpayers with more favourable CGT, losses, etc. Such deeds can be used to rewrite a will within two years of the date of death as long as all the beneficiaries agree. They are effective for IHT purposes and therefore by extension to CGT as a result of s 62 but it should be remembered that deeds of variation are ineffective for income tax purposes. Advisers should be aware that the instrument varying a disposition must contain a statement that it is intended that the appropriate CGT provision will apply. Deeds of variation are also considered in CHAPTER 15.

Probate values and CGT

11.3   From a CGT planning perspective, where an asset stands at a substantial gain there can be an advantage in retaining certain assets until the time of death so that they can benefit from the probate value uplift. In such cases it is important to consider the IHT business property relief (BPR) and agricultural property relief (APR) status of an asset. Advisers need to take care to avoid creating wider tax problems as a knock-on result of CGT planning especially as things can look very different in hindsight.

From an estate planning perspective it is good to transfer high growth assets out of an estate but it should be borne in mind that such assets could also fall in value. It was fashionable during the stock market boom to transfer quoted shares to discretionary trusts using hold-over relief under s 260. However, if death occurs within seven years then the value of the gift is fixed at the time of transfer (even though the shares may have fallen in value) and no probate value uplift is available on death.

Since personal representatives, legatees or other persons are deemed to acquire assets at the time of death for a consideration reflecting market value, the determination of that probate value is important. Section 274 provides that where the value of an asset has been determined on death for IHT purposes, this will also establish the market value to be used for CGT. (This is subject to an anomaly regarding the related property rules for IHT purposes. In such cases there will be a mismatch between the rules for the two taxes with the value for IHT being higher than the new base cost for CGT.)

Where IHT is payable, the executor may seek to try and use the lowest value possible in order to minimise the IHT due. However, advisers should consider that a low value may be disadvantageous when calculating chargeable gains in the future. This is particularly relevant if a sale is intended in the future and the additional amount of IHT payable, if any, is less than the potential reduction in CGT due on a subsequent disposal.

A not very pleasant CGT planning approach that can be undertaken arises in situations where a married client or one in a civil partnership has been diagnosed as having a terminal illness. In such a case the approach is for the healthy spouse to transfer assets to the terminally ill spouse on a no gain/no loss basis under s 58 in the knowledge that the assets will be passed back to them under the terms of the will of the terminally ill spouse.

Example – Terminal illness

Eva has been diagnosed as having terminal cancer. Her husband, Albert, transferred his personal share portfolio to Eva as it is pregnant with capital gains. He also transfers to Eva a let investment property which has a large pregnant gain. Eva's will provides for a nil rate band discretionary trust and for the residue of her estate to pass to Albert and so benefit from the spouse exemption. The assets are re-valued on death for probate value.

Realisation of estate assets

11.4   Assets forming part of a deceased person's estate will frequently be realised by the personal representatives and the surplus proceeds, after the satisfaction of IHT and other outgoings, distributed to legatees. Alternatively, assets may be distributed in specie to the legatees who can either retain those assets or sell them. Where a sale is contemplated it may be possible to arrange for this to be carried out by either the personal representatives or the legatees themselves. This type of planning is likely to be particularly appropriate where the administration of an estate takes some time so that the value of property in the estate has risen significantly. As estates are subject to CGT at 40% and only have a single annual exemption it may be beneficial for the executors to transfer chargeable assets standing at a gain to beneficiaries in specie so that the beneficiaries then realise the gain on sale. This could mean benefiting from any basic rate tax bands and annual exemptions available to the joint owners which would invariably be more beneficial than CGT being paid by the executors at 40%.

Careful planning is required here though. In some cases it may still be more beneficial for a sale to be made by an executor particularly where there are losses or reliefs that are only available to the executor or where all of the beneficiaries are higher-rate taxpayers and utilise their annual exemptions every year. Advisers may wish to consider such planning combined with a deed of variation.

Example – Sale of asset by personal representatives or beneficiaries

Mrs Bohan died on 1 April 2005 (2004/05) leaving an estate of £750,000 jointly between her four children, each of whom have an annual income of

£10,000. The estate included amenity land with no business use and a derelict building, valued in total, at £25,000 at the date of death. The executor received an offer of £400,000 from developers to redevelop the land and derelict building, subject to planning permission being available. Planning permission is secured on 1 May 2007.

If the executor sells the property in 2007/08 for £400,000, then the CGT liability is as follows:

	Notes	£	£
Proceeds			400,000
Base cost (probate)		25,000	
Cost of obtaining probate	1	(200)	
			(24,800)
Annual exemption	2		—
Taxable gain			£375,200
CGT at 40%			£150,080

1In accordance with Statement of Practice 2/04, for estates valued between £500,000 and £1 million, 0.8% of the cost of the asset is allowed as a deduction. This is considered further below.

2Annual exemptions are only available in the year of death and the following two tax years.

Alternatively, the executor could distribute the property to the beneficiaries prior to sale, who could then sell the asset together, as a jointly-owned asset. The CGT liability would then be calculated as follows:

	£	£
Proceeds		400,000
Base cost (probate value)		(25,000)
		£375,000
1/4 share thereof	93,750	
Less: annual exemption	(9,200)	
Taxable gain	£84,550	
Tax		
£29,825 x 20% =	5,965	
£54,725 x 40% =	21,890	
	£27,855	
Total CGT liability (£27,855 x 4)		£111,420

The CGT saving on a disposal of the property jointly by the beneficiaries, rather than by the executor, is £38,660.

No deduction is allowed under Statement of Practice 2/04 when the asset is sold by the beneficiaries as it only applies to the executor or personal representatives of the deceased. Statement of Practice 2/04 should always be considered as part of any CGT planning where estates are concerned. Specifically, it allows for relief to be given for a proportion of valuation costs and the costs of obtaining probate. The relief is calculated on a scale linked to the gross value of the estate. The higher the gross asset value, the lower the percentage relief entitlement.

Planning whereby assets are distributed to beneficiaries and then sold will most commonly be used for quoted shares and securities and for property assets. Where property assets are concerned, particular issues arise on the former principal private residence (PPR) or where a property is occupied by a beneficiary during the administration of the estate. The issues covered below are also relevant to trustees.

Private residences

11.5 It is possible for a claim to be made for PPR relief to apply to a property owned by trustees. This is provided that the property is occupied as a main residence by a beneficiary who is entitled to do so under the terms of the settlement. This is set out in s 225. HMRC's view is that s 225 can only apply where there is an interest in possession and so is not available to discretionary trusts. Their view, however, is on the basis that Statement of Practice 10/79 is still current and this is not universally accepted by the profession.

Under s 225A, PPR relief also extends to a property held by an executor but occupied as a main residence by one or more individuals entitled to an absolute interest or an interest in possession in a substantial part of the sale proceeds. For this purpose HMRC interpret this as 75% or more of the proceeds. The PPR relief in such a case must be claimed.

In both cases, the availability of PPR can provide distinct CGT planning opportunities for advisers. Further, as well as for more formal trust arrangements, s 225 is, in practice, used in implied trusts both from conduct and divorce arrangements. Implied trusts can arise from conduct such as where a property may be bought to be occupied by a relative but with no intention of an absolute gift to that person. This is particularly the case then where the property may be owned by different persons from the occupant. In such cases, advisers will need to take care. Given that any such implied trusts can only ever represent an interest in possession, these arrangements would not previously have given rise to any IHT consequences unless death occurred within seven years of the life tenant giving up their interest in the property. However, if such trusts are now implied in order to take advantage of CGT exemptions, there are likely to be immediate IHT consequences and possible liabilities following the changes to trust legislation in FA 2006. This is explored further in CHAPTER 15.

In terms of CGT planning, advisers should also be aware that PPR relief is denied following a hold-over relief claim. This is by virtue of s 226A and this may now impact more widely because of the greater scope for claiming s 260 hold-over relief. Section 226A provides that PPR relief is not available if the allowable expenditure on the disposal would be reduced as the result of a hold-over claim under s 260 on one or more earlier disposals of the property. Prior to 10 December 2003, discretionary trusts could be used to 'wash out' gains on second homes. The capital gain could be held over when the property was transferred into the settlement and the property could then be lived in by the beneficiary. Alternatively, the property could be transferred out to a beneficiary, again using hold–over relief, and then used as a private residence. However, this is no longer the case although for disposals on which hold-over relief was claimed and occurred before 10 December 2003, transitional relief is available. PPR relief may be given as if the property had ceased to be occupied as a PPR on 10 December 2003 but without the last 36 months of ownership. The issue of hold-over relief in such circumstances is considered in further detail in CHAPTER 8 and also in CHAPTER 9.

Example – Sale of asset by personal representatives or beneficiaries and PPR

Romeo died in June 2007 leaving a property in his estate. Juliet lived with Romeo and is continuing to occupy the property. The property is now worth £500,000 having been valued at £400,000 for probate purposes. The estate is to be divided between two beneficiaries (Juliet and Susie). Susie is a higher-rate taxpayer. Should the property be distributed to the beneficiaries prior to any sale?

	Sale by Personal Representatives	Sale by Beneficiaries	
		Susie	Juliet
	£	£	£
Expected proceeds	500,000	250,000	250,000
Probate value	(400,000)	(200,000)	(200,000)
Gain	100,000	50,000	50,000
PPR relief			(50,000)
Annual exemption	(9,200)	(9,200)	
	£90,800	£40,800	£Nil
CGT @ 40%	£36,320	£16,320	£Nil

(This example ignores the deduction under Statement of Practice 2/04).

No PPR relief is due to the personal representatives as Juliet is only entitled to half the proceeds and not the 75% level required for s 225A. If the beneficiaries sell the property, then the CGT reduces to £16,320 compared with £36,320 if the property is sold by the personal representatives. However, there may be issues between Juliet and Susie in terms of the distribution of the estate as Susie will have a CGT liability and Juliet will not. This raises some of the possibilities that may arise if a deed of variation is also considered. For instance, if Susie is married or in a civil partnership then her share of the property could be appointed out to both her and her husband. There may be capital or trading losses available to one or other. She might be non-resident.

Advisers should also bear in mind that s 225A can pose further problems in that a further condition stipulated is that immediately before and immediately after the death of the deceased person, the property must be the only or main residence of those individuals.

In cases where a gift has been subject to a reservation of benefit there is also no probate value uplift. This issue is particularly common where a house has been given away (usually to try and avoid care home fees) and the former owner has continued to occupy the property. The dramatic rise in house prices over the last decade has meant that often the new owners have a substantial liability to CGT if the house is sold either prior to, or before, the occupier's death. If the arrangements amount to a trust arrangement then it may be possible to claim PPR relief under s 225 or otherwise benefit from the probate value uplift for trustees under s 73.

Termination of an interest in possession

11.6 Under s 72, the position for many years has been that on the death of a person entitled to an interest in possession and the termination of the trust at that stage, there is a deemed disposal by the trustees together with a deemed reacquisition at market value. However, no chargeable gain arises. Following the widespread changes to the treatment of trusts contained in FA 2006 the position is now that when the life tenant dies s 72 will only apply if the interest in possession is one of the following:

(a) an immediate post death interest (IPDI);

(b) an interest to which the beneficiary became entitled before 22 March 2006;

(c) a transitional serial interest (TSI);

(d) a trust for a bereaved minor (TBM) where the minor has an interest in possession;

(e) a disabled persons trust; or

(f) an 18–25 trust where the deceased unusually has an interest in possession and dies under the age of 18.

Where the interest is within any of the above, then:

(i) to the extent that the property continues to be settled property there is a deemed disposal and reacquisition by the trustees at market value, but no chargeable gain or allowable loss will arise because of the probate value uplift;

(ii) to the extent that it ceases to be settled property the disposal under s 71(1) generates neither chargeable gains nor allowable losses; and

(iii) if the settled property passed into trust which is subject to a hold-over claim, the above exemptions are lifted, but the chargeable gain is restricted to the amount held over.

No chargeable gains arise on a beneficiary where he or she disposes of an interest in a settlement unless the interest was acquired for money or monies worth.

Person becoming absolutely entitled to capital

11.7 In accordance with s 71(1), trustees are deemed to dispose of trust property and immediately reacquire it at current market value when a person becomes absolutely entitled to trust property. For instance this would commonly have occurred on a beneficiary of an accumulation and maintenance settlement achieving age 21 or 25.

A person becomes absolutely entitled as against the trustees of the trust if he has the exclusive right to direct how the property is to be dealt with. If the trustees still hold the land partly for other beneficiaries of the trust, the beneficiary who would normally have become absolutely entitled only has an undivided share in the land, effectively an entitlement to a share of the proceeds of sale when the land is sold. As such the beneficiary has not become absolutely entitled to the share at this time so there is no deemed disposal.

If the deemed disposal takes place other than on a death, the disposal is usually charged to CGT. Hold-over relief under s 260 is available if:

(a) IHT is chargeable (eg an appointment out of a relevant property trust);

(b) a beneficiary of a TBM or age 18–25 trust becomes absolutely entitled to capital (s 260(2)(da) and (db)); or

(c) a beneficiary of an accumulation and maintenance trust becomes absolutely entitled to capital before 6 April 2008 (but only if they have previously had an interest in possession) or after 5 April 2008 if they must take capital at or before age 18 (s 260(2)(d)).

Where the death of the beneficiary also triggers an IHT charge (ie because the trust assets are included in his death estate as his settled property) the gain may be able to be held over again under s 260. If s 260 does not apply (eg because the assets are passing to a surviving spouse/civil partner and the assets are therefore exempt from IHT for the beneficiary) and the assets are business or agricultural property, gift relief may be available under s 165.

Where a loss arises on the deemed disposal, this must be offset first against the gains for the trustees. Excess losses may be passed down to beneficiaries under s 71(2) but may only be offset against future gains on the same assets and are therefore 'clogged losses'.

Sub-funds

11.8 A trust with several funds is a single settlement for CGT purposes, even if the assets and beneficiaries are entirely separate. Further, as confirmed by *Roome v Edwards* [1982] AC 279, [1981] STC 96, it would be possible for different funds of the same settlement to have different trustees. On a practical level, this can cause difficulties, as it means that the capital gains will have to be returned on one tax return and there are issues on how the annual exemption should be utilised between the funds as well as treatment of losses, etc. Such a situation of different funds can easily arise where a grandchildren's settlement was set up and there are different groups of cousins representing the funds in the settlements. Those cousins may not feel that they want much to do with the other family members outside of their immediate siblings.

As part of the trust reforms which were introduced in FA 2006, the ability to separate out sub-funds into separate trust funds was introduced. This had been much lobbied for and the new legislation is contained in s 69A and Sch 4ZA. A sub-fund election is possible where two conditions are satisfied:

(1) The sub-fund must not include an interest in an asset, where other interests in the asset are held elsewhere in the settlement.

(2) A person cannot be a beneficiary under both the sub-fund and the rest of the settlement.

It is necessary to elect for sub-fund treatment under Sch 4ZA, para 2 and the election must be made by the anniversary of 31 January following the year of assessment in which the date of the election is to take effect.

Whilst there was much hope that the ability to elect for sub-fund treatment would simplify trust administration and provide greater flexibility for families, no form of hold-over relief has been introduced with the sub-fund election such that the date of the election is deemed to be a disposal for CGT purposes. As no new form of hold-over relief is available it will be necessary to satisfy the conditions of ss 165 or 260 in order to avoid a CGT liability. As a result, so far, the ability to elect for sub-fund treatment has not been widely adopted, although it may become more widespread as entitlement to s 260 hold-over relief broadens as a result of the FA 2006 changes.

Example – Sub-funds

The Red Fund, Orange Fund, Yellow Fund and Green Fund are the four sub-funds of the Rainbow Trust.

For 2006/07 the annual CGT exemption for trusts was £4,400. This exemption belongs to all sub-funds of the Rainbow Trust collectively rather than being split equally between them (ie they do not get £1,100 each).

The sub-funds make gains after losses and taper relief, etc as follows:

Red	£Nil
Orange	£100
Yellow	£900
Green	£100,000

Agreement is reached with HMRC for the total gains to be reported on the tax return for the Yellow Fund and CGT is calculated as follows:

	£
Capital gains	£101,000
Less: annual exemption	(4,400)
Taxable gains	£96,600

CGT @ 40% = £38,640

Agreement needs to be reached between the trustees of the sub-funds as to how the CGT is split. It would seem unfair to pro-rate the exemption by reference to the gains as this would mean that the CGT is split as follows:

Red	£Nil (CGT £Nil)
Orange	£100/101,000 x 4,400 = £4 (CGT £38)
Yellow	£900/101,000 x 4,400 = £39 (CGT £344)
Green	£100,000/101,000 x 4,400 = £4,357 (CGT £38,258)

The Orange and Yellow Funds have a CGT liability only because the Green Fund has made such a large gain. This scenario makes it very difficult for the trustees of the sub-funds to carry out any CGT planning as they do not know what their share of the exemption will be.

A fairer approach is more likely to be for the exemption to be initially split equally (£1,100 each for 2006/07) and then to the extent that any of the sub-funds have a balance of their entitlement unused, the balance can be shared equally between the other funds and so on. Therefore in this example, the Orange and Yellow funds' gains will be covered by their share of the exemptions and the Green fund will receive the unused exemptions of £1,100 from Red, £1,000 from Orange and £200 from Yellow. The CGT position becomes as follows:

Red	£Nil
Orange	£Nil
Yellow	£Nil
Green	£38,640

If gains were made as follows:

Red	£Nil
Orange	£1,000
Yellow	£9,000
Green	£100,000

Then the CGT position would become:

Red and Orange have unused exemptions of £1,100 and £100 respectively = £1,200. This is then split equally (£600 each) between Yellow and Green so they then have exemptions of £1,700 each to offset their share of the gains.

This approach ensures that each sub-fund has an equal entitlement to a share of the annual exemption but if the trustees do not use it all it is recycled between the other sub-funds so it is not wasted. Advisers should note that the allocation of the exemption needs to be agreed by each set of trustees (who may require guidance from their advisers).

Taper relief considerations

11.9 For trustees, business asset status for taper relief purposes can also be by reference to an 'eligible beneficiary'. This was originally relevant in terms of the full-time working requirement and is now still relevant by reference to employment. There are some apportionment rules in Sch A1, para 8 where the trust assets relate to a mix of eligible and non-eligible beneficiaries.

The effect of s 62 is to treat the shares as acquired on death. However, a legatee does not actually become entitled to the shares until either the residue of the deceased's estate is ascertained or the executor agrees to the transfer of the shares. As such there is a period of the legatee's deemed ownership when it is the personal representatives who have the voting rights. Therefore, Sch A1, para 4(5) provides that:

'the asset shall be taken to have been a business asset ... [during the period between death and transfer] if at that time:

(a) it was held by the personal representatives of the deceased; and

(b) the relevant company was a qualifying company by reference to the personal representatives.'

Offshore trusts

11.10 As a result of tax changes introduced throughout the 1990s, CGT planning for offshore settlements is now fraught with difficulties. In particular, opportunities are very limited where the settlor is a UK resident and domiciled individual. For the purposes of this book and for completeness it is worth briefly recapping on the anti-avoidance regime applying to non-UK resident settlements. Specifically, tax advisers may have clients with attributed gains under the following rules and need to consider the implications as part of some wider tax planning. As will be clear from the following, the rules are complex and what follows is intended to be a straightforward guide rather than a detailed analysis. As will be seen, there are planning opportunities for non-UK domiciled individuals. Domicile is considered further in CHAPTER 14.

For CGT purposes, trustees are treated as a 'single and continuing' body of persons in accordance with s 69. Hence, if the trustees (as a body) are UK resident then they will be liable to UK CGT and if they are non-UK resident there will be no such liability. In accordance with s 69 the trustees will be treated as non-UK resident if:

(a) all the trustees are non-UK resident; or

(b) if at least one trustee is non-UK resident and the settlor was not resident, nor ordinarily resident and the settlor was not domiciled in the UK at the relevant time.

A trustee who is not resident in the UK is treated as UK resident if he acts as a trustee in the course of a business carried on through a branch, agency or permanent establishment in the UK.

Protectors, appointed by the settlor (such as in the Isle of Man), can also offer some reassurance to clients uncomfortable with the concept of an offshore trust, as they can supervise the actions of the trustees and ensure they are acting in accordance with the trust deed and in the best interests of the beneficiaries. A protector is, therefore, a useful mechanism for a settlor who has some concern about giving away his assets to a third party. However, care must be taken when deciding on the extent of the protector's powers. Extensive powers can, aside from making a trust difficult to administer, also carry the risk of HMRC arguing that the administration of the trust is carried on by the protector in the UK – if the protector is UK resident.

Trust emigration from the UK

11.11 If a UK resident trust becomes non-resident, then in accordance with s 80, the trustees are deemed to have sold the trust assets at market value and reacquired, so that a deemed disposal takes place. If the UK resident trustees fail to pay a s 80 charge within six months of the due date, HMRC can require any unpaid tax and interest to be paid by any trustee who had resigned in the 12 months before the trust become non-UK resident.

The charge does not apply to UK assets used by the trustees for a trade carried on in the UK through a branch or agency immediately after emigrating as they remain chargeable under s 10. Exemption from charge also applies to assets which would have been exempt under a double tax agreement had the trustees disposed of them immediately before emigrating. Roll–over relief under s 152 is not available for gains realised before emigration where the replacement asset is acquired after emigration unless it is situated in the UK and used in a trade carried on by the trustees through a branch or agency. In order to prevent CGT planning which made use of double tax treaties, s 83A was introduced in 2005. This applies to disposals by trustees provided that:

(a) they are made in a year in which the trustees are 'within the charge to CGT'; and

(b) the trustees are non-resident at the time of the disposal.

A year 'within the charge to CGT' is defined in s 83A(3), as one during any part of which the trustees are resident (or ordinarily resident) in the UK but not 'treaty non-resident'.

Trustees are non-UK resident at a particular time if they are:

(i) neither resident nor ordinarily resident in the UK; or

(ii) resident or ordinarily resident, but 'treaty non-resident'.

If the above conditions apply, then nothing in a double tax treaty is to be read as preventing the trustees being chargeable to CGT on that gain or to cater for settlor interested trusts within s 77 as preventing a tax charge arising whether or not to trustees.

Under s 85(1) the exemption for gains on disposals of interests in trusts does not apply to interests in non-UK resident trusts. Therefore, if a beneficiary disposes of his interest whilst the trust is non-UK resident, even if the beneficiary is one for whose benefit the interest was created, or who acquired the interest otherwise than for consideration in money or money's worth, a chargeable gain may arise. However, where the trust was UK resident and then becomes non-UK resident so that a charge arises on the trust under s 80, then under s 85(3) there is an uplift in value of the base cost of the beneficiary's interest to the market value of the interest immediately before the emigration of the trustees.

The uplift in value under this provision was exploited by certain offshore trusts. Trustees of offshore trusts which had realised but not attributed gains ('stockpiled gains') brought the trust onshore and then re-exported it. The stockpiled gains were not subject to UK tax since they were made whilst the trust was offshore and the trustees usually had no or little gains under s 80. The beneficiary, however, could sell his interest once the trust was offshore again and would have a high base cost. The uplift in the beneficiary's interest on emigration did not apply in such circumstances.

In the absence of any particular anti-avoidance legislation, the UK will generally not seek to impose a liability to CGT on foreign trustees, as they will fall outside the initial scope of the charge being neither UK resident nor UK ordinarily resident. This does not extend to the situation of the trust trading in the UK through a branch or agency as this is covered by s 10. This is unlikely to be common in practice but would catch, for example, such trustees owning and farming UK farmland. However, the legislation does impose CGT charges firstly on the settlor who has retained an interest if he is domiciled and resident in the UK (a s 86 charge) or otherwise on gains attributed to beneficiaries who are domiciled and resident in the UK (a s 87 charge).

Liability to CGT of beneficiaries of an offshore trust

11.12 Trust gains are only assessed on beneficiaries if they are not already assessed on the settlor in the tax year. The trustee's gains are calculated as if they were resident in the UK but no annual exemption is available. To these gains are added those brought forward from earlier years resulting in trust gains for the year. Capital payments made to the beneficiaries are then matched against these gains. In each year all capital payments made in that year are added together and gains are matched to capital payments on a first in/first out basis. There is a supplementary charge under s 91 on beneficiaries receiving capital payments where there is a delay between the time that the gain arose and the distribution of capital to the beneficiaries.

The gains are attributed under s 87 to a beneficiary who received a capital payment from the trust. Gains are only chargeable on beneficiaries who are both UK domiciled and either resident or ordinarily resident in the UK in the year of attribution. There is no form of remittance basis where the beneficiary is resident but not domiciled as in that case the attributed gains are simply not charged. The gains attributed to a beneficiary cannot exceed the amount of capital payments received by him. Gains attributed to a beneficiary are deemed to be gains realised by him in the year of assessment in which attribution takes place (ie not necessarily the year in which the gain was made). Care is required where beneficiaries are only temporarily non-resident under s 10A.

A capital payment is any payment from the trust (if received by a beneficiary who is resident or ordinarily resident in the UK) that is not charged to income tax in the hands of the beneficiary or (if received by a beneficiary who is not resident or ordinarily resident in the UK) is not received as income. It includes the transfer of an asset from the trust, the conferring of any benefit (eg a loan) and a beneficiary becoming absolutely entitled against the trustees.

A beneficiary is deemed to have received capital payment from the trust if:

(a)   he receives it directly or indirectly;

(b)   it is applied, either directly or indirectly, for his benefit; or

(c)   it is received by a third party at his direction.

The amount of capital payment made by way of loan or as a payment or something other than money is the value of the benefit conferred by it.

For example, if a loan is made on beneficial terms the capital payment is not the amount of the loan but the value of the beneficial terms of the loan as they differ from normal commercial terms appropriate to the circumstances, eg interest foregone if the loan is interest free. In practice, HMRC usually use the official rate of interest as an indication of commercial interest.

Example – Attributed gains

A non-UK resident trust has the following gains/losses:

Years		Gain £	Loss £
1996/97		12,000	6,000
1997/98		25,000	37,000
1998/99		104,000	2,000

The two beneficiaries, Alan and Brian, are resident and ordinarily resident in the UK. Alan is domiciled in the UK. Brian was not domiciled in the UK before 6 February 1999. He then became domiciled in the UK.

The trustees make the following payments to Alan and Brian:

Years		Alan £	Brian £
1996/97		Nil	Nil
1997/98		20,000	30,000
1998/99		35,000	35,000

The position for each year is as follows:

1996/97: The trust gains are £6,000 (£12,000 – £6,000). As there are no capital payments, the gains go forward to 1997/98.

1997/98: The trust gains are £6,000 (brought forward from 1996–1997). The losses must reduce gains of the same or later years therefore the loss of £12,000 (£37,000 – £25,000) must go forward to 1998/99. The trustees made capital payments of £50,000. Trust gains are attributed to the beneficiaries in proportion to the payment each received.

Alan 20,000/50,000 x 6,000 = £2,400

Brian 30,000/50,000 x 6,000 = £3,600

Alan is chargeable on £2,400. Brian is not chargeable on the £3,600 attributed to him if not remitted. This is because he is not domiciled in the UK. The process has not used up all the capital payments. The balance goes forward to 1998/99 (Alan £17,600 (£20,000 less 2,400), Brian £26,400 (£30,000 less £3,600)).

1998/99: The trust gains are £90,000 (£104,000 – £2,000 – £12,000). The capital payments are:

Description	Amount £
Made 1998/99	70,000
Brought forward	44,000
Total	114,000

Alan's share of payments is £52,600 (£35,000 + £17,600) and Brian's share of payments is £61,400 (£35,000 + £26,400). The attributed gains are:

Alan 52,600/114,000 x 90,000 = £41,526

Brian 61,400/114,000 x 90,000 = £48,474

Alan is chargeable on £41,526. Brian is chargeable on the £48,474 attributed to him. This is because he was domiciled in the UK at some time in the year.

The process has used all the gains and losses, however, there is still a balance of unused capital payments. This balance goes forward to 1999/2000 as follows:

Alan £11,074 (£52,600 – £41,526)

Brian £12,926 (£61,400 – £48,474)

Gains attributed under s 87 are treated as the lowest slice of the individual's gains which is important for the supplementary charge under s 91. The supplementary charge applies to effectively charge interest where there is a timing difference between the trustees realising the gain and a later capital payment to a beneficiary. For example a gain is made in 1999/2000 but is not attributed to the beneficiary until 2003/04.

The supplementary charge under s 91 is 10% per annum, up to a maximum of six years. The supplementary charge cannot exceed six years and cannot exceed the amount of the capital payment. For a higher-rate taxpayer, the maximum effective supplementary charge is therefore 64%. This extra charge does not apply if the beneficiary is non-UK resident or non-UK domiciled. There is no form of remittance basis if the beneficiary is resident but not domiciled in the UK. The gains are not charged.

In an attempt to monitor trust gains and capital payments, HMRC issue forms 50FS asking for details of a possible tax liability of the settlor and beneficiary. HMRC use the forms to calculate tax liabilities and pass this information onto the individual's self-assessment office. The aim is that HMRC are able to verify returns without having to open an enquiry.

Settlor-interested settlements

11.13   As already explained, from a tax planning perspective the objective is usually to want to gift assets into trust so as to reduce a person's estate for IHT purposes. As such, advisers need to be aware that it is vital to avoid a trust being settlor interested. Previously, and as explained in CHAPTER 8, it was possible to restart the taper relief clock by transferring an asset to a settler-interested life interest settlement. Such tax planning can still be relevant where the desire is to crystallise a CGT disposal for other CGT planning purposes such as to use losses or to claim another relief. Therefore the definition of 'settlor-interested' is important.

Where either the settlor or his spouse retains an interest in a UK resident trust, then s 77 provides that a CGT charge will arise on the settlor, rather than the trustees. A settlor is regarded as having an interest in the trust property if the trust property is (or will or may become) payable to or applicable for the benefit of the settlor or his spouse/civil partner or a minor child in any circumstances whatsoever. Specifically, s 77(2) stipulates that:

'a settlor shall be regarded as having an interest in a settlement if:

(a)   any property which is or may at any time be comprised in the settlement, or any derived property is, or will or may become, payable to or applicable for the benefit of the settlor or his spouse or civil partner in any circumstances whatsoever, or

(b)   the settlor or his spouse or civil partner enjoys a benefit deriving directly or indirectly from any property which is comprised in the settlement or any derived property.'

The extension to spouse/civil partner does not include a person to whom the settlor is not for the time being married but may later marry, or is separated from under a court order or separation agreement in such circumstances that the separation is likely to be permanent, or the widow or widower or surviving civil partner of the settlor.

A minor child is a person under the age of 18 years, including both a stepchild and an illegitimate child. Trust income that is paid to or for the benefit of a minor child of the settlor is treated as the income of the settlor. A capital distribution to a child of the settlor is also taxed as the settlor's income to the extent that it exceeds retained income in the settlement that has not been allocated to income expenses or otherwise treated as income of the settlor.

The settlor and his or her spouse should avoid providing any kind of benefit or the making of arrangements in favour of the settlement which involve the settlor being reimbursed out of settlement income or capital. A capital distribution from the settlement to the settlor will also be treated as the settlor's income to the extent that it matches income received by the settlement in the tax year in which the capital distribution is paid. This includes any sum paid otherwise than for full consideration, and any loan, or any loan repayment.

The concept of derived property in s 77 (or related property in ITTOIA 2005, s 624) in relation to any property, means income from that property or any other property directly or indirectly representing proceeds of, or of income from that property or income from it. The leading case on the meaning of derived property is the House of Lords decision in *West v Trennery* [2005] STC 214, HL. This case concerned a 'flip flop' scheme on the sale of shares which involved use of two settlements with a transfer between them funded by borrowing prior to the actual sale of the asset.

Specifically in this case, the taxpayers owned shares in an unquoted bus company, which were to be sold to a quoted company for a substantial cash consideration and which were pregnant with gain that would be taxed at 40%. If a settlor or his spouse had an interest in a settlement then the gains would be taxed on him. The taxpayer and his advisers sought to arrange matters so that the gains on the disposal of the shares would accrue to the trustees of a settlement in which he had no interest, while a substantial financial benefit accrued to a settlement in which he did enjoy an interest. If the shares could be transferred (subject to hold–over relief) to the trustees of the first settlement in whose property the taxpayers had no interest, those trustees could then realise the gains at the rate of tax applicable to trusts (25% at that time).

Shortly before 5 April 1995 the taxpayer made a nominal settlement for £10 upon trust for himself for life with remainder to his children. The trustees had power to pay or transfer capital to the trust fund of any other settlement for the benefit of any of the beneficiaries. The trustees were also empowered to exclude any beneficiary. The trustees of this settlement, the taxpayer and his wife, then borrowed £770,000 from their bank in their capacity as trustees of that settlement. The taxpayer then transferred the shares, which would be sold to himself and his wife as trustees of that settlement, claiming hold-over relief. They charged those shares with repayment of the £770,000.

At the same time, before 5 April 1995, the taxpayer made a second similar settlement of which the trustees were two of the partners in a firm of solicitors. The £770,000 borrowed by the first settlement was then appointed to the trustees of the second settlement. Finally, before the end of the tax year 1994/95, the trustees of the first settlement, exercised their power to exclude the taxpayer as a beneficiary of that settlement. Shortly after 6 April 1995, the first settlement sold the shares to the quoted company and repaid the borrowings.

In broad terms then the specific steps of the flip flop scheme were:

(1) The taxpayers created a trust of which they were trustees and beneficiaries. The trust instrument contained powers to enable the trustees to exclude beneficiaries and transfer capital of the trust fund to any other settlement for the benefit of the beneficiaries.

(2) Then the taxpayers transferred their shares to this settlement claiming hold-over relief.

(3) A second trust was settled by the taxpayers, whose trustees were independent professionals, on similar trusts and powers to the first trust.

(4) The trustees of the first settlement then borrowed from a bank (on the security of the shares) and transferred the advance of £770,000 to the trustees of the second settlement.

(5) The taxpayer trustees of the first settlement then executed a deed which excluded them from any beneficial interest under the first trust.

(6) In the subsequent tax year the trustees sold the shares in the first trust and paid off the bank loan using the sale proceeds.

On these facts, the taxpayers hoped that the capital gains on the sale of the shares would not be attributed to them via s 77(1) because they had no interest in the first settlement by the time that the taxpayers sold the shares. Meanwhile, the value in the shares had been extracted and was held in the second trust, in which the taxpayers held beneficial interests.

As such the fundamental issue in *West v Trennery* was whether property of the first 'taxpayer settlement' could remain 'derived property' once it had passed out of that settlement into a separate settlement. The House of Lords unanimously held that it did remain derived property. The result was that the gain realised by the trustees of the first settlement was attributed to and taxed in the hands of the settlors of that settlement even though they had no interest in the property directly held in that settlement. The scheme (which was widely used on share sales at the time) therefore failed.

Vulnerable beneficiaries

11.14 Special CGT rules apply to trusts for vulnerable beneficiaries under FA 2005, ss 30 to 33. Specifically the vulnerable beneficiary is treated as if he were the settlor of the trust. As a result, the gains of the trust are attributed to the beneficiary. For the purpose of ss 30 to 33 a 'vulnerable person' is defined as:

(a) a disabled person; or

(b) a relevant minor.

A disabled person is defined as:

(a) a person who, by reason of mental disorder, is incapable of administering their property or managing their affairs; or

(b) a person in receipt of attendance allowance or disability living allowance at the highest or idle rate. A relevant minor means a person who has not yet reached the age of 18 and at least one of whose parents are dead.

The special treatment applies until the earliest of the following three events:

(a) the beneficiary ceases to be a vulnerable person (eg because he attains the age of 18);

(b) the trust ceases to be a qualifying trust (eg because of a change of beneficiary); or

(c) the trust is wound up.

For the treatment to apply, it is necessary for the trustees to make a joint election with the vulnerable beneficiary under FA 2005, s 37(3). This election, which is irrevocable, must specify the date from which it is to have effect and must be made no later than 12 months after the next 31 January following the tax year in which the effective date falls. The trustees are obliged to notify HMRC within 90 days if one of the above events occurs.

Advisers should be aware that when the trust is also a settler-interested trust because the vulnerable beneficiary is a 'dependent child' of the settlor, the gains will not be taxed on the settlor but will instead by subject to the above rules (FA 2005, s 30(1A)).

A statutory trust for a minor child(ren) under the intestacy laws will be a qualifying settlement under FA 2005, s 35(1)(a). If the trust was set up by a will then further conditions need to apply in that:

 (i) the capital can only be applied for the vulnerable beneficiary,

 (ii) they must be entitled to income from the trust, and

 (iii) they become absolutely entitled to the trust capital at 18.

Whilst outside the scope of this book, for income tax purposes the trustees can use the personal allowance, lower and basic rate tax bands of the vulnerable beneficiaries. The trust income tax liability is reduced to take account of this special treatment ie the income tax charge will be, at most, what it would have been if it were taxed on the vulnerable beneficiary as an individual rather than on the trustees.

In accordance with s 77, the capital gains of the trust are taxed on the vulnerable beneficiary, and therefore do not form part of the trust tax return. Instead gains need to be declared by the beneficiaries. Strictly, the CGT is payable by the vulnerable beneficiary but the tax is fully recoverable from the trustees.

Example – Vulnerable beneficiary

The Lady Sapphire Bowen Family Settlement was set up for two very young children following the death of their parents in a car crash. The children are both vulnerable beneficiaries. As a result the trust is very tax efficient as it benefits from the income tax and CGT regime applicable to the two children. Neither of the children have significant other income or gains.

It is important that this preferential status is appreciated as it is relevant to the nature of the investment approach of the trust assets. If the vulnerable beneficiary rules did not apply then the trust monies would probably be best structured through bonds. However, in this case direct equity, property and fixed-interest investment is appropriate.

Alternative structures to trusts for CGT planning

11.15   As will be clear from the foregoing, the use of trusts for CGT planning is now very limited both because of anti-avoidance provisions and a 40% tax rate. Advisers therefore need to consider whether there are better alternative structures.

One possibility for clients is the use of limited partnerships. A limited partnership is the traditional private equity fund raising and investment structure. Participants in these investments are partners of the limited partnership and their commitments vary, depending on their role within the structure. Limited partnerships have particularly been used where there would be concern in relation to central management and control issues if a corporate entity was used. A group of investors can form a limited partnership with themselves as limited partners and appointing a manager who will be a general partner. The general partner manages the firm's business of venture capital or property investment and the limited partners collect a return on their investment.

It can be hard to determine the treatment of overseas partnerships. If the partners are based in different jurisdictions, then it will be necessary to consider the rules of each jurisdiction in order to ascertain whether the partners themselves will be taxable or if the partnership itself is taxable. As an example, a UK limited partnership is tax-transparent, so that its members are taxed on its profits as they arise. If different jurisdictions tax the partnership differently, then double taxation could arise and treaty relief may be available.

Tax Bulletin 83 provides some useful guidance on the UK taxation of foreign entities, such as limited partnerships. HMRC states within this bulletin that entities are described as either fiscally 'transparent' or 'opaque' for the purposes of deciding how a member is to be taxed on the income they derive from their interest in the entity. In the case of a 'transparent' entity, the member is regarded as being entitled to a share in the underlying income of the entity as it arises. In the case of an 'opaque' entity, the member generally is taxed only on the distributions made by the entity.

HMRC's view on offshore limited partnerships arose of *R v IRC, ex parte Bishopp* [1999] STC 531. Both PricewaterhouseCoopers and Ernst & Young had been considering setting up Jersey limited liability partnerships. They approached HMRC for confirmation that such partnerships would be treated as partnerships for UK tax purposes. HMRC were unwilling to provide the necessary confirmation and indicated that in their view a Jersey limited liability partnership was a company for tax purposes.

Another idea is foundations which can also be seen as a possible solution for advisers with clients from civil law countries who are uncomfortable with the concept of trusts. A foundation is a separate legal entity comparable with a company, in that it normally needs to be registered and its constitution will consist of charters and articles. The founder can reserve rights over the management of the foundation. The foundation concept has begun to be introduced into common law countries. Jersey is considering introducing foundation legislation and the Bahamas has enacted the Foundations Act 2004, which is strongly based on the successful Panamanian model.

A family investment company may be a good holding vehicle for investment or family assets: with an adjustment of share rights, the next generation can be given an interest in the assets, as well as participating in management, while leaving the settlor and spouse with ultimate voting control for as long as they see fit. It is likely to be a settlement for income tax purposes and there may be a chargeable transfer for IHT. As far as the company itself is concerned, it will be subject to corporation tax if it is in the UK, whilst if it is overseas the participators in the company are subject to s 13.

Conclusion

11.16 It is difficult to tackle the subject of CGT planning for trusts and estates in isolation. Fundamentally the tax planning involving such entities is based around IHT planning. This chapter must therefore be considered as providing supporting planning advice to other chapters in this book and to Tolley's Inheritance Tax Planning.

Checklist

	Cross Reference
Trusts and Estate Planning	

Significant CGT issues and planning opportunities arise in respect of estates and trusts. There are also areas of interaction with inheritance tax.

These include consideration of:

• Probate values.	11.3
• Sale of an asset by personal representatives or beneficiaries.	11.4
• Entitlement to principal private residence relief.	11.5
• Changes to entitlements under trusts.	11.6

Some of the more complex trust issues to consider include:

• Sub-funds	11.8
• Offshore trusts.	11.10
• Settlor-interested settlements.	11.13
• Vulnerable beneficiaries.	11.14
Advisers should consider all possible structures including alternatives to the traditional trust models.	11.15

Chapter 12

Losses

Capital loss planning – general principles

12.1 When advising on capital gains tax (CGT) planning, it is important to consider the potential for losses to be incurred and to assess downside risk. Most clients are anxious to avoid losses unless they are intentional as part of the planning. Where losses are incurred as a result of commercial decisions or economic factors, then an ability to utilise them to offset and mitigate tax liabilities that would otherwise arise is likely to be appreciated by the recipient of the advice.

A capital loss arises where an asset realises proceeds that are lower than the base cost. As such, capital losses are inevitably a fact of life. However, the ability to optimise tax relief on capital losses is restricted by the following factors:

(a) whilst capital gains are taxed as an addition to income, capital losses cannot (in general) be set off against income;

(b) indexation allowance cannot be used to augment a loss such that losses are not adjusted for inflation – nor is any indexation available on capital losses carried forward over time;

(c) rebasing to March 1982 does not universally apply to losses;

(d) losses have to be offset prior to taper relief;

(e) losses arising on disposal between connected parties can only be used against gains arising on transactions between the same parties; and

(f) losses cannot be transferred between spouses/civil partners.

Therefore, in general, capital losses can only be set off against capital gains made by the same person in the same year of assessment in the first instance and then against gains arising in following years. Where unused losses are brought forward from a previous year of assessment, these will be dealt with on a basis similar to that used for current gains, with taper relief being available on the balance remaining. However, losses brought forward do not reduce the net gains for a year of assessment below the annual exempt amount. This can lead to an effective wasting of taper relief.

Capital losses must be claimed and it is important that a taxpayer making a gain considers whether any unclaimed losses may have arisen in the past that should now be claimed.

All statutory references in this chapter are to TCGA 1992 unless otherwise stated.

Losses arising on assets held prior to 31 March 1982

12.2 It is often said that CGT does not apply prior to 31 March 1982 and so one only needs to calculate capital gains from that date. Whilst this is true, it is something of a simplification as in the absence of a global rebasing election under s 35(5) (or prior to TCGA 1992 under FA 1988, s 96(5)) then it is strictly necessary to calculate CGT both under the rebasing principles and under the original FA 1965 rules. This is rarely done as it is time consuming and usually unnecessary. However, where a loss arises by reference to a calculation using a March 1982 value, it is still necessary to do the calculation on the former basis because if a gain arises on that calculation then the loss is denied.

A s 35(5) election must be made by notice in writing to an officer of the Board. If an election has not been submitted then an election can now only be made by individuals and trustees within the period ending on the first anniversary of the 31 January next following the year of assessment in which the first relevant disposal after 5 April 1988 is made. There is an HMRC Statement of Practice (SP 4/92) covering rebasing elections and this sets out the scope for a late election. The position on late elections is also covered in the HMRC Capital Gains Manual at CG 16820.

It should be remembered that it is no longer possible for indexation allowance to create or augment a loss. Whilst this may be widely known, the point is often overlooked if a shortcut calculation is performed, which does not correctly split out the chargeable assets. The apportionment of consideration say between freehold land and buildings and goodwill can be important in this context. Overall there may have been no gain but the calculation is in respect of each chargeable asset. The nature of the chargeable asset is considered in CHAPTER 3.

Share options prior to 10 April 2003 and brought forward capital losses

12.3 Also when considering events of some years before, it is worth considering whether the individual concerned ever benefited from a share option arrangement. The case of *Mansworth v Jelley* [2002] EWCA Civ 1829; [2003] STC 53 exposed a flaw in the legislation whereby it was possible to make an error or mistake claim in respect of unclaimed capital losses arising following the exercise of the share option. Such capital losses were available to the employees of many public companies. An error or mistake claim may still be possible in respect of any years of assessment prior to 10 April 2003 for which no chargeable gain arose.

It is particularly important for advisors to question a new client about whether there are any brought forward capital losses as many tax software packages are prone to errors in this area. As a result, capital losses unutilised are not automatically carried forward from one year to another.

Taper relief and losses

12.4   Section 2A(6) establishes the order of set-off for allowable capital losses against gains eligible for taper relief. Where losses arise, these must be offset against any chargeable gains arising in the same year to produce net chargeable gains. Taper relief is then limited to the net chargeable gains and any available annual exemption is then deducted. As such, much of the planning involving losses is based on allocating losses between gains to maximise the amount of taper relief that can be obtained. The allocation may be made on whatever basis preserves maximum taper relief. Brought forward losses are offset against untapered gains sufficient to reduce them to the amount of the annual exempt amount.

Taper relief is applied to net chargeable gains and so losses are effectively tapered and are allocated in the manner that produces the lowest overall tax charge. The tapering of losses is particularly an issue where an individual is making gains on business assets and varying gains and losses on non-business assets. The objective is that any losses should be set against gains on the non-business assets first in order to minimise the wastage of losses.

Example – Taper relief and losses

Rory has worked for a number of years for Q plc and has acquired shares in it through various share options and SAYE schemes. He benefited from the *Mansworth v Jelley* case and as a result had £31,000 in capital losses brought forward at 6 April 2004.

As Rory is an employee of Q plc, his shares are treated as business assets for taper relief purposes.

Rory was also in partnership operating a small shop which was sold in July 2007. Rory received proceeds of £62,500 for his share, split £50,000 for the premises and £12,500 for the goodwill. The business was acquired in May 2002, with Rory's base costs being £36,000 for the premises and £1,500 for the goodwill.

Rory also decided to sell some of his Q plc shares in order to realise proceeds of £30,000 to spend on doing up his home. He was aware that he had significant losses available and also that he would qualify for maximum business asset taper relief (BATR) on some of his Q plc shares so was not concerned about making gains that would exceed his annual CGT exemption.

Rory sold three parcels of shares in Q plc on 10 February 2008 as follows:

(1)   4,000 shares sold for £16,000. They were acquired on 6 April 2007 and have a base cost of £11,500. They were owned for less than one year and so do not qualify for any taper relief.

(2)   500 shares sold for £2,000. They were acquired on 10 December 2006 and have a base cost of £1,500. They were owned for between one and two years and so qualify for 50% BATR.

(3) 3,000 shares sold for £12,000. They were acquired on 8 June 2005 and have a base cost of £7,500. They were owned for over two years and so qualify for the maximum 75% BATR.

If Rory could apply his brought forward losses to bring the pre-taper gain down to his annual exemption, his CGT calculation would be:

Description of asset	Taper relief rate	Pro-ceeds	Indexed cost	Pre-taper gain	Less losses b/f	Net gain	Taper relief	Tapered gain
	£	£	£	£	£	£	£	£
Shop:								
Premises	75%	50,000	(36,000)	14,000	—	14,000	(10,500)	3,500
Goodwill	75%	12,500	(1,500)	11,000	—	11,000	(8,250)	2,750
4,000 Q plc shares	Nil%	16,000	(11,500)	4,500	(2,925)	1,575	—	1,575
500 Q plc shares	50%	2,000	(1,500)	500	—	500	(250)	250
1,500 Q plc shares	75%	12,000	(7,500)	4,500	—	4,500	(3,375)	1,125
		£92,500	£(58,000)	£34,500	£(2,925)	£31,575	£(22,375)	£9,200
Less annual exemption								(9,200)
						Chargeable gain		£Nil

Rory would have used only £2,925 of his available losses to reduce his net chargeable gains to a level whereby taper relief reduced his total gain to the same amount as his annual exemption. Rory would therefore have £28,075 of losses to carry forward.

However, the rules say that brought forward losses must be used to the extent that the gains are reduced to the annual exemption before applying taper relief. In Rory's case, this therefore has the following effect:

Description of asset	Taper relief rate	Pro-ceeds	Indexed cost	Pre-taper gain	Less losses b/f	Net gain	Taper relief	Tapered gain
	£	£	£	£	£	£	£	£
Shop:								
Premises	75%	50,000	(36,000)	14,000	(14,000)	—	—	—
Goodwill	75%	12,500	(1,500)	11,000	(1,800)	9,200	(6,900)	2,300
4,000 Q plc shares	Nil%	16,000	(11,500)	4,500	(4,500)	—	—	—
500 Q plc shares	50%	2,000	(1,500)	500	(500)	—	—	—
1,500 Q plc shares	75%	12,000	(7,500)	4,500	(4,500)	—	—	—
		£92,500	£(58,000)	£34,500	£(25,300)	£9,200	£(6,900)	£2,300
Less annual exemption								(2,300)
						Chargeable gain		£Nil

Rory has therefore used £25,300 of his available losses, leaving only £5,700 to carry forward. If Rory had had no losses brought forward he would only have been taxable on gains of £2,925 after deduction of his annual exemption. It is therefore important that calculations are carefully prepared before advice on loss utilisation is given. Otherwise it is easy to miscalculate the tax liabilities arising.

As taper relief has bedded in, advisors have continued to consider how best to maximise the benefits of losses in order to also make the most of available taper relief. In particular, as far as share portfolio management is concerned, the timing of gains and losses is crucial (as is true throughout CGT) and collective investment funds are favoured. Unit trusts and OEICs or offshore funds can maximise the use of losses within the fund whilst taper relief is maximised on the fund wrapper. This point is considered further in CHAPTER 4. A further idea has been to take advantage of the connected party loss rules so as to channel appropriate gains through the same route.

The idea is to channel certain asset sales through a connected trust or a company. In theory, this is undoubtedly a sensible approach, however, the practicalities are not so apparent. There are various anti-avoidance provisions that could apply to prevent this type of planning. However, even ignoring the possibility of a challenge by HMRC on *Furniss v Dawson* ([1984] AC 474, [1984] 1 All ER 530, HL) or sham principles, such a policy is reliant upon being able to predict future gains with minimal taper relief.

The main difficulty with tax planning for losses is that it is inevitably based on assumptions about future investment performance. For those that have stock market investment portfolios with large losses, both crystallised and inbuilt, the priority will be to utilise them as early as possible rather than worrying about how best to avoid any tapering effect on the losses.

Losses and attributed gains

12.5   The interaction between losses and attributed gains under the non-resident trust legislation is complicated because of the requirement not to taper losses. Settlement gains are assessed on the settlor or on the beneficiaries under the following provisions:

(a)   settlor of UK resident trust (s 77);

(b)   settlor of non-resident trust (s 86); and

(c)   beneficiary of non-resident trust (ss 87 and 89(2)).

These 'attributed' gains are referred to as 'the section 2(5)(b) amount'. New rules apply from 2003/04 which enable a settlor assessable on gains under ss 77 or 86 to set personal allowable losses against them but no changes were made to the position for beneficiaries.

Attributed gains are considered further in CHAPTER 11.

Utilising trading losses against capital gains

12.6 There are specific provisions enabling trading losses and certain other expenditure for income tax purposes to be set off against chargeable gains to the extent that they cannot be relieved against income (due to an insufficiency of income) for the year of assessment in question. Where trading losses arise and an individual makes a claim for relief under s 261B (formerly FA 1991, s 72) he may make a claim for the loss to be treated as an allowable loss for CGT purposes. This means that in effect capital losses flowing from a claim are treated as current year losses rather than losses brought forward from prior years. However, an amount treated as an allowable loss is not allowed as a deduction from chargeable gains accruing to a person in any year of assessment beginning after he has creased trading. For the purpose of applying this rule, any such losses brought forward are treated as set against gains in priority to genuine capital losses (HMRC Capital Gains Manual CG 3519).

'*The relevant amount for the year*' is so much of the trading loss as:

(a) cannot be set off against the claimant's income for the year; and

(b) has not already been taken into account for the purposes of giving relief (under ICTA 1988, s 380, this relief provision or otherwise) for any year.

'*The maximum amount*' is the amount on which the claimant would be chargeable to CGT for the year disregarding the annual exemption and taper relief.

A claim for roll-over relief in a later year has the effect of reducing the amount chargeable for the year and, in such a case, the allowable capital losses flowing from a claim under the provision would be displaced by the effect of the roll-over claim but would be available to carry forward to subsequent years. A claim for relief is not deemed finally to be determined until the relevant amount for the year can no longer be varied.

The tax years for which relief may be claimed under ITA 2007, s 64 against income and consequently under s 261B against gains are the year in which the trading loss is incurred or the preceding year. The relief must be claimed no later than the first anniversary of 31 January following the tax year in which the loss is incurred. Although strictly the two claims should be made in the same notice, HMRC are prepared to accept a separate claim under s 261B where a claim has already been made under ITA 2007, s 64 (HMRC Tax Bulletin August 1993).

Example – *Offset of trading losses against capital gains*

Jack has carried on a trade for some years, preparing accounts to 30 June each year. For the year ended 30 June 2007 he makes a trading loss of £17,000. His taxable profit for 2006/07 is £5,000 and his other income for both 2006/07 and 2007/08 amounts to £2,000. He makes a capital gain of £20,000 and a capital loss of £1,000 for 2007/08 and has capital losses brought forward of £2,800. The gain qualified for the maximum non-business asset taper relief of 40%. Jack makes a claim for loss relief, against income of 2006/07 and income and gains of 2007/08 under s 261B and ITA 2007, s 64.

Calculation of 'relevant amount'

	£	£
Trading loss – year ended 30.06.07	17,000	
Relieved against other income for 2007/08	(2,000)	
Relieved against income for 2006/07	(7,000)	
	£8,000	

Calculation of 'maximum amount'

	£	£
Indexed gain	20,000	
Capital loss	(1,000)	
Unrelieved losses brought forward	(2,800)	
Maximum amount	£16,200	

Relief under s 261B

	£	£
Indexed gain pre-taper		20,000
Capital loss in the year	1,000	
Relief under s 261B	8,000	
Capital loss brought forward	1,800	
		(10,800)
Gain covered by annual exemption		£9,200
Capital losses carried forward		£1,000

Loss memorandum

	£
Trading loss	17,000
Claimed under ITA 2007, s 64	(9,000)
Claimed under s 261B	(8,000)
	£Nil

The example shows how various aspects of the relief interact. Typically, it would be unattractive to claim s 261B relief in such cases because the income loss is tapered and it is usually preferable to preserve the income tax loss at the expense of the capital loss. If the relief was not claimed then the assessable gains for the year would be as follows:

	£
Capital gain	20,000
Capital loss in the year	(1,000)
Capital losses brought forward	(2,800)
	16,200
Non-business asset taper relief @ 40%	(6,480)
	9,720
Annual exemption	(9,200)
	£520

Section 261B relief is extended to include post-cessation expenditure and post-employment deductions.

Negligible value claims

12.7 A negligible value claim can be made under s 24. This is particularly relevant in terms of unquoted shares. The HMRC Capital Gains Manual states (CG 13131) that a negligible value claim can be considered where the following conditions are satisfied:

(a) the company is registered in the UK;

(b) the company is not registered as a PLC;

(c) the capital loss arising from the deemed disposal of shares following the negligible value claim is under £100,000; and

(d) the company was in liquidation and insolvent, or had ceased trading and had no assets at the date of the claim and at any earlier date specified in the claim.

In other cases involving unquoted shares the Inspector is instructed to refer the case to the Shares and Assets Valuation Division.

In addition, a taxpayer can ask for a post transaction valuation check after the negligible value claim has been made and before the return showing the loss arising from the deemed disposal is filed. You may accept that the post transaction valuation check is made after the claim is made if form CG34 is submitted at the same time as the claim. The guidance in this paragraph only applies to the acceptance that shares are of negligible value at the time the taxpayer makes a claim and at any earlier date specified in the claim.

Relief for losses on loans to traders

12.8 Section 253 provides relief for irrecoverable loans where:

(a) the money lent has been used by the borrower wholly for the purposes of a trade, profession or vocation;

(b) the borrower is a UK resident; and

(c) the loan is not a debt on a security (s 132).

Further, the relief extends to guarantee payments made in respect of such a loan. This extends to guarantees made in respect of overdrafts but not hire purchase agreements and an indemnity is not a guarantee.

A claim is possible in respect of the outstanding principal if it has become irrecoverable and the claim can be backdated for up to two years as long as the loan was irrecoverable at that time. The claim must be made on or before the fifth anniversary of 31 January next following the year of assessment. There is therefore considerable flexibility as to the offset of any such capital loss.

This is a very useful relief and should be considered when planning an investment in a small business. It helps mitigate the downside risk of the investment but it is only of assistance where the lender has other capital gains against which to offset the loss. By contrast, the relief for capital losses on unquoted shares is much more flexible and beneficial.

Losses on shares in unlisted trading companies

12.9 ITA 2007, s 131 (formerly ICTA 1988, s 574) allows a capital loss to be offset against income and so enables the loss to be fully utilised without any effective tapering. This is important because the relief gives the potential for 40% tax relief on a loss (for a higher-rate taxpayer) with only a 10% tax rate on a gain (because of BATR). This is only bettered by qualifying for full income tax relief under the Enterprise Investment Scheme (EIS) where loss relief is available but any gain is exempt. However, such EIS relief is limited to holdings of less than 30% (see CHAPTER 6).

Where an individual who has subscribed for shares in a qualifying trading company incurs an allowable loss on the disposal of the shares he may, by written notice given on or before the first anniversary of 31 January following that year, make a claim for relief from income tax against:

(1) current year income; and/or

(2) income of the preceding year.

Relief for a loss may be claimed for the current year or the preceding year or both years – the taxpayer may choose which year takes priority and should make this clear in his claim (HMRC Helpsheet IT 286). Any part of the loss remaining unrelieved against income reverts to being a capital loss for the year of disposal.

Relief is available only if:

(a) the disposal is at arm's length for full consideration;

(b) it is by way of a distribution on a winding up or dissolution; or

(c) the value of the shares has become negligible under s 24.

An individual subscribes for shares if they are issued to him by the company for money or money's worth, or if they were so issued to his spouse or civil partner, who transferred them to him under s 58.

For shares issued after 5 April 1998, a qualifying company:

- is an eligible trading company at the date of disposal; or

- has ceased to be an eligible trading company within three years before that date and has not since that cessation been an excluded company, an investment company or a non-eligible trading company; and either

- has been an eligible trading company for a continuous period of at least six years prior to the disposal (or prior to the cessation, as the case may be); or

- has been an eligible trading company for a shorter continuous period ending with the disposal or cessation and has not previously been an excluded company, an investment company or a non-eligible trading company; and

- has carried on its business wholly or mainly in the UK throughout the relevant period.

For shares issued before 7 March 2001, it was also a condition that the company be an unquoted company throughout that part of the relevant period that falls before 7 March 2001.

As regards shares issued before 6 April 1998, a qualifying trading company is an unquoted company which either:

- is a trading company at the date of disposal; or

- has ceased to be a trading company within three years before that date and has not since that cessation been an excluded company or an investment company; and either

- has been a trading company for a continuous period of at least six years prior to the disposal (or prior to the cessation as the case may be); or

- has been a trading company for a shorter continuous period ending with the disposal or cessation and has not previously been an excluded company or an investment company; and

- has been resident in the UK throughout the period from incorporation to the date of disposal.

The relevant period is the period ending with the disposal of the shares and beginning with the incorporation of the company, or if later, one year before that date on which the shares were issued (one year before they were subscribed for as regards shares issued before 6 April 1998).

An eligible trading company is a company which is or would be a qualifying company for the purposes of EIS. A trading company is a company (other than an excluded company) whose business consists wholly or mainly of the carrying on of the trade or trades. The 'holding company' of a 'trading group' is also within this definition.

An excluded company means a company the trade of which consists wholly or mainly of dealing in land, in commodities or futures or in shares, securities or other financial instruments (as regards shares issued before 6 April 1998, dealing in shares, securities, land trades or commodity futures). A company which does not carry on its trade on a commercial basis and with a reasonable expectation of profit is within this definition, as is the holding company of a non-trading group.

Trading group means a 'group' the business of the members of which, taken together, consists wholly or mainly in the carrying on of a trade or trades. Any trade carried on by a subsidiary which is an excluded company (or, as regards shares issued before 6 April 1998, which is non UK-resident) is disregarded.

The above represents a narrowing of the loss relief against income rules as regards shares issued after 5 April 1998 in that the company which issued the shares must satisfy the EIS requirements. However, there are no conditions that the company must have issued the shares under the EIS, that the shares have been held for a minimum period, or that any EIS income tax relief has been, or could have been, claimed in respect of them.

Where an individual who has subscribed for shares in a company has also acquired shares of the same class in the same company by other means, and both the subscription shares and the other shares form part of the same holding (ie the number of shares of the same class held by one person in one capacity, whether or not pooled for CGT purposes), then in determining the extent (if any) to which a disposal relates to shares subscribed for (qualifying shares), disposals are to be identified with acquisition on a last in/first out (LIFO) basis.

For disposals after 5 April 1998, there is an exception to the above rule where the holding includes any of the following:

- shares in respect of which Business Expansion Scheme (BES) relief has been given and not withdrawn;

- shares to which EIS income tax relief is attributable.

In such a case, disposals are identified in accordance with the identification rules generally applicable to EIS and BES shares (first in/first out (FIFO)). Loss relief under these provisions on the disposal of qualifying shares forming part of the larger holding is restricted to the sums that would have been allowable as deductions in computing the loss if the qualifying shares had been acquired and disposed of as a separate holding.

HMRC Venture Capital Schemes Manual (VCM47150) identifies four steps in the computation of loss relief under these provisions where a holding does not entirely consist of qualifying shares. Step 1 is to compute the allowable loss for CGT purposes under normal CGT principles and identification rules. Step 2 is to identify the qualifying and non-qualifying shares in the disposal. If it is found that the disposal comprises both, Step 3 is to apportion the loss, on a just and reasonable basis, between qualifying and non-qualifying shares. Step 4 is to compare the loss so attributed to the qualifying shares with the actual allowable expenditure incurred on those shares and to apply restriction.

Relief is not available in respect of a new holding within s 127 unless relief could have been given (assuming the legislation to have been in force) on the disposal which would have occurred on the reorganisation but for s 127.

Example – ITA 2007, s 131 relief for losses on unquoted share

Laura subscribed for 3,000 £1 ordinary shares at par in Builders Limited, a qualifying trading company, in June 1988. In September 1995, Laura acquired 2,200 shares at £3 per share from another shareholder. In December 2006, Laura sold 3,900 shares at 40p per share.

Share pool	Shares	Qualifying expenditure	Indexed pool
		£	£
June 1998 subscription	3,000	3,000	3,000
Indexation to September 1995 £3,000 x 0.413			1,239
September 1995 acquisition	2,200	6,600	6,600
	5,200	9,600	10,839
Indexed rise: September 1995 to April 1998 £10,839 x 0.080			867
	5,200	9,600	11,706
December 2006 disposal	(3,900)	(7,200)	(8,780)
Pool carried forward	£1,300	£2,400	£2,926

Step 1 – Calculate the CGT loss in the normal way, as follows:

Disposal consideration 3,900 x £0.40	1,560
Allowable cost	
	7,200
$\dfrac{3,900}{5,200} \times 9,600$	
Allowable loss	£5,640

Step 2 – Applying a LIFO basis, identify the qualifying shares (1,700) and the non-qualifying shares (2,200) comprised in the disposal.

Step 3 – Calculate the proportion of the loss attributable to the qualifying shares.

Loss referable to 1,700 qualifying shares

£2,458

$\dfrac{1,700}{3,900} \times 5,640$

Step 4 – Compare the loss in Step 3 with the actual cost of the qualifying shares, viz:

Loss referable to 1,700 qualifying shares

£1,700

$\dfrac{1,700}{3,000} \times 3,000$

The loss available against income is restricted to £1,700 (being lower than £2,458).

The loss not relieved against income remains an allowable loss for CGT purposes.

£5,640 – £1,700 =	£3,940

This relief is a very flexible and useful form of loss utilisation but only where shares have been subscribed for. It is usually the case that small trading companies have minimal share capital with the balance of capital advanced as a loan. In such cases, relief will only be available for a loss under s 253 rather than ITA 2007, s 131. In view of this, consideration is often given to capitalising a loan where there is a possibility that the company may become worthless. As such, the approach is to capitalise the loan by the issue of shares. HMRC may dispute the value of the shares subscribed for on the grounds that the loan is already worth less than the face value of the debt. It is therefore important that appropriate documentation is put in place including formal independent valuations on any such conversion.

Earnouts and other deferred unascertainable consideration

12.10   For the purposes of CGT, the date of the disposal is the date of the contract in accordance with s 28. It then follows that the person making the disposal is taxable on the gain in the year of assessment of the disposal. This will be the case even if the proceeds have not yet been turned into cash such that the tax can be paid. A particular issue arises where part of the proceeds are not quantifiable or ascertainable at the time. The best example of this is where shares in a company are sold and part of the consideration is in the form of an earnout.

The case of *Marren v Ingles* [1980] STC 500 established that the earnout right is a chose in action (ie a separate legal asset) that must be valued at the time of the disposal and forms part of the proceeds at that point in time. The amounts taxed at that time become the base cost of this notional asset. As the earnout comes to fruition then further gains or losses will arise. However, the loss may arise in the future and at that point in time could only be carried forward. As a result of lobbying, s 279A was introduced. This provides for an additional form of loss relief.

Where a person disposes of a right to future unascertainable consideration, acquired as consideration for the disposal of another asset, and a loss accrues, he may, subject to conditions, make an election under s 279A for the loss to be treated as arising in the year in which that other asset was disposed of. Accordingly, where the election is made, the loss on disposal of the right can be set against the gain arising on the disposal of the original asset.

Where an election is made under the above provisions, the relevant loss is treated for CGT purposes as if it were a loss accruing in the earliest tax year which is an eligible year. The amount of the relevant loss that can be deducted from chargeable gains of that year is limited to the amount (the *'first year limit'*) found by taking the following steps:

Step 1—Take the total amount of chargeable gains accruing to the taxpayer in the year.

Step 2—Exclude from that amount any amounts attributable to the taxpayer under ss 77, 86, 87 or 89(2).

Step 3—Then deduct any amounts in respect of allowable losses except for any losses falling to be set against gains attributable to the taxpayer under ss 77 or 86. Account must be taken of any previous elections made under these provisions, but no account must be taken of the relevant losses.

Where attributed gains have been received, two further steps must be taken to arrive at the first year limit, as follows:

Step 4—Add to the remaining amount every amount attributed to the taxpayer as a chargeable gain under ss 77 or 86.

Step 5—Deduct any losses falling to be set against such attributed gains.

To the extent that the relevant loss exceeds the first-year limit (and so is not utilised in the first eligible year), it may be carried forward for set-off against gains of later years. In the case of tax years falling between the first eligible year and the year of the loss, any remaining part of the relevant loss can only be deducted if the year is an eligible year. For such years, the amount of loss which may be deducted is limited to the amount (the *'later year limit'*) in respect of which the taxpayer would be chargeable to CGT for the year:

- on the assumption that no part of the relevant loss, or any other loss in respect of which an election under these provisions could be made, but which immediately after the making of the election in question, has not been made, falls to be deducted from the gains for the year;

- taking account of any previous elections under these provisions; and

- apart from any available taper relief and any gains from which the taxpayer's personal losses are not deductible.

A right is a 'right to unascertainable consideration' if, and only if, it is a right to consideration the amount or value of which is unascertainable when the right is conferred because it is referable in whole or part to matters which are uncertain at that time because they have not yet occurred. The amount or value of any consideration is not regarded as unascertainable by reason only:

- that the right to receive all or part of the consideration is postponed or contingent to the extent that the consideration is brought into account in accordance with s 48;

- in a case where the right to receive all or part of the consideration is postponed and may be to any extent satisfied by the receipt of alternative types of property, that some person has the right to select the property or type of property that is to be received; and

- that either the amount or the value of the consideration has not been fixed, if either the amount will be fixed by reference to the value, and the value is ascertainable, or the value will be fixed by reference to the amount, and the amount is ascertainable.

An election under the above provisions is irrevocable and must be made by notice in writing in the prescribed form on or before the first anniversary of 31 January following the year of the loss.

This is a useful relief although it has become common to structure earnouts such that the risk is avoided. In particular, for disposals after 10 April 2003 an election to treat the earnout right as a security under s 138A is available. The CGT issues in respect of earnouts and planning considerations are covered further in CHAPTER 2 and CHAPTER 5.

Losses and capital allowances

12.11 Section 38 provides that unless otherwise specified in the legislation, the amount or value of consideration in money or money's worth, given by the taxpayer wholly and exclusively for the acquisition of the asset is deductible in computing the gain or loss. Section 39 excludes from s 38 any expenditure allowable as a deduction in computing the profits or gains of a trade for the purposes of income tax or allowable as a deduction in computing any other income or profits or gains or losses for the purposes of the Income Tax Acts.

Section 41 restricts any capital loss arising to the extent that capital allowances or renewals allowance have been claimed. Therefore, any calculation of a capital loss is after adjusting for the benefit of any capital allowances that have been obtained. This is relevant to plant and machinery assets where the item concerned would otherwise come within the CGT legislation. From 1988 to 1998 it was possible for indexation allowance to augment a loss. Hence, during that period losses could (and did) arise on assets where capital allowances had been claimed.

Example – Capital gains and capital allowances

John acquires in 1998 a printing press costing £100,000. It is sold in 2003 for £27,000.

The capital allowances, after deducting the balancing charge, amount to £73,000. The computation, if s 41 did not apply, would be:

	£
Disposal proceeds	27,000
Less: cost	100,000
Capital loss	£(73,000)

The computation under s 41 is as follows:

	£	£
Disposal proceeds		27,000
Less: cost	100,000	
Deduct capital allowances	(73,000)	
		(27,000)
		£Nil

If the person making the disposal acquired the asset at its capital allowances written down value by a transfer by way of a sale in relation to which an election under CAA 2001, s 569 was made (sales without change of control or between connected persons) or by a transfer to which CAA 2001, s 268 applies (succession to trade on death) any adjustment of the loss accruing to the transferee is to take account of any capital allowances made to both the transferor (including previous transferors) and the transferee.

Where allowable expenditure on the building or structure has been fully covered by capital allowances, no loss relief is available. In these circumstances, it is not necessary to compute the loss on the disposal of the building or structure.

More recently, the interaction of capital allowances and the CGT legislation has been relevant in the case of *Revenue and Customs Commissioners v Smallwood* [2007] STC 1237. This case concerned entitlement to a loss on the disposal of a property within an Enterprise Zone. Enterprise Zones were introduced in the 1980s to provide favourable tax status for areas requiring regeneration. The taxpayer claimed a loss in 1999/2000 on the disposal of an interest in a property even though a 100% first-year allowance had been claimed on the vast majority of the property in 1989/90. The Special Commissioners, the High Court and the Court of Appeal have now ruled in favour of the taxpayer, although this would seem to be due to the fact that the legislation is flawed where the ownership of an asset is via an Enterprise Zone Property Unit Trust (EZPUT).

Section 99 requires that for the purposes of the CGT legislation a unit trust scheme must be treated as if:

(a)   the scheme is a company; and

(b)   the rights of the unit trust holders are the same as those of shareholders in a company.

The effect of s 99 is that Mr Smallwood, in the case mentioned above, was deemed to be in the same position as a shareholder in a company. The base cost of shareholdings are not adjusted for capital allowances claims made by the company itself. This outcome could have been avoided if HMRC had included EZPUTs in the CGT (Definition of Unit Trust Schemes) Regulations 1988 (SI 1988 No 266) but for whatever reason EZPUTs were not excluded from the provision of s 99.

Disallowance of losses – anti-avoidance provision

12.12   The Finance Act 2007 introduced a new s 16A into TCGA 1992. This is a Targeted Anti–Avoidance Rule (TAAR). This provides that a loss on the disposal will not be allowable against gains if:

●   the loss accrues as a result of, or in connection with, any arrangements; and

●   the main purpose, or one of the main purposes, of the arrangement is the securing of a tax advantage.

The term 'arrangements' is very widely drawn and 'includes any agreement, understanding, scheme, transaction or series of transactions (whether or not legally enforceable)'. 'Purpose' is not defined but reference can be made to the position on transfers of assets abroad and in particular to Tax Bulletin 40 (April 1999). 'Tax advantage' can be taken to have a similar meaning to that used in the Transactions in Securities legislation. However, in the context of tax advantage for s 16A, tax means CGT, corporation tax and income tax only.

The legislation is clearly targeted at certain tax marketed schemes that HMRC finds unacceptable. However, the legislation is more widely drawn and will effect transactions not being entered into as part of a marketed scheme. In order to try and overcome this, HMRC has issued detailed guidance to narrow down the scope. This states that 'the legislation is intended to have effect where a person enters deliberately and knowingly into arrangements to avoid tax'. It also states that 'because it is targeted at arrangements that are intended to avoid tax, most persons will not be affected, nor will it apply to the majority of transactions undertaken by such persons'. A concern is as to whether or not the Guidance is legally enforceable particularly in the light of the Wilkinson case, (*R (on the application of Wilkinson) v Inland Revenue Commissioners* [2005] UKHL 30. [2006] STC 270), which confirmed that it is up to Parliament to make the law and not HMRC.

Those advising clients on utilising capital losses against gains should make reference to the Guidance Notes and consider whether or not the proposed planning could be impacted upon. The areas of advice where the new rules are most likely to apply are:

- inter-spouse transfers;

- transactions involving trusts and beneficiaries; and

- transactions between connected parties.

Concerns have been expressed with respect to the position on transactions between spouses as follows:

Example – Spouse transfer and possible application of TAAR

A husband sells at a loss, with his wife buying back the same amount. The wife sells when the price improves.

	Husband £	Wife £	Combined £
Buy	(1,000)	(200)	(1,000)
Sell	200	500	500
Gain/(loss)	£(800)	£300	£(500)
Overall gain after TAAR applied			£300

The result is a combined economic loss of £500 but a taxable gain of £300.

Should the legislation apply then the husband's loss has gone for good so that not only are husband and wife worse off overall than if there had been no transfer of shares, but the wife cannot redeem the situation by routing her sale via her husband. The outcome is worse than the general treatment of losses between connected persons.

However, it is clear from the attempts by HMRC in drafting the Guidance and the many examples contained in it concerning inter-spousal transfers, that the intention is not to catch such transfers. Further, during the Finance Bill Committee Debate on this clause, the Economic Secretary to the Treasury, Ed Balls, explained some of the examples in the Guidance concerning inter-spousal transfers and concluded that he had 'explained the straightforward way in which statutory tax relief can be passed between husband and wife in a way that allows a loss to be set against the gain. The clause does not interfere with that normal tax practice and planning'. At this time, this should be taken to mean that it is not Treasury policy to seek to prevent minimisation of CGT by making spouse transfers. However, government policy in this area is unclear and could change in the future. In possible cases advisors should refer to the guidance and caveat their advice accordingly.

The Guidance also states that the 'legislation will not apply where there is a genuine economic transaction that gives rise to a real economic loss as a result of a real disposal'. Further, HMRC states in the Guidance that they will give advice under Code of Practice 10 (COP10) where there is genuine uncertainty about the interpretation of the legislation.

Conclusion

12.13 Capital loss planning involves the interaction of a number of complex reliefs. In addition it is necessary to closely question the client to identify opportunities that may otherwise have been overlooked. Losses may have been incurred at times when professional advisors were not instructed and the client may be embarrassed to mention business failures, unwise guarantees and poor investment decisions. It is also important not to overlook the potentially adverse impact of rebasing, indexation allowance and taper relief on losses.

Checklist

	Cross Reference
Capital Loss Planning	
The usage of capital losses is very restrictive for CGT purposes. The interaction of losses with other reliefs leads to many different potential outcomes. Careful organisation of losses is required especially in respect of:	
• assets held prior to 31 March 1982;	
• share options;	
• entitlements to taper relief; and	
• attributed gains for offshore trusts.	
It is possible to offset trading losses against capital gains.	**12.6**
It is possible to offset capital losses on certain shares in unlisted trading companies against income.	**12.9**
A loss carry back is possible where an initial earnout calculation turns out to be excessive.	**12.10**
A targeted anti-avoidance rule now applies to restrict loss relief for CGT.	**12.12**

Chapter 13

Anti-Avoidance, Enquiries and Disclosure

Introduction

13.1   Other chapters of this book cover the details of various tax planning ideas, including specific anti-avoidance provisions written into legislation. However, it is also necessary to consider the wider anti-avoidance provisions, including the following:

(a)   Is the transaction subject to capital gains tax (CGT) or is it instead subject to income tax as trading income, employment income or dividend income?

(b)   Has the matter previously been contested before the courts, such that there is relevant case law to consider?

(c)   Is the planning covered by more general anti-avoidance legislation and case law provisions, such that it is prevented by the Ramsay principle in respect of a pre-ordained series of transactions?

(d)   Other anti-avoidance provisions that apply to such a transaction for the purpose of other taxes in case they provide an insight as to the possible methods of countering the planning.

Any planning advice should consider the potential scope for HMRC to challenge the approach being adopted and to consider the above. The advice should also consider the potential implications of other taxes and interaction with other taxes, principally inheritance tax (IHT), which is considered in **CHAPTER 15**, income tax and Stamp Duty Land Tax (SDLT). In addition, any planning advice should consider how the transaction is to be disclosed to HMRC and how the risk of a tax investigation can be minimised or, if an enquiry is likely to be opened, then how it can be best managed.

This chapter concerns itself with more general anti-avoidance principles and issues that should be considered as part of any planning advice. It is also concerned with the particular difficulties raised by valuation issues and the scope of such matters to undermine the advice given.

All references in this chapter are to TCGA 1992 unless stated otherwise.

Requirement for anti-avoidance rules

13.2   CGT was introduced as a new code in 1965 and was not built on any previous legislation or case law. It is a very artificial tax, with a large number of deeming provisions and notional disposals. It exists for reasons of equity and so can be viewed as anti-avoidance legislation in its entirety. However, the desire for equity in a tax system has to be balanced with a desire to limit complexity.

The various anti-avoidance rules that apply seek to limit the tax planning opportunities that might otherwise naturally present themselves. These are:

(a) to convert income into capital gains and so avoid income tax and pay CGT at lower tax rates;

(b) to extend the period of ownership in order to benefit from a higher rate of taper relief;

(c) to convert non-business assets into business assets in order to benefit from a higher rate of taper relief;

(d) to attempt to obtain a relief that was not intended to be available by Parliament; and

(e) to try to shift value to a connected party with a more favourable tax status.

Prior to the introduction of CGT, there was considerable effort exerted into trying to convert income into capital gains in order to avoid income tax. This led to the development of much of the well known anti-avoidance provisions during the 1950s and 1960s. Even after the introduction of CGT, capital gains continued to benefit from lower tax rates compared to the highest rates of income tax. This was the case right up until 1988 when Nigel Lawson introduced symmetry into the system (although even then there remained certain generous reliefs such as CGT retirement relief).

However, as a result of Business Asset Taper Relief (BATR) and the possibility of a 10% tax rate, the motivation is now to try and convert revenue profits into capital gains. Potential anti-avoidance provisions available to HMRC include:

 (i) transactions in securities (ITA 2007, ss 682 and 607);

 (ii) the transfer of assets abroad (ITA 2007, s 714) and non-residency;

(iii) transactions in land (ICTA 1988, s 752 and pre-CGT cases);

(iv) the sale of a right to income (ITA 2007, s 773);

 (v) value shifting (s 29); and

(vi) a pre-ordained series of transactions.

Transactions in securities

13.3   ITA 2007, Pt 13, Ch 1 sets out the anti-avoidance provisions in connection with transactions in securities. It is a very complex piece of legislation and even though it has been in existence for nearly 50 years, it is difficult for tax advisers to feel entirely comfortable with what it means. It applies where there is a transaction in securities and a tax advantage is obtained. A transaction in securities is defined to include:

(a) the purchase, sale or exchange of securities;

(b) the issue of new securities; and

(c) the altering of rights attaching to securities.

It is designed to prevent the conversion of an income profit into a capital gain, eg by making profits in a company and then liquidating the company so as to receive a capital distribution rather than withdrawing the profits by way of dividend. It was not until the House of Lords decision in *Inland Revenue Commissioners v Laird Group plc* [2003] 4 All ER 669 that it was established that a dividend by itself does not constitute a transaction in securities. However, other transactions involving abnormal dividends, such as the Universities Superannuation Scheme case (*Inland Revenue Commissioners v Universities Superannuation Scheme Ltd* [1997] STC 1), are still transactions in securities. The provision applies where:

  (i) income tax or corporation tax is reduced or avoided (ie a tax advantage is obtained); and

 (ii) any of the five circumstances (A to E) in ITA 2007, ss 686–690 apply. Of these, A and B are unlikely to be relevant with the main circumstances of interest being D but with E and C also having implications.

For the purposes of this legislation it is important to understand that 'tax' means income tax or corporation tax. Therefore, as long as income tax or corporation tax is avoided or reduced then a tax advantage is obtained.

The legislation is so wide ranging that there had to be a let out – often referred to as the 'escape clause'. This is that it will not apply where 'the transaction or transactions were carried out either for bona fide commercial reasons or in the ordinary course of making or managing investments, and that none of them had as their main object, or one of their main objects, to enable tax advantages to be obtained'.

The best way to get a feel for this provision is to read some of the principal decided cases of which the two best examples are:

(1) *CIR v Cleary* [1967] 2 All ER 48 – Cleary and her sister owned all the shares in two companies – M Ltd and G Ltd. In 1961 the sisters sold their shares in M Ltd to G Ltd for its market value satisfied in cash. The sisters had entered into a transaction in securities that gave rise to a tax advantage as income tax and surtax was avoided. The transaction was not undertaken for bona fide commercial reasons. The sisters therefore lost the case and the tax assessment to counteract the tax advantage was upheld.

(2) *CIR v Joiner* [1975] 1 All ER 755 – Joiner owned 75% of J Ltd. The other 25% was owned by a family trust. In 1964, J Ltd sold its business to a new company, A Ltd, which was controlled by Joiner. J Ltd was then placed into liquidation. Joiner had entered into a transaction in securities that gave rise to a tax advantage as income tax and surtax was avoided. The transaction was not undertaken for bona fide commercial reasons. Joiner lost the case and the tax assessment to counteract the tax advantage was upheld.

The *Joiner* case is noteworthy because one sees many taper relief promoted schemes that would appear to have similar facts.

Lord Denning MR said of the original legislation in *CIR v Clearly*:

> 'Previously, when … a company had money available for distribution by way of dividend, there were means whereby the money could be taken out in the form of capital so as not to attract income tax. Now Parliament strikes at those transactions. It enables the Commissioners of Inland Revenue to counteract the tax advantage by making an assessment as if the money were received as income and not capital.'

In order to provide certainty, Parliament introduced a clearance procedure so that a taxpayer would know the tax position before undertaking a transaction. It is this clearance unit that has progressively developed over the years into the Business Tax Clearance Team. The approach to clearances is considered further below. Given that the main incentive for the structuring of certain transactions will be to take advantage of a 10% tax rate, it will be imperative that there is not only good commercial justification for the method of structuring the transaction but also that clearance is obtained.

The transfer of assets abroad and non-residency

13.4 ITA 2007, Pt 13, Ch 2 is concerned with the transfer of assets abroad in order to avoid tax. This includes a charge under ITA 2007, s 727 where a capital sum is received as a result of a series of transactions.

There is also the possibility of avoiding a liability to CGT by becoming non-resident. The tax issues in connection with this, including anti-avoidance aspects, are considered in CHAPTER 14.

Transactions in land

13.5 ITA 2007, Pt 13, Ch 3 is concerned with the avoidance of income tax by persons concerned with land or the development of land. It was formerly ICTA 1988, s 776. The old title for the section was 'artificial transactions in land' which is a better description of its impact. Its scope is in fact fairly limited and it is designed to tax property dealing profits and development profits as income even if they are disguised as capital.

One of the main reasons why it is unlikely to apply is that most of the situations that would otherwise be caught by it will in fact fall within the badges of trade and fall to be taxed as trading transactions. This was an area where there was a considerable body of case law prior to the introduction of CGT and any attack by HMRC is likely to be based around those cases with the principal determining factors being:

(a) the nature of the occupation of the taxpayer. If he is a builder or developer then any capital gain is likely to be held as falling within his trading activities; and

(b) the intention of the taxpayer on acquiring the land site.

The issue of whether an activity is on trading or capital account is considered further in CHAPTER 1 and CHAPTER 9.

A sale of a right to income

13.6 ITA 2007, Pt 13, Ch 4 charges to income tax the sale of occupation income. It counters schemes which turn income from an occupation (a profession or vocation) into capital. This provision was originally introduced to counter the sale of personal services by actors, etc for a capital sum in order to avoid income tax.

Anti-avoidance provisions also exist to counter structured finance arrangement schemes involving the factoring of income receipts. The schemes involve the transfer of an asset on which there is a predictable income stream or a transfer of the right to such an income stream and interest. The transferor then claims that the income or receipts arising during the period of the arrangement are not taxable on him and that the lump sum is either a capital receipt giving rise to a chargeable gain only or is not taxable at all. Broadly, the provisions operate by deeming the intended effects of the arrangements not to have effect for tax purposes.

For capital gains purposes, where the borrower or a person connected with him (other than the lender) makes a disposal at any time of any security under the arrangement to or for the benefit of the lender or a person with him (other than the borrower) and either:

(a) the person making the disposal subsequently reacquires the arrangement the asset disposed of; or

(b) that asset subsequently ceases to exist, having been held continuously by the lender (or connected person) from the time of the disposal,

then the disposal of the security and any subsequent reacquisition of the asset are disregarded.

Value shifting

13.7 In accordance with s 29, the following transactions are treated as giving rise to a disposal of an asset for CGT purposes:

(a) If a person having control of a company exercises his control so that value passes out of his shares or those of connected persons, or out of rights over the company exercisable by him or connected persons and passes into other shares in or rights over the company, then a disposal is deemed to have been made out of those shares or rights.

(b) Where an owner of property enters into a transaction whereby he becomes the lessee of that property (eg a sale and lease back) and there is a subsequent adjustment of the rights and liabilities under the lease, which is favourable to the lessor.

(c) If an asset is subject to any right or restriction – the extinction or abrogation, in whole or part, of that right, etc.

The aim of the legislation is to tax the amount of value passing into the transferee holdings – not (if different) the amount passing from the transferor. The disposal value is thus the value received by the transferee (HMRC Capital Gains Manual CG58855). This is relevant where value passes from a majority shareholding into one or more minority holdings.

Example – Value shifting

Fiona owns all of the 1,000 £1 ordinary shares in New Homes Limited. The shares were acquired on subscription in 1998 for £50,000. In December 2006, the trustees of Fiona's family settlement subscribed at par for 250 £1 ordinary shares in New Homes Limited thereby acquiring 20% of the voting power of the company. It is agreed that the value per share of Fiona's holding immediately before the December 2006 share issue was £175 and immediately afterwards was £150. The value per share of the trust's holding, on issue, was £97 per share.

The proceeds of the deemed disposal are computed as follows:

The value passing out of Fiona's 1,000 shares is £25,000 (1,000 x £25 per share (£175 – £150)).

The value passing into the trust's 250 shares is £24,250 (250 x £97 per share), less the subscription price paid of £250 (250 x £1 per share) = £24,000.

The proceeds of the deemed disposal are equal to the value passing into the new shares, ie £24,000 (the trust's acquisition cost is £24,250, ie actual plus deemed consideration given).

	£
Proceeds of sale	24,000
Allowable cost	
$\dfrac{24,000}{24,000+150,000}$ x 50,000	
	(6,897)
Gain pre-taper	£17,103

A pre-ordained series of transactions

13.8 During the 1970s a number of tax planning schemes were developed which were based around a pre-determined set of events which took advantage of a loophole in the CGT legislation. These schemes were considered in the cases of *WT Ramsay v CIR* [1981] STC 174, *Furniss v Dawson* [1984] AC 474, [1984] 1 All ER 530, HL, and *Craven v White* [1989] AC 398, [1988] 3 All ER 495, HL. These were all heard in the 1980s and have led to a refined code of 'substance over form' to set aside a pre-ordained series of transactions.

Under this approach, a pre-ordained series of transactions may sometimes be considered as a whole. The result is that, when determining the fiscal consequences of the transactions, any steps inserted in the series of transactions with no business purpose apart from the avoidance of tax may be disregarded. This approach has since been developed and reviewed in further cases, the most recent House of Lords decision being *MacNiven v Westmoreland Investments Ltd* [2001] STC 237.

In *Furniss v Dawson*, Lord Brightman summarised this principle as follows:

> 'There must be a pre-ordained series of transactions; or, if one likes, one single composite transaction ... Secondly, there must be steps inserted which have no commercial (business) purpose apart from the avoidance of a liability to tax – not 'no business effect'. If these two ingredients exist, the inserted steps are to be disregarded for fiscal purposes.'

The issue of the pre-ordained series of transactions was further refined by Lord Oliver of Aylmerton in that there must be no practical likelihood that the pre-ordained series of transactions would not take place precisely in the order contemplated.

The HMRC practice in applying the approach to certain common tax saving situations was outlined in a published exchange of letters (ICAEW TR 588). The exchange was published on 25 September 1985 and so is now somewhat dated. However, it is still worthy of reference. It was confirmed that inspectors have been asked to refer to Somerset House cases involving disputed application of the Ramsay approach, especially where an appeal was pending or where a change of established HMRC practice was involved. Where there had been full disclosure of facts and documents, the inspector was required to analyse the relevant transactions and identify the composite transaction before advancing a formal contention based on the Ramsay approach.

The situations relevant to CGT covered by the exchange of letters are:

(a) Bed and breakfasting, see **CHAPTER 4** – subject to the provisions which have specifically limited the effect of this practice, the bed and breakfasting of shares would not be challenged using the Ramsay

approach provided the transactions effectively transferred the beneficial ownership of the shares. Similar transactions affecting other
assets could, however, be more liable to attack.

(b) Husbands and wives – in most instances, the transfer of assets
between spouses/civil partners to ensure that relevant assets were
owned by the spouse carrying on the trade in order to qualify for
roll-over relief or retirement relief would not be questioned. But it
might be necessary to compare the relief claimed by the trading
spouse with that which could have been claimed by the transferor
spouse if the trade had been carried on by him for the whole period
concerned.

Therefore, over and above all the more detailed anti-avoidance rules, there
remains an all encompassing general anti-avoidance rule to deal with any
contrived tax planning schemes. The principle has been developed through
subsequent cases and has most recently been considered by a Special
Commissioner in *Drummond v HMRC* (2007) SpC 617.

This case involved a tax scheme that (if it worked) enabled individuals
with capital gains to generate offsetable capital losses without suffering a
real economic loss (apart from the costs of implementing the scheme).
Essentially, the scheme worked as follows:

(1) On 23 February 2001, an employee of a finance company called
L&O took out five life policies for single premiums of £250 on her
own life. On 26 March 2001, she assigned the policies to L&O which
topped each of the policies up with a further premium of £349,750
on 30 March 2001.

(2) On 4 April 2001, the taxpayer, Mr Drummond, contracted to buy the
five secondhand policies from L&O for £1,962,233. He paid £1
million up front and agreed to pay the balance of £962,233 to L&O
on the following day.

(3) On 5 April 2001, when the surrender value of the five policies was
£1,751,376 and before he had paid the balance of the price of the
policies, Mr Drummond asked L&O to surrender the life policies
(L&O was still the legal owner of the policies because there had been
no legal assignment of them to Mr Drummond). L&O duly surrendered the policies to the life company.

(4) The life company paid £1,751,376 cash on surrender to L&O (a net
amount of £789,143 after taking into account his liability for the
balance of the purchase price of £962,233).

The intended tax result for Mr Drummond was to have been as follows:

For income tax purposes, a small chargeable event gain in respect of the
policies arose as follows:

	£
Surrender proceeds	1,751,376
Less: Initial premia	(1,250)
Additional premia	(1,748,750)
Previous gains	(25)
Chargeable event gain	£1,351

For CGT purposes, an allowable loss of £1.96 million arose because in the disposal computations the surrender proceeds of £1,751,376 had to be excluded under s 37(1) because this amount had already been taken into account as a receipt in computing the 'income or profits or gains or losses of the person making the disposal' for income tax purposes. Essentially, the scheme relied on a perceived mismatch between the income tax and the CGT treatment of the proceeds of surrendering secondhand life policies, which appeared to allow the surrender proceeds to be excluded from the disposal of the computation for CGT.

HMRC had amended Mr Drummond's self-assessment tax return to deny the claimed loss for CGT on the following grounds:

(a) the £1,751,376 surrender proceeds had not already been taken into account in computing Mr Drummond's income and as such did not fall to be excluded from the CGT calculation;

(b) the difference between the £1,962,233 which Mr Drummond agreed to pay for the policies and the surrender proceeds of £1,751,376 (some £210,000) was to be excluded as acquisition consideration in the CGT computation because it was not given by Mr Drummond 'wholly and exclusively for the acquisition of' the life policies as required by s 38(1); and

(c) in any event, no part of the £1,962,233 was acquisition consideration because it was not incurred 'wholly and exclusively for the acquisition of' the life policies as required by s 28(1).

The Special Commissioner held that surrender proceeds were not monies taken into account as receipts in computing Mr Drummond's income. Whilst the proceeds had been brought into account in the calculation of the income gain treated as arising in connection with the policies under ICTA 1988, s 541 for the purpose of determining the amount deemed to form part of Mr Drummond's total income for the year ended 5 April 2001, they were nevertheless not taken into account as a receipt in computing his income.

The Special Commissioner found for HMRC on all three points and that there was no purpose in the sale and purchase of the life policies other than the facilitation of a tax avoidance strategy and that the £1.96 million consideration was not given 'wholly and exclusively' for the life policies but on acquiring a tax shelter. Even if he was wrong in that, the Special

Commissioner would also have held that the difference of £210,000 was not incurred 'exclusively' on the life policies but was in reality a fee for the services of the advisers involved.

In deciding that the surrender receipts had not been taken into account as a receipt in computing Mr Drummond's income, the Special Commissioner relied on a technical form of reasoning. The calculation of the gain on the surrender of the policies brought into account amounts that may not have been incurred by Mr Drummond, namely the premium paid by the original holder of the policies and the top-up premiums paid by L&O and the surrender proceeds paid to L&O. The only amount actually taken into account in computing Mr Drummond's income is the resulting chargeable event gain, namely £1,351. This is a stand-alone figure deemed to form part of Mr Drummond's income. The surrender proceeds were too remote from the computation of Mr Drummond's income to enable them to be disregarded for CGT purposes under s 37(1).

The case is expected to go to appeal and so the principle of a pre-ordained series of transactions is likely to be further clarified in the coming years. The case further demonstrates the risks involved in the pre-packaged CGT planning scheme.

Valuation issues and CG34 procedure

13.9 The nature of CGT is that it contains a number of notional disposals and deeming provisions. In such cases, it is necessary to use valuations as there is no third party arm's-length sale. In addition, even where there are arm's-length sales, it is often the case that there are a number of assets being disposed of, such that it is necessary to apportion the consideration between various assets. These factors mean that valuations are a crucial aspect of CGT, and in many cases planning advice is dependent upon the valuation being used.

Whilst valuations are relevant to all assets, they typically involve the following:

(a) properties;

(b) unquoted shares; and

(c) goodwill.

HMRC accept some of the inherent difficulties in connection with valuations and so it is possible to seek to agree the value being used prior to the submission of the relevant tax return. However, the valuation cannot be agreed in advance of the transaction. This facility is used in terms of planning and is not just relevant to compliance procedures. That is because it enables a valuation to be agreed when other planning actions are still possible. For instance, it may be that the value being agreed is part of a series of possible transactions and that the value will be relevant in terms of subsequent decisions to be made. Equally, if the value can be agreed early on in the tax year, then there may still be time to undertake other planning in the remainder of the tax year, such as realising losses or making a pension contribution.

Under the CG34 procedure, the relevant valuation is referred to either the District Valuer or the Shares Valuation Division and HMRC advise that they may expect it to take a minimum of 56 days to agree a valuation or to provide an alternative. It is necessary to submit a full computation with the CG34 application, although it is only an advance agreement on the valuation and the inspector will not comment on other aspects of the computation or any relief claimed at that point in time. Also, where a valuation is agreed for, say, a small shareholding, this does not necessarily provide much assistance or any binding precedent should a disposal of a large holding be contemplated.

It is also important to remember that the valuation for CGT purposes must be on the appropriate basis. For CGT purposes, the valuation required is the open market value of the asset being transferred or where the transaction concerns shares, the actual shareholding which is the subject of transfer. This is different to the valuation required for IHT purposes where the diminution principle applies or where related party rules could apply. It is also important that the relevant asset is identified and appropriate discounts applied – see CHAPTER 3.

Example – Valuation basis for CGT and IHT

Chris and Sue own 76 out of the 100 shares in issue in Foundry Limited. They each own 38 shares. They both decide to give 30 in total (15 each) to Harriett.

For CGT purposes, it is only necessary to look at a value of a 15% shareholding as that is the subject of transfer by each of them. For IHT purposes, it is necessary to do a combined valuation of a 76% shareholding and a combined share valuation of a 46% shareholding and the total gift is the difference between the two.

This can be very relevant in terms of planning, especially if s 260 hold-over relief is being considered and IHT business property relief may not be available.

Disposal of goodwill

13.10 Valuation issues can be particularly difficult where the disposal involves goodwill or other intangible assets. There has been a common CGT planning approach where businesses are incorporated or otherwise where intangible assets are retained in the personal ownership of the shareholders. The aim of the planning is to introduce the goodwill or other intangible assets into the company for a value such that profits can be extracted from the company at a 10% tax rate on the basis that maximum BATR applies.

Example – Goodwill on incorporation

Catherine decides to incorporate her business. She has no other disposals in the year and after taking advice, puts a value on the transfer of goodwill of £36,800.

On the basis that maximum BATR is available, then this amount can be extracted from the company without a tax liability arising as follows:

	£
Proceeds on disposal of goodwill	36,800
Taper relief (75% BATR)	(27,600)
	9,200
Annual exemption	(9,200)
	£Nil

As long as the goodwill is worth more than £36,800, then a s 165 hold-over relief claim can always be entered into such that no additional liability to CGT arises. Even if a tax liability did arise, then it would only arise at an effective tax rate of 10% if Catherine is a higher-rate taxpayer. However, problems will arise if the value of the goodwill cannot be substantiated to be at least £36,800 as in that case, monies have been extracted from the company which will form a distribution subject to income tax.

The view of HMRC on this issue was set out in Tax Bulletin 76 issued in April 2005 which states that:

'where the goodwill was deliberately overvalued when it was sold to the company as an inducement for the individual to take up employment with the company, or in return for future services to be provided by the individual to the company, the excess payment will be taxable as earnings within s62 ITEPA 2003. Where, exceptionally excess value is paid in respect of the transferor's employment but it cannot be characterised as 'earnings' the overvalue may be chargeable as a benefit under s203 ITEPA 2003'.

'The excess value is also liable for Class 1 National Insurance Contributions (NICs) because it derives from the employment and is therefore a payment of 'earnings' as defined in s3(1)(a) Social Security Contributions and Benefits Act 1992. This treatment applies irrespective of how the payment has been characterised for income tax purposes. There is no provision for 'making good' for NICs. So even if the tax charge on the benefit is reduced by making good, Class 1 NICs must be accounted for on the original excess value.'

'But in many cases, the goodwill will have been transferred from a sole trader to the company before the company has commenced trading. There may be no evidence that any excess value constitutes earnings (or is a benefit)'.

'So, in the majority of cases in which goodwill is transferred from the sole trader to a company we expect that the transferor will have received any overvalue in his capacity as shareholder, rather than as an employee/director. In such cases, the excess value will for tax purposes be treated as a distribution by virtue of ICTA88/s209(2)(b) or s209(4)'.

'Because of the uncertainties in establishing the value of goodwill there will clearly be occasions where a transfer is inadvertently caught by ICTA88/ s209(4). If it is clear that there was no intention to transfer the goodwill at excess value, and reasonable efforts were made to carry out the transfer at market value by using a professional valuation, then the distribution may be 'unwound'.

'The distributions may not be unwound if there is attempted (or actual) avoidance, or if the overvaluation was intentional, or no professional valuation was obtained'.

'In this context, we would normally regard 'professional valuation' as including one carried out by a named independent and suitably qualified valuer on an appropriate basis. But in some instances it may be necessary to establish what steps were taken to arrive at the value, what instructions/information were given to the valuer, whether it was reasonable to the parties to rely on the valuations provided, etc before an application for unwinding can be accepted'.

Depending on the level of withdrawals from the company, then it may be that, in any case, the director's loan account is still in credit and the agreement could simply be amended so that a lower goodwill valuation is used. In such a case, one could see the attraction of the CG34 procedure in order that matters are agreed as soon as possible. It is also important to make sure that the company law position is fully considered and documented and the appropriate board minutes and general meeting resolutions are put in place including that under CA 1985, s 32. It is also important that the ownership period and acquisition details of the goodwill are fully considered.

However, it is not only the value of goodwill that needs to be considered but also whether or not there is any transferable goodwill in the first place. This has implications in terms of interaction with other taxes, notably SDLT and the intangible asset regime in FA 2002 for corporation tax purposes. In this context, HMRC seek to distinguish between goodwill and categorise it into the following types:

(a) free goodwill;

(b) inherent goodwill;

(c) adherent goodwill; and

(d) personal goodwill.

Where the goodwill is personal to the individual concerned, the HMRC view is that it cannot be transferred such that no disposal has taken place. In other cases, HMRC argue that the goodwill is part of the property value and cannot be separated from it. This is relevant on the value of hotels, restaurants, etc. There are also businesses where it is accepted that no goodwill exists such as where goodwill is prevented by law (eg, medical GP practices).

The HMRC Capital Gains Manual at CG67990 provides the following analysis of the goodwill types:

(1) Personal – related to the skill and personality of the proprietor of the business;

(2) Inherent – related to the location of the business premises; and

(3) Free – related to the overall worth of the business and subdivided into:

    (a) free adherent goodwill – this arises not from the location of the premises but the carrying out of a particular business for which those premises have been or are specifically adapted or licensed; and

    (b) free separable goodwill – true free goodwill which is entirely separate from the business premises and can be transferred independently from them.

According to HMRC, when a business is sold as a going concern, the only types of goodwill which can pass will be any free separate goodwill and if the premises are also sold, any adherent free goodwill and any inherent goodwill. In HMRC's view, inherent and adherent goodwill cannot exist independently of the land to which they are attached. Therefore, these types of goodwill are part of the land for CGT purposes.

HMRC's classification of goodwill is derived in part from the decision of the Court of Appeal in *Whiteman Smith Motor Co Ltd v Chaplin* [1934] 2 KB 35 which identifies four types of customers:

(i) the cat – who stays faithful to the location not the person;

(ii) the dog – who stays faithful to the person and not the location;

(iii) the rat – who is casual and is attracted to neither person nor location; and

(iv) the rabbit – who comes because it is close by and for no other reason.

However, the legislation refers only to goodwill and does not distinguish between any categories of it. Goodwill is fundamentally an accounting concept and any modern court is likely to take heed of specialist accounting opinion and what constitutes generally accepted accounting practice (GAAP). In this context, Financial Reporting Standard (FRS) 10 defines purchased goodwill as:

> 'the difference between the cost of an acquired entity and the aggregate of the fair values of that entity's identifiable assets and liabilities. Positive goodwill arises when the acquisition cost exceeds the aggregate fair values of the identifiable assets and liabilities. Negative goodwill arises when the aggregate fair values of the identifiable assets and liabilities of the entity exceed the acquisition cost.'

The approach of HMRC was not accepted by the Special Commissioner, Michael Tildersley, in the case of *Balloon Promotions Ltd v Wilson (Inspector of Taxes)* [2006] STC (SCD) 167. This case concerns franchised operations of Pizza Express and whether the franchisee had any goodwill of their own. The Special Commissioner's view is that:

'The authorities caution against an over-analytical approach to goodwill (see *IRC v Muller & Co's Margarine Limited and Whiteman Smith Motor Company*). In view of these authorities, I question the applicability of the approach adopted by the respondents in their Capital Gains Tax manual and by their counsel which categorises goodwill into three types with the third type broken down into sub-categories. The thrust of the categorisation is to restrict roll-over relief to specific categories of goodwill. The categorisation is partly derived from the zoological definition of goodwill which was considered to be of limited value in *Whiteman Smith Motor Co*. I prefer the approach adopted by the appellant's counsel that goodwill in TCGA 1992 should be looked at as a whole which I consider to be consistent with the authorities and confirms with the principles of statutory construction.'

The Special Commissioner also makes it clear that '*Whiteman Smith Motor Co* was not authority for the proposition that the value of net adherent goodwill will as a matter of course be incorporated into the valuation of premises sold'. The Special Commissioner then went on to state:

'I accept that adherent goodwill is associated with a property and will not be passed to the purchaser if the property is not sold with the business. However, where the sale of the business incorporates the interest in the property, it does not automatically follow that the value of the adherent goodwill would be subsumed within the value of the property.

I say this because:

(1) I consider that Counsel has extended too far the ratio of *Whiteman Smith Motor Co*, upon which his proposition was based. *Whiteman Smith Motor Co* stated that net adherent goodwill will only arise if the property is sold with the business. *Whiteman Smith Motor Co* was not authority, however, for the proposition that the value of the net adherent goodwill in all circumstances would be subsumed within the property valuation. The value of the adherent goodwill was included in the property valuation in *Whiteman Smith Motor Co* because that was the requirement of the Landlord and Tenant Act which is not the statute under consideration in this appeal.

(2) The present edition of the Respondent's Capital Gains Tax manual classified adherent goodwill with free goodwill and not with inherent goodwill which suggests that adherent goodwill will be valued separately from the property. *Butler v Evans* recognises this fact.

(3) Counsel produced no evidence to support his proposition that Pizza Express and the appellants included adherent goodwill in their valuations of the leasehold interest transferred. The available evidence from the sales agreement suggested that the only type of goodwill not included in the vendor's goodwill was that inherent in the property.'

What has been established by the case law is that whether or not there is goodwill that is saleable is a question of fact. However, HMRC are still resisting this conclusion and stand by the approach adopted in the Capital Gains Manual. Their view on *Balloon Promotions* was set out in Tax Bulletin 83 where HMRC states:

'We do not accept that the term goodwill in TCGA 1992 embraces all of the various types of goodwill described in the CG Manual. We will continue to treat inherent and adherent goodwill as part of an asset in the form of a freehold or leasehold interest in land and buildings.'

Enquiries

13.11　In the early days of self-assessment, HMRC seemed to have limited staff resource to raise enquiries into CGT matters. As a result, in many cases where an enquiry from HMRC may have been expected, none was forthcoming. However, as a result of more recent reorganisations within HMRC there is now more likelihood of appropriate enquiries being raised into the capital gains pages of tax returns. This will particularly be the case where high net worth individuals are concerned who are dealt with by one of the complex personal tax units. In addition, as part of the HMRC crackdown on perceived tax avoidance, there would appear to be a higher level of TMA 1970, s 9A enquiry notices being issued on CGT computations where planning is involved such as computations involving claims for principal private residence relief and in particular where elections have been made – see CHAPTER 9.

The likelihood of an HMRC challenge needs to be considered when the planning advice is being given and the approach to disclosure of the computations and the information required should be considered at that point in time.

The normal enquiry window available to HMRC is 12 months after the tax return filing deadline. So, for tax returns for the year to 5 April 2007 the filing deadline is 31 January 2008 and the normal enquiry window closes on 31 January 2009. However, in the case of a 'discovery' enquiry, this window is extended by a further four years making it five years after the filing deadline – 31 January 2013 for 2006/07 tax returns. A discovery assessment can be made by an inspector under TMA 1970, s 29 where a loss of tax is discovered, ie the self-assessment made by the taxpayer was insufficient.

The tax case of *Langham v Veltema* [2004] STC 544, CA highlighted that the enquiry window can be extended beyond the normal 12 months after the filing deadline not only in cases where there is fraud or negligence on behalf of the taxpayer but also where the taxpayer does not provide enough information for the inspector to realise within the enquiry period that the self-assessment is insufficient.

Although the tax return only asks for basic information, there is a need to ensure that sufficient information is provided either in the additional information 'white box' or by way of attachments so that clients can have certainty of closure after 12 months following the filing deadline, not uncertainty for up to five years. However, simply filing every available piece of paper, calculation and supporting documents will not be sufficient and attention must be drawn to the appropriate detail. An inspector has to have all the information he would need, without having to carry out detailed research, to be able to decide whether or not the self-assessment is sufficient before the end of the normal 12-month enquiry window.

There is some HMRC guidance available as to what disclosure would normally provide protection against a later discovery assessment and this was issued following discussion with the professional bodies after the *Langham v Veltema* case.

If a valuation has been used then the white space note, or attached copy valuation, should state that a valuation has been made, who carried it out and that they are a named, independent and suitably qualified valuer (if that is the case) and that it was carried out on the appropriate basis. Where a judgment has been made then it is necessary to disclose what the judgment relates to and the basis of the judgment. Where a differing view from the published HMRC view has been adopted then it is necessary to disclose that HMRC guidance has not been followed and to quantify the financial impact as far as possible.

Capital gains calculations should be attached in cases where the calculation is more than a very straightforward 'proceeds less indexed cost, losses and taper relief' calculation. This includes where there is a complex calculation of the base cost – e g quoted shares with complex pooling or where there have been demergers, etc.

Disclosure of Tax Avoidance Schemes (DOTAS)

13.12   There are provisions requiring promoters of, and in some cases taxpayers making use of, tax avoidance schemes to disclose details to HMRC. The detailed provisions are mostly contained in regulations. Originally, the provisions required disclosure only of schemes connected with employment or involving financial products but the provisions were extended to cover the whole of income tax, CGT and corporation tax. Disclosure can be made online via HMRC's Anti-Avoidance Group website (www.hmrc.gov.uk) or alternatively, forms for making disclosures can be downloaded from the same location.

DOTAS is unlikely to apply to the bespoke types of planning for clients that is covered in this book. However, it may be that a client would wish to contact their personal tax adviser to discuss the specifics of a scheme. In that case, it is important that the adviser highlights the DOTAS rules to the client and the disclosures that will need to be made on the tax return.

Getting clearance

13.13   Disclosure is not just an issue for the filing of the tax return after the event but is also very relevant where a clearance application is to be made. The danger is that in order to get clearance the adviser gives insufficient information for HMRC to fully understand the position. If that is the case, then the clearance given cannot be relied upon.

HMRC has a one-stop shop for most clearance applications, which are dealt with by the Business Tax Clearance Team (BTCT). Clearance applications under the capital gains reorganisation provisions, demergers, purchase of own shares, intangible assets and transactions in securities should be sent as one application to the BTCT, 5th Floor, 22 Kingsway, London, WC2B 6NR. Clearance applications under the Enterprise Investment Scheme (EIS) do not go to the BTCT but instead to the Small Company Enterprise Centres.

A large number of clearance applications are submitted to BTCT each year. Whilst there is some evidence of an increasingly hard line on clearance applications where there is extraction of value subject to CGT, it would seem that the number of refusals is still less than 5% of the total submitted.

From a tax practice point of view, and from that of running a business, the objective is to obtain clearance as quickly and cheaply as possible. In order to do that, the clearance application must:

- clearly disclose all relevant information; and

- be as concise and as user-friendly as possible in order to facilitate a quick response from the BTCT.

It is not possible to provide definitive guidance on the format of clearance applications for all scenarios, but some general comments are as follows:

- The heading of the letter should state the legislative sections for which clearance is sought.

- It should provide full details of all the companies and individuals involved – tax reference, company number, residence position, membership of any group and details of shareholders. It may be better to provide these details in an appendix and, if relevant, also include before and after group structure diagrams.

- It should include a short summary of the overall plan together with a detailed step by step explanation of the transaction(s).

- It should include an explanation of the bona fide commercial reasons as to why the relevant steps do not form part of a scheme or arrangement one of the main purposes of which is to avoid tax.

- It should include specific technical information in respect of the statutory conditions for the sections concerned.

For applications in respect of demergers and the purchase of own shares, further guidance is provided in Statements of Practice 13/80 and 2/82. For other sections where clearance is required, there is currently no such guidance.

Clearance applications under ss 135, 136 and 139 are concerned with whether the relevant anti-avoidance legislation will be invoked. The granting of clearance does not mean that all the conditions for relief under the legislation are satisfied.

Some of the common problem areas in applications are in the transaction failing to satisfy the following requirements:

- the 25% share capital holding requirement in s 135(1);

- the minimum six month term for loan notes and redeemable shares (see ICAEW TR657 issued in April 1987);

- the reconstruction conditions in Sch 5AA; and

- the definition of business (ie what is transferred must amount to more than a transfer of assets).

These technical points should be worked through before an application is submitted and a second opinion should be sought on complex issues to ensure that risk is minimised. It is also important that company law issues are considered and this is best achieved by involving commercial law specialists.

It is also important to appreciate the significance of the FA 2002 changes and the introduction of Sch 5AA. Prior to 16 April 2002, the legislation referred to 'reconstruction or amalgamation' and these terms were not defined in statute. This vagueness has now been replaced by specific conditions in order for s 136 to apply. Sch 5AA requires that a scheme of reconstruction must consist of:

- the issue of ordinary share capital;

- equal entitlement to new shares; and either

- continuity of business; or

- a compromise or an arrangement with members.

The Stamp Office will accept clearance by the BTCT as satisfying the bona fide commercial reason tests in FA 1986, ss 75, 76 or 77. Given the potential impact of stamp duty or SDLT, the tax savings under these reliefs can be substantial. However, these reorganisation reliefs are very limited and in all but straightforward scenarios there is likely to be some liability.

The obtaining of clearance will also ease the path when subsequent tax returns are made as an inspector will accept that the overall commercial justification for the transaction has already been considered by HMRC and so some of the anti-avoidance provisions above cannot be invoked.

Conclusion

13.14 Whilst this book demonstrates that there are still plenty of opportunities available for CGT planning, tax advisers should be wary of the potential scope for such planning to be caught by specific as well as wider anti-avoidance provisions. As detailed in this chapter, the adviser should take particular care when advising on transactions in land or securities, value shifting, international aspects, a sale of a right to income or a pre-ordained series of transactions. Further, the adviser should consider whether such planning is appropriate in light of case law as well as anti-avoidance provisions that apply to such a transaction for the purpose of other taxes.

Whilst the adviser and taxpayer alike may feel there is little shelter from the ravages of the scope for anti-avoidance there are specific procedures in place to aid them. The ability to apply for clearance on certain transactions as well as the CG34 valuation check procedure can be highly useful. That said such methods can only be advantageous if the disclosure is carefully considered by the adviser and is adequate. This not only applies to the clearance application and the CG34 form themselves but equally to the self-assessment return and specifically the capital gains pages. It is only when matters are adequately disclosed that the client can seek comfort 12 months after the filing date that an HMRC enquiry is unlikely to ensue.

Checklist

	Cross Reference
Anti-Avoidance, Enquiries and Disclosure	
CGT was introduced to prevent the conversion of income into capital gains. Over the years (both before and after CGT was introduced) a number of anti-avoidance rules have been introduced. These need to be considered as part of any planning:	
• transactions in securities;	13.3
• transfer of assets abroad;	13.4
• transactions in land;	13.5
• sale of right to income;	13.6
• value shifting; and	13.7
• care law rules.	13.8
Valuation issues and disclosure on tax returns are important considerations in terms of minimising enquiries by HMRC.	
Particular problem issues arise on the valuation of goodwill.	13.10

Chapter 14

International Aspects of Capital Gains Tax Planning

Overview of International aspects of CGT

14.1   It is appropriate in this book to consider the international aspects of capital gains tax (CGT) planning within the context of advisers situated in the UK. Detailed cross-border tax advice is beyond the scope of this work as it requires advice from the overseas jurisdiction. This chapter is instead concerned with more general planning ideas and in particular for those currently, or soon to be, resident in the UK. Specifically it covers the following areas:

(a)   residency and CGT;

(b)   domicile considerations;

(c)   becoming non-resident for CGT planning purposes;

(d)   foreign assets;

(e)   overseas taxes and double tax agreements; and

(f)   the use of non-UK resident companies.

All statutory references in this chapter are to TCGA 1992 unless otherwise stated.

CGT and residence

14.2   CGT is assessed by reference to residence. Non-residents are not subject to the tax although consideration must be given to the tax regime in their country of residence. A person is chargeable to CGT if he is resident or ordinarily resident in the UK in a tax year in which disposals are made. A person may also be chargeable to UK CGT on gains made whilst he is temporarily non-resident. If a person is non-UK resident, he is not liable to CGT, even on UK situate assets, unless he is carrying on a trade through a UK branch or agency. If the person is also domiciled in the UK, he is chargeable to CGT on all aspects of his assets, regardless of where the assets giving rise to those gains are situated. He may be subject to foreign tax on non-UK gains and double taxation relief is available. If the person is not domiciled in the UK, he is assessed on his UK gains on an arising basis and on his non-UK gains on a remittance basis.

Extra-statutory concession (ESC) D2 provides that when a person first becomes resident in the UK, he is charged to CGT only on those gains which arise after his arrival provided he has not been resident or ordinarily resident in the UK in the previous five tax years before the year of arrival. Similarly, a person permanently leaving the UK will be charged to CGT only on those gains which arise before his departure. However, if the individual has been resident or ordinarily resident in the UK for the whole of at least four out of the seven tax years before the year of departure, the concession does not apply. The split-year concession in ESC D2 does not apply to trustees or the settlor where ss 77 or 86 applies.

The emigration of an individual does not give rise to a deemed disposal of assets, unlike that for trustees. A CGT charge will be levied where assets have been acquired within the previous six years and a capital gain has been held over. This is broadly where assets have been acquired by way of gift or purchase at undervalue (see s 168 regarding held-over gains and s 80 regarding the emigration of trustees).

In earlier years a device frequently used to avoid CGT involved relatively temporary absence from the UK. An individual would cease to be both resident and ordinarily resident, and undertake the disposal of an asset before returning to the UK at a later date. If the individual was working full-time overseas for a period including a complete fiscal year this might well have been sufficient to avoid liability. Others usually had to contemplate residing overseas for a minimum period of 36 months. In accordance with s 10A, where an individual leaves the UK but subsequently returns to the UK, gains made by him whilst he is non-resident may be assessed on him in the year of return. In order for this provision to apply, the individual must:

(a) be resident or ordinarily resident in the UK in the year of return;

(b) not have been resident or ordinarily resident in the UK for one or more years before that, but was resident or ordinarily resident in the UK in some previous year;

(c) have been outside the UK so that there are less than five tax years between the year of departure and the year of return; and

(d) have been UK resident or ordinarily resident for four out of the previous seven years of assessment immediately before the year of departure.

This section does not apply to assets acquired in the non-resident period nor assets disposed of to a spouse/civil partner, nor to assets already chargeable under s 10.

All the gains and losses which would have accrued to the individual in the non-resident period (together with trust gains under s 86 and company gains and losses under s 13) will be taxable on the individual in the year of return as if they were gains or losses of that year. Taper relief applies at the time of the actual disposals, not until the date that the gains became chargeable on return.

Example – Temporary non-residence

Fred is resident in the UK until January 2007. He then leaves the UK and ceases to be resident and ordinarily resident in the UK until 2011/12. In July 2008, he disposes of a business asset that he acquired on 9 August 2006. The proceeds are £150,000 and the cost of the asset was £87,000. In June 2009, he disposes of an asset acquired in May 2006 for £100,000. The proceeds are £80,000. He has no other chargeable assets.

	£
Gain in 2008/09	
Proceeds	150,000
Less: cost	(87,000)
Gain	£63,000

Taper relief from 9 August 2006 to 8 August 2007 will be available. However, the relief will be given after the loss of 2009/10 is relieved. This is because they are treated as a gain and a loss respectively of 2011/12.

	£
Loss made 2009/10	
Proceeds	80,000
Less: cost	(100,000)
Loss	£20,000

	£
Gains chargeable after 2011/12	
Gain	63,000
Less: loss made in 2009/10	
(Treated as loss of 2011/12)	(20,000)
Net gain	43,000
Gain after taper relief 50% x £43,000	£21,500

Section 10A was introduced in 1998 to prevent a liability to CGT from being avoided by becoming non-resident for a short period. This could perhaps have been achieved by disposing of shares in exchange for loan notes and then becoming non-resident before the loan notes were redeemed. Prior to 1998 the short period could be only one year if it was to take up a full-time contract of employment abroad. Whilst s 10A sought to block this, there was still a way to avoid this anti-avoidance provision by taking advantage of an applicable double tax treaty. As a result s 10A was amended in 2005 to counter this type of tax planning.

Determining residence and domicile

14.3   Residence is a question of fact and *IRC v Zorab* (1926) 11 TC 289 is the prime authority for this. The issue is how those facts are to be determined. The Special Commissioners' case of *Gaines-Cooper v HMRC* (2006) SpC 568 has had a significant impact on the approach of professional advisers when advising on residence as traditionally they have based their advice upon IR20. (IR20 represents HMRC's practice governing the fiscal consequences of emigration and immigration since the 1920s and HMRC applies it almost as if it is statute.)

Mr Gaines-Cooper was born in Reading in 1937, and was domiciled and brought up in England. He ran a successful juke-box business in the late 1950s and 1960s. Several other businesses followed, some of them based abroad, and from 1979 to 1986 he lived with his first wife in California. Mr Gaines-Cooper visited the Seychelles for the first time in 1973 and said that he 'immediately fell in love with the Seychelles and wanted to make his permanent home there'. He established a factory there, manufacturing plastic goods, in order to obtain his residency permit. In October 1975 Mr Gaines-Cooper purchased a property in the Seychelles.

During the 1970s Mr Gaines-Cooper spent about five months a year in the Seychelles and no more than two months a year in the UK. However, in the 1980s he only made, on average, three trips a year to the Seychelles, some of them quite short. There was evidence that Mr Gaines-Cooper enjoyed life in the Seychelles and had a good circle of friends there but he maintained a home in the UK at virtually all times, had many friends in the UK and attended regular social functions here.

In 1993 Mr Gaines-Cooper married his second wife who was from the Seychelles, although she took British citizenship and generally lived in the UK as her residence. In April 1998 Mrs Gaines-Cooper gave birth to their son, James, in England and she lived with her son in the UK, generally spending only school holidays in the Seychelles. Mr Gaines-Cooper was a truly mobile individual. He would make about 150 flights each year and had business interests in many jurisdictions.

For the period from 1990 to 2000, if days of arrival and days of departure are ignored then Mr Gaines-Cooper averaged just under the 91-day limit in the UK (provided that time spent in the UK for a heart bypass operation and sixteen days at the time his son was born are excluded). However, this is because there were many trips being of short duration and so the days of arrival and departure are very significant. The Special Commissioners calculated the nights spent in the UK as an average of about 130 a year. The time spent in the Seychelles was to be 'measured in weeks rather than months' and even though he had a close attachment to the Seychelles, the UK constituted his primary residence.

The Commissioners were asked to decide whether Mr Gaines-Cooper was domiciled in England during the tax years from 1992/93 to 2003/04, and whether he was resident and ordinarily resident in the UK for the same periods.

The Commissioners noted that residence is not defined in the legislation, so the word should be given its natural and ordinary meaning. They commented that no number of days spent in the UK is prescribed by statute and that one must take into account numerous factors including presence in the UK, regularity and frequency of visits, birth, family, business ties and connections with this country. On the basis of all these factors, the Commissioners determined that Mr Gaines-Cooper was indeed UK resident.

Mr Gaines-Cooper argued that he had abandoned his English domicile of origin in favour of a Seychelles domicile of choice and that during this period he was not domiciled in the UK. The Commissioners 'regarded as significant' that Mr Gaines-Cooper had his connections with the UK located in a comparatively small area of Berkshire/Oxfordshire, as did his second wife. They found it significant that his will was prepared by English solicitors and that it was subject to English law, and also that James's guardians under the Will lived in the UK. They also found it relevant that he retained his British citizenship without applying for citizenship in the Seychelles and that his second wife, although of Seychelles origin, obtained British citizenship.

In order to justify a domicile of choice in the Seychelles, Mr Gaines-Cooper had to show that the Seychellois residence was his main one. Also, although the burden of proof on the taxpayer to show that he had acquired a domicile of choice was the civil standard of balance of probabilities, the level of intention which had to be established on those principles was a 'clear and unequivocal' one to establish a new domicile and to 'reject' England. On the basis of the facts, they thought that he had not done so. He had clearly established many connections with the Seychelles, and the property he had there was the one which he had owned the longest, but he had always maintained close connections with the UK, and indeed with the particular area in which he had been brought up.

Following the *Gaines-Cooper* case, HMRC issued a guidance note saying that they had not changed their interpretation of IR20, and that the 91-day test was still valid, but that it only applied when the taxpayer had 'left' the UK. This case demonstrates that individuals who are from the UK, wishing to claim that they have lost their UK residence, will need to be more cautious than they might previously have been. Such individuals, especially if they wish to keep their UK home and even more so should their wife and children still be based in the UK, must seriously consider whether they can lose their UK residency and will probably want to at least start counting their days spent in the UK on the basis of whether they are here overnight, rather than being able to ignore days of arrival and departure. Realistically, it may be difficult to show non-residence unless an individual's spouse and young children are also abroad.

For individuals who come to the UK for limited periods merely to work and who have their home, spouse and family outside of the UK, then the case is less significant. HMRC view the case as being about establishing whether someone has left the UK. Advisers should be wary and IR20 must be viewed as a concession and so cannot be used for tax avoidance purposes.

Tax return questions and disclosure

14.4   The Self-assessment Tax Return question on residence asks for the box to be ticked 'if you consider that you are non-resident', etc for the year, and also asks for a factual statement as to whether you are non-resident. There is no question of a claim being made, which would imply an element of choice. An individual cannot elect for non-residence.

The Tax Return now also includes some much more specific questions on domicile and these should also be considered as part of any advice based on a non-UK domiciled status. It is on the basis of these responses that any assessment is determined. The four key questions asked are as follows:

(i) Is this the first year you have claimed to have a domicile outside the UK?

(ii) If so, and you have a domicile of origin within the UK, when did your domicile change?

(iii) If you have never been domiciled in the UK, were you born here?

(iv) If you were born outside the UK, when did you come to live here?

Hold-over relief and non-residence

14.5   Section 168 provides that a held-over gain under ss 165 or 260 crystallises if the donee emigrates within six years of the end of the tax year in which the gift took place. The gain is chargeable on the transferee but recoverable from the transferor if not paid within 12 months of the due date (except that a transferor is not to be charged more than six years after the end of the tax year in which the gift took place). The transferor has a right of recovery from the transferee. The crystallised gain is proportionately reduced where the transferee has disposed of the assets in whole or part before becoming non-resident. On a subsequent actual sale of the asset by the donee, the held-over gain is not deducted from the base cost in order to avoid a double charge to CGT.

There can be no liability if the loss of UK residential status occurs more than six years following the end of the year of assessment in which the transfer took place. Liability as a temporary non-resident under s 10A does not displace the application of s 168 but the possibility of double liability is removed by treating the transferee as having acquired the asset at market value without any deduction for hold-over relief at the time of the original transfer.

However, s 168(5) does provide that exemption from tax under s 168(1) is available if the donee is absent from the UK for a period not exceeding three years whilst carrying out full-time duties of an office or employment overseas.

Shares qualifying for Enterprise Investment Scheme relief

14.6   In accordance with Sch 5B, para 3(1), the deferred gain or part of the deferred gain in relation to qualifying shares will be brought back into charge when the investor becomes non-resident within five years of the issue of shares under the Enterprise Investment Scheme (EIS) or where a person who received the shares on a no gain/no loss transfer from their spouse or civil partner becomes non-resident within five years of the issue of the shares.

As for s 168, no chargeable event will arise where the non-residence is due to a person being in employment, all the duties of which are performed outside the UK and that person again becomes resident or ordinarily resident in the UK within a period of three years calculated from the time when the person became non-resident without having meanwhile disposed of any of the shares.

The taper relief on the deferred gain is calculated by reference to the original deferred gain as set out in CHAPTER 6.

Avoiding CGT on the sale of shares by becoming non-resident

14.7   The concessional 'split year' basis in ESC D2 does not generally apply for CGT (unless, exceptionally, the individual has only been a short-term UK resident). HMRC give some guidance in their manuals as to what they would consider to be exploitation of ESC D2. Paragraph CG25982 of the Capital Gains Manual states:

> 'In straightforward cases where the contract of sale is delayed until after the date of emigration, the Board have decided that they will not withhold the concession merely on the grounds that the disposal was arranged to take place after the date of departure from the UK. On its own, a genuine postponement of the disposal is not regarded as an attempt to use the concession for tax avoidance, but where coupled with other arrangements it might be so regarded.'

Similar comments are made at CG26040 and CG26050 concerning options and cross options respectively. However these comments need to be interpreted in the light of the recent *Gaines-Cooper v HMRC* (2006) SpC 568 decision which is considered above.

Therefore, in general, if the shares are sold after the date of departure, but in the same tax year, then the gain will be taxed in that year under normal rules. To escape CGT using the 'five-year' absence rule, the vendor must be commercially able to finalise the sale negotiations and complete the sale contract after they leave the UK (also requiring a cooperative purchaser). Great care must be taken to prevent a binding contract being created before the end of the tax year of departure – hence, any communications between the parties and heads of agreement, etc must clearly be stated as being 'subject to contract'.

In the vast majority of cases, an individual vendor must ensure that he is neither resident nor ordinarily resident for at least five complete tax years after the tax year of departure. In practice, this means that the vendor must leave the UK before the tax year of disposal and ideally remain entirely absent from the UK throughout the tax year in which the shares are sold.

To avoid being treated as resident or ordinarily resident in (at least) the following four tax years, return visits to the UK should be minimised. An individual will be regarded as tax resident in the UK if he spends 183 days or more here in any tax year or an average of 91 days or more each tax year.

Vendors also have to show that they have taken up permanent residence elsewhere and their case is strengthened by selling or granting a long lease of their UK home and acquiring a permanent home abroad. Of course, it must also be ensured that no overseas tax liability arises in the destination country.

The disruption caused by spending at least five years away from the UK is perhaps only likely to appeal to those selling out at the end of their business career. Others may well seek more realistic solutions. For example, if the company has substantial reserves, it may be appropriate for the vendor to emigrate for a shorter period (at least one complete tax year) with a view to extracting a dividend from the company whilst non-resident. As the vendor would be a non-UK resident, there should be no further UK income tax liability in respect of the dividend.

Example – Dividend stripping

Lester owns 100% of the shares in Cash Cow Limited, a call centre operator. He goes non-resident during 2006/07. Cash Cow Limited has retained reserves of £2 million and has minimal fixed assets with most of the assets in cash. The company is still trading profitably but trading operations are now at a lower level because some large contracts have been lost.

Lester wishes to extract the value from the company and has been considering a sale. On taking local advice Lester establishes that the dividend will not be taxed in the jurisdiction in which he is resident. The retained profits can therefore be extracted in 2007/08 with no further tax liability.

In the fairly rare event that an individual vendor has only been UK tax resident for less than four years out of the last seven tax years, before the year of departure, they will be able to avoid a UK CGT charge on selling their shares by either:

(a) going abroad under a full-time contract of employment spanning at least one tax year; or

(b) leaving the UK before the tax year of disposal and going abroad for at least three tax years (so as to be neither resident nor ordinarily resident in the UK in the tax year of disposal).

If the vendor intends to emigrate at some future date, then it is very difficult to defer the tax charge where the acquiring company issues loan stock (or shares) in exchange for the vendor's shares. Clearance applications are invariably refused where the issue of loan notes is purely designed to avoid tax. If the vendor has indicated an intention to emigrate after the sale this must be fully disclosed in the clearance application.

Trading in the UK through a branch or agency

14.8 A person who is neither resident nor ordinarily resident in the UK will be subject to CGT in any year of assessment in which he is carrying on a trade, profession or vocation in the UK and in which he makes gains on the disposal of assets situated in the UK:

(a) which are used in or for the purposes of the trade at or before the time of disposal (eg plant and machinery);

(b) which are used or held for the purposes of the branch or agency at or before the time of disposal or are assets acquired for use by or for the purposes of the branch or agency (eg office premises).

An individual emigrating from the UK is strictly still UK resident in the year of departure so s 10 cannot apply to make UK branch assets chargeable until after the year of departure. If ESC D2 is applied in this situation, it would effectively exempt gains in the year of departure made after departure, thus creating a loophole. Therefore, ESC D2 specifically does not apply to gains on UK branch assets in the year the taxpayer emigrates.

It would be possible to avoid a charge under s 10 either by ceasing to trade through a UK branch before selling the assets or by removing the assets from the UK (where possible) whilst still trading. Therefore, where a non-resident person ceases to trade in the UK through a branch or agency, he is deemed to have disposed of any chargeable asset used in the trade immediately before it ceases. Furthermore, if such a person exports such an asset before the trade ceases, he will be deemed to have made a chargeable disposal of such an asset immediately before export. For both of these situations giving rise to a deemed disposal, use market values for the calculation of the chargeable gain.

Roll-over relief is not available to relieve chargeable gains on UK assets unless the replacement assets are chargeable assets immediately after they are acquired. In this context, a dual resident person is treated as non-resident where replacement assets would be exempt from UK CGT by virtue of a double tax relief agreement.

From a practical perspective and one that can give more tax planning flexibility, where an individual has a sole-tradership which is to continue after becoming non-resident then an incorporation prior to becoming non-resident should be considered.

Non-domiciliaries and CGT

14.9 Individuals resident and ordinarily resident in the UK normally pay UK tax on all of their income and capital gains, as and wherever they arise in the world. However whilst a non-domiciliary is assessable on all UK income and capital gains arising, the non-UK source income and capital gains are only subject to UK tax to the extent that they are remitted to the UK. The CGT provisions do not contain the need to make a claim for the remittance basis and as a consequence of this the arising basis cannot apply to gains on the sale of non-UK assets.

Domicile is a common law principle and attaches an individual to a legal system. It is a concept of where one truly belongs regardless of physical presence. Individuals have a domicile of origin but can acquire a domicile of choice. However, the domicile of choice is acquired in addition to the domicile of origin and will fall away if the individual decides to give up the domicile of choice. Tax advice based on those domiciled within the UK adopting a domicile of choice outside of the UK is fraught with difficulty. However, by the same token it is equally hard for non-UK domiciled individuals to acquire a UK domicile. It is therefore important when advising clients not to assume the domicile status and to properly question the client to establish the position.

The domicile status of the individual at the time of the disposal and the date of remittance is important. For example, a capital gain realised when non-domiciled but remitted when UK domiciled is still liable to tax. That said, the residency status of the individual is also a key factor in establishing UK liability. For the UK to impose a liability, the individual must be within the charge to CGT, ie resident or ordinarily resident during any part of the tax year, at both the date of disposal and the date of remittance. If the individual is non-resident at the time an asset is disposed of and remits those funds after he has subsequently acquired a UK residency, the UK will impose no liability to CGT. Similarly, the UK will not impose a liability on a gain realised by the individual when he is UK resident but the proceeds of which are remitted when he becomes non-resident.

It is possible for a non-domiciled vendor to defer CGT on the disposal of an asset and avoid it altogether by setting up the 'right' structure when a company is first incorporated. Typically, this would entail establishing a foreign incorporated company (which would be UK tax resident on the grounds of being centrally managed and controlled here). Shares in the foreign company would be regarded as non-UK assets (and hence, when sold, CGT would only be payable on a remittance basis). Alternatively, if a UK company is used, some or all of the shares can be placed in a non-resident trust while their value is relatively low.

Non-domiciled individuals are not subject to the settlor charge on non-UK resident trusts. However, gains arising in trusts created by non-domiciled individuals (whenever created) are taxed when received by the UK domiciled individual. If the gains are retained in the trust, they cannot be taxed in the UK (and it may be possible for the settlor to extract them on a subsequent emigration).

Gains remitted to the UK

14.10 An amount is treated as being a gain remitted to the UK if it is paid, used or enjoyed in the UK, or is transmitted or brought into the UK in any manner or form. Constructive remittances to the UK are treated as if they were remittances and the rules for determining this in relation to overseas income and income tax are also applied to CGT.

Losses incurred by a chargeable person who is domiciled abroad are not allowable. It is important therefore to segregate gains and losses because remitted gains are assessed even where there is a net loss.

It can happen that gains made in one tax year are subject to tax in a later tax year. The gain is computed according to the rules in force in the tax year in which it is made, but CGT is payable on that gain at the rate applying in the tax year in which the gain is remitted. Taper relief applies to remitted gains, but only up to the date of the actual gain, not until the time of remittance (if later).

What is a remittance?

14.11 Significant planning opportunities are possible within the remittance rules. An individual can maintain separate overseas bank accounts to hold income and capital and remit to the UK only from the capital account. Overseas income can also be paid abroad to meet non-UK expenditure. This can be achieved by ensuring that there are three accounts maintained offshore, for the following purposes:

(a) a capital deposit account;

(b) an income account into which deposit interest is credited; and

(c) a dealing account to receive the proceeds for the sale of assets.

The use of overseas income to pay a UK credit card bill is a taxable remittance. So too is (in HMRC's opinion) the use of overseas income to repay the debt on a foreign credit card if that card has been used for purchases in the UK. On a practical level this can be very messy to sort out in terms of matching gains and remittances. The use of funds to buy assets abroad which are then brought to the UK will not constitute a remittance. Examples that are commonly encountered are cars and yachts. However, if the asset is subsequently sold in the UK then the proceeds will be treated as a remittance. Arrangements which import overseas income by a sequence of transactions run the risk of being treated as a remittance.

Example – Remittance basis planning for non-domiciles

Dixon is UK resident but domiciled in Kenya. He maintains funds with a bank in the Isle of Man as follows:

Bank Account One – Capital balance prior to becoming resident. This was a balance paid into the account prior to Dixon becoming UK resident. Money is paid from this account to Dixon in the UK.

Bank Account Two – Overseas income receipts. No transfers are made from this account to Dixon in the UK. Transfers from this account are used to fund personal expenditure outside of the UK.

Bank Account Three – Receipts from foreign gains. This account could be combined with the income account but it is easier on a practical level to keep it separate as long as there are significant gains. Its usage is the same as the income account (Bank Account Two).

Delayed remittances

14.12 A taxpayer may be unable to remit proceeds arising from the disposal of a foreign asset for legal and other reasons. A taxpayer may claim relief under s 279 where the delay arises because of a provision of the law of the territory where the asset was situated, or due to the action of its government, or due to the impossibility of obtaining foreign currency in that territory, and the inability to transfer the gains was not due to any want of reasonable endeavours on the part of the taxpayer. The claim must be made by the fifth anniversary of 31 January following the tax year in which the gain arises. The effect of the claim is to remove the gains from charge in the year they arise. Taper relief applies up to the date of the actual disposal. When the proceeds, and thus the gain, become transferable, it is treated as being a chargeable gain arising in that year.

Example – Remittance of gains

Rufus is UK resident but not UK domiciled. In 2006/07 he has the following gains and losses:

	£
Gain on sale of UK shares (non-business asset – no taper relief)	10,000
Gain on sale of overseas shares (business asset – 1 year taper relief)	9,000
Loss on sale of villa in Cyprus	(4,000)
Loss on sale of holiday home in Devon	(1,000)

The proceeds of sale of the overseas shares were £25,000 and Rufus remits £5,000 during the year from the proceeds to the UK. Therefore, the part of the gain remitted is £1,800 (5,000/25,000 x 9,000).

For the purposes of calculating Rufus' chargeable gains, the loss on the villa in Cyprus is not allowable. Rufus' chargeable gains for 2006/07 are therefore as follows:

	Business assets	Non-business assets
	£	£
Gain on UK shares	—	10,000
Gain on overseas shares	1,800	—
Loss on Devon holiday home	—	(1,000)
Gain before taper relief	1,800	9,000
Less taper relief @ 50%	(900)	—
	900	9,000

Summary of total chargeable gains:	£
Total gains	9,900
Less: annual exemption	(8,800)
Chargeable gains	£1,100

Gains and losses on foreign currency

14.13   In accordance with s 251, no chargeable gain accrues on a withdrawal from a sterling bank account. However, by virtue of s 252 this rule does not apply to credit balances of foreign currency accounts, unless the currency was acquired by the holder for the personal expenditure outside the UK of himself or his family and any dependants.

Where overseas gains arise, it is common for the proceeds to be paid into an offshore bank account denominated in a currency other than sterling. If this is the case, then it will also be necessary to consider the movements on such a foreign bank account from a CGT perspective. It may be that a loss arises which can be offset against the gain on the original overseas asset.

If the foreign currency is subject to CGT, any withdrawal from the account potentially gives rise to a gain or loss, depending on currency fluctuations unless, in accordance with Statement of Practice 10/84, it is a transfer to another account in the same currency held by the taxpayer.

Foreign currency is dealt with for CGT purposes as though it were shares and securities (s 104) with additions (including interest), and withdrawals being computed in sterling at the exchange rate prevailing at the time of the transaction.

Location of assets

14.14 The legislation at s 275 sets out rules for determining where an asset is located for the purposes of this relief. These rules were amended in 2005 to counter avoidance. For example, it was previously possible for non-UK domiciled individuals to avoid CGT on bearer shares by arranging for the bearer instrument to be outside the UK at the time of disposal, since under common law the shares were situated where the bearer instrument was held. This is no longer the case.

Double tax treaties

14.15 The domestic tax legislation of different countries can conflict in terms of the rates of taxation applied, whether an item is taxed, the manner of taxation and the tax year or other period over which the tax is applied. Double taxation of capital gains can arise whilst in many countries there is no separate CGT and gains are added to taxable income. In particular:

(a) a UK-resident individual who disposes of assets situated abroad may be liable both to foreign income tax and to CGT;

(b) a person may be resident in more than one country and liable to tax on worldwide gains in both countries.

Assets situated in the UK which are owned by a person neither resident nor ordinarily resident in the UK are not normally liable to CGT. However, CGT does apply if:

(a) the assets form part of the business property of a branch or agency in the UK; or

(b) an individual is a temporary non-resident.

To try and overcome these difference in tax treatment, double tax agreements (or treaties) have been entered into between countries. The approach of tax authorities to the taxation of capital gains differs widely and therefore so do the agreements on this issue. For example, where both countries tax capital gains on a broadly similar basis, it is not uncommon to exempt a resident of one country from tax in the other, except to the extent that the gains are derived from a permanent establishment in the latter country. However, in order to try and achieve more uniformity of approach, the Organisation for Economic Co-operation and Development (OECD) produces a model convention of which Article 13 concerns capital gains. Despite this, it should not be assumed that there is a treaty between the UK and another country which adopts this article and specific reference should be made to the relevant treaty itself. Article 13 reads as follows:

'1 Gains derived by a resident of a Contracting State from the alienation of immovable property referred to in Article 6 and situated in the other Contracting State may be taxed in that other State.

2 Gains from the alienation of movable property forming part of the business property of a permanent establishment which an enterprise of a Contracting State has in the other Contracting State, including such gains from the alienation of such a permanent establishment (alone or with the whole enterprise), may be taxed in that other State.

3 Gains from the alienation of ships or aircraft operated in international traffic, boats engaged in inland waterways transport or movable property pertaining to the operation of such ships, aircraft or boats, shall be taxable only in the Contracting State in which the place of effective management of the enterprise is situated.

4 Gains derived by a resident of a Contracting State from the alienation of shares deriving more than 50 per cent of their value directly or indirectly from immovable property situated in the other Contracting State may be taxed in that other State.

5 Gains from the alienation of any property, other than that referred to in paragraphs 1, 2, 3 and 4, shall be taxable only in the Contracting State of which the alienator is a resident.'

This model article provides that capital gains on the disposal of immovable property may be taxed in the country in which it is situated and this is extended to include gains from movable property that is part of a permanent establishment or of a fixed base. Any other capital gains are then taxable only in the country of residence of the person making the disposal. Some agreements provide, however, that one country may apply CGT to the disposal of any property situated in that country. Immovable property is to be construed in accordance with the law of that country and means not only land but also property ancillary to the use of the land including livestock, agricultural and forestry equipment.

The disposal is often referred to in the article as the 'alienation of property'. This will include gains arising not only from sale but also from exchange, expropriation, transfer to a company in exchange for shares, the granting of a right, transfer by gift, and even the passing of property on death. It will also include partial disposal in similar situations.

Double tax relief

14.16 Where a UK resident is taxable to CGT and to foreign tax on gains, relief is available either under a double taxation treaty, or by virtue of unilateral credit relief under s 277. The relief given cannot exceed the UK CGT on the asset.

In accordance with Statement of Practice 6/88, it is not necessary for the foreign tax to be exactly the same nature as CGT (eg if it treats the gain as income), payable at the same time as CGT or by the same person, as long as the tax relates to the same source. Credit relief is also available in relation to tax paid by an overseas company on gains apportioned to UK-resident participators.

Where credit relief is not advantageous, a taxpayer may instead treat any foreign tax paid as a deduction in computing the gain on disposal under s 278. A case where this may be useful is where the gain will be rolled over so that no CGT is actually payable. The foreign tax can be used to reduce the gain rolled over, thus resulting in a higher base cost for the new asset. Deduction relief may also be advantageous where losses exceed gains for the year as this relief will enable higher losses to be carried forward.

Example – Foreign tax as a deduction

> Norman sells an apartment in Spain. He acquired the property in 2004 for £100,000 (based on the exchange rate at the time). He sells the asset in summer 2007 for £90,000 on conversion into sterling (after costs). Before accounting for foreign tax there is a loss of £10,000. However, Norman finds out that in Spain he is liable to tax on the gain of £2,000. There can be no claim for credit relief as there is no liability in the UK. By claiming the foreign tax as a deduction his allowable loss to be carried forward is increased to £12,000.

Double tax relief in practice can be very messy as the overseas tax regime is unlikely to be identical to that in the UK. This is particularly the case when dealing with share portfolios where it is likely that a practical and cost-effective approach will be necessary. It is also problematic when providing tax advice both because of language difficulties and because the foreign tax treatment (and therefore the level of double tax relief) may not be clear at the time.

Gains made by a non-UK resident company

14.17 Section 13 provides that gains realised by non-resident companies, whilst not chargeable on the company itself, can be taxed on the participators on an apportioned basis if the company would be 'close' were it UK resident. It applies where:

(a) gains accrue to a company which is non-resident in the UK;

(b) the company would be a close company if resident in the UK; and

(c) the gains are not distributed by the company within two years from the date the gain arose by dividend, distribution of capital or dissolution of the company.

Gains are calculated using the corporate capital gains calculation rules (ie full indexation allowance with no taper relief). The charge depends on whether a person is a participator in the company as defined for income tax purposes in ICTA 1988, s 417 and ITA 2007, s 253. Interests of beneficiaries under settlements are treated as interest of trustees of that settlement, not of the beneficiaries. No charge can arise on a non-domiciliary who is a participator.

The gains of the company will be apportioned, in the year the gain arises, to each participator who is UK resident or ordinarily resident, if individuals are UK domiciled at that time, in relation to the extent of the participator's interest as a participator in the company. No apportionment is made if the part of the gain attributable to the participator does not exceed one tenth of the gain, ie a participator must have over 10% of the shares in order to be charged under s 13. Holdings of associates are taken into account in determining whether the participator has more than a 10% shareholding.

Example – Application of s 13

Bruce is a UK resident and domiciled shareholder who owns half the shares in a non-resident close company. In July 2007 the non-resident company sells an asset realising an indexed gain of £100,000. Bruce has no other gains in 2007/08 and is a higher-rate taxpayer.

In accordance with s 13, half the gain of £100,000 is attributable to Bruce because he is a 50% shareholder and he is assessable to CGT in 2007/08. The CGT due is:

	£
Gain under s 13	50,000
Less: annual exemption	(9,200)
	£40,800
CGT @ 40%	£16,320

If the company distributes the gain within the earlier of three years of the end of the period of account of the company in which the gain accrued or four years from the date the gain accrued, by dividend or distribution of capital or otherwise, a deduction is given against any tax payable on this later event in respect of the tax paid on the attribution of gains, to reduce or extinguish the later liability. No repayment of tax is allowed. Any tax reimbursed by the company to the participator is not treated as a payment by the company (ie it is not a distribution) for tax purposes. Any CGT paid by the participator (to the extent it is not reimbursed by the company nor applied to reduce any subsequent liability to CGT) is an allowable deduction in computing a gain on any asset representing his interest in the company as a participator in respect of which the apportionment of the gain arose. There are rules to decide which of the gains (or income if the distribution is by way of dividend) is to be treated as the highest part of gains (or income) for a tax year.

The provisions do not apply to:

(a) gains accruing on the disposal of any asset only used either for the purposes of the trade carried on by the company wholly outside the UK or for the purposes of the non-UK part of a trade carried on partly within and partly outside the UK;

(b) gains arising on a disposal of currency or a foreign currency bank account where the money is used for the purposes of a trade of the company carried on wholly outside the UK; or

(c) gains charged on a UK permanent establishment.

Losses may also be apportioned under these provisions in the same proportion as gains. However, such losses can only be used to reduce or extinguish gains apportioned to the participator under these provisions in the same year of assessment. There is no carry forward of unutilised s 13 losses.

Section 13(10) extends this anti-avoidance provision to non-resident trustee participators which, while not within the charge to CGT, could be 'looked through' and imputed charges under ss 86 and 87 would follow. Section 79B prevents trustees from using tax treaties to prevent gains of offshore companies being attributed to resident UK settlors and beneficiaries.

Central management and control

14.18 If a company is non-resident for UK corporation tax purposes, it is not chargeable to UK tax on the capital gains it makes. This can afford protection from UK taxation on gains. In practice, it can be difficult to ensure that the company is and remains non-resident for corporation tax purposes because of the effective control and management test, under which even a non-UK-incorporated company can be regarded as a UK tax resident.

The leading case for determining a company's tax residence is *De Beers Consolidated Mines Ltd v Howe* [1906] AC 455 during which Lord Loreburn said:

'A company resides ... where its real business is carried on ... and the real business is carried on where the central management and control actually abides.'

The issue of central management and control was recently considered in the Court of Appeal case of *Wood v Holden* [2006] EWCA Civ 26. The facts of the case are quite complex but in essence concern Mr and

Mrs Wood who wished to sell their greeting cards business which was pregnant with a £30 million gain. The business operated through Ron Wood Greetings Card Ltd (Greetings), a trading company operating the 'Birthdays' chain of card shops. Mr and Mrs Wood owned between them approximately 96% of the ordinary share capital in Greetings.

On 27 March 1995 Mr and Mrs Wood engaged PriceWaterhouseCoopers (PWC) Corporate Finance to locate a buyer for the company. On the advice of PWC a number of tax-geared steps were taken thereafter.

- On 22 September 1995 — Ron Wood Greetings Card Holdings Ltd (Holdings) was formed. The shares were held by Mr and Mrs Wood.

- On 18 October 1995 — Mr and Mrs Wood set up a number of family settlements. The trustees of these settlements were Barclays Private Trust (BVI) Ltd, a wholly-owned subsidiary of Barclaytrust, based in Geneva.

- On 31 October 1995 — the trustees incorporated Copsewood Investments Ltd (CIL), a company registered in the British Virgin Islands. Mr and Mrs Wood had gifted 49.99% of their Holdings shares to CIL.

- On 26 October 1995 — Mr and Mrs Wood gifted their Greetings shares to Holdings.

- On 27 October 1995 — Mr and Mrs Wood gifted a small number of shares in Holdings to a UK-resident accumulation and maintenance trust for the benefit of their children.

- On 18 July 1996 CIL purchased all the shares in a dormant Dutch company Eulalia Holdings BV (Eulalia). ABN AMRO Trust Company (ABN AMRO) was appointed as sole managing director of Eulalia.

- On 23 July 1996 CIL disposed of its shareholding in Holdings to Eulalia for £23.7 million plus, in the event of a sale within three years in excess of that amount, 95% of such excess. Eulalia paid for the shares by way of an interest-free loan from Holdings.

- On 21 October 1996 Eulalia sold its shares in Holdings for £30,799,384. The other shareholders in Holdings and Greetings also sold their shares at the same time.

In short, acting at the instigation of PWC, the Netherlands directors of Eulalia had purchased the UK company from an offshore company (CIL) in July 1996, and sold the UK company in October 1996 to an arm's-length purchaser.

HMRC assessed Mr and Mrs Wood to CGT under s 13 on gains which, it contended, accrued on the 23 July disposal. The contention for Mr and Mrs Wood was that the disposal was brought within the 'no gain/no loss' provisions of s 17 by virtue of s 14. To succeed on this argument, the taxpayers had to demonstrate that both CIL and Eulalia were non-resident companies. HMRC accepted that CIL was a non-resident entity but maintained that Eulalia was centrally managed and controlled in the UK such as to make it UK-resident for tax purposes.

The Commissioners nonetheless held that, by itself, the purchase of the Holdings shares did not give rise to a finding that central management and control lay in the UK. They were so persuaded by two additional factors. These were as follows:

(i) Eulalia had no business other than the acquisition, holding and sale of the shares in Holdings, and

(ii) although there were strong commercial reasons for Eulalia to accept the offer to sell the shares in Holdings in October 1996, no 'real consideration' was given by ABN AMRO to the terms of that sale. The Commissioners found that ABN AMRO 'simply fell in with the wishes of Mr Wood expressed by his advisers'.

In the Court of Appeal, Chadwick LJ held that the Special Commissioners had made two crucial findings of fact that led necessarily to the conclusion that Eulalia was non-UK-resident. Firstly, the Commissioners found that 'the directors of Eulalia ... were not bypassed nor did they stand aside since their representatives signed or executed the documents'. This took 'the present case outside the class exemplified by the facts in *Unit Construction Co Ltd v Bullock*' (where the parent company had usurped the powers and functions of the local board of directors). Secondly, the Commissioners found 'nothing surprising in the fact that [Eulalia's] directors accepted the agreement prepared by Price Waterhouse'. The managing director of Eulalia, ABN AMRO, did sign and execute the documents 'and so must, in fact, have decided to do so'.

Chadwick LJ went on to conclude:

'Those two facts make it impossible to treat this case as one in which ABN AMRO, as managing director of Eulalia, made no decision. There was no evidence that Price Waterhouse (or anyone else) dictated the decision which ABN AMRO was to make; although as the Special Commissioners and the judge pointed out, Price Waterhouse intended and expected that ABN AMRO would make the decisions which it did make ... there were two critical decisions for Eulalia to make — the decision to purchase the Holdings shares in July 1996 and the decision to sell those shares in October 1996 — and both decisions were, in fact, made by ABN AMRO as managing director. There was nothing else to manage. A further flaw in the Special Commissioners' approach was to treat the decisions which were made by ABN AMRO as not "effective decisions" because they were reached without proper information or consideration. But a management decision does not cease to be a management decision because it might have been taken on fuller information; or even, as it seems to me, because it was taken in circumstances which might put the director at risk of an allegation of breach of duty. Ill-informed or ill-advised decisions taken in the management of a company remain management decisions.'

It was undoubtedly helpful to the taxpayers' case that all the correspondence showed that PWC did not give orders when writing to the Netherlands' directors. When PWC put documents before the directors the language used was along the lines of 'could you review these documents and let us know if you are happy to sign them?'.

Chadwick LJ helpfully expanded upon the requirements in terms of the role of the non-resident company directors and company formalities by stating:

> 'it is essential to recognise the distinction between cases where management and control of the company is exercised through its own constitutional organs (the board of directors or the general meeting) and cases where the functions of those constitutional organs are ... exercised independently of, or without regard to, those constitutional organs ... It is essential to recognise ... between the role of an "outsider" in proposing advising and influencing the decisions which the constitutional organs take in fulfilling their functions and the role of an outsider who dictates the decisions which are to be taken.'

The phrase 'constitutional organ' reveals why central management and control is to be defined by the actor rather than the actions. It is the nature of a corporate board to take decisions on behalf of a company. Whether a board takes wise or well-informed decisions may be a matter for debate, but it is not a relevant debate in establishing the abode of central management and control. HMRC were refused leave to appeal the case to the House of Lords.

With careful planning, a non-domiciled individual may be able to mitigate UK CGT on the disposal of UK property by holding it through a suitably structured offshore trust in an appropriate jurisdiction.

Example – Offshore structuring

Mike is a UK resident but non-UK domiciled client who wishes to acquire UK investment property with significant growth potential. If he acquires this property in his personal name, then any capital gain realised on the sale of the investment property will be liable to UK CGT. If an offshore company is used to acquire the investment property then it will, if the residence of the company is situated offshore, ensure that any gain from the sale of the property will not be taxable in the UK.

He sets up a Jersey company the shares of which are held by a Jersey discretionary trust. The Jersey company has two Jersey resident directors and a corporate secretary who is also resident in Jersey. The UK settlor has no legal or beneficial interest in the company and so no constitutional or legal powers whatsoever over the company, its officers and shareholders, or its affairs. He is neither a director nor a shareholder and so it is difficult for HMRC to contend that he exercises actual management and control of the business of the company or the company itself, as these powers are reserved exclusively to the professional directors, and to the trustees as shareholders. The settler should if possible avoid direct contact with the directors, and should communicate his wishes solely to the offshore trustees. There should also be a directors' service agreement between them and the offshore trustees.

Conclusion

14.19   It is much more common for UK-resident individuals to acquire properties overseas and there has also been an increase in both immigration to, and emigration from, the UK over the last decade or so. International CGT planning issues are increasingly commonplace amongst mainstream private client work, however, there is a danger that the issues are not picked up. In particular it is important that domicile status is properly enquired into when all new clients are taken on.

Checklist

	Cross Reference
International Aspects of CGT	
CGT is assessable on UK residents. It is therefore necessary to consider residency issues. Non-domiciled individuals are taxable on a remittance basis in respect of foreign gains.	14.2
It is possible to avoid CGT by becoming non-resident.	14.7
Section 13 taxes participators of non-UK resident companies on gains made by those companies.	14.17

Chapter 15

Interaction with Inheritance Tax

Importance of inheritance tax issues in capital gains tax planning

15.1 Inheritance tax (IHT) planning is considered separately in Tolley's Inheritance Tax Planning. This chapter is not intended to seek to replicate that work, nor to unduly focus on the interaction between capital gains tax (CGT) planning and IHT to the exclusion of other taxes, such as income tax, corporation tax, VAT and Stamp Duty Land Tax (SDLT) but rather to highlight some specific circumstances in which the IHT issues should be borne in mind by advisers. In the main, these relate to areas where CGT planning has been covered elsewhere in this book. Whereas income tax planning relates to monies being earned or received each year, and so the benefits are immediate, the point about CGT planning is that because of decisions made for short-term reasons, there may be unfortunate consequences in the long term when an asset is sold, leading to the client having a large tax liability at that point in time. The same points are very true of IHT planning.

As such, the long-term implications of CGT planning need to be considered at the outset given that outcomes will not be known for sometime. This chapter will cover some of the significant CGT issues covered elsewhere in this book where it is particularly important that associated IHT planning issues are also considered. Specifically, the following points are considered:

(a) In CHAPTER 4 and CHAPTER 6 investment in tax-efficient schemes was considered. The IHT position also needs to be considered here – such schemes may have IHT advantages such as business property relief (BPR) being available on the Alternative Investment Market (AIM).

(b) In CHAPTER 5 and CHAPTER 8 the CGT position on company reorganisations, including incorporation and dis-incorporation as well as de-mergers was considered. The position in respect of property transactions and whether items are transferred into a company or kept outside of the company was also highlighted. This will have implications for BPR and is considered in this chapter.

(c) In CHAPTER 3 and CHAPTER 9 the position on properties provided to family members under dependent relative relief (and whether or not a constructive trust applies) was considered. There are significant IHT implications of such planning and advisers need to be aware of these.

(d) In CHAPTER 11 and CHAPTER 14 the position of domicile and CGT planning in relation to trusts was considered. Again, such planning has IHT implications that need to be borne in mind.

All statutory references in this chapter are to TCGA 1992 unless otherwise stated.

Business property relief and unquoted businesses

15.2 The impact of IHT is greatly reduced because of the availability of business property relief (BPR) and agricultural property relief (APR). However, these reliefs are not always as extensive as may first be assumed. In particular, the ownership structures required to achieve these reliefs may conflict with CGT planning objectives.

For advisers dealing with individuals with business interests, the principal categories of business property qualifying for BPR in IHTA 1984, s 105 are:

(a) a business or an interest in a business;

(b) unquoted shares in a company; and

(c) assets used in the business of the owner's company or his/her partnership.

Categories 1 and 2 qualify for 100% BPR. 50% relief is available on assets used by a company (as long as the owner has control of the company) or by a partnership in which the owner is a partner. No relief is available in respect of assets used by a company if the owner of the asset only has a minority shareholding.

As such, IHT issues will arise where property is retained outside of a company. This is usually done to avoid SDLT and CGT as the aim is to retain the benefit of business asset taper relief (BATR). If the property is let to the company or partnership then the maximum rate of BPR will be 50% but only as long as the owner retains control. This is likely to be a problem if the aim is to pass the business on to the next generation.

Example – Property retained outside of a company

Tim and Charlie each own 50% of a small manufacturing company. The business premises are owned personally by both of them jointly outside of their company. A rent is charged for the use of the premises and the property is intended to be used as a retirement fund by Tim and Charlie and their respective wives.

As a result of this structure, no BPR will be available against the business premises as neither Tim nor Charlie has control of the company.

In such a case, advisers will need to consider the IHT implications alongside any CGT advice. The interest in the freehold property could be left to a nil rate band discretionary trust on a first death by Tim or Charlie or Tim and Charlie could consider transferring their each half share of the property into joint ownership with their wives now BATR would continue to be available after such a transfer. Alternatively Tim and Charlie could consider taking out insurance against the IHT liability especially as part of a wider shareholder protection arrangement or they could consider establishing a Small Self Administered Scheme (SSAS) and transferring the property into it. By this means the retirement income could in due course be taken from the fund rather than from direct ownership of part of the property.

Advisers will particularly need to take care in considering whether assets are retained outside of a company when a business is looking to incorporate. Incorporation is considered in CHAPTER 5. CGT planning may dictate that incorporation utilising the provisions under s 165 is appropriate whereby the majority of business assets are transferred to the company but a property, say, is then retained outside of the company. In such cases advisers should not overlook the IHT position.

Example – Incorporation and BPR

Fiona owns an unincorporated hairdressing business which trades from freehold premises worth £500,000 in Narrow Street, a secondary location. In order to expand the business, she decides to relocate to larger and more prestigious leasehold premises in Wide Street. At the same time, Fiona decides to incorporate the business. The Narrow Street property is to be let and Fiona is advised to keep the property outside of the company because of the CGT and SDLT position.

In such a case the 100% BPR that was available on the Narrow Street property will be lost when the business incorporates. It may still be appropriate to keep the property outside of the company but Fiona may wish to consider some of the advice that was given to Tim and Charlie with regards to her IHT position.

When advising on incorporations advisers should also take care when determining the consideration for the assets transferred to the company. Where a business is incorporated and the consideration is satisfied in the form of shares under s 162 then the replacement property provisions apply and the entitlement to BPR in respect of the business continues uninterrupted. If the business is transferred to a company for a consideration in the form of a loan account then entitlement to BPR of the value of the loan is lost. To what extent this is a concern will depend upon the age and health of the business owner.

Extent of non-trading activities

15.3   Where individuals own shares in a company which has both trading and investment assets, it will often be necessary to consider the trading status of the company in seeking to establish the availability of BATR. This is considered in detail in CHAPTER 2. In such cases, advisers should be wary that what is deemed to be a trading company for CGT and IHT purposes is different in the view of HMRC. The CGT legislation provides that where a company has some non-trading activities, such companies still count as trading if their activities '... do not include to a substantial extent activities other than trading activities'. HMRC consider that substantial in this context means more than 20%. This is considered in Tax Bulletin 53 and in HMRC's Capital Gains Manual at CG17950. For BPR, there is no such substantial requirement and hence trading activities have to only be more than 50%.

A further point to note is that BPR is concerned with the businesses as a whole, whereas BATR only provides relief on trading assets. As a result, BPR may be available but not BATR. This can have significant implications when undertaking will and trust planning. If BATR is not available then there will not be an entitlement to s 165 hold-over relief. This means that a gift will only be eligible for hold-over relief if structured as a gift into trust and, as such, the BPR qualification is very important.

Case Study – Trendy Fashion Shops Limited and Hold-Over Relief

This case study is considered with slight variations in CHAPTER 2, CHAPTER 5 and CHAPTER 8. For ease of reference the scenario is again repeated here.

Trendy Fashion Shops Limited has been incorporated for 29 years. It originally had a single shop (Homestore) but then expanded to have a chain of five shops. Following a strategic review in 2004, a decision was made to cease trading from two of the shops (Old Town and New Town) which were then let to tenants. The trading shops are now Homestore, High Street and Retail Village. The company owns all of the shops with the exception of Retail Village which is leasehold.

The directors and shareholders are:

	No of shares (£1 ordinary)
Alan and Barbara Hazel (husband and wife)	4,500
Thomas Hazel (son)	5,500
	10,000

The directors have obtained planning permission to redevelop the top two floors of the Old Town shop and also to extend the property. This will create five apartments in addition to the letting shop. Alan Hazel intends to occupy one of the apartments.

The intention is to convert the New Town shop into two luxury apartments. No decision has yet been made as to whether these apartments are to be let or sold.

On a turnover basis, and by reference to the management time, the company is clearly a trading business. What is the position on the asset basis?

Trendy Fashion Shops Limited
Balance Sheet as at 30 June 2007

	£000s
Fixed assets:	
Homestore	1,250
High Street	750
Old Town	500
New Town	400
Goodwill	500
Fixtures and fittings	100
	3,500
Working capital	(250)
Long-term bank loans	(600)
	£2,650
Represented by:	
Share capital	10
Profit and loss account	2,390
Revaluation reserve	250
	£2,650

After redevelopment, the Old Town property will be worth £1 million and £700,000 for New Town. The conversion costs are £250,000 for Old Town and £150,000 for New Town. The conversion costs are to be funded by additional bank debt. The apartment to be occupied by Alan Hazel will be worth £200,000.

Profitability of the trade is declining such that the goodwill value may fall.

*Forecast
Position after
Redevelopment*

	Total	Alan Hazel's apart-ment	Remain-der of Old Town	New Town	Trading Assets
	£000s	£000s	£000s	£000s	£000s
Homestore	1,250				1,250
High Street	750				750
Old Town	1,000	200	800		—
New Town	700			700	—
Goodwill	500				500
Fixtures and fittings	100				100
					2,600
Working capital	(250)				(250)
	4,050	£200	£800	£700	£2,350
Long-term bank loans	(1,000)				
	£3,050				

The pure trading assets represent £2,350,000 out of gross assets of £4,050,000 – 58%. Depending on the allocation of the bank loans, the proportion of trading to investment assets could vary. However, the intention is to use the rental income to repay the bank borrowing and so the bank debt should reduce over time in any event.

If the usage of the apartment by Alan Hazel is part of his remuneration arrangements, then it could be considered to be part of the trading assets of the business.

If the letting of the Old Town shop is only temporary and it could be brought back within the trade at a later date, then it could be a trading asset. A sale of the New Town apartments with reinvestment of the proceeds in the trade would increase the proportion of trading assets.

Overall the conclusion must be that there is potential tainting of the BATR position. For BATR purposes it is necessary to look at the position over the period of ownership such that a short period of tainting may not be disastrous to the tax position. Further, on a sale there will be at least cash proceeds and the seller of the shares may well be prepared to accept the risk of tainting in order to conclude the deal. Different considerations apply to a family gift of shares. The client will want to be assured that hold-over relief will be available before the gift is made.

Possible Gift of Shares by Alan and Barbara Hazel on 31 October 2007

Number of shares	4,500
% shareholding	45%

	£
Valuation (assumed to be the same for both CGT and IHT purposes)	600,000
Less: base cost (31/03/82)	(82,000)
	518,000
Less: gain held over under s 165 (restricted – see below)	(383,320)
Untapered gain	134,680
Taper relief at 75%	(101,010)
	£33,670

The claim to hold-over relief is restricted as there are non-trading assets. The current restriction could be calculated as follows:

	£000s	
Homestore	1,250	Business asset
High Street	750	Business asset
Old Town	500	
New Town	400	
Goodwill	500	Business asset
Homestore	£3,400	

Hold-over relief is available but will be restricted to:

CBA = chargeable business assets – £2,500

CA = all chargeable assets – £3,400

CBA/CA = 74%

On the above basis, there would be a restriction to the hold-over relief claim but this assumes that the company qualifies as a trading company for BATR at the time of the gift. There is clearly a risk that it does not. If it ceased to qualify as a trading company at, say, 30 June 2004, then no hold-over relief will be available and the chargeable gain would then increase as follows:

	£
Gain pre hold-over and taper relief	518,000
Taper relief	
06.04.98 – 30.06.04 – 75% (2,277 days)	
01.07.04 – 31.10.07 – 40% (1,218 days)	
Total days 3,495	
Overall taper rate 62%	(325,304)
Chargeable gain	£192,696

If the shares are transferred into a discretionary trust then no CGT liability should arise. This is because CGT can be avoided on the transfer to the trust by claiming hold-over relief under s 260 (which is available). As well as considering the CGT position, it is necessary to ensure that the value of the shares transferred into the trust does not exceed the nil rate band (£300,000) for IHT purposes. In this example, the value of a 45% shareholding is £600,000. However, BPR should also be available to restrict the chargeable transfer of value for IHT purposes.

Therefore a transfer routed via a discretionary trust or trusts can be made without a tax liability arising as long as the trust is not settlor-interested. Care is required that there is no reservation of benefit (this is considered further below) and so it is also important to ensure that if Alan and Barbara are to remain as directors that their remuneration arrangements are wholly commercial. If Thomas has children then such a discretionary trust could in any case be tax efficient for school fees planning purposes.

The issue of whether a company was carrying on a business that was eligible for BPR was tackled in the Special Commissioner's decision in *Farmer v CIR* [1999] STC SCD 321. This case concerned an individual who died leaving a large farm with many properties which were let to third parties, because they were surplus to requirements. The thrust of the case was not just to look at the five relevant factors, namely the context of the business, the capital employed, the time spent by the employees, the turnover and the profits – individually, but to take the whole business 'in the round'. Although one of the important factors, the net profit, could be seen to lean more towards investments, the overriding view was that the activities as a whole amounted to a business and therefore qualified for the relief.

On the basis of the decision in *Farmer*, it is possible to argue that the overall activities of Trendy Fashion Shops Limited amount to a business in totality. This is as long as IHTA 1984, s 105(3) is satisfied. This section reads as follows:

'A business or interest in a business, or shares in or securities of a company, are not relevant business property if the business or, as the case may be, the business carried on by the company consists wholly or mainly of one or more of the following, that is to say, dealing in securities, stocks or shares, land or buildings or making or holding investments.'

The legislation therefore provides that BPR applies to unquoted companies which are carrying on a business, with the exception of those where the business is wholly or mainly one of dealing with investments or properties or the making or holding of investments. An asset is only excepted under IHTA 1984, s 112 if it has not been used for the purposes of a business conducted by the company for the previous two years, nor required for the future use of that business.

As confirmed by *American Leaf Blending Co Sdn Bhd v Director-General of Inland Revenue* [1978] 3 All ER 1185, 'any gainful use to which [a company] puts any of its assets prima facie amounts to the carrying on a business'. Therefore, a portfolio of quoted investments held by a company will normally represent an investment business conducted by it, and so long as this is not the main business of the company, BPR will be due on the whole value of the company.

There is a useful summary of the law in this area in *Land Management Ltd v Fox (Inspector of Taxes)* [2002] STC (SCD) 152. In this case, a company owned and let a freehold residential property, held and received dividends from shares in various companies, made an interest-bearing loan to a connected company, and received interest on a bank deposit. The Special Commissioner held that each of its activities, and all four in combination, amounted to carrying on business. As a result, it is possible to have an investment activity together within an otherwise trading company so that in total the combined activities amount to an overall business.

In CHAPTER 5 the possibility of a s 110 Insolvency Act reorganisation was explored. Whilst such an approach would achieve BATR status on the ongoing trading company, there is no doubt that the investment company would then be caught by IHTA 1984, s 105(3). Given that in the case study considered in that chapter (and above), it was Alan and Hazel taking on the investment business, this would seem to be very unwise from an IHT planning perspective (and therefore an overall tax planning perspective).

Tax-efficient investing

15.4 Whilst CGT will often be the driving force behind an investment decision, the desire to also obtain BPR for IHT purposes will also be relevant. As is the case so often with CGT planning, IHT considerations are interlocked. By investing in shares in companies listed on AIM qualifying for BPR for IHT purposes, investors receive the following tax advantages:

(a) 100% relief from IHT when shares are held for two years or more; and

(b) business asset taper relief (BATR) on share sales for CGT purposes.

An AIM portfolio is likely to be attractive to the following:

 (i) investors with a potentially large IHT liability (and possibly a CGT liability to defer);

 (ii) investors who wish to retain control over and have access to their assets;

(iii) investors looking for a short IHT mitigation qualification period of only two years; and

(iv) investors looking for further diversification of their investments.

This can be further considered with Enterprise Investment Scheme (EIS) relief if shares are subscribed for in a qualifying company on a new issue. EIS is considered in CHAPTER 6. Where an EIS investment is made (and assuming a gain chargeable at 40% without any taper relief) then it is possible to achieve 100% tax relief on the investments.

Example – Maximising tax relief on investing

Miss Faversham, a higher-rate taxpayer, makes a large gain on the sale of some fully quoted shares which she had only owned for less than three years. She decides to reinvest in such a way that she qualifies for full EIS relief. The shares will also qualify for BPR after two years.

Miss Faversham invests £50,000 and obtains tax relief as follows:

	£
Initial investment	50,000
CGT deferral relief @ 40%	(20,000)
EIS income tax relief	(10,000)
Cost of investment after tax relief	£20,000

Two and a half years after investment, Miss Faversham dies. The shares are still valued at £50,000. Miss Faversham's estate is large and so is subject to IHT at 40%. Her estate obtains 100% BPR on the shares, so obtaining a further £20,000 of tax relief.

A further point to note with regards to tax-efficient investing is that trustees can also qualify for CGT deferral relief through EIS under Sch 5B, para 17. Many trusts comprise quoted share portfolios which over the years have become heavily pregnant with gains. Tax planning is limited by the small amount of the annual exemption available to trusts and this can particularly be the case where there are related settlements. This has been exacerbated by the increase in the income tax rate on trusts as dividend income is particularly severely taxed, especially where it is distributed to income tax paying beneficiaries.

These considerations have led to different approaches to investing for trusts which seek to avoid CGT rules and to minimise the income subject to 40% tax each year. The objective is therefore to try and achieve 'gross roll-up', ie so that income is allowed to accumulate without suffering income tax. One of the attractive ways this can be done is for the trustees to invest in an offshore bond with a view to assigning the bond out to the beneficiary on, say, the 18th birthday. The aim of this approach would also be to avoid the chargeable event gain such that the beneficiary can then encash the bond and so pay income tax at a lower rate.

In terms of maximising tax relief, the same principles can apply where someone doesn't want to invest in shares but is keen to invest in quasi-investment assets such as qualifying let property or farmland. Advisers may wish to bear in mind that where an individual has made a gain on a business asset, it is possible to roll over the gain into a furnished holiday letting property, say. Subject to meeting the necessary conditions for BPR on a holiday letting business, the rolled-over gain will drop out on death and no IHT liability will arise.

Example – Roll-over into holiday lets

Basil sells a business asset which qualifies for roll-over but not maximum BATR. He is elderly and decides to buy a furnished holiday letting complex in which a manager is employed on site.

He rolls over the gain and qualifies for BPR immediately because of replacement property rules.

CGT planning involving the use of a deed of variation

15.5 Where appreciating assets are included in an estate, there may be significant capital gains on a later sale of such property. As can be seen in the example in CHAPTER 11, it is often beneficial for the asset to be appointed to the beneficiaries in specie, rather than the sale taking place by the executors, in order to reduce the exposure to CGT through the use of individual annual exemptions and basic rate bands. This planning can be extended further even where the beneficiaries are higher-rate taxpayers.

Deeds of variation are effective for CGT purposes under s 62. This means that the beneficiaries of a particular asset may be amended so that any CGT liability on a future sale is minimal. Such planning needs to be made within two years of death and appropriate consideration needs to be made within two years of death and appropriate consideration needs to be made to IHT also.

Example – Deed of variation

Mrs Gunn inherited shares valued at £100,000 on the death of her husband, which qualified as business property for IHT purposes. After 18 months, the family company was bought out and Mrs Gunn received £250,000 for the shares. As a higher-rate taxpayer, with no remaining annual exemption, she will pay £60,000 in CGT on these. However, as the takeover occurs within two years of her husband's death, planning may be undertaken by deed of variation. By appointing the shares to her three children, there could be significant tax savings. Say Mrs Gunn's son and daughter left the UK and moved to Ireland some time ago then there would be no CGT in the UK on the takeover on their shares. Her UK-resident son will pay CGT on only 1/3 of the total gain, ie £50,000. If he has no other income, after exemptions, the total tax liability is just £9,117.

As BPR is available, there is also no IHT on the deed of variation provided there were no pre-existing agreements regarding the takeover at the time of death.

Planning in connection with private residences

15.6   For those dealing with private clients, a significant amount of work involves advising on the minimisation of CGT and IHT in connection with private residences. This is particularly relevant in terms of will planning for a surviving spouse and providing a home for family members. Specifically in this context, it is necessary to consider the following areas:

(a)   gifts with reservation of benefit under FA 1986, s 103 and in particular the implications of *Phizackerley (personal representative of Phizackerley, deceased) v Revenue and Customs Commissioners* (2007) SpC 591;

(b)   dependant relative relief under s 226;

(c)   occupation of a property under the terms of a trust – formal, constructive or implied.

Gifts with reservation of benefit and the Phizackerley case

15.7   Mr Phizackerley was an Oxford professor and until 1992 he lived in college accommodation and had no other property. In 1992, he retired and he and his wife purchased a house as joint tenants. The purchase price was £150,000. Mrs Phizackerley did not work during the time that they were married and the funds therefore must have been provided by Mr Phizackerley (probably to a large extent from his tax-free cash on retirement). On 1 May 1996, the joint tenancy was severed as part of some IHT planning and the property was then owned as tenants-in-common in equal shares.

Mrs Phizackerley died in April 2000 with an estate of less than the nil rate sum. She left her estate of £150,000 to a discretionary settlement, the trustees of which then entered into an IOU scheme with Mr Phizackerley such that the half share in the property was transferred onto him and he agreed to pay to the trustees the liability of £150,000 (index linked).

Mr Phizackerley died in July 2002 and left an estate of £529,654 before deducting the IOU, which at the time of death was £156,013.

The IOU approach works by giving a power in the will to allow the trustees of the discretionary trust to accept an IOU from the surviving spouse in satisfaction of all or part of the nil rate sum. This enables the nil rate band to be utilised on a first death where there are insufficient liquid assets in the estate to otherwise satisfy the legacy. This is typically the case where the estate consists of principally the half share of the house. As a result the trustees end up with an IOU and the surviving spouse ends up with the deceased's tenants-in-common share of the property. The IOU is expressed to be repayable on demand but in practice will not usually be called in until the second death or the sale of the property if the surviving spouse downsizes.

On second death, the debt in the widow/er's estate is repaid to the trust and accordingly deducted from the taxable estate as a personal liability. It is the deduction of this personal liability that is prevented by FA 1986, s 103 where there have been lifetime gifts. This was the issue in the *Phizackerley* case.

FA 1986, s 103 provides that a liability is not deductible from the value of a person's estate if it derives directly or indirectly from a disposition previously made by him. In the *Phizackerley* case it would seem clear that this would prevent the deduction of the debt as the assets in Mrs Phizackerley's estate were primarily the half share of the house that was derived from a gift made to her by her husband in 1992. The Special Commissioner held this to be the case.

IHTA 1984, s 11 provides that a disposition is not a transfer of a value if it is made by one party to a marriage in favour of the other party and is for the maintenance of the other party. As such, the argument in the *Phizackerley* case was whether or not the gift of the half share of the property amounted to a disposition by Mr Phizackerley for the maintenance of Mrs Phizackerley. At issue, therefore, was the definition of 'maintenance'.

Dr Avery-Jones, the Special Commissioner, referred to previous case law and concluded that it seemed to him 'that the ordinary meaning of maintenance has the flavour of meeting recurring expenses'. He did, however, feel that it was wide enough to cover the transfer of a house or part interest in a house but only if it relieves the recipient from incurring expenditure, for example on rent. Overall, he concluded that he did 'not consider that when a husband puts a house in joint names for himself and his wife during their marriage, it is within the ordinary meaning of maintenance'.

Implications of the Phizackerley case

15.8 The *Phizackerley* case does not change the position in respect of IHT planning involving the use of the family home, ownership as tenants-in-common and the use of a nil rate band discretionary trust in a will. It simply confirms the position that if an IOU arrangement is utilised between the trustees of the discretionary will trust and the surviving spouse, then the deduction of that debt for tax purposes will be restricted or prohibited to the extent that there have been lifetime gifts. As such, if considering this type of planning, questions need to be asked about any inter-spouse gifts made since March 1986.

But what other options are available where there are insufficient liquid assets in the estate to otherwise satisfy the nil rate sum? The IOU scheme was developed because if the half share of the property itself is left within the discretionary settlement then, in the view of HMRC in Statement of Practice 10/79, this is likely to create an interest in possession settlement.

An alternative is to use an equitable charge arrangement. This works by including a power in the will for the executors to satisfy the nil rate band legacy by imposing a charge on the home, in favour of the trustees, in lieu of the legacy. The trustees have no right to enforce payment of the amount of the legacy against the surviving spouse (ie the widow/er is not made personally liable for payment of the debt). This approach gets round the gift with reservation of benefit problem as the debt is deductible as a legal charge on the property.

However, the downside with the equitable charge approach is that if the property is subsequently sold, then the debt must be repaid at that point in time. If a further loan is advanced, then this is a personal liability of the recipient and so comes within the same rules as IOU arrangements. Therefore, before this approach is used, it is necessary for the trustees and the surviving spouse to consider his/her future accommodation requirements.

The attraction of using an index-linking arrangement for the loan on the equitable charge approach is that this takes the arrangement outside of the income tax legislation as it represents a security for CGT purposes.

Example – Equitable charge and CGT

Mr Kirby deceased having left a legacy in his will to a nil rate band discretionary trust. The legacy was satisfied by an equitable charge over the private residence. The equitable charge was in the sum of £200,000 and was indexed to a national house price index. The property was sold in March 2007 when the value of the charge had increased to £325,760.

By linking the value of the nil rate band in the trust fund to a property index, it is an excluded indexed security and so taken outside of the income tax provisions of ITTOIA 2005. As such, the gain on the disposal of the security is subject to CGT. Non-BATR at the rate of 15% is available.

The CGT computation is as follows:

	£
Gain	125,760
Non-business asset taper relief @ 15%	(18,864)

	106,896
Less: annual exemption	(4,600)
Taxable gain	£102,296

Dependent relative relief

15.9 This relief was phased out in April 1988, however, it does still apply to those cases that satisfy the requirements on a transitional basis and advisers must therefore consider whether it applies. The qualifying conditions for this relief are quite narrowly defined. The exemption from CGT applies to all periods before 6 April 1988 when the property is occupied by a dependent relative and also any period after that date, where it was occupied by the same dependent relative. A dependent relative includes a widowed mother, so long as they were widowed before 6 April 1988. It also includes a parent who is aged 65 or older on that date. Where an individual has more than one qualifying dependent relative, for example, where both parents were aged over 65 on 6 April 1988, the claim should be made by reference to the longest surviving spouse who occupied the property.

Family homes – constructive trusts and PPR relief

15.10 It was fairly common during the early/mid 1990s for the legal ownership of properties to be transferred from parents to their children (perhaps in an attempt to avoid nursing home fees having to be paid). At the time property values were low and CGT and IHT issues were not considered to be an issue (or not considered at all).

In the absence of any trust arrangement, the gift of the property will be subject to the reservation of benefit rules with the following consequences:

(a) the property continues to be in the estate of the donors at its current market value, and

(b) CGT will be payable on the sale without the benefit of PPR relief.

Where a gift of the property was made subject to reserving the right to occupation by the donor(s), then it is clearly a gift with reservation of benefit. However, where a gift of the property was made and the recipients subsequently granted a right of occupation for life to the donors, then the arrangements could amount to a constructive trust. If the arrangements do amount to the donors being entitled to occupy the property as beneficiaries under the terms of a trust then PPR relief will be available under s 225. Usually, no formal trust deed will have been prepared and it is necessary to consider the documentation that is available and the basis of occupation of the property by the donor(s) in conjunction with the client's legal advisers.

If the arrangements do amount to a trust, then it will be an interest in possession arrangement, such that the value of the property will have to be included in the beneficiary's estate for IHT purposes. Where the arrangement commenced prior to 22 March 2006 then on the death of the life tenant, no liability to CGT will arise because of the probate value uplift under s 73. However, it is important that the correct returns are made to HMRC both on the first and second death. For new arrangements then the IHT arrangements need to be carefully considered in light of the FA 2006 changes.

Where a person(s) has occupied a property rent free for their lifetime, it may be possible to argue that they are beneficiaries of a constructive trust and that they were entitled to live in the property under the terms of that trust. The HMRC Capital Gains Manual at CG65423 says that where there is no lease and the occupier pays no rent, then the property is likely to be occupied under a licence. However if the licence is completely gratuitous then the occupier is not considered to have an interest in the property, hence a constructive trust is not implied. It is therefore necessary to show that any licence that may exist is not gratuitous. If a constructive trust is established, then entitlement to occupy should follow.

This would mean that any gain would be exempt for the entire period of occupation by such persons and there would not be any chargeable period. Advisers should take care though as this argument is often challenged by HMRC. As the trust is not explicit, usually it would be sensible to get a solicitor to confirm that in their opinion such a trust is implied and to prepare a deed of arrangement evidencing this. It is also necessary to consider the implications of the pre-owned asset tax regime.

Under s 225A, the beneficiaries occupying a property as their main residence must have a relevant entitlement of 75% or more of the net proceeds of disposal, as legatee of the deceased person, or to an interest in possession in the net proceeds of disposal. However, s 225A(2) poses a problem in that a further condition stipulated is that immediately before and immediately after the death of the deceased person, the property was the only or main residence of those individuals. This can be a problem if a beneficiary of the estate moves in to a second property following the death.

IHTA 1984, s 191 provides that in certain cases where property is sold within three years of death, the probate value of those properties can be substituted with the sale value to provide relief from IHT. The substituted sale value is also used for CGT purposes. The idea is to give relief for falls in value, from IHT, but the legislation does not make reference to this being the only application.

This would mean that CGT would not be chargeable on the subsequent sales, and as the substitution of the sale values does not increase the chargeable estate above the nil rate band for IHT purposes, then no IHT would become due either.

In the view of HMRC a claim under IHTA 1984, s 191 is only possible where IHT is payable. This is because if there is no IHT payable then in their view there is no 'appropriate person' to make a claim. IHTA 1984, s 190 defines the appropriate person to make the claim as the person liable to IHT on the asset. The case of *Stonor and another (executors of Dickinson, deceased) v IRC* [2001] STC (SCD) 199 concluded that there can be no adjustment of the probate values to the sales values in order to minimise CGT under IHTA 1984, s 190 if there is no IHT due. As a consequence, it is not possible to make a claim under IHTA 1984, s 191 to save CGT where no IHT is payable because, for instance, the spouse exemption applies.

Example – Estate issues and PPR

Mr and Mrs Pinochet own two properties:

(i) Homefield – their main residence

(ii) Hillside – a let property

Following the death of Mr Pinochet, Mrs Pinochet no longer wishes to occupy Homefield and obtains vacant possession of Hillside. Both Homefield and Hillside were owned solely by Mr Pinochet. The probate values were as follows:

(i) Homefield – £360,000

(ii) Hillside – £385,000

Both properties are sold as Mrs Pinochet wishes to move back to live with her daughter. Homefield is sold for £320,000 and Hillside £425,000. Overall there is no gain on the sale of both properties. However, the loss on Homefield is not allowable as PPR applies. Under s 225A no relief is available on Hillside as Mrs Pinochet did not live in that property before the death.

If the will provided for Mrs Pinochet to inherit Hillside the PPR would be available under s 222. If the will provided for Hillside to be included in a trust of which Mrs Pinochet was a beneficiary then the trustees would qualify for relief under s 225. If the will provided for Hillside to pass as a specific legacy to another beneficiary then there could possibly be a claim as a constructive or implied trust although that would depend upon the intentions and conduct of the legatee of the Hillside property. In such cases the position could perhaps be improved by a deed of variation. If there was no will then it would depend upon how the assets of the estate were treated for the purposes of the intestacy rules as to whether or not any PPR claim is possible under either ss 222 or 225.

Conclusion

15.11 In terms of CGT planning then it is always necessary to consider the wider tax position of the client. The purpose of this chapter has been to explore some of the CGT planning ideas covered elsewhere in this book as far as IHT is concerned. In addition to the comments and examples above a further very important issue is domicile which should never be overlooked. However, the points made above are considered to be of the widest relevance as they relate to business interests, investment assets and family homes.

Checklist

	Cross Reference
IHT	
Inheritance tax (IHT) planning focuses on lifetime gifts, optimising the usage of the nil rate band and maximising business property relief. If lifetime gifts are to be made then CGT must be considered. In such cases, CGT is typically a barrier to gifting.	**15.2**
Gifts of assets are possible where a hold-over relief applies.	**15.3**
Tax-efficient investing through usage of EIS enables both deferral of CGT and avoidance of IHT because of the availability of business property relief.	**15.4**
There is also interaction between IHT and CGT where a nil rate band discretionary trust uses an equitable charge scheme.	**15.8**

Chapter 16

Pre-Year End Capital Gains Tax Planning

Introduction

16.1 When advising on capital gains tax (CGT) planning the timings of gains and losses are crucial. Pre-tax year end planning is therefore fundamental to ensure that clients are well placed to mitigate and offset any potential CGT liability. Whilst the key planning points outlined in this chapter (such as utilising annual exemptions and crystallising losses) are often known, advisers all too often overlook the opportunities that are available on a yearly basis, and that once 5 April has passed, are no longer available.

Effective CGT planning relies upon the adviser knowing his or her clients and having a good understanding of their objectives. Ideally, there is ongoing dialogue and communication with the client on the CGT tax planning issues throughout the year and all deadlines are appropriately marked and updated on the permanent file records. However, in addition (and as a failsafe) it is sensible to review all the CGT planning provided during a tax year just prior to the year end. This is a pro-active approach and should be appreciated by clients.

This chapter is intended to provide a 'one stop' practical summary of these planning points. It is not deemed to be an exhaustive list and in each case the planning points identified will often be relevant throughout the year, collectively though they provide a practical guide to the key CGT considerations pre-year end.

All statutory references in this chapter are to TCGA 1992 unless otherwise stated.

Utilising annual exemptions

16.2 Clients often fail to realise that each individual is entitled to an annual exemption for CGT purposes (which is currently £9,200 – 2007/08). This means that an individual and their spouse/ civil partner can make chargeable gains of up to £18,400 (2007/08) without giving rise to a CGT liability. If the annual exemption is not used by 5 April, it is lost, so it makes sense to crystallise a gain up to this level if possible.

The old practice of 'bed and breakfasting' (see **CHAPTER 4**) is no longer allowed; however, it is possible to buy back shares in the same company after 30 days. This can still present planning opportunities for investors if the commercial risk is acceptable. Alternatively, the client could buy shares in the same sector (ie sell Barclays and buy Lloyds TSB shares).

The practice of 'bed and spousing' could also be appropriate. This entails an individual selling their shares at a gain prior to 5 April and their spouse/civil partner making an equivalent purchase (the repurchase must be on the open market). As such an individual can utilise their annual exemption without having to entirely surrender the asset. Their spouse/civil partner then holds the shares, with a higher base cost for CGT purposes. Share pooling rules should be considered, see below and CHAPTER 4.

'Bed and ISAing' can also offer a sensible CGT planning route for individuals who stand to make a gain on their investments. In the same way, the taxpayer could sell their shares prior to 5 April in order to utilise their annual exemption and then buy them back (on the open market) through an Individual Savings Account (ISA). It is unlikely that the whole annual exemption could be used in this way though due to the limits applied to the amounts an individual can invest in an ISA each year. However, this type of planning could be appropriate where a client stands to make a number of smaller chargeable gains.

Trusts and the annual exemption

16.3   Trusts set up prior to 7 June 1978 are entitled to an annual exemption of one half of that due to an individual. For the tax year 2007/08 this amounts to £4,600.

Trusts made after 6 June 1978 are subject to special group provisions. The half exemption of £4,600 is divided between all of the settlements made by the same settlor. This is, however, subject to a minimum of one tenth of that due to an individual (£920 for the tax year 2007/08). For the purpose of calculating the annual exemption under these group provisions, charitable trusts, retirement annuity schemes and non-resident trusts are excluded.

It should also be noted that trusts for a mentally disabled person, a person in receipt of an attendance allowance or the middle or highest disability living allowance are treated differently. For these types of trusts the annual exemption entitlement is the same as it is for an individual.

In terms of pre-year end tax planning, it is advisable where trusts are in place to consider what capital distributions have been made during the year and to what extent the trustees annual exemption has been utilised. As the trust exemption is smaller, the failure to maximise sales each year can eventually lead to a very limited room for manoeuvre from a CGT perspective.

Trusts are considered in further detail in CHAPTER 11.

Minimising income

16.4   Net chargeable gains over the annual exemption are chargeable to CGT as if the gains were an extra slice of savings income for the tax year concerned. As such, net gains are charged at 10%, 20% and 40%.

As part of any pre-year end tax planning, the overall income position of an individual is therefore relevant. Where possible, advisers should look to minimise an individual's income in any given year where capital gains have arisen in excess of the annual exempt amount. This could entail changing the accounting reference date for a sole trader or partnership for example, in order to minimise an individual's overall income in a year when chargeable gains have arisen.

Other possibilities include choosing annual interest payment dates for the proceeds on deposit such that it falls into a later tax year and care over income receipts from estates or trusts. It is important to look at the wider investment portfolio issues for the client in order to minimise exposure to higher rate tax rather than only focusing on the gain.

Alternatively, advisers could look to achieve additional tax relief for an individual (thus potentially mitigating tax paid at the higher rate), for example, through pension contributions or gift aid payments. This is considered further below.

Making the most of gift aid

16.5   If an individual gives assets other than money (such as land and buildings or shares) to a UK charity, and that asset is given as an outright gift, the disposal is treated as being at such a price that there is neither a chargeable gain nor an allowable loss. This means that a liability to CGT is avoided.

Relief is available from CGT under s 257 which combined with a special form of gift aid relief under ITA 2007, s 431 (formerly ICTA 1988, s 587B) is extended to provide exemption from CGT on gifts to charity of shares, securities, land and buildings and other real property.

Gift aiding of shares and real property is treated differently to cash gifts which are deemed to have been made net of basic rate tax. For gifts of real property, the value of the gift is deducted from total income in the year of the gift and tax worked out accordingly.

If a charity is unable to accept the gift because it does not maintain a share portfolio then the gift could be structured through the Charities Aid Foundation (CAF) or another such organisation. The issue of valuation is also important in tax planning for gifts of land and buildings or unquoted shares. Appropriate valuations should be obtained and a formal certificate obtained from the charity. The issue of valuations is considered further in CHAPTER 13.

Gifting of assets is considered further in CHAPTER 8.

Example – Gifting of shares to charity

Audrey wishes to give £25,000 of quoted shares to a registered charity in March 2008. The shares have a negligible base cost and Audrey has already utilised her annual exemption for 2007/08. Audrey has annual employment income of £60,000 from her catering business and only minimal other income from her shares and investments.

As a result of the gift, Audrey's income tax liability for the year will be reduced by £10,000 (£25,000 gift x 40%).

Careful planning of income tax on sources of income is required to maximise the benefit of gift aid under ITA 2007, s 431. In particular where there is dividend income or if pension contributions are being made.

Payments on account will also be reduced (if appropriate). It may also be beneficial to spread gifts over several years.

The gifting of an asset to charity can therefore be very attractive not only in terms of CGT planning but in terms of the income tax relief it attracts in any given tax year. The timing here can be crucial if an individual's income is likely to fluctuate.

The tax adviser should, however, be wary that if a charity were to pay for an asset and the amount received by the individual is less than they originally purchased the asset for, then the disposal is also treated at such a price that there is neither a chargeable gain, nor an allowable loss for CGT purposes. It is not therefore possible to generate capital losses through the disposal of an asset at undervalue to a charity.

On the other hand if a charity purchases an asset for more than the individual originally paid, it will be necessary to calculate the capital gain on the basis of the proceeds received from the charity. The fact that the disposal is to a charitable body does not exempt the individual from any CGT liability.

Crystallising losses

16.6 Whilst the utility of capital losses is somewhat restricted, see CHAPTER 12, it can still be beneficial from a CGT perspective to deliberately crystallise a loss before the end of the tax year. If a client has chargeable gains arising in the year they should be advised to review their portfolio of investments for any assets standing at a loss in order to reduce the clients overall net gains.

It may also be advisable for individuals to delay the sale of some investments until after 5 April in order to qualify for more taper relief. For non-business assets held since before 16 March 1998 the maximum level of taper relief is achievable from 6 April 2007. For business assets, it will often be very important to consider the timing of any disposal to ensure that full business asset taper relief is available, see CHAPTER 2. In this context, it is important to maximise the benefit of the losses that have been crystallised. The aim will be to utilise them against gains with minimal taper and not against assets qualifying for maximum BATR.

Watch share purchases

16.7 The major problem with computing chargeable gains on the disposal of shares is identifying which shares have actually been sold.

There are specific rules which require the matching of disposals with particular acquisitions. These rules are considered in more detail in CHAPTER 4. In broad terms:

(a) Shares acquired after 6 April 1998 are matched with disposals on a last in/first out basis.

(b) Shares acquired after 6 April 1982 are pooled.

(c) Shares acquired between 6 April 1965 and 5 April 1982 are also aggregated in a separate pool.

Whilst this applies to all CGT planning where shares are concerned, particular care should be taken prior to 5 April when it is likely that share disposals and acquisitions are being made for CGT purposes. Advisers should be acutely aware of the share matching rules and the impact of purchasing new shares should always be considered, including shares acquired through reinvesting dividends.

Enterprise Investment Scheme (EIS)

16.8 The reinvestment of capital gains is still important to private investors who may be making gains on shares or property that are subject to a rate of CGT of 40% or not much less. The particular attraction for this group is that Alternative Investment Market (AIM) company shares can still qualify for EIS because AIM is treated as unlisted for these purposes. As such, private investors can invest in EIS shares which do have an exit route. It is particularly relevant to consider the timing of any EIS investment. A further benefit is that shares in AIM may qualify for business property relief for IHT purposes after two years.

Types of EIS relief

16.9 It is important to appreciate that there are two types of EIS relief:

(1) The 'full EIS relief' which includes exemption from CGT on any gain, the potential for CGT deferral relief and a 20% income tax credit.

The maximum up front tax relief under this relief is 60%. In order to qualify for this relief, the maximum ownership of the shares and loan stock by the new investor is limited to 30%. Understandably there are also a large number of further restrictions that can apply. The maximum subscription in any one tax year is £200,000.

(2) The more limited form of EIS relief which is a CGT only relief and is referred to as 'deferral relief'. It is not necessary for the shares acquired to be subject to the EIS income tax relief. Under this relief, there is no restriction as to the percentage ownership of the shares and loan stock but there are still a number of complex restrictions to consider. The maximum tax benefit is 40% of the investment although the tax relief percentage is typically lower because of the likelihood of taper relief being available on the original gain. There is no maximum subscription.

A gain arising on the disposal of any kind of asset may be deferred by an individual if he invests in a company which is qualifying company under the EIS rules.

The amount of the gain (before taper relief) that can be deferred is the lower of:

(a) the amount subscribed by the investor for his shares, which has not previously been matched under this relief (or Venture Capital Trust relief); and

(b) the amount specified by the investor in the claim. This can take into account the availability of losses, taper relief and the annual exemption.

Example – EIS investment

Andrew made a gain of £156,000 (before taper relief) on the disposal of a property in 2007/08. The property qualifies for taper relief as a business asset but was only held for between one and two years. He subscribed for some shares in a company which qualified under EIS.

If, say, Andrew had no other chargeable gains a claim can be made to defer £137,600 to utilise Andrew's annual exemption as follows:

	£
Gain before deferral relief	156,000
Less: EIS reinvestment relief	(137,600)
Gain before taper relief	18,400
Gain after taper relief at 50%	9,200
Less: annual exemption	(9,200)
Chargeable gain	£Nil

It is likely that a key driver to investing in an EIS investment will be CGT deferral (otherwise a Venture Capital Trust investment would be better from an income tax perspective). However, from a pre-tax year end planning angle, the income tax relief may be significant in terms of the timing of the investment. It needs to be borne in mind that there may be some time delays in making the necessary EIS investments and it is best not to leave it too late before taking action.

EIS is considered in further detail in CHAPTER 6.

Pension planning

16.10 It will often be the case that individuals faced with a CGT liability will be paying a significant amount of tax at the higher rate of 40%. Pension planning could be an attractive option for some individuals to mitigate this higher rate tax.

A personal pension contribution or an additional voluntary contribution (AVC) is paid net of basic rate tax and the additional tax relief is achieved through self-assessment. This can mean that additional tax relief at 20% (giving total relief of 42%) is available as the pension contribution could mean that CGT is payable at 20% instead of 40%. This is because a pension contribution extends the basic band.

Example – Pension contribution and CGT

Jenny sells a property, which was not her principal private residence, in January 2008. The chargeable gain arising on the property is £31,512. Jenny has £30,000 profits from her self–employment as a solicitor and has some other investment income but is not ordinarily a higher-rate taxpayer.

Her total CGT liability is £11,538, calculated as follows:

	£
CGT at 20% (£5,335 x 20%)	1,067
CGT at 40% (£26,177 x 40%)	10,471
Total CGT liability	£11,538

Approximately £26,000 of Jenny's chargeable gain is being taxed at 40%. This could be mitigated if Jenny were to make a personal pension contribution of £20,280 before 5 April 2008. This would achieve a gross contribution of £26,000.

The same principles apply to gift aid as well, although that of course depends upon the charitable motives of the client. For all clients, timing is important where a gain pushes an otherwise basic rate taxpayer into higher rates. For those making regular pension contributions or gift aid donations, then merely accelerating such payments can achieve a tax saving. This type of planning is ideal for clients like Jenny especially if they are concerned about their pension funding position and if the gain arises on an investment asset such as a buy to let.

Advisers should also bear in mind that a combination of pension and EIS planning may be attractive to the client.

Gift aid carry back

16.11   A gift aid contribution made before the tax return is filed can be treated as though it was made in the tax return year. For example, if a gift aid contribution is made on 17 August 2007 and the 2006/07 tax return has not been filed, then the gift aid contribution can be treated as if it was made in 2006/07. The gift aid payment must be before the 31 January tax return filing deadline.

Where a capital gain has been made, then consideration should be given to the possibility of relating back a gift aid contribution *before* the filing of the tax return. It may be worth delaying the submission of the tax return if appropriate.

Roll-over relief

16.12   Roll-over relief extends to gains arising on the disposal of qualifying business assets and gains from the transfer of an interest in land to authorities (and others) able to exercise compulsory purchase powers. In addition, claims are available to effectively roll over gains attributable to the receipt of capital sums derived from assets. The various forms of roll-over relief are considered further in CHAPTER 7.

In essence, CGT deferral can be achieved if a qualifying replacement asset is purchased within the prescribed time limits. Whilst these time limits relate to the disposal date of the original asset, the availability of roll-over relief is something that advisers should be keen to detect as part of any pre-year end tax planning. A provisional claim for roll-over relief may be appropriate, again see CHAPTER 7.

The pre-tax year end planning season is a good time to review roll-over relief deadlines where provisional claims have been made and to remind clients of the relevant reinvestment dates.

Conclusion

16.13   As part of pre-tax year end planning, it is sensible to revisit CGT planning advice given to clients earlier in the tax year. The list of action points outlined in this chapter provides a checklist for planning ideas to raise with clients to ensure they are well placed to mitigate and offset any potential CGT liability.

Table of Cases

Table of Statutes

Table of Statutory Instruments

Index